JUVENILE JUSTICE
TODAY

JUVENILE JUSTICE
TODAY

Gennaro F. Vito
University of Louisville

Julie C. Kunselman
Northern Kentucky University

Prentice Hall

Boston   Columbus   Indianapolis   New York   San Francisco   Upper Saddle River
Amsterdam   Cape Town   Dubai   London   Madrid   Milan   Munich   Paris   Montréal   Toronto
Delhi   Mexico City   São Paulo   Sydney   Hong Kong   Seoul   Singapore   Taipei   Tokyo

Senior Acquisitions Editor: Vernon R. Anthony
Acquisitions Editor: Eric Krassow
Development Editor: Megan Moffo
Editorial Assistant: Lynda Cramer
Director of Marketing: David Gessell
Senior Marketing Manager: Adam Kloza
Marketing Assistant: Les Roberts
Senior Managing Editor: JoEllen Gohr
Project Manager: Alicia Ritchey
Operations Specialist: Pat Tonneman

Art Director: Diane Ernsberger
Text and Cover Designer: Candace Rowley
Cover Art: Darwin Wigget/Getty Images
Media Editor: Michelle Churma
Lead Media Project Manager: Karen Bretz
**Full-Service Project Management
   and Composition:** Integra
Printer/Binder: Edwards Brothers
Cover Printer: Lehigh-Phoenix Color/Hagerstown
Text Font: Garamond

Credits and acknowledgments borrowed from other sources and reproduced, with permission, in this textbook appear either on the appropriate pages in the text or on pages 411–412.

Many of the designations by manufacturers and seller to distinguish their products are claimed as trademarks. Where those designations appear in this book, and the publisher was aware of a trademark claim, the designations have been printed in initial caps or all caps.

Library of Congress Cataloging-in-Publication Data

Vito, Gennaro F.
   Juvenile justice today/Gennaro F. Vito, Julie C. Kunselman.
      p. cm.
   ISBN-13: 978-0-13-515148-8
   ISBN-10: 0-13-515148-1
   1. Juvenile justice, Administration of—United States.   2. Juvenile delinquents—United States.
   I. Kunselman, Julie C.   II. Title.
   HV9104.K86 2012
   364.360973—dc22

2010035613

10 9 8 7 6 5 4 3 2 1

Prentice Hall
is an imprint of

www.pearsonhighered.com

ISBN 10: 0-13-515148-1
ISBN 13: 978-0-13-515148-8

This book is dedicated to Clifford E. Simonsen; Anthony, Gina, and Mary Vito; and Alex, Davis, Lacie, Lauren, Logan, Jordyn, Kaitlyn, and Will Kunselman.

brief contents

contents

2

Juvenile Statistics: Measurement and Analysis   40

3

Dealing with Delinquency: Theories, Issues, and Practice   64

part II
The Juvenile Justice System   103

4
The Juvenile Justice Process   104

5

Juveniles and the Police: Where the System Starts 126

6

Juvenile Assessment and Classification 162

7

Legal Rights of Juveniles 198

8

Juvenile Probation and Diversion   226

10

Juvenile Parole   314

part III
Special Populations: Juvenile Victims and Juvenile Gangs   335

11

Juvenile Victimization   336

12

Juvenile Gangs   366

preface

Juvenile Justice Today is written for the student beginning to develop an interest in the juvenile area of the criminal justice system. It focuses on the system itself, the processes within it, and the young people who become involved in it. We also present a historical view of the juvenile justice system and how it relates to the entire criminal justice system.

This text is based on a specific model emphasizing concise chapters that logically build upon each other. It is designed to keep the reader's attention and interest by presenting each chapter in self-contained yet interrelated parts that can be easily read in short sessions without excessive effort. **Key Terms**, **Discussion and Review Questions**, **MyCrimeKit Lessons**, and **Endnotes** are contained at the end of each chapter for students to answer, study, and consult. The text also includes **Video Profiles,** which are videos that highlight real-life cases of juveniles in contact with the juvenile justice system. Videos are called out in the margins and can be watched on the MyCrimeKit site. End-of-chapter questions ask students to review and analyze each video case and to link to key concepts and issues in the chapter.

The true purpose of any textbook is to transmit and clarify ideas and information to students in a clear and understandable writing style as well as to impart real-life examples. Thus:

- Readability is a key feature of this text. We have taken steps to make this text easy for the instructor to use and to make it a pleasant and worthwhile learning experience for the reader.

- The inclusion of research and evaluation summaries of juvenile programs, as well as forms used in the field, provides opportunities for real-life learning.

- The videos that accompany the text are true-to-life, actual scenes of juveniles in the juvenile justice process along with all of the principal actors: police, probation officers, judges, and other juvenile justice personnel at work in the system. They give a dramatic picture of the process at work, with all of the attendant pressures that the individuals involved face.

- Along with readability, the organization of the text makes the content clear to the reader. The subject matter flows in a logical and planned fashion following the system as a whole and the process to which juveniles are subjected.

- Attention is given to special populations by including separate chapters focusing on juvenile gangs and juvenile victims.

ORGANIZATION OF *JUVENILE JUSTICE TODAY*

This text is divided into three major sections and twelve chapters. Part I presents the history of the juvenile justice system and offending. It examines the handling of juveniles by justice systems from ancient times up to the present, along with the slow emergence of a separate system of juvenile justice. Chapter 1 traces the development of juvenile justice from Babylon to the treatment of juveniles through the establishment of and changes in the operations of the juvenile court in the twentieth century. Chapter 2 examines statistics on juvenile justice and crime today, providing a basis for the examination of issues covered in the remainder of the text. Chapter 3 presents the connection between theory, issues, and juvenile justice practice. Here, theory is integrated with a serious problem presented by juveniles and a practice that is proposed to deal with them.

Part II is an extensive coverage of the entire juvenile justice process. It examines the parts of the juvenile justice system that are both similar to and different from the adult criminal justice system. Chapter 4 reviews the process model of juvenile justice and the specialized language and terminology used to handle juvenile cases. A handy lexicon of related phrases is provided to help the student understand the differences between the adult and juvenile justice models. Chapter 5 deals with the relationships that exist with the juvenile in trouble and his or her first point of contact: the police. The development of police organizations to deal with juveniles is reviewed, with special attention given to community and problem-oriented policing. Chapter 6 examines the systems of classification and assessment that are designed to put juveniles into groups to facilitate custody and treatment plans in both the institution and the community. Chapter 7 traces the development of the juvenile court and the modern pressures for change, primarily to make it more like the adult system with regard to both due process and accountability. It also provides a review of the legal rights of juveniles, tracing the significant legal decisions that have begun to shape and change the juvenile justice process. Chapter 8 examines the problems and hopes that lie in juvenile probation, a system that is splintered into so many jurisdictions that it seems to be no system at all. Special attention is given to innovations in juvenile probation, such as electronic monitoring and school probation. Chapter 9 traces the history of juvenile institutions as a response to delinquency. In particular, the serious issue of disproportionate minority confinement and the holding of juveniles in adult jails and prisons are examined. Chapter 10 examines juvenile parole and its less-than-fulfilled promise to return the juvenile to the community successfully. The model of Intensive Aftercare is also presented.

Part III considers two special populations in the juvenile justice system: juvenile victims and juvenile gangs. Chapter 11 covers juvenile victimization and also looks at group homes, foster care, and adoption as potential ways to place juveniles in productive environments rather than the formal juvenile justice process. Chapter 12 presents the nature and extent of the juvenile gang problem in the United States. The chapter describes attributes of gang members and characteristics of the gang, including risk factors and models for gang entry, as well as the development of gang-related programming.

SUPPLEMENTS

Instructor Supplements

- A PowerPoint presentation is available for each chapter.
- The Instructor's Manual with Test Bank contains a chapter summary, outline, key terms, and test questions to accompany each chapter of the text.
- The test bank is also available in the form of MyTest (a computerized test bank) and in Blackboard and WebCT formats.
- An e-book version of the text is available in the form of CourseSmart.
- The Video Profiles accompanying the text are available through the MyCrimeKit Web site at www.mycrimekit.com.

To access these supplementary materials online, instructors must request an instructor access code. Go to **www.pearsonhighered.com/irc**, where you can register for an instructor access code. Within 48 hours after registering, you will receive a confirming e-mail, including an instructor access code. After you have received your code, go to the site and log on for full instructions on downloading the materials you wish to use.

Student Supplements

The online MyCrimeKit study guide at www.mycrimekit.com offers practice quizzes, essay questions, flashcards for key terms, Web quest activities, and related Web links to accompany each chapter of the text. MyCrimeKit also houses the video profiles that accompany the text, as well as career information and research tools (the Prentice Hall Criminal Justice Cybrary and Research Navigator). Students can submit the practice quizzes, essays, and Web quest activities to instructors through the Web site for grading.

ACKNOWLEDGMENTS

We are indebted to many people for the preparation and production of this text. It has been reviewed by several of our colleagues around the country; their thoroughness, attention to detail, and expertise in juvenile justice was a tremendous help. The Kentucky Department of Juvenile Justice provided many of the illustrations in the text and is the hope of juveniles in the Commonwealth. Eric Krassow was our editor at Prentice Hall. Elisa Rogers supervised the preparation of the manuscript, and she has our sincere appreciation for her encouragement and patience. Thanks to the Kunselman kids—Alex, Davis, Lacie, Lauren, Logan, Jordyn, Kaitlyn, and Will—for sharing their love of laughter, exploration, and learning; their spirit and beautiful smiles are gifts of energy for sacrifices made. Mary Vito put up with her husband's absences and gave Gennaro the time away from his chores and families to do the work necessary to complete the text. Of course, a great deal of this text contains the words of the original author, Clifford E. Simonsen. We owe him a debt that cannot be repaid. His scholarship lives on in these pages.

We also acknowledge our reviewers: Wendie Johnna Albert, Keiser University; Eric G. Anderson, Chippewa Valley Technical College; James J. Drylie, Kean University; Melissa Ricketts, Shippensburg University; Pamela Tontodonato, Kent State University; John Vivian, Arizona State University–West Campus; Ivy Yarckow-Brown, Missouri State University; and Maryann Zihala, Ozarks Technical Community College.

We hope that this text helps children in trouble and those persons who work so hard in the juvenile justice system and elsewhere on their behalf.

G. F. V.
J. C. K.

about the authors

Gennaro F. Vito is a Distinguished University Scholar and Professor in the Department of Justice Administration at the University of Louisville. He also serves as a faculty member in the Administrative Officer's Course at the Southern Police Institute, Vice Chair. He holds a Ph.D. in Public Administration from The Ohio State University. Active in professional organizations, he is a past President and Fellow of the Academy of Criminal Justice Sciences. He is also the recipient of the Educator of the Year Award from the Southern Criminal Justice Association (1991) and the Dean's Outstanding Performance Award for Research and Scholarly Activities from the former College of Urban and Public Affairs at University of Louisville (1990), the Dean's Award for Outstanding Research from the College of Arts and Sciences and the President's Distinguished Faculty Award for Excellence in Research (2002). He has published on such topics as capital sentencing, police consolidation, police traffic stops, policing strategies for drug problems in public housing, attitudes toward capital punishment, and the effectiveness of criminal justice programs, such as drug elimination programs, drug courts, and drug testing of probationers and parolees. He is the coauthor of nine textbooks in criminal justice and criminology, including *Criminology: Theory, Research and Practice* (Jones & Bartlett) and *Organizational Behavior and Management in Law Enforcement* (Prentice Hall).

Julie C. Kunselman is a Professor in the Department of Political Science and Criminal Justice at Northern Kentucky University. She earned her bachelor's degree in Mathematics from Gannon University and a Master's of Public Administration and Ph.D. in Urban and Public Affairs from the University of Louisville. She has published more than 25 articles in areas of leadership and administration, public policy, and student engagement and pedagogy, as well as coauthored two textbooks: *Research Methods in Criminal Justice* (Charles C. Thomas) and *Statistical Analysis in Criminal Justice and Criminology: A User's Guide* (Waveland). She has also contributed to more than 20 monographs, grants, and community research partnerships.

JUVENILE JUSTICE
TODAY

PART I

History of the Juvenile Justice System and Offending

1

The History of Juvenile Justice

*O*ur whole society is organized to separate child from adult and to provide a host of ways for taking the presumed developmental stages of childhood into account. The invention of delinquency, the creation of the juvenile court, the drafting of child labor laws, the legal requirements regulating the school-leaving age, pediatricians, child psychiatrists, and elementary and secondary school teachers are all a reflection of our modern construction of childhood.

LAMAR T. EMPEY[1]

LEARNING OBJECTIVES

1. Identify the historical trends in the views of how children should be handled to avoid the problems of crime and delinquency.

2. Identify how society's view of children changed throughout history.

3. Identify how the American juvenile justice system was influenced by its historical predecessors in Europe and England.

4. Identify the influence of the "child savers" on the creation of the American juvenile court.

5. Define the concept of *parens patriae* and identify its influence on the American juvenile justice system.

6. Identify how the "due process revolution" shaped the American juvenile justice system.

7. Describe the deinstitutionalization process promoted by Jerome Miller.

CHAPTER OVERVIEW

Is the concept of juvenile justice as a system something new? How did this concept evolve to the juvenile justice system we have today? Have children always received more lenient treatment than adults from those who make and enforce the law? How did early societies control the child who got outside the boundaries of their folkways, mores, and laws? In this brief overview, these and many other questions will be explored. We examine the ancient as well as the more recent antecedents of juvenile justice, from 2000 B.C. to the end of the nineteenth century. It should be noted that this is not a history text; but, as the writer Studs Terkel said, "A society that doesn't know its past cannot understand its future." It is important for students of juvenile justice and juvenile crime to be familiar with the rich history of this segment of the criminal justice system. These examples demonstrate the timelessness of the problems both presented and caused by juveniles and their behavior. We will try to show how the complaints of adults in ancient times mirror those made about juveniles today. We sincerely hope this survey will stimulate the student to seek other volumes to fill in the blanks of the brief history presented herein. We shall start with development of the concept of laws to control the order and structures of early societies.

PRIMITIVE LAWS

proscribed Acts or behaviors that are universally forbidden. Some examples are rape, incest, murder, treason, kidnapping, and rebellion. These acts fall at the forbidden end of the behavioral continuum.

folkways Socially acceptable behaviors

mores Societal norms and customs

Behaviors can be viewed as points on a continuum, as shown in Figure 1.1: Continuum of Behavior (*Source:* Simonsen, Clifford E., *Juvenile Justice in America,* 3rd ed.). From the earliest times, certain acts have been universally forbidden, or **proscribed**. Some examples are rape, incest, murder, treason, kidnapping, and rebellion. These acts fall at the forbidden end of the behavioral continuum. Approved or prescribed acts, such as getting married, having children, or having a job fall at the opposite, or approved, end. Most socially acceptable behaviors fall somewhere near the middle and were generally referred to as **folkways. Mores** or societal norms and customs were generally enforced through the use of strong social

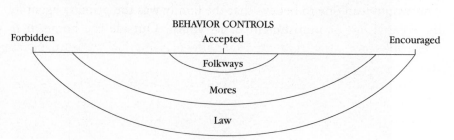

Figure 1.1
Continuum of Behavior

Source: "Behavior Controls" from *Juvenile Justice in America,* 3rd Edition, by Clifford E. Simonsen. Copyright © 1991 by Clifford E. Simonsen. Reprinted by permission of Pearson Education, Inc., Upper Saddle River, NJ.

disapproval, such as ostracism, exile, punishment, and even death. Mores were also reinforced through the use of rewards or strong social approval, such as money and lands, dowries, and fertility rites.

As societies progressed, their loosely structured sanctions became codified and referred to as law. However, enforcement was gradually taken out of the hands of the general citizenry and given to special law enforcement groups ranging from witch hunters to the Magistrates Court of England.

The Old Testament concept of an "eye for an eye" (Exodus 21:24) best describes how ancient humans dealt with wrongs committed against themselves or their property. Although this concept of revenge cannot be considered to have been "law," it has had a strong influence on the development of most legal systems throughout history.

As early societies developed language and writing skills, they began to record their laws. The **Hammurabic Code**, which dates from c. 2270 B.C., is considered by many historians to be the first comprehensive attempt at codifying such laws. This code recorded the laws of Babylon. It was an attempt to regulate business transactions, property rights, rights of master and slave, and family relationships.[2]

Hammurabic Code Dates from c. 2270 B.C., and is considered by many historians to be the first comprehensive attempt at codifying laws.

In the period of the Code of Hammurabi, the husband and father was decidedly in charge of the family. A part of that code was written as follows: "If a son strikes his father, one shall cut off his hands."[3] Compared with such early bloody forms of punishment of children by their parents, today's practice of referring the juvenile to court for rebellion or misconduct (status offenses) seems very mild.

The code also provided for the adoption of children. However, in return for a home, adopted children were expected to be loyal to their adoptive parents. If such an adopted child were to deny the parentage of his adoptive family, he could have his tongue cut out, and if she were to return to her natural father's or mother's home, she could have an eye plucked out.[4]

The code also had many regulations regarding the care of children by parents and marital arrangements. However, these laws involved behavior within the family unit; public offenses were not mentioned. This would lead one to believe that the family was the primary agent in the supervision or punishment of its youth. Outside the home, it is reasonable to assume that children suffered the same punishments as adults.

At that time, boys attended school twelve hours a day all year long from the time they were very young through early manhood. Liberal use of corporal punishment helped to encourage their industriousness. Fathers wanted their sons to stay in school, do their homework, respect their elders, and use their spare time constructively. In other words, the father admonished his son to do just what most parents today still want their children to do: get a good education.

Little has been recorded about crime that may have been committed by youths in early human history. Our knowledge of the time consists primarily of examples of some of the punishments. The types of court systems employed, what jails or prisons were like, and how the policing of juveniles was conducted remain on the whole an historical mystery. What we do know is that discipline and control of children was generally considered the responsibility of parents. Because there was no juvenile court, a royal court or a local magistrate dealt with juveniles outside their family. Persons, including children, were not generally imprisoned in early history as a form of punishment. They were normally detained only until their punishment was determined and applied.

In fact, one of the first prisons in the world was designed to incarcerate juveniles. In 1704, Pope Clement XI built the **Hospice at San Michele** in Rome to rehabilitate wayward youth. Of course, the Holy Father was interested in saving youthful souls and having them atone for their sins. This early institution housed the two sets of juvenile clients that remain with us today: those sentenced for actual crimes and "incorrigible" boys who could not be controlled by their parents. Thus, the desire to "save the children" was evident from the very beginning of juvenile institutions.

Hospice at San Michele One of the first prisons in the world; was designed to incarcerate juveniles and rehabilitate wayward youth

European and British Views of the Origins of Delinquency

American definitions of delinquency were influenced by those of their European and British forebears. Up through the Age of Enlightenment, the treatment for children in trouble seemed to be corporal punishment and tough discipline. Children during that long period were treated more as property than as small human beings with their own rights. Of course, this era also provided little but severe punishment as the primary response to adults who broke laws. The prevailing method of treatment for adults and juveniles alike seemed to be to try to "beat the devil" out of the offender. Often this resulted in a death sentence for the person being "treated," if the devil was reluctant to leave. In the eighteenth century, as Old World practices were imported to the New World, problems with children began to gain at least some attention from the criminal justice systems of the colonies and then from the fledgling United States of America.

Similarly, a British report on crime among youths cited the chief causes of delinquency as poverty, lack of education, and poor parental guidance.[5] Not surprisingly, studies in the mid-1990s show that children from low-income families, who do not get an education, and are from bad or broken homes are much more likely to get into trouble with the law by the age of 18 years than are youths from middle- or high-income families.[6]

In addition, the British public was also blamed for the failure of the "Poor Laws" of the time to provide adequate homes and care for destitute children. However, poor children did not make up the entire population of England's delinquents. As in the present day, reforms are made and public interest aroused only when the problem of crime and delinquency creeps out of the ghettos of poverty and racism and begins to affect the middle-class or wealthy.[7]

History of Childhood

We take for granted modern views of juveniles and the stages of life that are the basis of the juvenile justice system. This limited view overlooks the fact that the juvenile justice system represented a radical change in how youths were treated by society. It was based on a changed view of childhood and how children should be handled. History shows us that children were not always valued by society. For example, infanticide (the killing of legitimate children) was only slowed in the Middle Ages. Illegitimate children were killed far into the nineteenth century.[8] In Roman society, children who were not physically perfect or who cried too much were routinely murdered. Sons were prized because they could provide for their parents in old age. Unlike girls, they would also make certain that the family name and lineage would continue. Both infanticide and abandonment were common methods of controlling family size, as abortion is viewed today. A high death rate among children due to disease was commonplace; therefore, close attachment to them was ill advised. The attitude of parents toward children was commonly one of indifference and detachment.

Views of child rearing were also quite different. Children were commonly sold into bondage and servitude to prepare them for the adult world of work. Indenture contracts to merchants and craftsmen were routinely signed. During the Middle Ages, children were apprenticed when still very young. Typically, they then lived in large, communal-like households. As a result, youths were exposed to all forms of adult depravity. The sexual abuse of children and promiscuity was the norm through the seventeenth century.

The modern view of protecting children is also a recent event. Children of all classes and stations were exposed to harsh punishments to instill discipline, including whipping and branding. Basically, there was no modern concept of childhood as a special and protected time of life. As is typically depicted in the arts, children were little more than miniature adults.

The modern conception of childhood gradually developed in Europe and the New World. Education and intellectual development were eventually prized as methods of moral training for youths. Among the Puritans, principles were established to govern the behavior of children[9]:

1. The first principle emphasized the importance of keeping a close watch over children and never permitting them to be alone.
2. The second stressed the importance of disciplining rather than pampering or coddling children. They must learn to exercise self-control and to exhibit appropriate manners in social situations.

3. The third principle stressed the importance of modesty. Children should not be permitted to go to bed in the presence of a person of the opposite sex. Young girls should be completely covered and not lie in an immodest position. Children of different sexes should not sleep together.

4. Parents were admonished to prepare children for the world of adult work. The work ethic was not only morally desirable but economically necessary for the continued existence of the family.

5. Respect for and obedience to all authority was expected. Children were warned to honor not only their parents but any authority figure. Disobedience inevitably led to destruction.

These principles became the basis for the attitudes toward children in the American colonies. Their purpose was to ensure the proper development of children to take their place in adult society. Childhood eventually became a transition point in life.

Examples of Penalties for Juvenile Crime

The Christian church continued to have an important role in regulating the behavior of disobedient children. As frequently as not, punishment for crimes in the Middle Ages was the same for children as for adults. For example, children convicted of *petie treason*, or willful murder, could be drowned, hanged, or burned alive, depending on their background. However, there were exceptions for severe punishments based on the age of the child. For example, children fourteen years of age and under could not be convicted of burglary[10] or larceny[11] in England.

In addition to the Magistrate's Court mentioned previously, children were also tried in the central court in London, which was commonly called the **Old Bailey**. Court records reveal that the numbers of children tried in this court were miniscule when compared with the number of adults. And, although court records indicate that many children were sentenced to death, it cannot be ascertained whether these death penalties were ever carried out. Many sentences were commuted or the judge pardoned the offender, and such events often went unrecorded.

There are many examples of punishment of children in this period. In 1682, Quaker children in Bristol were put in the **stocks** and whipped for misbehavior. In Halifax, in 1691, children were thrown into debtors' prison; to avoid their rotting in jail and dying of starvation, these children were compelled to work for their creditors until the debt was paid. Many were less than 14 years of age. In 1716, in England, a mother and her 11-year-old daughter were executed for witchcraft.

Other juvenile issues dealt with during this period parallel the problems of the present day, including dealing with children in need due to homelessness and poverty. Later in the same century, other methods of

Old Bailey The central court in London, England, which also tried juveniles

stocks A wooden structure used in the 1600s for restraining criminals; usually used in a public setting

dealing with delinquent or vagrant youth were tried. One of them, as explained here, could well be an early forerunner for our present trade or industrial school: It entailed sending vagrant and delinquent boys to service as apprentices on British warships.[12]

In 1758, construction was begun in London on a prototype of what has come to be known today as a "group home." It was established by Sir John Fielding and was called the "**House of Refuge** for Orphan Girls." The purpose of this home was to rescue vagrant girls from almost certain lives of prostitution.

Public asylums for the children of convicts and other destitute or neglected children, such as that founded by the Philanthropic Society in London, were proposed in 1786. Records from the Report of the Select Committee Appointed by the House of Commons show that between 1787 and 1797, ninety-three delinquent children were transported for crimes from England to Australia. This practice continued into the early 1800s. During transportation, the children were kept in confinement on the various decrepit ships ("**hulks**") that took them from their native land.[13] By 1829, **transportation**[14] for life was the recommended punishment for the growing number of juvenile delinquents.

Imprisonment of children, though frowned upon by early social reformers, did exist, although the social reformers had a hand in changing some of the more deplorable conditions of the time, including the treatment and confinement of young criminals. The Warwick County Asylum, instituted in 1818, was the result of the united endeavors and generous contributions of concerned, benevolent citizens. The proposed object of the asylum was to make available to the criminal boy a place where he could escape the ways of vice and corruption. As is the case today, early efforts at reform suffered from the lack of sufficient funds. The public soon lost interest in the asylum, and the only way it survived was by showing the franchised public that it could save them money.

By 1815, juvenile crime in London had reached serious proportions, and inquiries were conducted to discover the causes. One of the earliest recorded surveys of juvenile delinquency took place in London between 1815 and 1816. According to the survey, juvenile delinquency in metropolitan London was epidemic. Organized gangs of homeless boys survived life on the streets by picking pockets and stealing. Actual figures on the number of delinquents in metropolitan London at the time of the survey are not available. However, the committee had reason to believe that there were thousands of boys under the age of 17 years who engaged daily in criminal activities.

The group formed to conduct the survey realized that inquiry alone would serve no purpose, so its members also set out to find ways of providing help so that these wayward youths might turn their paths from vice to virtue. In this effort, they often ran into problems similar to those

House of Refuge A "group home" in London constructed in 1758 to rescue vagrant girls from almost certain lives of prostitution

hulks Ships used to confine and transport delinquent children from England to Australia

transportation In the late 1700s and early 1800s, there were delinquent children transported for crimes from England to Australia. During transportation, the children were kept in confinement on the various ships.

encountered today. They had to find funding sources for suggested reforms. They had to convince the parents or guardians of a delinquent youth that leaving him or her in the community and not imprisoning the child might serve the best interests of the juvenile. Having a child or children put in jail was cheaper for the parents—and many of them would prefer to have extra money for alcohol or gambling.

THE EARLY AMERICAN EXPERIENCE

Colonial youth did not escape the wrath of secular law or of strict Puritanical thinking and preaching, nor was their treatment much different from that of the youth of "Jolly Old England." Punishment being dealt out to delinquent children in the early era of the New England colonies (1641–1672) included: trials for burglary and theft of fruits from gardens, corporal punishment (whipping) for stealing clothing, the death penalty for children over 16 for "cursing or smiting" their parents, and the removal of children from their homes if their parents failed to provide training and instruction to obtain honest work.[15]

The American colonies were quick to catch up with and even surpass the English at incarcerating criminals, including juveniles. In Philadelphia in 1790, the Quakers were instrumental in founding the nation's first true correctional institution in a section of the Walnut Street Jail. Although the present method of using a separate court for juveniles had not yet been implemented at that time, juvenile delinquents did come before Colonial Courts and early American Courts. It seems that court judges faced the perplexing problem of what to do with these children then, just as they do now.

America, too, had its reform movements. Several citizen groups tried to deal with the problem of the rising number of juvenile delinquents. In 1823, the New York Society proposed a house of refuge for juvenile delinquents for the prevention of pauperism. To plead for their cause, the society obtained statistics on persons brought before the police magistrates during 1822: There were 450 persons, all under the age of 25 years, and a considerable percentage of these were both boys and girls from ages 9 to 16 years. None of these children had actually been charged with a crime other than vagrancy; they had no homes and were forced to fend for themselves. Eventually, the view of the proper role of government in the guidance of children adopted a more caring and thoughtful process of intervention.

Parens Patriae

Like most of America's criminal justice system, our juvenile justice system derives from the common law of England. *Parens patriae* gave the state the right and responsibility to take control over children from the natural

---

mycrimekit™

Review: Difference between Adult and Juvenile Justice System

parens patriae The state has right and responsibility to take control over children from the natural parents when they prove to be unable to meet their responsibilities or when the child is a problem for the community.

parents when they proved to be unable to meet their responsibilities or when the child was a problem for the community. In England, this responsibility was fulfilled by the chancery courts as a part of their legal authority under the feudal system. The needful child became a ward of the state under the authority of *parens patriae* doctrine.[16] The chancery court was designed to act more flexibly than the more rigid criminal courts. The main concern was for the welfare of the child, and legal procedures that might hamper the court in its beneficial actions were either circumvented or ignored. Thus, there were two concepts under the common law: (1) that children from birth to age 7 years were not responsible for their actions and (2) that a certain category of children was in need of protection by the state. It was not until the ages of possible responsibility were raised to 16 and 18 years that these two concepts merged into the idea of juvenile delinquency.

From the ages of 8 through 14 years, offenders were not held responsible unless the state could prove that they could clearly distinguish between right and wrong. Last, when offenders were over the age of 14 years, they were assumed to be responsible for their acts and therefore deserving of punishment. In this last case, the burden rested with the defendants to prove that they were not legally responsible.

In 1838, the doctrine of *parens patriae* became a part of the American juvenile justice system in the court decision *Ex parte Crouse*. This decision justified the commitment of a juvenile offender to a house of refuge. The court intervened on behalf of a child whose parents were too poor to ensure her education and to control her behavior. Thus the state was recognized as an official agent that could assume the control and care of children in the face of deficient families.[17]

The Age of Reform and Reform Schools: 1825 to the Early 1900s

With the creation of the juvenile justice system, new institutions became the central instrument to discipline and control children. Strict laws regulated behavior, and the penalties for juvenile offenders were severe. The first of the early juvenile **reform schools** was the New York House of Refuge, which opened in 1825. Their numbers grew during the nineteenth century, and eventually, the administration of the schools was overtaken by the state. The first state juvenile reform school opened in 1846, and by 1876 the country had 51 reform schools. Facility administrators determined the length of stay and had broad discretion in transferring disruptive youths to adult prisons.[18] During the first half of the twentieth century, separate facilities for girls were created. The schools emphasized deference to authority and physical labor, which has remained central to reform schools throughout their history.[19] In fact, administrators built juvenile facilities in rural areas, assuming that farm

reform schools Juvenile institutions that emphasized formal training and were administered by municipal and state governments in the mid-1800s

work would aid the reform process. When conditions of confinement deteriorated sharply after the Civil War, many states established boards to oversee their facilities.

The goal of these institutions was to provide "a good dose of institutionalization" to "benefit" the juvenile offender, the wandering street arab, the willfully disobedient child, and the orphan to "shield them from the temptations of a sinful world."[20] For example, the Philadelphia House of Refuge sought to expose its youthful charges to "a course of rigid but not cruel or ignominious discipline," including "unrelenting supervision, mild but certain punishments for any infraction of the rules, and habits of quiet and good order at all times."[21] The hope was that institutionalization would repair the damage caused by the outside environment.

As the Industrial Revolution began, many secular and Puritanical laws against truancy and vagrancy were conveniently forgotten so that industrialists could take advantage of cheap child labor and to make way for the urban sweatshops that lay just around the corner. Unfortunately for adults as well as children, the expanding, exploitative economy of young America provided less protection for the individual. In an attempt to keep pace with the newly emerging economy and its needs, the prison movement's search for the causes of delinquency soon gave way to merely dealing with the physical manifestations of delinquency and exploiting the child labor potential.

In the first decade of the nineteenth century, legislatures began to delegate the *parens patriae* role to the legal structure, which temporarily served to mask the vast differences between the Puritan-like "reformer" and the "child saver" outcomes expected for children and families. The reformers used tradition and the concept of social order as a basis for reducing state intervention at the expense of child-saving efforts. The child-savers expounded the Protestant work ethic, were primarily philanthropic, and supported the rehabilitation model. They had little real interest in the law or legal issues. Any overreach of the legal rights of the children was excused under the concept of *parens patriae*.

By 1828, the first institution for juvenile delinquents in the United States came into existence. It had taken more than five years of careful planning and maneuvering for public support on the part of the Society for the Prevention of Pauperism, which went on to become the Society for the Reformation of Juvenile Delinquents in the City of New York. The concept of this early institution was sound; it provided juveniles with a place of imprisonment or punishment that separated them from adults. However, what it did not provide was separate kinds of punishments. Children were still bound and fettered as adults with such things as handcuffs, the ball and chain, leg irons, and the "barrel."[22] Sporadic attempts were made to expose the deplorable conditions in those "houses of refuge" to the public and the press. Some reforms were brought about by the efforts of such men as Elijah Devoe, the assistant superintendent of the New York House of Refuge; William Sawyer, a magistrate in Massachusetts who decried sending children to places that turned them out in worse condition than when they were put in; and Edward Everett Hale, whose 1855 essays on juvenile delinquency offered the suggestion of guilt and stigma-free alternatives to the "criminal rules" of the day.

The depression of 1837 rekindled the flame of "nativism." Again, foreign-born paupers were victims of abuse and neglect at the hands of the politicians—and victims of worse at the hands of refuge house managers. Refuge houses went so far as to publish the names and native citizenship of juveniles and their parents. In the beginning, African Americans were barred from admittance to houses of refuge or, if admitted, were treated badly. The superintendant of Philadelphia's house of refuge stated that "It would be degrading to the white children to associate them with beings given up to public scorn." Eventually separate houses were opened for African American youths; the new inmates were characterized as "the offending offspring of the poorest, most ignorant, most degraded and suffering members of our community."[23]

The goal of refuge managers was to indoctrinate the poor unfortunates who passed through their doors with "good solid middle-class values." Those who were slow to get the point in the beginning soon learned to play the game. The transformation of institutionalized young people into streetwise youth is nothing new.

Offending juveniles were often apprenticed to farmers or others offering an honest trade in return for hard work. The idea then, just as it remains today, was to get a child a job and keep him or her busy; after all, "idle hands are the devil's workshop." In fact, about 90 percent of the children released from houses of refuge each year entered into apprenticeships. By the mid-1800s, houses of refuge were enthusiastically declared a great success. Managers even advertised their houses in juvenile magazines such as the *Youths Casket* (1851). Managers took great pride in turning seemingly total misfits into productive, hard-working members of society. Redeemed children even wrote managers letters of testimony: "I seem plucked as a brand from the burning. I am a guilty rebel, saved by grace,"[24] stated one lad.

However, these exaggerated claims of success were disputed from both without and within. Managers and administrators often disagreed over methods of discipline. By the 1850s, there was a proliferation of reform schools in most Eastern seaboard states. The houses of refuge had failed to prevent the growth of juvenile delinquency by reforming delinquents, and there arose a need to identify certain children as a special class of deviants known as juvenile delinquents.

PREVENTIVE AGENCIES AND REFORM SCHOOLS

In 1849, George Matsell, the New York City police chief, publicly warned that the numbers of vicious and vagrant youth were increasing and that something must be done. And done it was. America moved from a time of houses of refuge into a time of preventive agencies and reform schools.

Philanthropists and others viewed the causes of delinquency differently behind this new movement. Refuge house managers had viewed children as inherently wicked and sought to change them. In the new system, children were thought most likely to be corrupted by their environments. Reformers of the day wanted to give children a break, a fresh start, and not condemn them for coming from the "wrong side of the tracks."

The church also took a strong hand in trying to deal with the problem of delinquency. The Methodist Episcopal Church, for example, opened a mission in New York City (called the Five Points Mission) to give vagrant and destitute children a basic education. The mission's director, Reverend Lewis Pease, even moved his wife and family into Five Points, which was in one of the poorest areas of New York City, and gave out clothing, food, and jobs to the poor. Child-saving societies employed agents to take groups of delinquent or vagrant children west by train. The children were then parceled out in towns along the way. Unlike the apprenticeships associated with the houses of refuge, there were no binding agreements between the child or the child placers and the families with whom they were to begin new lives.

Young Inmates at the State Agricultural and Industrial School, Monroe County, ca. 1910

Thus, agrarian work ethic emerges as the panacea for delinquency. Reformers sought to empty the streets of the slum children and put them all on farms. No one epitomized this movement more than Charles Loring Brace (1826–1890), the founder of the Children's Aid Society in 1853. In one of his many speeches, Brace told of the speech of one of his "westernized" newsboys to fellow "newsies": "Do you want to be newsboys always, and show blacks, and timber merchants in a small way selling matches? If ye do you'll stay in New York, but if you don't you'll go out West, and begin to be farmers, for the beginning of a farmer, my boys, is the making of a Congressman, and a President."[25]

Placing out encountered strong opposition, even though, as Brace claimed, a survey of Western prisons and almshouses in 1875 proved that his "children" had gotten into very little trouble in their new environments. The opposition came from the institutions that were deprived of the labor of children in training. Others argued that it was senseless to send a child all the way out West when there were adequate facilities for them in the East.

Beginning in the mid-1800s, municipal and state governments became interested in founding and administering juvenile institutions. They were called "reform schools," and they emphasized formal training. States and municipalities initially sought private support for their reform schools, but eventually the majority of the costs were paid out of state or city revenues.

Also in the mid-1800s, cottage reform schools emerged, which divided children into classes based on their criminal profiles. However, the majority of school operators did not use this method, stating, for example, "You may divide these boys into classes, and the vicious will grow more vicious, . . . but when mixed with the rest, and when they see a public opinion in favor of reform, they will reflect, improve, and in the end be reformed."[26] The proponents of the cottage reform schools contended that mixing different classes of delinquents would simply multiply the crime problem and not solve it.

During the Civil War, penitentiaries and jails were practically empty, whereas reform schools were filled beyond capacity. This latter situation was attributable to the absence of parental authority when fathers were called into the service. Many of the reform schools made room for younger boys by releasing the older ones to the military.

Post–Civil War economic conditions forced institutions for juvenile delinquents to curb many of their nonbasic activities. During the late nineteenth and early twentieth centuries, governments of Western and Northern states were given the responsibility for the control and care of many additional categories of indigent persons, including children in orphanages, almshouses, insane asylums, and mental hospitals. This shift in responsibility forced the juvenile institutions into competition with these other agencies for the funds they needed. As a result, many of the juvenile correctional facilities were forced to operate on deficit budgets that reduced them to nothing more than delinquent warehouses.

Although the number and variety of institutions for delinquents did recover from this economic setback and resumed their growth, the severity of the problems that they faced also grew. As a result of poor management and lack of adequate resources both during and following institutionalization, the state institutions founded after the turn of the twentieth century offered very little in the way of adequate treatment and subsequent planned reentry for youths into the community when it was determined that they were ready to be discharged. All too often, youths were forced out of institutions for lack of space and without any other alternative than to turn them loose unsupervised and back on the streets.

In the dark history of the treatment of juveniles in trouble, up through the Age of Enlightenment, the answer seemed to be punishment and tough discipline. Children through that huge span of history were treated as property, rather than as small humans with the rights and privileges of adults. It should be noted, however, that this long period also delivered harsh and cruel punishment to adults. It seems that a prevailing philosophy for adults and juveniles was to "beat the devil out of them." As was shown, this method usually resulted in the demise of the offending person if the devil was reluctant to depart. It was not until the eighteenth century that children with problems began to gain at least some attention from the new nation called the United States regarding some separation of juvenile and adult miscreants.

The early efforts at a juvenile court system in 1899 began the movement toward a truly separate system for juvenile justice. Before the start of the modern era, several circumstances molded the future of the juvenile justice system in America. Among them was the practice of dealing with delinquent and dependent youth that has come to be known as the **mother image**, in which women crusaded for children's rights and for treatment of children different from that accorded adult criminals. These social activists became known as "the **child savers**." Modern practices of social work with neglected and dependent youths owe much to this movement, which was strictly a female domain. These women, including Jane Addams, Louise Bower, Ellen Herotin, and Julia Lathrop, were usually well traveled and well educated, and they had access to financial and political resources.

However, scholars have questioned the motives of these activists. Platt (1969) was one of the first to suggest that their humanitarian efforts disguised the paternalistic and severely punitive system of correction for juveniles.[27] Eventually, their reforms created a number of policies that thwarted juvenile rehabilitation.

Another practice that began before the start of the modern era but that has carried over into the present-day juvenile justice system is that of

mother image The practice of women dealing with delinquent and dependent youth before the start of the modern era. These women, including Jane Addams, Louise Bower, Ellen Herotin, and Julia Lathrop, were usually well traveled and well educated, and they had access to financial and political resources.

child savers Before the start of the modern era, these individuals crusaded for children's rights and for treatment of children different from that accorded adult criminals.

Elmira Reformatory, Exercise Yard, 1900

providing alternatives (resources and conditions permitting) to institutionalization for dependent and neglected juveniles. However, despite the existence of houses of refuge, reform schools, special institutions, and the practice of placing out children into apprenticeships, children were still jailed or imprisoned with little or no consideration of whether they had committed a crime. The incarceration of dependent and neglected youths (**status offenders**) today is comparable to the practice in the late 1800s and early 1900s.

status offenders Conduct by the juvenile that would not be defined as a criminal act if committed by an adult; Nondelinquent youth, including those who commit offenses that would not be considered "criminal" if the youth were an adult (e.g., runaways), as well as dependent and neglected youths

DELINQUENCY AND DELINQUENTS: THE LATE 1890S AND THE EARLY 1900S

The years preceding and following the turn of the century did see some basic though often crude attempts to explain delinquency and the emergence of various treatments for changing human behavior patterns. These attempts accompanied the introduction of the social science approach in the field of juvenile corrections. Granville Stanley Hall (1846–1924), for example, developed an evolutionary explanation of delinquent behavior based on the notion that childhood years are a period of savagery in which the forces of good and evil constantly do battle with one another for the possession of the child's soul. Hall categorized juveniles in trouble as victims of circumstances who deserved pity, understanding, and love. When forces of good had won the child, he was considered "born again." Thus, this theory came to be known as the "recapitulation theory": Through proper guidance and influence, social reformers could transform evil youths into "angels of virtue." Again, we encounter the "child savers." As mentioned previously, these reformers were primarily females who crusaded for children's rights and treating them differently from adult criminals.

As a prime example, Jane Addams (1860–1935) was a noted child saver and founder of a famous social settlement in Chicago known as Hull House. Influenced by recapitulation theory, Addams believed that juveniles had naturally free spirits in quest of joy and happiness. She felt that the urban environment that placed commercial interests above creative fun and recreation stifled this quest. Addams viewed delinquents as actually being good children who were turned bad by the urban environment and poverty. Unfortunately, her belief could not explain why some juveniles were incarcerated and why others from similar backgrounds were not. This quandary led to a search for other explanations for delinquent behavior.

For example, one of Addams' contemporaries, William Forbush, believed that juveniles who were struggling with the forces of good and evil became stuck in what he called **psychic arrest**. Psychic arrests were considered periods of continued tendencies toward crime. Forbush believed that if the period of his or her psychic arrest did not pass, a juvenile could be permanently locked into a life of crime. However, this theory, like those before it, lacked empirical verification and was based almost entirely on speculation.

psychic arrest Periods of continued tendencies toward crime. Forbush believed that if the period of his or her psychic arrest did not pass, a juvenile could be permanently locked into a life of crime.

Despite their humanitarian intentions, the child savers have been criticized for imposing their class, ethnic, and racial biases on the poor, immigrants, and minorities.[28] For example, Kasinsky states that minority mothers were labeled "unfit" because their style of care did not conform to those of the child savers. Thus, these mothers were the objects of state control and their children were often removed from their homes.[29]

Scientific explanations of delinquency advanced very little toward proof during this period. There were some attempts to apply scientific principles of study to delinquents, but these were conducted more as laboratory experimentation than as scientific attempts to explain delinquent behavior. For example, in the early 1900s special institutions for defective delinquents offered scientists and behaviorists a captive population for their experimental use. In Indiana, in 1907, the first sterilization statute in America was passed; other states followed suit, and by 1936, twenty-five states had similar laws allowing for the sterilization of defective delinquents.[30] Often the result of economic pressures, contemporary views of morality, and political manipulations, these nonscientific ideas and attitudes brought the advancement of significant, scientifically based, causal theories of delinquency to a standstill.

mycrimekit™

Review: Historical Treatment of Children and the Juvenile Justice System

THE JUVENILE COURT MOVEMENT BEGINS

Despite concern for their children's welfare, most communities have a tolerance point for the disruptive behavior of juveniles. When children go beyond this point, they can be taken into custody and recorded as delinquents and placed in institutions. The mixing of juvenile offenders and adult felons was a practice that had existed for centuries, though in America's early history, it was looked on as repugnant. However, it was not until 1899 that the delinquent juvenile began to receive differential attention in the courts. The first **juvenile court** was established in that year in Cook County (Chicago, Illinois). The delinquent then joined the dependent and neglected child as a ward of the state.[31]

> **juvenile court** The first juvenile court was established in 1899 in Cook County, Illinois, which began the movement toward a truly separate system for juvenile justice.

When the juvenile delinquent was thus placed under the cloak of *parens patriae,* he or she was removed entirely from the formal criminal justice system of adults. Juvenile courts spread rapidly across the nation. By 1919, juvenile court legislation was a reality in all but three states. By 1932, there were estimated to be more than 600 independent juvenile courts in the United States. By 1945, there were juvenile courts in every state in the Union.

The early juvenile court system was part of a general movement toward the separation of juvenile offenders from adult felons. It was regarded as one of the greatest advances in the crusade to protect children's welfare and revolutionize the treatment of delinquent and neglected youths. But the juvenile court system, although revolutionary in theory, was not the hoped-for panacea that it was first thought to be. Eventually, major problems developed as a result of this combination of delinquent, dependent, and neglected children as wards of the state (*parens patriae*) under the same rubric. From the 1920s through the 1970s, the emphasis in dealing with juveniles had shifted from punishment and imprisonment to an attempt to understand the delinquent as a member of society.

Video Profile: Kids Today

Juvenile Justice during the Depression: A Bleak Era

The 1930s—the period of the Great Depression—brought a disruption in the progress and development of the juvenile justice system. As a result of the Depression, institutional and reform school budgets were cut back, and skilled and knowledgeable administrators were let go when staffs were reduced. Once again the philosophy of control and repression, accompanied at times by cruel and unnecessary punishment, became dominant.

During the Great Depression, new explanations of juvenile delinquency were proposed. One of these was the causal theory championed by Virginia P. Robinson and Jesse Taft, two maverick social workers. They believed that delinquency was the result of family disintegration and conflict: Because of conflict and maladaptation within the family unit, the child does not develop the ability to differentiate between right and wrong and therefore exhibits unacceptable social behavior. Psychiatric treatment became the cure of the day. From this approach, many forms of psychoanalytic treatment, including those developed by Freud, were used.

Yet it was still a generally accepted belief that the family alone was responsible for delinquency, and this led to demands that parents of delinquents be punished for failure to control the behavior of their children. For about ten years (1937–1946) the systematic punishment of parents was tried. Parents were fined heavily and even jailed for the acts of their offspring. However, the social effects of punishing parents were often disastrous, with the mother or father in prison and the home broken up. Children were placed in institutions or foster homes, or often left to shift for themselves.

It was also found that judges began to rely on punishing the parents instead of attempting to deal with the rehabilitation of the children. It became evident that blaming delinquency entirely on the family and punishing the parents for the "sins" of their children was not the answer to the problem. It was simply one of the many serious attempts to find a single, simple cause of delinquency.

Courts did continue a tendency toward treatment of children that was lenient compared with the punishment of adults for similar offenses. Unfortunately, courts and law enforcement agencies across the country varied widely in their treatment or punishment of juveniles who had committed like offenses. Punishment ranged from horsewhipping to prison terms.

The Depression era was also plagued by many of the problems faced currently. For example, a large number of juveniles are arrested today on drug charges. In the 1930s, juveniles were arrested with equal zeal for drinking—a violation of the prohibition of alcoholic beverages.[32] Not unlike the casualties of today's drug culture, Prohibition had its own casualties.

It is interesting to note that the parents of the juveniles involved bemoaned the fact that their children could not acquire "innocuous light wines and beer" instead of the "vile bootleg whisky." One wonders how many parents of juveniles spaced out on crack, angel dust, crystal methamphetamine, ecstasy, or heroin today might bemoan the fact that their children could not legally acquire "innocuous supplies of marijuana" instead of "vile" and potentially fatal doses of the hard drugs.

The Post-Depression Era: The 1940s and 1950s

Although the Illinois Court Act of 1899 did much to lead the way toward individualized treatment of the juvenile delinquent and dependent child, its practicality and efficacy came into question in the post-Depression era of the 1940s and 1950s. Although the courts in fact gave the youths treatment, the informality of proceedings under *parens patriae* deprived the juvenile of the same legal rights provided to adults who committed similar acts.

Deprived of equal protection under the Constitution, juveniles were subject to the discretionary authority of the courts, the police, and child service agencies. The courts, therefore, did what they could to process the ever-increasing number of juvenile cases coming before them.

The post-Depression era also spawned large detention facilities for juvenile offenders. The Youth House, a "kid Big House for big and little kids" in New York City, was typical of large juvenile detention facilities of this era. It soon acquired the reputation of being a poorly equipped, understaffed dumping ground for delinquent and dependent children. All the cruelties and brutalities that could be imagined in a "kid prison" took place in the original Youth House and its equally notorious successor. It has been claimed that Youth House and detention facilities and institutions like it destroyed more children each year than any known disease. Youth House processed thousands of children in New York each year, and although conditions there periodically become a public issue, it continued to operate with the same destructive force as in the past.

In the 1940s and 1950s, with a growing number of crimes committed by juveniles, police forces began to set up specialized juvenile units made up of specially assigned officers. For example, in 1944 the Chicago Police Department's Crime Prevention Bureau provided increased educational opportunities for juvenile officers. Juvenile personnel, especially policewomen, were given a special twelve-week course of instruction on the treatment of juveniles, including the subject of their referral to social agencies.[33]

The growing number of crimes committed by juveniles in this period meant a growing institutional population. Although an effort was made to provide juveniles with facilities to keep them separated from adult criminals, in most large cities these new juvenile detention facilities became little more than juvenile jails. And, when they became filled, dependent delinquents and status offenders were often moved to adult jails, which defeated the purpose of separate facilities.

In the post-Depression era, belief that the disintegration of the family was the prime cause of delinquency faded, and environmental factors and individual personalities were seen as its main cause. Many authorities of the day believed that "official" delinquency was primarily a lower-class phenomenon. However, the findings of several studies conducted during the 1950s indicated that there was not a universal causal relationship between social class and law-violating behavior.

Some current attempts to cope with and/or prevent delinquency are not so different in scope and design from those of the 1940s and 1950s. For example, the concept of a youth authority such as that in California and several other states had its beginnings in 1940 with the development of the American Law Institute's Model Youth Correction Authority Act. The major concern was for the treatment of those juvenile offenders who fell outside the age of most juvenile court jurisdictions and who, as a result, were often tried in adult criminal courts and sentenced to adult prisons. The model act was published in an attempt to urge various states to adopt a similar body of procedures and guidelines.[34]

> California adopted this concept for both adults and juveniles; Wisconsin and Minnesota followed suit, as did a number of other states, although they made several modifications. To date, although many such modifications have been made, states have been reluctant to implement the full provisions of the youth authority movement; however, the concept of parole release and aftercare supervision of children...did get a tremendous boost in the 1940s and 1950s from the youth authority model.[35]

It is often assumed that the idea of community-based treatment, diagnosis, and planning in the field of juvenile delinquency is the brainchild of the 1960s and early 1970s. As the passage cited indicates, community involvement in juvenile justice is far from new.

The post-Depression era gave rise to many studies and causal theories, including a book by Sheldon and Eleanor Glueck, *Unraveling Juvenile Delinquency*. The Gluecks found three factors prevalent among the 500 delinquents studied:

- The boys generally had poor family relations. Their fathers were needlessly harsh or completely lax in maintaining discipline, seldom firm but kindly. They received little parental love.
- They clashed with other people and were highly assertive, defiant, suspicious, destructive, and impulsive.
- They had turbulent personalities and were adventurous, extroverted, suggestible, stubborn, and emotionally unstable.

The authors made two conclusions in the article. First, detecting delinquency in its earliest stages is a job for specialists. It cannot be done, the Gluecks admitted, by any simple, easily interpreted pencil-and-paper test. Second, the husband and wife team believed that in delinquency, society is faced not with predestination, but with destination. And destination can often be modified by intelligent early intervention.[36]

The literature of the 1940s and early 1950s was filled with reports of **intervention strategy**, in which there was introduced into the life of a juvenile some outside intervening factor, such as intensive counseling. The influence of this intervening factor on the juvenile's future delinquent behavior was then evaluated. Dr. Edwin Powers described an experiment that utilized one such intervention strategy in an attempt to prevent delinquent behavior

intervention strategy Refers to reports from the 1940s and early 1950s when some outside "intervening factor" was introduced into the life of a juvenile in an attempt to evaluate the influence of this intervening factor on the juvenile's future delinquent behavior among a population of 650 boys. The conclusion of the study was somewhat vague in that the counselors were unable to stop the rapid advance of young boys into delinquency with any greater success than the usual deterrent forces in the community. Some of the boys were evidently deflected from delinquent careers that, without the counselors' help, might have resulted in continued or more serious violations. The researchers felt that although they were not completely successful in the first stage of delinquency prevention, in working with boys ages 8–11 years, later and more serious stages were to some degree curtailed.[37]

In the 1950s, several intervention strategy programs for youths were set up, providing job training and creating jobs. In 1956, for example, the Citizens Union of New York for the Prevention and Cure of Delinquency recommended the establishment of work camps for delinquent boys. The basic idea behind these camps and similar programs was to divert juveniles from exhibiting delinquent behavior by providing them opportunities for good jobs. This idea was expanded on in the early 1960s and thereafter through the establishment of such programs as (1) the Job Corps under Title 1-A of the Federal Poverty Program, (2) the Neighborhood Youth Corps under Title 1-B of the same program, and (3) the work-study program for college students under the same program. Through these programs, underprivileged youths are given an opportunity to upgrade their education and learn a trade or a skill that might lead to a decent, steady job. It should be noted that although the primary goal of these programs is to provide opportunities to juveniles in need, the prevention of delinquency is often a secondary objective and result. This differs somewhat from the concept of the work camps of the 1950s, whose primary objective was the prevention of recurrent delinquent behavior in juveniles who had already exhibited such behavior before coming into the programs.

The 1960s and 1970s: Chaos and Construction

In the 1960s and 1970s there were revolutionary legal, social, and procedural changes in the development and scope of the juvenile justice system. At the end of the 1970s, the United States had disengaged from the unpopular war in Vietnam; seen confrontations, riots, and killings on college campuses; witnessed major political assassinations; and gone through radical changes in all areas of social intercourse and activity.

During this era, men had been put on the moon, planes had been perfected that traveled faster than sound, surgeons had transplanted human organs and performed other almost unbelievable feats in medicine. Humanity had advanced technically and scientifically beyond previous generations' wildest dreams.

But had these technical and social advances solved the problem of juvenile delinquency in this country? Had scholars, writers, and researchers found any revolutionary new theories regarding the cause, cure, or prevention of this major problem? Unfortunately, the answer to both questions is no.

The ethical issues that face the juvenile justice system are essentially the same as those faced by society in general. Because of the highlighting of this system, however, the ethical dilemmas are exacerbated by observers and participants alike. If members of the healing professions (e.g., psychologists, psychiatrists) find that certain treatments have promise, they are again faced with an ethical kind of Catch-22: Is it ethical to treat those in the juvenile justice system, or is it preferable to divert them from the system completely?

> The importance of delinquency prevention was reflected by the growing concern of the federal government during the 1960s. In 1961, the President's Commission on Juvenile Delinquency and Youth Crime was established. This committee recommended the enactment of the Juvenile Delinquency and Youth Offenses Control Act of 1961. Originally authorized for three years, the act was later extended through fiscal year 1967. In 1967, the President's Commission on Law Enforcement and the Administration of Justice highlighted the importance of prevention in dealing with crime and delinquency.[38]
>
> In the following year (1968), Congress enacted both the Juvenile Delinquency Prevention and Control Act and the Omnibus Crime Control and Safe Streets Act. In 1972, the Juvenile Delinquency Prevention Control Act of 1972 was passed with funding remaining under the auspices of the U.S. Department of Health, Education, and Welfare. Two years later, Congress enacted the Juvenile Justice and Delinquency Prevention Act of 1974. It established the Office of Juvenile Justice and Delinquency Prevention (OJJDP) within the Law Enforcement Assistance Administration of the Department of Justice. The concern of the federal government regarding delinquency and the importance of prevention is evidenced not only in the title of the 1974 act, but in the attention given to prevention as an important strategy of forestalling the antisocial behavior among adolescents and young adults.[39]

THE DUE PROCESS REVOLUTION

We have indicated that adults are getting more protection under the law than are juveniles. The courts have attempted to rectify this situation by concentrating on bringing about reforms in the treatment given to both delinquent and nondelinquent juveniles. It should be pointed out, however, that the question of children's rights is multidimensional and complex. It involves not just procedural rights in juvenile courts and the applicability of constitutional rights to juveniles, but also the complex issues of the political, economic, and social position of minors in society.

This subject is made even more complex by the ever-changing status of youth and the resulting confusion reflected in adult attitudes toward them. The key issue here is the previously discussed doctrine of *parens patriae*. Although this doctrine called for the protection and treatment of children differently from adults, it also meant that children would not have the basic rights of adults held in criminal proceedings.

BOX 1.1 **HOW DO WE ADDRESS THE EVER-CHANGING STATUS OF YOUTH?**

Not unlike the changing definitions of "youthful offender," "delinquency," and "status offender," throughout the history of the juvenile justice system, shifts in agency or state policy add to the ever-changing status and definition of youth. Making things more complex are differences in state laws, that is, laws that name a youth at age 17 years a juvenile in one state but an adult if in another state.

MOBILE COUNTY SHERIFF'S OFFICE

STANDING OPERATING PROCEDURE	FILE INDEX NUMBER: SOP# 27	PAGE: 1 OF 13
EFFECTIVE DATE: 06-14-99	DATE OF ISSUE: 06-01-99	RESCINDS:
SUBJECT: Youth and Juvenile Procedures	AMENDS: SOP# 27, Issued 10-01-96	DISTRIBUTION: All Personnel

PURPOSE:

The purpose of this Standing Operating Procedure is to establish guidelines for the handling of juvenile offenders, neglected, abused, missing, or runaway children, and for the identification, investigation, processing, referral, and custody of minors.

DISCUSSION:

It is the policy of the Mobile County Sheriff's Office (MCSO) to promote public safety and reduce juvenile delinquency by maintaining the integrity of the substantive laws prohibiting certain socially unacceptable behavior and by developing individual responsibility for lawful conduct. This policy shall be pursued through means that are fair and just, that recognize the unique characteristics and needs of children, and that give children access to opportunities for personal and social growth.

DEFINITIONS:

A   Adult. Anyone eighteen (18) years of age or older.

B.   Age of Criminal Culpability. The age at which a person becomes subject to prosecution for violation of state laws. In the State of Alabama, this is seven (7) years of age.

C.   Age of Consent. The age at which a person may legally consent to have sexual relations. In the State of Alabama, this is sixteen (16) years of age.

D   Child in Need of Supervision (CHINS).

1.   A child who, being subject to compulsory school attendance, is habitually truant from school.

2.   A child who disobeys the reasonable and lawful demands of his/her parents, guardian or other custodian, and whose behavior is beyond their control.

Example Standard Operating Procedures for Working with Juveniles

E. Competent Adult.

1. A parent.

2. A legal guardian or custodian.

3. Another relative, neighbors or adult whom the detaining Deputy may reasonably believe will notify the juvenile's parent or custodian of the offense and detention, and who will assume responsibility for, and custody of, the juvenile.

F. Dependent. Title 12-15-1 (Juvenile Proceedings) of The Code of Alabama defines a dependent child as a child:

1. Who is destitute, homeless or dependent upon the public for support.

2. Who is without a parent or guardian who is able to provide support, training and education.

3. Whose custody is the subject of controversy.

4. Whose home, or in whose care the child may be, is an unfit and improper place for him/her.

5. Whose parent (s), guardian, or custodian neglects the care necessary for the child's health and well-being.

6. Whose condition or surroundings endangers the child's morals, health or general welfare.

7. Who has no proper parental care nor guardianship.

8. Whose parent (s), guardian or custodian fails, refuses or neglects to send such child to school.

9. Who has been abandoned by his/her parents, guardian, or other custodian.

10. Who has been physically, mentally or emotionally abused by parent (s), guardian or other custodian, or who is without proper care and control because of the faults of his/her parent (s), guardian or custodian, and they are unable to discharge their responsibilities to, and for, the child.

Example Standard Operating Procedures for Working with Juveniles (continued)

What is the solution? Juvenile justice practitioners and others working closely with juveniles or directly involved in the juvenile justice system may closely follow shifts in policy related to juvenile victims and offenders. Others who come in contact with youth but are not necessarily focused only on them may not; one example is law enforcement. In such cases, a law enforcement agency may develop standard operating procedures (SOPs) for handling juveniles as well as providing definitions. The first two pages of an example SOP is included here. Do you think the SOP presented would benefit you as a deputy? Why or why not? What is the difference between a child in need of supervision and a dependent? Is it possible that a juvenile delinquent may also be identified as a dependent or status offender? Beyond the pages presented, what do you think a law enforcement SOP should include?

Source: Mobile County Sheriff's Office, Mobile, Alabama.

As noted previously, early American practices did not reflect such a parental concern for juveniles. In colonial times, children who committed crimes were often punished more severely than adults. However, by the nineteenth century, several champions had surfaced to lead the crusade for children's rights. Americans were recognizing that children might not be as responsible for their criminal behavior as adults. By 1858, in California, a youth industrial school was established as an institution for children under the age of 18 years who were leading "idle or immoral" lives. In 1887, California held that it was unlawful to confine children under the age of 16 years to jails.

However, under *parens patriae,* confinement was also different for children from that for adults sentenced to institutions. For example, in 1870, boys could be sent to the Chicago Reform School under an indeterminate sentence and be held until they were 21 years of age. Boys could be committed for an offense or be sent by their parents or guardians for their own protection and benefit. Such an extended sentence, of course, is not possible for adults. The nature of this type of a commitment became the basis for the case of *People v. Turner* (55 Ill. 280, 1870). The Illinois Supreme Court declared that the petitioner had been denied basic due process of law and declared the commitment to an "infant penitentiary" unconstitutional. Protection could easily become punishment under *parens patriae.*[40]

Table 1.1
HELPING FAMILIES OF YOUTH IN 2000: PJAC COMMUNITY ENHANCEMENTS PROGRAM

The Pinellas Juvenile Assessment Center (Florida) Community Enhancements Program is "helping families access specialized services in their community." The table below highlights services offered to families with children.

Services Offered
Personal Interviews
Assessment of Child
Treatment Coordination
Resource Identification
Follow-up Contact
Drug Screening

Outreach Services	
Ages 11 to 18 years old	Ages 11 and younger
Assessment	Crisis Intervention
	Educational Materials
	Personal Interviews
	Follow-up Contact

Source: Pinellas, Florida, Juvenile Assessment Center brochure.

Nevertheless, the juvenile court movement pressed forward. The nation's first juvenile court was established in Cook County, Chicago, in 1899. *Mill v. Brown* (Utah, 1907) highlights the significance of the laws establishing early juvenile courts: "The juvenile court law is of such vast importance to the state and society that, it seems to us, it should be administered by those who are learned in the law and versed in the roles of procedure, effective and individual rights respected. Care must be exercised in both the selection of a judge and in the administration of the law."

In 1923, the National Probation Association's Annual Conference proposed a Standard Juvenile Court Act. The last state to adopt this act was Wyoming, in 1945. Between 1925 and 1945, various states defined their own juvenile code.

The "new" court system, which was more than 100 years in coming, defined all procedures of the juvenile courts as civil rather than criminal. (*Civil* suits relate to and affect only individual wrongs, whereas *criminal* prosecutions involve public wrongs.) It is evident, therefore, that the greatest effort in the juvenile justice system has been aimed at creating a separate court system for youths and delinquents. This separate system and the perpetuation of the doctrine of *parens patriae* have resulted in a system that largely ignored the legal rights of juveniles. Those rights accorded to adults—such as the right to speedy trial, to trial by jury, to bail, to confront one's accusers, and to protection from self-incrimination—were seen as unnecessary for juveniles.

However, due process rights for juveniles were not clearly established until the rulings of the U.S. Supreme Court under the leadership of Chief Justice Earl Warren. Landmark cases of the Warren Court, such as in *Miranda v. Arizona,* were decisions that did have a bearing on both adult and juvenile rights. The decision in *Gideon v. Wainwright,* 372 U.S. 335 (1963), set the stage for legislation regarding legal representation in the criminal process. Although this case involved the right of legal counsel in adult, noncapital felony cases, several states have required that indigent children who request counsel be so provided and at public expense. *Gault* established this right for juveniles. Chapter 7 contains a review of landmark cases in juvenile justice.

Institutions in the 1960s, 1970s, and 1980s

The institutionalization of delinquent children continued in the 1980s. Juvenile institutions were the norm until the Commissioner of the Department of Youth Services, Jerome Miller, convinced the Governor of Massachusetts to approve the closing of all but one juvenile correctional institution (the Shirley Training School, which served a few remaining girls) and placing all other adjudicated juveniles into community-based programs. This bold move, supported by the media and politicians, has been copied in many states since that time and proved that the large majority of adjudicated juveniles could be better dealt with in the community.

The Massachusetts Experiment

In 1969, Dr. Jerome Miller took over as youth commissioner for Massachusetts and made some revolutionary changes in that state's juvenile justice system. One of the more radical actions was closing the Lyman School for Boys in January 1972. The Lyman School for Boys was opened in 1846 and was the first institution of its kind in the nation. Its closing was the finale of an intense drama that had been going on in Massachusetts for more than two years. The era of confining children in large correctional institutions was dead, and a new age of decent, humane, community-based care for delinquent youngsters was beginning. The idealistic young reformers who had worked so hard to close down the institutions cheered. But juvenile justice professionals, both in Massachusetts and other states, were stunned and, in many cases, horrified at what Jerome Miller had done.

Miller is not without his critics. In fact, most juvenile corrections administrators outside Massachusetts, when queried in the mid-1970s, were generally in disagreement with the closing of institutions. Several very important figures in the field were interviewed by *Corrections Magazine* in 1975 and had mostly criticism for the actions of Miller. These ranged from "Very tragic and I'd hate to see other states imitate it" to "[Only] when you've got training schools that are brutalizing kids, then you should close them."[41] Whether from this lack of support from his peers or from the somewhat inconclusive results from the early years of the experiment in Massachusetts, Jerome Miller was finally a victim of his own turbulent actions and left the state in 1973. What were the results of this "crusade" in Massachusetts? Did closing down the larger juvenile correctional institutions make a difference? Miller had contended that training schools were not only ineffective at reforming juvenile lawbreakers but profoundly destructive and that those children who went through them were more likely to commit new crimes when they left than when they were admitted.[42]

A team of researchers from Harvard University found, after eight years of intensive examination of youngsters released from institutions and youngsters released from community programs, that the experiment was successful. They examined the recidivism rates of boys released from the traditional institutions in 1968 with a sample of boys placed under community supervision in 1974. The rates for both reappearance in court (74 percent versus 66 percent) and for either probation or commitment (55 percent versus 47 percent) were slightly higher for the boys

BOX 1.2 **WHAT DO YOU THINK ABOUT JUVENILE FACILITIES?**

Discussion of whether juvenile facilities are instructive/rehabilitative or destructive continues in 2010. An editorial published in *The Times-Picayune* identified problems of overcrowding, violence, and sexual abuse in Monroe, Louisiana's Swanson Center for Youth. The editorial cites the head of the state Office of Juvenile Justice as saying, "I think we are doing a much better job" at curbing assaults and sexual contact by staff. However, self-reports from juveniles collected between June 2008 and April 2009 by the Federal Bureau of Justice Statistics estimate that one out of six "either had forced or consensual sexual conduct" at the center.

The Bureau of Justice Statistics report highlights findings from the National Survey of Youth in Custody (NSYC) which included approximately 26,550 adjudicated youth confined in state and large locally or privately operated juvenile facilities (pp. 1, 14):

- An estimated 12% of youth in these facilities reported experiencing one or more incidents of sexual victimization;
- About 2.6% reported the incident involved another youth, and 10.3% reported the incident involved facility staff;
- About 4.3% of youth reported having sex or other sexual contact with staff as a result of some type of force;
- 10.8% of males and 4.7% of females reported sexual activity with facility staff;
- An estimated 88% had been victimized more than once by the staff; 27% had been victimized more than 10 times;
- Thirteen facilities were identified as "high rate" based on the lower bound of the 95%-confidence interval of at least 35% higher than the average rate among facilities by type of consent; and
- 18% of the juvenile facilities had no reported incidents of sexual victimization.

The percent of youth reporting sexual victimization in Louisiana's Jetson Correctional Center for Youth is 8%, while 16.6% reported sexual victimization at Louisiana's Swanson Center for Youth. These numbers approximate youth reports of staff sexual misconduct (8% and 15.6% respectively) at each facility. *The Times-Picayune* editorial reports the director of the Juvenile Justice Project of Louisiana having concerns about the large number of juveniles housed at the Swanson Center for Youth, as well as an increase in incidents of fighting at the center. The editorial also notes the director's additional concerns about the state's grievance procedure given the gap between reported incidents in the national report and official reports.

What is the solution? In the juvenile justice system there are struggles between the balance of rehabilitation and punishment, as well as the best interests of the child and the interest of the community. Indeed, as discussed in this chapter, these historical struggles continue. What advice would you give to Louisiana's Office of Juvenile Justice? What is the responsibility of the state and the administration at the Swanson Center for Youth? As a future juvenile justice practitioner, how would you address this struggle?

Source: Allen J. Beck, Paige M. Harrison, and Paul Garrison, *Sexual Victimization in Juvenile Facilities Reported by Youth, 2008–09: Bureau of Justice Statistics Special Report* (Washington, DC: U.S. Department of Justice, January 2010), Available: http://bjs.ojp.usdoj.gov/content/pub/pdf/svjfry09.pdf.; "Juvenile justice setback." (January 15, 2010). *The Times-Picayune.* Page B6.

who were released from the institutions. Girls had a lower rate of reappearance (37 percent versus 24 percent) and probation/commitment (25 percent versus 10 percent).[43] Some of the researchers' conclusions were that the community programs did not go far enough and in many cases merely replaced institutionalization with a similar condition in small group homes.

> Instead of having "institution kids" we now have a new group of "agency kids." They are generally treated better, but their experience in these agencies is still quite foreign to the worlds in which they live. If these private agencies are to prevent recidivism better than the training school model, they must take the risk of becoming involved in the community to a more significant degree than simply retaining a "community board."[44]

Services were often lacking and support systems weak. Because of these findings and the fact that the community group was probably older and tougher, the researchers warned against quick conclusions that the community approach does not work. On the contrary, they cautioned those who still used institutions extensively to look in depth at the extent of services and the results (favorable) that were obtained when services were not available. Miller believes that the harsh institutional approach is at least as ineffective as the community programs that provide no services, and that both should be avoided in favor of community programs that address the full range of client needs.[45]

Yet, there are those in the field of juvenile corrections who believe that simply closing an institution is not enough. They believe that as institutions are closed, they should also be torn down. For example, there are many old prisons that have been "abandoned" for new ones, only to be reopened in a short while. Americans are great at finding a use for vacant buildings. If not used as prisons, they are used as facilities for the mentally ill or other social misfits.

However, the aims of Miller's deinstitutionalization reforms had far reaching effects. Deinstitutionalization was the basis of the 1974 Juvenile Justice and Delinquency Prevention Act. This movement was not overcome until conservative political rhetoric led to punitive legislative reforms in the 1980s.[46]

The 1990s and Beyond

The provisions of the Federal Anti-Gang and Youth Violence Act of 1997 outline the problems both presented and faced by juveniles during this decade. The Act was intended to deter and punish serious gang and violent crime, promote accountability in the juvenile justice system, prevent juvenile and youth crime, and protect juveniles from various forms of abuse. Its provisions include the following:

- Targeting violent gang, gun, and drug crimes (includes targeting illicit gun markets and protecting children from guns and drugs)
- Protecting witnesses to help prosecute gangs and other violent criminals (includes penalties for obstruction of justice offenses involving victims, witnesses, and informants)

- Protecting victims' rights (includes the extension of the Victims of Child Abuse Act)
- Federal prosecution of serious and violent juvenile offenders
- Rules governing the incarceration of juveniles in the adult Federal system
- The creation of the Office of Juvenile Crime Control and Prevention (including Juvenile Crime Assistance, and Missing and Exploited Children).

The Act reflects the dichotomy present in the juvenile justice system since its inception. The intent is to protect children from harm but also to hold them accountable for serious crimes.

During the present decade, the rehabilitative nature of juvenile justice has been called into question. The **"Get Tough" movement** featured stricter penalties for youths including the sentencing of juveniles as adults and the death penalty. This new model focuses on such issues as punishment, justice, and accountability. This terminology reflects the view that juveniles must bear individual responsibility for their crimes, particularly serious crimes, as adults do. It represents a movement away from the original doctrines of the child savers and the juvenile court. Traditionally, the juvenile justice system should not punish youths because they are not responsible actors. The "Get Tough" viewpoint holds the opposite view—that juveniles should be punished to make them more responsible. Thus, this movement represents a revolution in the philosophy and operations of the juvenile justice system.[47]

Whereas the juvenile offenders of the past were considered wayward youth rather than hardened criminals, juvenile offenders are considered ruthless and unconcerned about the consequences of their actions. The "Get Tough" movement focuses on the crimes committed rather than the underlying causes of delinquency. As a result, more youths are being tried in criminal courts and sent to adult prisons. Juvenile facilities were also made more secure. In addition, budget cutbacks in the 1980s resulted in a reduction of programs for juveniles. Special education programs were developed, but crowding became a problem, increasing pressure to sentence juveniles as adults. Yet, many juvenile justice experts emphasize the need to work with families and communities to reduce problems before they are out of hand and to put more emphasis on treatment programs.[48]

"Get Tough" movement Movement featuring stricter penalties for youths—including the sentencing of juveniles as adults and the death penalty—that is focused on such issues as punishment, justice, and accountability. This terminology reflects the view that juveniles must bear individual responsibility for their crimes, particularly serious crimes, as adults do.

SUMMARY

From the era of the Depression and Prohibition through the post-Depression era and into the 1960s, 1970s, 1980s, and 1990s, U.S. society has been faced with social, moral, and economic problems caused by juveniles. They commit crimes, run away from home, or simply refuse to be treated as children any longer.

Drugs, alcohol, and the pressures of a thermonuclear society all pressed in on the juvenile of the 1980s. What are they really? Researchers and experts in the field of juvenile corrections continuously debate typologies and treatment modalities. Institutions and prisons for juveniles are seen as ineffective by reformers such as Jerome Miller and his followers. Others see them as worthwhile and appropriate and still others as necessary evils. Police forces have become "specialized" in attempting to deal with delinquents. Some are trying to prevent juvenile crime by working closely with the community in developing diversions for children who might otherwise get into trouble.

Supreme Court decisions such as *In re Gault* have brought some constitutional protection and redress from legal wrongs to young people, but many other court actions are still in progress.

It seems that the definition of delinquency and standardization of semantic meanings for other terms commonly used in the field of juvenile justice still need to be resolved. Also, we have seen that the procedures of a juvenile court in one county in a state may differ significantly from those of a neighboring county in the same state.

Lest we become too depressed by the situation, it is important to note that the percentages of persons under age 18 involved in crimes cleared by arrest has been coming down steadily since their peak in the mid-1970s. Most young people are not juvenile delinquents. The juvenile justice system, however, is set up to deal with those that deviate from societal standards of conduct. Not all deviant behavior is criminal or delinquent, but all criminal and delinquent behavior is deviant. It is this latter behavior that we shall discuss for the remainder of this text, now that we have a broad overview of the history of how we got to where we are today and where we seem to be going in the new century.

Increasing caseloads and restricted budgets have now produced deteriorating conditions of confinement. Although the current situation has many similarities to that of 100 years ago, the Office of Juvenile Justice and Delinquency Prevention is exercising a national leadership role in blending treatment and public safety concerns. Renewed interest also exists in upgrading professional standards, professional associations are speaking out against punitive rhetoric, and private philanthropy is supporting progressive juvenile justice reform.[49]

We have presented this review to consider the impact of history on the future. Bernard has identified an historical "cycle of juvenile justice" that has been repeated throughout American history. This cycle begins with the official and public perception that juvenile crime is exceptionally high. This perception is coupled with the belief that punishments are too harsh and that more lenient treatment is in order for juveniles. In turn, such changes fuel the next cycle, in which officials and the public blame these lenient treatments for the latest increase in juvenile delinquency. The predictable reaction is that punishments are increased and juveniles are subjected to the same penalties as adults.[50] It seems that the United States is in the midst of a punitive cycle at the present time. Time will tell if Bernard's prediction for the next turn in juvenile justice policy will be toward treatment over punishment.[51]

Another noted historian, Randall Sheldon, worries that the juvenile justice system is returning to its more punitive past. Sheldon notes that juvenile justice initially emphasized institutionalization as the solution to delinquency. One of the problems with this approach is what Sheldon terms the "Field of Dreams Syndrome"—the construction of institutions that are filled soon after they are built. The result is that institutions become cemented into the system, even in the face of the optimistic evidence from the Massachusetts experiment that institutions are unnecessary.[52]

Several experts have called for continuing reform in the system to adapt to changing times. For example, Watkins has suggested that juvenile court, as a separate entity, is still valuable. However, it must adapt to both the nature and the problems faced by today's youths. He calls for a reinvigoration of the juvenile court to offer methods of child saving relevant to twenty-first century children.[53] He concludes by documenting the jurisprudential shift in sentencing policy from treating delinquent offenders to punishing them. For example, Feld outlines three alternatives to the current juvenile justice system: restructuring juvenile courts to fit their original therapeutic purpose, combining appropriate punishment with criminal procedural safeguards, and abolishing juvenile co-jurisdiction over criminal conduct and trying young offenders in criminal courts after making certain substantive and procedural changes.[54]

KEY TERMS

child savers	mother image
folkways	*parens patriae*
"Get Tough" movement	proscribed
Hammurabic Code	psychic arrest
Hospice at San Michele	Old Bailey
House of Refuge	reform schools
hulks	status offenders
intervention strategy	stocks
juvenile court	transportation
mores	

DISCUSSION AND REVIEW QUESTIONS

1. What is meant by the term *parens patriae?* Where does it come from?
2. Were the problems of delinquency in early societies different from those faced today? If so, how?
3. How did the penalties for juvenile misbehaviors and delinquency differ from those used today?
4. How did the "due process revolution" affect the rights of juveniles? How did the doctrine of *parens patriae* affect the legal rights of juveniles?
5. How did child savers like Jane Addams view the problem of juvenile delinquency?
6. What were the aims of the first juvenile court? How do the procedures for handling juveniles under *parens patriae* compare with how adults are treated in the criminal justice system?
7. What are the elements of the "Get Tough" movement? How do they represent a change in operations of the juvenile justice system?

VIDEO PROFILES

Kids Today video profile in MyCrimeKit highlights issues associated with the development of the juvenile court and the system's focus on the "best interests" of both juvenile victims and delinquents. Compare and contrast the juvenile justice system as presented in the video with the early juvenile justice system as described in this chapter. Then, discuss the pros and cons associated with the evolution of the system; is the system "better" today? Why or why not?

At a Glance: The Juvenile Justice Process video profile in MyCrimeKit shows the process of a juvenile entering and moving through the initial steps of the juvenile justice system. Discuss whether the intake, detention, and initial hearing steps, as well as the interactions between juvenile justice professions and the juvenile as presented in the video, align with the early juvenile justice system or current system as described in this chapter. Then, discuss whether you think these steps and interactions are grounded in *parens patriae*. Why or why not?

MYCRIMEKIT

mycrimekit™ Go to MyCrimeKit.com to explore the following study tools and resources specific to this chapter:

- Practice Quiz: Test your knowledge with multiple-choice, true–false, fill-in-the-blank, and essay questions.
- Flashcards: 20 flashcards to test your knowledge of the chapter's key terms.

- Web Quest: Review the Web sites of the Office of Juvenile Justice and Delinquency Prevention as well as your state's Juvenile Justice agency.
- Web Links: Check out sites related to the content presented in this chapter.

ENDNOTES

1. LaMar T. Empey, *American Delinquency: Its Meaning and Construction* (Homewood, IL: The Dorsey Press, 1978), p. 66.

2. For a thorough and comprehensive look at the Code of Hammurabi and other early laws, see Albert Kocaurek and John H. Wigmore, *Evolution of Law, Select Readings on the Origin and Development of Legal Institutions,* Volume 1: Source of Ancient and Primitive Law (Boston: Little, Brown and Company, 1951).

3. Code of Hammurabi, item 195. Richard R. Cherry, Barrister-at-law, Reid Professor of Constitutional and Criminal Law in the University of Dublin. Reprinted from *Lectures: Growth of Criminal Law in Ancient Communities* (London: Macmillan & Co., 1890).

4. Ibid, pp. 192–193.

5. Sanders, *Juvenile Offenders for a Thousand Years*, p. 135.

6. See, for example, Scott H. Decker and Barik Van Winkle, *Life in the Gang: Family, Friends, and Violence* (London: Cambridge University Press, 1996).

7. Barry Krisberg and James F. Austin, *Reinventing Juvenile Justice* (Newbury Park, CA: Sage, 1993), pp. 112–139.

8. Lloyd de Mause, *The History of Childhood* (New York: Psychohistory Press, 1974), p. 25.

9. Empey, *American Delinquency*, pp. 54–55.

10. Wiley B. Sanders, ed., *Juvenile Offenders for a Thousand Years* (Chapel Hill: University of North Carolina Press, 1970), p. 11.

11. Ibid., p. 14.

12. Ibid., pp. 52–53.

13. Ibid., p. 70.

14. For a thorough and insightful history of transportation, see Robert Hughes, *The Fatal Shore* (New York: Knopf, 1987).

15. Sanders, *Juvenile Offenders for a Thousand Years*, p. 46.

16. Barry C. Feld, *Bad Kids: Race and the Transformation of the Juvenile Court* (New York: Oxford University Press, 1999), p. 52.

17. Ibid., p. 53.

18. Barry Krisberg, "The Legacy of Juvenile Corrections," *Corrections Today,* Vol. 57 (5) (August, 1995), p. 122.

19. S. Schlossman, "Delinquent Children: The Juvenile Reform School," in Norval Morris and David J. Rothman, eds. *The Oxford History of the Prison: The Practice of Punishment in Western Society* (Oxford: Oxford University Press, 1995), pp. 363–389.

20. David J. Rothman, *The Discovery of the Asylum* (Boston: Little, Brown, 1971), p. 215.

21. Ibid.

22. The child was tied with arms and legs around a barrel, thus exposing his or her backside quite readily to the whip.

23. Robert M. Mennel, *Thorns and Thistles: Juvenile Delinquents in the United States 1825–1940* (Hanover: University of New Hampshire Press, 1973), p. 17.

24. Mennel, *Thorns and Thistles*, p. 24.

25. Compare this practice with the program of sending ghetto children to summer camps once a year.

26. Mennel, *Thorns and Thistles*, pp. 56–57.

27. Anthony M. Platt, *The Child Savers: The Invention of Delinquency* (Chicago: University of Chicago Press, 1969).

28. Ibid.

29. Renee G. Kasinsky, "Child Neglect and 'Unfit' Mothers: Child Savers in the Progressive Era," *Women and Criminal Justice,* Vol. 6 (1994), pp. 97–129.

30. See Alexander W. Pisciotta, *Benevolent Repression: Social Control and the American Reformatory–Prison Movement* (New York: New York University Press, 1994).

31. John C. Watkins, *Juvenile Justice Century: A Sociological Commentary on American Juvenile Courts* (Durham, NC: Carolina Academic Press, 1998).

32. The Prohibition Act, or the Eighteenth Amendment (ratified January 16, 1920), banned the sale of alcoholic beverages. *U.S. Statutes at Large,* Volume 41, p. 305.

33. Eliot Ness of Chicago's Police Department Crime Prevention Bureau, and later of television fame, advocated that instead of apprehending young delinquents as offenders, police or juvenile officers should be trained to make referrals to proper social agencies for guidance and treatment. See Eliot Ness, "New Role of the Police," *Survey* (March 1944), p. 77.

34. See Clifford Shaw and Henry D. McKay, *Juvenile Delinquency in Urban Areas* (Chicago: University of Chicago Press, 1942); Cletus Dirksen, *Economic Factors in Delinquency* (Milwaukee: Bruce, 1948); William W. Wattenburg and J. J. Balistrieri, "Gang Membership and

Juvenile Delinquency," *American Sociological Review,* Vol. 18 (1950), pp. 631–635; Ernest W. Burgess, "The Economic Factor in Juvenile Delinquency," *Journal of Criminal Law, Criminology, and Police Science* (May–June, 1952), pp. 29–42; Albert K. Cohen, *Delinquent Boys: The Culture of the Delinquent Gang* (New York: Free Press, 1955); and Sol Rubin, "Changing Youth Correction Authority Concepts," *Focus,* Vol. 29 (1950), pp. 77–82.

35. Elizabeth Fajen, "Curing Delinquency at the Source," *Survey* (October 1946), pp. 261–262.

36. Gary B. Adams, ed., *Juvenile Justice Management,* (Springfield, IL: Charles C. Thomas Publisher, 1973) pp. 323–324.

37. Edwin Powers, "An Experiment in the Prevention of Delinquency," *The Annals of the American Academy,* (January 1949), p. 81.

38. President's Commission on Law Enforcement and Administration of Justice, *The Challenge of Crime in a Free Society* (Washington, D.C.: U.S. Government Printing Office, 1967), p. 58.

39. *Juvenile Justice and Delinquency Prevention Act of 1974,* Public Law 93-415, 93rd Cong. S. 821, September 7, 1974, p. 2.

40. Platt, *The Child Savers,* pp. 103–104.

41. "Moving the Kids Out: A Unique Experiment," *Corrections Magazine* (November–December 6, 1975): 29.

42. Robert B. Coates, A. D. Miller, and Lloyd E. Ohlin, *Diversity in a Youth Correctional System: Handling Delinquents in Massachusetts* (Cambridge, MA: Ballinger, 1978), pp. 149–154.

43. Ibid.

44. Ibid., p. 173.

45. "Moving the Kids Out," p. 30.

46. Krisberg, "Legacy," p. 152.

47. H.R. 810, the Anti-Gang and Youth Violence Act of 1997.

48. M. E. Blomquist and M. L. Forst, "Punishment, Accountability, and the New Juvenile Justice," in Barry W. Hancock and Paul M. Sharp, eds. *Criminal Justice in America: Theory, Practice, and Policy* (Upper Saddle River, N.J.: Prentice Hall, 1996), pp. 356–369.

49. S. Gluck, "Wayward Youth, Super Predator: An Evolutionary Tale of Juvenile Delinquency from the 1950s to the Present," *Corrections Today,* Vol. 59 (June, 1997), pp. 62–64, 66.

50. Krisberg, "Legacy," p. 154.

51. Thomas J. Bernard, *The Cycle of Juvenile Justice* (Oxford: Oxford University Press, 1992).

52. Randall G. Shelden, *Juvenile Justice in Historical Perspective: Confronting the Edifice Complex and Field of Dreams Syndrome* (from Dan Macallair and Vincent Schiraldi, *Reforming Juvenile Justice: Reasons and Strategies for the 21st Century* (Dubuque, IA: Kendall/ Hunt Publishing Co., 1998), pp. 7–28.

53. Watkins, *Juvenile Justice Century.*

54. Barry C. Feld, "Criminalizing the American Juvenile Court," in Michael Tonry, ed. *Crime and Justice: A Review of Research* (Chicago: University of Chicago Press, 1993), pp. 197–280. See also Jerome G. Miller, *Last One over the Wall: The Massachusetts Experiment in Closing Reform Schools* (1998).

2

Juvenile Statistics: Measurement and Analysis

The state and federal government must take a closer look at the problems that are entrenched in the juvenile justice system. These problems often include harsh or abusive conditions; pervasive disparities in the treatment of youth by race and ethnicity; and disproportionate sanctions for minor and predictable misbehavior. We know and there is evidence to prove that with effective interventions, systems reforms, and more effective policies, the system can produce better outcomes for young people.

DOUGLAS W. NELSON, PRESIDENT
AND CHIEF EXECUTIVE OFFICER,
ANNIE E. CASEY FOUNDATION[1]

LEARNING OBJECTIVES

1. Identify the juvenile crime arrest trends from the Uniform Crime Report.
2. Identify the patterns of status offenders in custody.
3. Identify the patterns of delinquency from the cohort studies.
4. Identify the patterns of juvenile crime victimization from all sources.
5. Identify the risk factors associated with delinquency and other juvenile problem behaviors.

CHAPTER OVERVIEW

Information is the lifeblood of any organization. To determine what is occurring in a system, it is necessary to create valid and reliable statistical information. In this chapter, we review several sources of statistical information on the juvenile justice system: information on crime and delinquency, crime victimization, and the risk factors that youths in America face. This information can serve as the basis for future operations and reform to improve the juvenile justice system.

Analysis of the data presented in this chapter conveys a picture of the extent and nature of juvenile crime. However, students should keep in mind that statistics, although important, do not always accurately represent the amount of delinquency and the nature of the delinquents. The data are imperfect and limited and must be considered with this in mind.

MEASURING DELINQUENCY

The measurement of the extent of juvenile crime (generally that committed by persons under the age of 18 years) is a problem that has vexed researchers from the beginning of their attempts to determine the extent of it. Because juvenile crime has been the domain of a highly splintered system, the only valid data have tended to deal with crime in a local area. Most tools now used to measure juvenile crime are from either official or unofficial sources. Variance in the numbers is great, depending on the source, time frame, and scope of the database. Most official figures come from the FBI's **Uniform Crime Report (UCR)**, reports from the National Criminal Justice Reference Service, reports of the Office of Juvenile Justice and Delinquency Prevention (OJJDP), juvenile court statistics, institutional and aftercare records, and cohort studies. Unofficial figures come from self-report studies, victimization surveys, and various academic studies conducted by universities and research organizations.

Uniform Crime Report (UCR)
A cooperative statistical effort of among city, county, and state law enforcement agencies and represents the amount of crime reported to the agencies in a given year

Juveniles as Offenders: The Uniform Crime Report

The UCR program is a cooperative statistical effort of among city, county, and state law enforcement agencies. They voluntarily report data on crimes that witnesses and victims bring to their attention or are uncovered by the police themselves. Thus, they collectively represent the amount of crimes known to the police (either through reporting by complainants or directly by the police themselves) in a given year. They are presented in their annual report, *Crime in the United States*. Thus, these figures are produced by the police and reflect their activities regarding juveniles. However, they do not present the complete extent of juvenile crime.

Juvenile Arrest Patterns, 2008

The OJJDP compiles and presents information on juvenile arrests, compiled from the UCR **Index crimes**. The following data represent violent crimes:

- **Juveniles were involved in 16 percent of all violent crime arrests and 26 percent of all property arrests in 2008.** One in eight violent crimes was attributed to juveniles in 2008, but juvenile arrests for violent crimes declined between 2006 and 2008. However, juvenile property arrests increased for the second consecutive year in 2008.[2]

- **By 2008, juvenile violent crime arrest rates were far below peak levels from the 1990s.[3]**

  - With the exceptions of 2001 and 2004, juvenile arrest rates for murder have fallen every year since 1993. In 2004, it was 74 percent lower than the peak year of 1993. But in 2008, it rose by almost 17 percent.

  - Since 1991, the juvenile arrest rate for forcible rape has declined every year. By 2008, this rate was 57 percent lower than the peak year of 1991.

  - The juvenile robbery arrest rate fell 62 percent between 1995 and 2002. But the 2008 figure was a 44 percent increase over the low point in 2002.

  - Unlike other juvenile violent crime arrest trends, the rate for juvenile aggravated assault arrests was not below the lowest levels registered in the 1980s. But by 2008, the juvenile aggravated assault arrest rate dropped 8 percent—its lowest point since the late 1980s.

  - Although they accounted for just 16 percent of the youth population (aged 10–17 years), African American youth accounted for 52 percent of the juvenile violent crime arrests in 2008.[4]

The following patterns were present for juvenile property crime arrests in 2008:

- **The juvenile arrest rate for burglary fell dramatically between 1980 and 2008: 68 percent.[5]**

- **The juvenile arrest rate for larceny-theft remained relatively constant between 1980 and 1997, then declined 45 percent by 2005.** However, this rate has increased 17 percent since 2007.

- **In 2008, the juvenile arrest rate for motor vehicle theft was lower than any year since 1980.** Between 1980 and 2008, it fell by 78 percent.

- **The juvenile arrest rate for arson has fallen 46 percent between 1994 and 2008.**

- **In 2008, African American youths accounted for 33 percent of the juvenile property crime arrests.[6]**

Index crimes Violent and property offenses for which data are collected in the Uniform Crime Reports. Violent Index crimes include murder, forcible rape, robbery, and aggravated assault. Property Index crimes include burglary, larceny-theft, motor vehicle theft, and arson.

Teen Being Arrested

status offenses Acts committed by juveniles that would not be considered crimes if committed by adults.

The great juvenile justice debate of the 1990s was framed by the supposed worsening of juvenile crime and what to do about it. Bernard examined juvenile crime statistics for roughly the same time period and concluded that there was no crime wave and thus no reason to make radical changes in juvenile justice policy.[7] The statistics are not wrong, but as always, they are open to interpretation. Overall, it seems that juvenile arrests for both violent and property crimes have decreased in recent years. It also seems that African Americans are overrepresented in both arrest groups. Again, it is important to note that these figures are produced by the police and may reflect enforcement priorities and patterns as well as the actual amount of juvenile crime in society. However, there are other sources of statistics to consider in the attempt to discover whether juvenile crime is getting worse.

STATUS OFFENSES

The OJJDP conducts two data collection programs that gather information about juveniles in custody. These sources provide information about status offenders in the juvenile justice system. **Status offenses** are behaviors that are not law violations for adults, such as running away, truancy, and ungovernability. Some residents were held in a juvenile residential placement facility but were not charged with or adjudicated for an offense (e.g., youth referred for abuse, neglect, emotional disturbance, or mental retardartion; those referred by their parents). The federal Juvenile Justice and Delinquency Prevention Act states that jurisdictions shall not hold status offenders in secure juvenile facilities for detention or placement—a policy known as the deinstitutionalization of status offenders. The one exception to this general policy is that a status offender may be confined in a secure juvenile facility if he or she has violated a valid court order, such as a probation order requiring the youth to attend school and observe a curfew.[8]

Although many status offenders enter the juvenile justice system through law enforcement, in many states the initial official contact is a child welfare agency. About half of all status offense cases referred to juvenile court come from law enforcement. In 2003, status offenders accounted for 5 percent of the juveniles held in custody nationwide (approximately 4,600 juveniles).[9] This proportion has declined 32 percent since 1991, reflecting a deemphasis on status offenses throughout the system.[10] However, 40 percent of the female juveniles held in custody in 2003 were status offenders.[11] Yet, the status offender proportion of female offenders in custody dropped from 33 percent in 1991 to 13 percent in 2003.[12]

mycrimekit™

Video Profile: Status Offender

COHORT STUDIES: ANOTHER WAY TO MEASURE DELINQUENCY

Another way to examine the rate of juvenile delinquency is the cohort study. A **cohort study** examines a selected group (cohort) of people who share a common experience in time. Delinquency research has featured the use of *birth cohorts*—persons born at the same time and living in the same place over a long period of time. Since World War II, there have been major cohort studies on delinquency conducted in several different locations. These studies present some interesting insights into the delinquency of a large group of juveniles in their specific settings and make possible some tentative generalizations about the larger population of juveniles.

cohort study Examines a selected group (cohort) of people who share a common experience in time (e.g., born in the same year)

The Philadelphia Birth Cohorts

In a massive effort to describe delinquency in Philadelphia, renowned criminologist Marvin Wolfgang and his colleagues studied two birth cohorts.[13] The first comprised all males born in 1945 in Philadelphia from age 10 to 18 years. The second consisted of all males and females born in 1958 that lived in Philadelphia from age 10 to 18 years. The two studies were designed to determine the effects of growing up in the 1960s and 1970s. The first cohort included almost 10,000 subjects, and the second included nearly 30,000 subjects. (This latter group reflects the rapid expansion of the Baby Boom generation after World War II.) These two groups are known as the **Philadelphia Birth Cohorts**.

Philadelphia Birth Cohorts Two birth cohorts; one included all males born in 1945 in Philadelphia from age 10 to 18 years, and one included all males and females born in 1958 that lived in Philadelphia from age 10 to 18 years. The two studies were designed to determine the effects of growing up in the 1960s and 1970s.

The first cohort study revealed the existence of a group of 627 chronic offenders who were responsible for the majority of the crimes committed by the entire cohort. Their criminal histories were related to the age at which they first committed a crime. The earlier juveniles in this study committed their first offense, the greater the number of offenses they committed by age 17. Race and family income also figured heavily in chronic delinquency. More than two-thirds of the chronic offenders were African American. However, family income had more of an impact than race. Nonwhites of low socioeconomic status were three times more likely to be chronic offenders than whites of the same status.[14] Chronic offending was also related to intelligence and educational performance. The chronic offenders had lower mean IQ scores, below-average school achievement, and a higher incidence of retardation.

The 1958 cohort had a higher rate of offending per 1,000 subjects. In addition, the members of this cohort committed almost twice as many Index offenses and three times as many violent crimes as the 1945 cohort. Moreover, the 1958 cohort had an offense rate that was five times higher for robbery, three times higher for homicide, twice as high for assault, and almost twice as high for rape. Finally, injurious offenses were much more prevalent and harmful in the 1958 cohort. In summary, the

1958 cohort members committed more and more serious offenses than the 1945 cohort.

Like the 1945 cohort, the 1958 cohort contained a group of chronic offenders. The chronic offenders in the 1958 cohort were a larger group, and they committed a higher percentage of the total number of offenses (61 percent versus 52 percent of all the crimes committed by the cohort). The chronic offenders of 1958 accounted for the majority of the serious violent crime committed by the group.

Once again, race and socioeconomic status had an effect on the rate of crime committed by the 1958 chronics. Among whites, chronic offenders committed 50 percent of the offenses. Among nonwhites, they accounted for 65 percent of the crime. Chronic offenders of high socioeconomic status committed 51 percent of the offenses for their subgroup, whereas chronic offenders of low socioeconomic status committed 65 percent of the offenses in their subgroup. The chronic offenders in the 1958 cohort evidenced the same social problems as those in the 1945 cohort. They moved more often, had lower achievement scores, had less schooling, and were more likely to have disciplinary problems at school.

The 1958 birth cohort study was designed to replicate the first with one significant difference: More than half of the cohort was female. Their offending patterns were substantially different from those of males. The number of boys who had their first police contact before age 18 years was two and a half times higher than that for females. Females were primarily one-time offenders (60 percent) who were less likely to commit serious crimes that involved injury and stolen money. Only 7 percent of the females were chronic offenders.

The relationship between race and socioeconomic status among the chronic offenders was similar for both males and females. Nonwhites and offenders with low socioeconomic status, both male and female, were most likely to be chronic delinquents. However, the size and impact of the female chronic delinquent group was much smaller than that of males.

A comparison of the research findings from both cohorts leads to several generalizations. Evidently, delinquency was prevalent among non-whites and subjects with low socioeconomic status. Delinquency was also related to residential instability, poor school achievement, and failure to graduate from high school.[15] The offenders in the 1958 cohort committed a greater number of crimes, and their crimes were more serious. Finally, in both cohorts, a core of chronic offenders was responsible for the bulk of serious crime.

A recent study examined the rates of adult offending within the 1958 cohort. Overall, the violent and chronic juvenile offenders had the highest rates of adult offending, with 63 percent of this subgroup having committed an adult offense. However, comparisons between rates of offending among males and females could be made within this cohort.

For example, 612 males were classified as both violent and chronic offenders. They represented more than 62 percent of the chronic offenders and 54 percent of the serious male delinquents. This group was smaller among females: For each serious and chronic female delinquent there were 7 such males. Yet, females in this subgroup committed a more disproportionate share of adult crime than the males.

Socioeconomic status also had an impact that overshadowed the effect of race and ethnicity on the rates of adult offending. Disadvantaged living conditions heightened the risk of future crime. The authors concluded that the risk factors associated with delinquency and adult crime must be identified to develop effective ways to treat juveniles and prevent crime.[16]

These studies became a model for several other efforts to determine the extent of delinquency through the use of official records, community studies, self-reporting data, and other sources to measure any large birth cohort.

The Columbus Cohort

Hamparian and her colleagues examined the records of all juveniles born between 1956 and 1960 in Columbus, Ohio, who had been arrested for a violent crime. They compared the backgrounds of 1,138 arrestees with various personal and social characteristics to determine who was most likely to commit serious crimes.[17] They found that males outnumbered females by about six to one (85 percent to 15 percent). African Americans outnumbered whites. Of the offenders, 85 percent fell below the median income level. However, a very small percentage of the cohort (2.5 percent) was involved in violent crimes. Among this group, a significant number (12.2 percent) had siblings who had also committed violent offenses. Finally, institutional treatment seemed to have a negative effect on the offenders.[18]

Unlike the Philadelphia findings, the **Columbus Cohort** did not progress from lesser to more serious types of crime, nor did they specialize in any specific type of crime. The researchers also followed the cohort members into adulthood. They found the following:

Columbus Cohort Included all juveniles born between 1956 and 1960 in Columbus, Ohio, who had been arrested for a violent crime

1. The frequency of arrests declines with age.
2. Most adult crimes committed by juvenile violent offenders were not violent.
3. Four out of ten adult offenders were arrested for at least one Index violent crime.
4. Almost half of the arrested cohort members were imprisoned as adults. More than 80 percent were released, and half went back a second time.

These findings did not identically match those from Philadelphia. It appears that juvenile offenders do not get a "clean slate" as adults. The adult system does not accord them the leniency usually given to first offenders.

Following the cohort into adulthood also gave the Hamparian research team the opportunity to explore some key policy issues. The findings are summarized for three categories: one-time-only offenders, juvenile assaulters, and chronic offenders.

1. One-time-only offenders:
   • These offenders were more likely to be white.
   • The group was disproportionately female.
   • They were usually not committed to training schools.
   • They were usually arrested for non-Index violent offenses (55.6 percent).
   • They were frequently charged with an assault occurring while police attempted an arrest for another, less serious crime.

2. Juvenile Assaulters:
   • Assault was the most serious juvenile violent offense arrest for nearly three-quarters of all female cohort members.
   • More than 51 percent were white, whereas only 42 percent of the Index violent offenders were white.
   • One-time-only offenders were less likely to be chronic offenders.
   • Both violent and nonviolent offenders were usually arrested for the first time before age 13 years.

3. Chronic Offenders:
   • This group was disproportionately male, first arrested by age 13 years, and had been incarcerated in juvenile training schools.
   • Three-quarters of juvenile chronic offenders were also adult offenders.
   • More than 50 percent of adult offenders were also chronic juvenile offenders.
   • Juvenile chronic offenders (8 percent) were also repeat adult Index violent offenders. They accounted for one-third of all adult arrests for Index violence.
   • Most juvenile chronic offenders had been incarcerated; 54 percent were committed at least once to training schools. Almost 64 percent had at least one adult imprisonment.[19]

It is interesting to note that the removal of chronic offenders from the cohort would have reduced the number of cohort arrests by 50 percent. This study demonstrates that the continuity between juvenile and adult crime is a reality and that policy decisions that affect these offenders *before* they become adults could have a drastic impact on future adult crime.

The Racine Cohort

Shannon and his colleagues conducted a longitudinal study that examined the criminal careers of 6,127 persons born in Racine, Wisconsin, in

1942, 1949, and 1959. The study examined the development of criminal careers within the three birth cohorts. Data on reported police contacts were collected through 1974. As in the Philadelphia studies, the goal was to identify those persons who were more likely to engage in delinquency, those who stopped committing crimes, and those who continued their criminal careers into adulthood. However, analysis of the **Racine Cohorts** indicates different findings from those in Philadelphia.

> **Racine Cohort** A longitudinal study that examined the criminal careers of persons born in Racine, Wisconsin, in 1942, 1949, and 1959

Shannon reported that the rates for serious felonies more than doubled from 1942 to 1955 for the age group 6–17 years. The rate more than tripled for the 18–20 year age group. Crime rates were highest in the inner city areas where unemployment and underemployment were commonplace. Offenders with a juvenile record were more likely to commit crime as adults. Yet, it was impossible to predict which juveniles would become adult offenders.[20]

Lab and Dorner (1987) compared female delinquency patterns with that of the males in the three Racine birth cohorts. They reported that, over time, female delinquency rose for status, victimless, and minor property offenses. Yet, in terms of major property and personal offenses, the female rates did not match those of their male counterparts.[21]

The Cambridge (UK) Study of Delinquent Development

The **Cambridge (UK) Study of Delinquent Development** followed 411 London (UK) working-class males from age 8 to 32 years, beginning in 1961–1962. Data were obtained from (1) tests and interviews conducted at ages 8, 10, and 14 years; (2) interviews conducted at ages 16, 18, 21, 25, and 32 years; (3) parental interviews; (4) questionnaires completed by the subjects' teachers; and (5) statistics compiled by the Criminal Record Office in London. These data were analyzed to identify predictors of (1) participation (prevalence) in officially recorded offending between ages 10 and 20 years; (2) early onset (between ages 10 and 13 years) versus later onset (ages 14 to 20 years) of offending; and (3) persistence versus desistance of offending in adulthood (ages 21 to 32 years).

> **Cambridge (UK) Study of Delinquent Development** Included working-class males from age 8 to 32 years, beginning in 1961–62 to identify predictors of prevalence, onset of offending, and persistence versus desistance of offending

Here, Farrington found that the peak age for the annual prevalence of convictions is 17 years (11.2 males per 100 convicted). The best childhood predictors (at age 10 years) of prevalence were childhood antisocial behavior, convicted parents, impulsivity and daring, low intelligence and attainment, low income and poor housing, and poor child-rearing practices (including separation from parents). The number of offenses committed per year peaked at age 17 years (16.8 per 100 males). The peak age of onset was 14 years (4.6 first convictions per 100 males) with a secondary peak at 17 years. The *age of desistance*—when the last offense is typically committed—was 23.3. Farrington also determined that violent offenders committed their crimes frequently. Therefore, measures designed to reduce future violence might as well be targeted on frequent as well as currently violent offenders.[22]

In particular, the early onset of offending was predicted by low paternal involvement with the boy in leisure activities. The same factor led to persistence in crime between ages 21 and 32 years, together with a low degree of commitment to school and low verbal IQ at ages 8–10 years.[23] A long-term follow-up study of the cohort found that nearly all subjects had been sent to prison. Most of the subjects thought imprisonment had no effect on them, although some believed it had made them less likely to reoffend. In general, chronic offenders led more dysfunctional lives in adulthood than other offenders. The most important childhood risk factors for chronic offending were troublesomeness, daring, and having a delinquent sibling or a convicted parent. On the basis of such features, Farrington and West believed that most of the chronic offenders might have been predicted at age 10 years and that treatment could have been identified.[24] Another study of the life course of these offenders revealed that several social variables (work history, relations with spouses) distinguished chronic and other types of offenders.[25]

The results of the Cambridge study emphasize the need to consider the different stages and elements of a criminal career as separate entities. It also seems that the most promising methods of preventing offending are behavioral parent training and preschool intellectual enrichment programs.[26]

In reaction to the findings of the cohort studies, experts have suggested that juvenile courts adopt a policy of close, intensive supervision perhaps for first-time and certainly for second-time juvenile Index offenders. After a third Index offense, incapacitation should become "the rule rather than the exception.…Juveniles can and should receive severe penalties in juvenile court when their most current offense and prior record warrant such action."[27] In addition, policies should be established to identify the chronic offender more effectively, and an enhanced system of record keeping should ease identification of them.[28] Hamparian and her colleagues recommended that chronic violent offenders be dealt with severely, not just with punishment but with a graduated series of programs. These programs should range from incarceration to work readiness projects providing sheltered employment in the form of a "Community Conservation Corps" for young adults. They stressed the importance of not waiting for chronic juvenile offenders to become adult criminals. Indeed, the existance of a core of chronic juvenile offenders is the key finding of the cohort studies. There is clear evidence that delinquency causes violent crime victimization.[29]

RESEARCH ON VERY YOUNG OFFENDERS

Also sponsored by OJJDP, current research by Loeber and Farrington examine the early involvement of very young children in delinquency. This research was spurred by the previously cited findings that most chronic and violent juvenile offenders begin their delinquency careers by ages 10–12 years. These studies have revealed some significant conclusions:

- **Young offending is serious business.** Very young delinquents engage in serious crime at high rates of involvement. In this study, they were responsible for one in three juvenile arrests for arson, one in five juvenile arrests for sex offenses and vandalism, and one in twelve juvenile arrests for violent crime.

- **There is no evidence that a new and more serious "breed" of child delinquent and young murderer exists.** Crime statistics do not indicate a dramatic shift in juvenile offending. Between 1980 and 1997, the number of murders committed by offenders age 12 years or younger remained fairly constant (about thirty per year).

- **These young offenders will not "grow out" of delinquency.** Child delinquents are twice as likely to engage in serious violent behavior and chronic offending. They have longer delinquent careers and are more likely to become gang members and engage in substance abuse.

- **Incarceration seems to be ineffective and may even make things worse.** There is no evidence that incarceration slows the development of a violent delinquent career. In fact, their early exposure to older, serious offenders may aggravate the situation.[30]

Researchers have also identified some "early warning signs" of serious delinquent behavior:

- **Disruptive behavior that is apparent during the preschool and certainly the elementary school years.** This is significant especially if this behavior is more disruptive and severe than that of other children.
- **Physical fighting.**
- **Cruelty to people or animals.**
- **Covert acts such as frequently lying, theft, and fire setting.**
- **Inability to get along with others.**
- **Low school motivation during elementary school.**
- **Substance abuse.**
- **Repeated victimization (e.g., child abuse, peer bullying).**[31]

To prevent the development of delinquency, programs should focus on "risk and protective factors" such as birth complications, hyperactivity, impulsivity, parental substance abuse, and poor child rearing practices, because these factors put children at the highest risk of becoming serious, violent, and chronic offenders.[32] Communities should engage in early intervention programs that encourage conflict resolution and violence

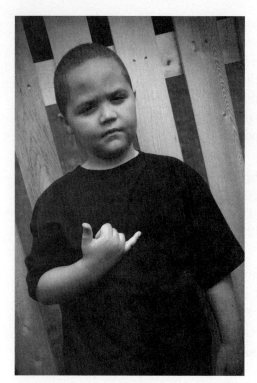

Juvenile Flashing a Gang Sign

prevention,[33] featuring partnerships between appropriate social agencies and the juvenile justice system.

JUVENILE VICTIMIZATION

Another vital source of information involves the nature of juvenile victimization. This information provides data on which, how, and where juveniles become victims of different types of crime.

Juvenile Homicide Victims

Crime information over a period of years generates trend data and avoids reaching erroneous conclusions that may occur when information is based on a short time frame. Examination of long-term (1993–2006) trends from the UCR also offers the following information about juveniles and homicide[34]:

- Homicides of juveniles peaked in 1993 at about 2,840. The number of juvenile homicide victims in 2006 was 39 percent below the 1993 peak, but 14 percent above the 2003 level. Juveniles represented about 10 percent of all murder victims in 2006.

- In 2006, 27 percent of murdered juveniles were female, 47 percent were African American, and 53 percent were killed with a firearm. Of the juvenile murder victims of known offenders in 2006, family members killed 39 percent; acquaintances, 46 percent; and strangers, 15 percent.

- Between 1980 through 2006, juvenile offenders participated in about one of every four homicides of juveniles in which the offenders were known to law enforcement. In about one-fifth of the juvenile homicides in which known juvenile offenders participated, adult offenders were also involved.

Juveniles were most likely to be murdered in large cities (Los Angeles, New York, Chicago, and Philadelphia).[35] Until their teenage years, boys and girls were equally likely to be murdered. However, between 1980 and 2006, approximately 9,815 seventeen-year-old males were homicide victims, compared with approximately 1,855 seventeen-year-old females.[36] African American youth accounted for about 16 percent of the juvenile population between 1980 and 2006 but were the victims in 47 percent of juvenile homicides during the 27-year period.[37]

National Crime Victims Survey (NCVS) Survey conducted by the Bureau of Justice Statistics to uncover unreported crime by surveying households

Juveniles as Victims of Violent Crime: The National Crime Victims Survey

A key source of information on crime victimization is the **National Crime Victims Survey (NCVS)**. The Bureau of Justice Statistics has conducted this survey since 1972. Its aim is to uncover unreported crime by going directly to the victim. The NCVS is a scientifically designed survey of U.S. households. In an attempt to best represent households across the nation, households are selected using a stratified, multi-stage cluster design. Approximately 60,000 households respond to the survey each year. Information in this report is also presented as a population rate: the number of victims per 1,000 households.

Again, consider victimization trends using long-term data. Analysis of violent crime victimization survey data from 1993 to 2003 reveals the following:

- **Juveniles 12–17 years of age were more than twice as likely to be the targets of violent crime.** The violent crime victimization rate for male teens was more than twice of that for adult males. Female teens were about twice as likely as adult females to be the victims of violent crime.[38]

- **Teens aged 15–17 years of age were about three times more likely than younger teens (12–14 years of age) to be the victims of violent crime with a firearm.** The older teens were also more likely to be victimized by strangers.

- **Both urban and suburban youths were at least twice as likely as their adult counterparts to be the victims of violent crime.**

- **More than two out of three violent crimes against juveniles were committed without a weapon.** Yet, about three out of ten violent crime victimizations resulted in an injury.[39]

- **School crime was not uncommon.** Most violent crime victimizations took place at school.

- **Overall, about one-quarter of the juvenile violent crime victimizations were reported to the police.**[40]

RISK FACTORS

The search for risk factors in delinquency is an attempt to provide information to guide juvenile programs and treatment. The hope is that treating the risk factor will provide more effective treatment for juveniles.

Drug Use: The Youth Risk Behavior Surveillance System

It is difficult to obtain accurate estimates of drug use. In 1990, the National Center for Chronic Disease Prevention and Health Promotion developed a nationwide, representative survey of ninth- through twelfth-grade students throughout the United States. The survey questions deal with several health risk behaviors. Table 2.1 presents results from the 2005 and 2007 surveys on drug use among these students.

Table 2.1
SURVEY RESULTS: *YOUTH ONLINE* NATIONAL CENTER FOR CHRONIC DISEASE PREVENTION AND HEALTH PROMOTION, 2005 AND 2007

Drug Question and Demographic

Students who had at least one drink of alcohol on at least one day during the 30 days before the survey.	2005 Percentage	2007 Percentage
Male	42.8	44.7
Female	43.8	44.6
Total	**43.3**	**44.7**
White	46.4	47.3
African American	31.2	34.5
Hispanic	46.8	47.6
Other	34.0	35.5
Total	**43.3**	**44.7**

Students who used marijuana one or more times during the thirty days before the survey.	2005 Percentage	2007 Percentage
Male	22.1	22.4
Female	18.2	17.0
Total	**20.2**	**19.7**
White	20.3	19.9
African American	20.4	21.5
Hispanic	23.0	18.5
Other	13.9	17.2
Total	**20.2**	**19.7**

Students who used any form of cocaine one or more times during their life.	2005 Percentage	2007 Percentage
Male	8.4	7.8
Female	6.8	6.5
Total	**7.6**	**7.2**
White	7.7	7.4
African American	2.3	1.8
Hispanic	12.2	10.9
Other	7.7	6.5
Total	**7.6**	**7.2**

Students who used heroin one or more times during their life.	2005 Percentage	2007 Percentage
Male	3.3	2.9
Female	1.4	1.6
Total	**2.4**	**2.3**
White	2.2	1.7
African American	1.5	1.8
Hispanic	3.6	3.7
Other	2.4	2.9
Total	**2.4**	**2.3**

Students who used methamphetamines one or more times during their life.	2005 Percentage	2007 Percentage
Male	6.3	4.6
Female	6.0	4.1
Total	**6.2**	**4.4**
White	6.5	4.5
African American	1.7	1.9
Hispanic	8.8	5.7
Other	6.4	5.2
Total	**6.2**	**4.4**

Source: Youth Risk Behavior System. http://www.cdc.gov/yrbss. Retrieved on August 11, 2008.

The table is divided into categories by year and by the sex and race of the respondents. The total percentage of drug use for each drug is also presented. In terms of alcohol use in the thirty days before the survey, the percentage slightly increased (1.4 percent) for the entire group between 2005 and 2007. Between the sexes, the percentage for males and females was about equal (44.7 percent) in 2007—a figure that was up 1.9 percent for males and 0.8 percent for females. Among racial groups, whites and Hispanics had the highest rates in 2007 (47.3 percent and 47.6 percent). Between 1991 and 2007, the prevalence of reported alcohol use had declined (50.8 percent – 44.7 percent = 6.1 percent).

Marijuana use had slightly decreased over time (0.5 percent). Males were more likely to report use during the 30 days prior to the survey than females. Among racial groups, African Americans recorded the highest percentage in 2007 (21.5 percent), and the greatest decrease over time was recorded by Hispanics (4.5 percent). From 1991 to 2007, reported marijuana use of this type increased 5 percent (14.7 percent versus 19.7 percent). However, this marijuana use figure peaked in 1999 (26.7 percent) and has since declined.

Reported cocaine use was also down slightly between 2005 and 2007 (0.5 percent). This figure has declined for both males and females and across all racial groups since 2005. However, between 1991 and 2007, reported life-time cocaine use has increased 1.3 percent (5.7 percent versus 7.2 percent).

Heroin use minutely declined (0.1 percent) since 2005, but its overall usage rate is the lowest of all the drugs considered in the survey. In 2007, males (2.9 percent) and Hispanics (3.7 percent) had the highest rates of heroin use.

Methamphetamine use has declined 1.8 percent since 2005. Both sexes and all racial groups recorded lower methamphetamine use rates in 2007 across the board. This decline has been even greater since 1999: 4.7 percent (9.1 percent versus 4.4 percent).

Teens with Marijuana Joint

Although these figures indicate a decline in the use of drugs by students, the Office of National Drug Control Policy reports troubling trends in the abuse of prescription and over-the-counter drugs.[41] Figures from the National Survey on Drug Use and Health reveal that more teens abuse prescription drugs than any illicit drug (except marijuana). In 2006, more than 2.1 million teens abused prescription drugs. One-third of these youths were 12 to 17 years of age. Typically, teens abuse pain killers (e.g., hydrocodone, oxycodone), depressants (e.g., sleeping pills, anti-anxiety drugs) and stimulants (e.g., drugs prescribed for attention deficit disorder).

This pattern was also present among some over-the-counter drugs, especially cough and cold medications containing dextromethorphan (DXM). From 1999 to 2004, the sevenfold increase in the abuse of DXM in poison control centers was largely due to 15- and 16-year-old teens.

One of the factors promoting this increasing pattern of abuse is the easy availability of these drugs. The majority of the teen respondents (64 percent) said that they received prescription pain relievers from friends or relatives. They noted that they are available everywhere and much easier to obtain than illegal drugs.

Part of the problem here is the attitudes of both youth and parents—underestimating and even denying the deleterious effects of abusing prescription and over-the-counter drugs. Teens believe that prescription drugs are much safer because they are given by doctors. They see nothing wrong with abusing them from time to time. About one-third of the teen respondents believed that pain killers were not addictive at all. They also reported that because prescription pain relievers are legal, there is less shame in their abuse. Compared with illicit drugs, they also noted that their parents were less concerned if they were caught. More than one-quarter of the parents believed that prescription and over-the-counter drugs were much safer to abuse than street drugs.

Other Risk Factors: The Youth Risk Behavior Surveillance System

Other risk factors are also reported in this survey. The patterns discussed in this section were recorded in "the prevalence of behaviors that contribute to violence." Weapon carrying by students decreased between 1991 (26.1 percent) and 1999 (17.3 percent). However, there was no change in this reported behavior between 1999 and 2007 (18 percent). Carrying a gun decreased between 1993 (7.9 percent) and 1999 (4.9 percent) and showed no change from 1999 to 2007. Rates of reported fighting declined between 1991 (42.5 percent) and 2003 (33 percent) but then increased through 2007 (35.5 percent).

In terms of sexual behaviors, engaging in sexual intercourse over their lifetime decreased between 1991 (54.1 percent) and 2007 (47.8 percent). Current sexual activity also declined over this time period (37.5 percent to 35.0 percent). Drinking or using drugs before intercourse among currently sexually active teens increased between 1991 (21.6 percent) and 2001 (25.6 percent) and then decreased through 2007 (22.5 percent).

In regards of suicide-related behaviors, the percentage of teens seriously considering attempting suicide in the twelve months before the survey declined between 1991 (29 percent) and 2007 (14.5 percent). The rate of teens who actually attempted suicide during the twelve months prior to the survey showed no change between 1993 and 2001 (about 8.8 percent) and then decreased through 2007 (6.9 percent).

Program of Research on the Causes and Correlates of Delinquency

In 1986, the Program of Research on the Causes and Correlates of Delinquency began under the sponsorship of the OJJDP. This program is a collaborative longitudinal effort that consists of three separate scientific surveys of youths in Rochester, New York (State University of New York—Albany research team); Denver, Colorado (University of Colorado research team); and Pittsburgh, Pennsylvania (University of Pittsburgh research team). For more than a decade, these researchers have interviewed 4,000 participants at regular intervals in an attempt to identify the risk factors associated with delinquency accurately.

In particular, they have examined the impact of three factors (drug use, school problems, and mental health problems) as they relate to serious delinquency (problem behavior lasting two years or more). Research from the three sites led to five conclusions about this relationship[42]:

1. **A great proportion of the serious delinquents did not have persistent drug abuse, school, or mental health problems.** The majority of the serious delinquents were not persistent drug abusers, but more than 50 percent of the drug-abusing males and 20 percent of the drug-abusing females were serious delinquents.

2. **Thus, even though less than half of the serious delinquents were persistent drug abusers, it is the problem that co-occurs most frequently with serious delinquency.** Between 34 percent and 44 percent of the seriously delinquent males were also drug abusers. Among seriously delinquent females, 46–48 percent were drug abusers.

3. **As the number of problem behaviors increase, the greater the likelihood that males will be serious delinquents.** The combination of drug, school, and mental health problems is a "reasonably strong risk factor" for serious delinquency.

4. **However, the findings also indicate that serious delinquency does not always co-occur with other problems.**

5. **The degree of co-occurrence between problem behaviors and serious delinquency is not consistently overwhelming.**

It is often difficult to determine the answer to the "chicken-egg question" here: Does the problem behavior relate to serious delinquency or does serious delinquency relate to the problem behavior? The research on risk factors emphasizes the need to direction attention to the careful determination of the problems faced by individual juveniles and how they may relate to delinquency if they go unchecked and untreated.

Risk factors must be considered when attempting to design policies and programs for juveniles. They must be addressed within the target population served while considering the behavior (delinquent or otherwise) to be addressed.

SUMMARY

Determining the level of juvenile crime and delinquency is a difficult task. In this chapter, we presented data from several sources to obtain a more complete picture. Each source has its own strengths and weaknesses in terms of ability to measure crime. The UCRs are the only true national measure of crime. Unfortunately, they consist only of crimes known to the police. Naturally, they cannot include crimes that go unreported or unseen. Therefore, to a certain extent, they reflect police operations. If the police are concentrating on a certain type of crime or targeting juveniles in one area, then the UCR statistics will reflect that emphasis. In other words, the UCR often represents what the police are doing rather than how much crime there actually is.

The National Crime Victims Survey is an attempt to get around this problem by interviewing victims directly. However, this source does not present data by state, county, or city. Although some breakdowns are provided by region of the county and level of urbanization, its findings are representative of the nation as a whole. Nevertheless, the results of the **Developmental Victimization Survey (DVS)** present a more accurate picture of the dangers that children and youth typically face.

The cohort studies are limited to the area in which they were conducted and by their reliance on official statistics. However, they do provide a long-term view of how juvenile delinquency develops over time and who is responsible for most of it.

Given these limitations, there are several conclusions that can be reached in our review of recent juvenile statistics on risk factors and delinquency:

Developmental Victimization Survey (DVS) Longitudinal study designed to assess a comprehensive range of childhood victimizations across gender, race, and developmental stage

1. Risk factors for children and teens must be carefully examined. Patterns are typically present across racial/ethnic groups and for different states. These individual patterns must be found so that proper plans can be made to prevent delinquency. They are the indicators of the "root causes" of juvenile delinquency that must be addressed to deal with the problem. Although some improvement in these factors has occurred over time, high rates still exist for subpopulations.

2. Statistics indicate that student use of illicit drugs has declined since 1999. However, this trend is counterbalanced by a shift to prescription and over-the-counter drug abuse. This problem will be especially difficult to address without increased vigilance by all persons concerned, including parents, relatives, and members of the medical and pharmaceutical communities. It is the major drug problem currently facing youths.

3. Other risk factors among teen survey respondents indicate that rates of violent, sexual, and suicide-related behaviors are on the decline. Only vigilance and education will enable this trend to continue.

4. Juvenile crime does not seem to be worsening. Although there were some increases in the 1990s, the levels of juvenile crime are declining or leveling off. This is true for both violent and property crimes.

5. Juvenile victimizations seem to be lessening officially, but the other problems they face are alarming and persistent.

Parents, teachers, church officials, family members, and all concerned citizens must be aware of the warning signs of delinquent behavior and attempt an appropriate intervention. Punishment after the fact is not as effective as prevention. Risk factors, like substance abuse and teen fatherhood, must be attended to.

Statistics themselves do not offer solutions to problems; they do provide direction—where to concentrate efforts and what to work on. Because juvenile delinquency, victimization, and other behaviors are always subject to change, it is important to continue research. Information is the key to effective program and policy development.

KEY TERMS

Cambridge (UK) Study of
  Delinquent Development
cohort study
Columbus Cohort
Developmental Victimization
  Survey (DVS)
Index crimes

National Crime Victims
  Survey (NCVS)
Philadelphia Birth Cohorts
Racine Cohort
status offenses
Uniform Crime Report
  (UCR)

DISCUSSION AND REVIEW QUESTIONS

1. What is the pattern of violent crime by juveniles presented from the UCR?
2. What is the pattern of property crime by juveniles presented from the UCR?
3. Compare your answers to Questions 1 and 2. Is there an overall trend for juvenile crime?
4. Among the data, what are the most common characteristics of juvenile offending?
5. What is the victimization pattern presented regarding school crime? What do the results of the Developmental Victimization Survey represent?
6. How do the findings of the cohort studies compare? Do they have anything in common?
7. In your opinion, what is the most significant risk factor revealed by the very young offender research?

VIDEO PROFILES

The *Status Offender* video profile in MyCrimeKit provides insights into the intake process as well as the initial hearing for a 17-year-old female status offender. The video highlights issues associated with both the "best interests" of the juvenile (e.g., "she does not understand what's in her best interests and needs the court to step in") and the rights of the juvenile (e.g., notification of rights, detention hearing, initial hearing). Discuss what the juvenile is charged with and how the charge might be captured in crime statistics.

Compare and contrast the mother's description of the case with the judge and probation officer's opinions of the case. Finally, identify the risk factors the client demonstrates. Are they being appropriately handled?

The *Delinquent Offender* video profile in MyCrimeKit shows the process of a juvenile detention hearing. The judge discusses the juvenile's rights, the process of determining probable cause, petition for delinquency, and determination of detention prior to the delinquency hearing. Discuss the offenses the juvenile is charged with and how the charges might be captured in crime statistics; how would the situation differ had the juvenile been charged with possession of a handgun? What risk factors does this client demonstrate? Finally, does the suggested program address the risk factors posed by the client appropriately? Why or why not?

MYCRIMEKIT

mycrimekit™ Go to MyCrimeKit.com to explore the following study tools and resources specific to this chapter:

- Practice Quiz: Test your knowledge with multiple-choice, true-false, fill-in-the-blank, and essay questions.
- Flashcards: 20 flashcards to test your knowledge of the chapter's key terms.
- Web Quest: Review the Web sites of the UCR and the National Crime Victimization Survey.
- Web Links: Check out sites related to the statistics presented in this chapter and update the statistics with the most current available.

ENDNOTES

1. *Essay Focuses on the Urgent Need to Reform Juvenile Justice.* Annie E. Casey Foundation. http://www.kidscount.org/datacenter
2. Charles Puzzanchera, *Juvenile Arrests 2008: OJJDP Juvenile Justice Bulletin* (Washington DC: Office of Justice Programs, December, 2009), pp. 1–4.
3. Ibid., p. 6.
4. Ibid., p. 1.
5. Ibid., p. 7.
6. Ibid., p. 1.
7. Thomas J. Bernard, "Juvenile Crime and the Transformation of Juvenile Justice: Is There a Juvenile Crime Wave?" *Justice Quarterly,* Vol. 16 (2, 1999), pp. 337–356.

8. Howard N. Synder and Melissa Sickmund, *Juvenile Offenders and Victims: 2006 National Report* (Washington, DC: National Center for Juvenile Justice and U.S. Office of Justice Programs, 2006), p. 107.

9. Ibid., p. 198.

10. Ibid., p. 200.

11. Ibid., p. 207.

12. Ibid.

13. Marvin Wolfgang, Robert Figlio, and Thorsten Sellin, *Delinquency in a Birth Cohort* (Chicago: University of Chicago Press, 1972), pp. 65–131.

14. Ibid., p. 192.

15. Paul Tracy, Marvin Wolfgang, and Robert Figlio, *Delinquency Careers in Two Birth Cohorts* (New York: Plenum Press, 1990), p. 292.

16. Kimberly Kempf-Leonard, Paul E. Tracy, and James C. Howell, "Serious, Violent, and Chronic Juvenile Offender: The Relationship of Delinquency Career Types to Adult Criminality," *Justice Quarterly,* Vol. 18 (2001), pp. 449–478.

17. Donna M. Hamparian, Richard Schuster, Simon Dinitz, and John P. Conrad, *The Violent Few: A Study of Violent Juvenile Offenders* (Lexington, MA: Heath, 1978), pp. 38–40.

18. Donna M. Hamparian, J. M. Davis, J. M. Jacobson, and R. E. McGraw, *The Young Criminal Years of the Violent Few* (Washington, DC: U.S. Department of Justice, 1985), pp. 14–15.

19. Ibid., pp. 19–20.

20. Lyle W. Shannon, *Criminal Career Continuity: Its Social Context.* (New York: Human Sciences Press, 1988).

21. Steven P. Lab and William G. Doerner, "Changing Female Delinquency in Three Birth Cohorts," *Journal of Crime and Justice,* Vol. 10 (1987), pp. 101–116.

22. David P. Farrington, "Criminal Career Research in the United Kingdom," *British Journal of Criminology,* Vol. 32 (1992), pp. 521–536.

23. David P. Farrington and J. David Hawkins, "Predicting Participation, Early Onset and Later Persistence in Officially Recorded Offending." *Criminal Behaviour and Mental Health,* Vol. 1 (1991), pp. 1–33.

24. David P. Farrington and David J. West, "Criminal, Penal and Life Histories of Chronic Offenders: Risk and Protective Factors and Early Identification," *Criminal Behaviour and Mental Health,* Vol. 3 (1993), pp. 492–523.

25. Daniel S. Nagin, David P. Farrington, and Terrance E. Moffitt, "Life-Course Trajectories of Different Types of Offenders." *Criminology,* Vol. 33 (1995), pp. 111–139.

26. David P. Farrington, "Implications of Criminal Career Research for the Prevention of Offending." *Journal of Adolescence,* Vol. 13 (1990), pp. 93–113.

27. Tracy, Wolfgang, and Figlio, *Delinquency Careers,* pp. 295, 297.

28. Kimberly L. Kempf, "Career Criminals in the 1958 Philadelphia Birth Cohort: A Follow-up of the Early Adult Years." *Criminal Justice Review,* Vol. 15 (1990), pp. 151–172.

29. Xiaojin Chen, "The Link between Juvenile Offending and Victimization." *Youth Violence and Juvenile Justice*, Vol. 7 (2009), pp. 119–135.

30. Ibid., pp. 3–4.

31. Ibid., p. 5.

32. See Stanton E. Samenow, *Before It's Too Late: Why Some Kids Get into Trouble and What Parents Can Do About It* (New York: Times Books, 1998).

33. See Jan Arnow, *Teaching Peace: How to Raise Children to Live in Harmony—Without Fear, Without Prejudice, Without Violence* (New York: Perigee, 1995).

34. OJJDP Statistical Briefing Book. Online. Available: http://ojjdp.ncjrs.gov/ojstatbb/victims/qa02304.asp?qaDate=2006. Released on October 24, 2008.

35. Ibid. Available: http://ojjdp.ncjrs.gov/ojstatbb/victims/qa02305.asp?qaDate=2006. Released on October 24, 2008.

36. Ibid. Available: http://ojjdp.ncjrs.gov/ojstatbb/victims/qa02311.asp?qaDate=2006. Released on October 24, 2008.

37. Ibid. Available: http://ojjdp.ncjrs.gov/ojstatbb/victims/qa02310.asp?qaDate=2006. Released on October 24, 2008.

38. Katrina Baum, *Juvenile Victimization and Offending, 1993–2003: Bureau of Justice Statistics Special Report* (Washington, DC: U.S. Department of Justice, August, 2005), p. 2.

39. Ibid., p. 5.

40. Ibid., p. 6.

41. Office of National Drug Control Policy, *Prescription for Danger: A Report on the Troubling Trend of Prescription and Over-the-Counter Drug Abuse Among the Nation's Teens* (Washington, DC: Executive Office of the President, 2008).

42. David Huizinga, Rolf Loeber, Terrence P. Thornberry, and Lynn Cohern, *Co-occurrence of Delinquency and Other Problem Behavior: OJJDP Juvenile Justice Bulletin* (Washington DC: Office of Justice Programs, November, 2001), pp. 5–6.

3

Dealing with Delinquency: Theories, Issues, and Practice

*N*othing fails like success.

SIMON DINITZ

LEARNING OBJECTIVES

1. Define juvenile delinquency and status offenses.
2. Describe various criminological theories associated with juvenile delinquency.
3. Identify the patterns of delinquency utilizing criminological theories.
4. Apply criminological theories to specific crimes or crime policy.

summary 2 pgs

CHAPTER OVERVIEW

Theories are attempts to explain events. They have two main functions: (1) They organize existing knowledge about a subject into a coherent framework, and (2) they help provide direction for future research on the topic. Kaplan reminds us that often theories are attempts to make sense of a disturbing situation (such as delinquency).[1] Thus, they provide a vehicle to interpret, criticize, and unify existing beliefs. Theories make the comparison of different approaches possible. They allow us to consider the question of causation by specifying the relationships between different social, physical, or even economic variables and a phenomenon like crime.

Like all theories, criminological theories have certain attributes. First, they exist at different levels of **generality**. Some theories, called **grand theories**, strive to explain all types of criminal behavior. For example, Charles Tittle contends that a number of different crimes (e.g., theft, burglary, rape, homicide, voyeurism) could be considered "instances of the same act—intrusion into private domains."[2] Other theories, more limited in their approach and scope, try to explain a specific area or type of crime (e.g., serial murder, white-collar crime). They are based on the belief that there is too much variation in human behavior, criminal motives, cultures, economic conditions, and historical contexts to expect a general theory to give an adequate explanation for crime. Merton calls these **middle-range theories** (see Box 3.1).[3]

Criminological theories also differ in focus. Some theories highlight the actor (i.e., the criminal or the victim). Others consider the social background (e.g., education) and relationships (e.g., family structure) among all people in society as potential crime-causing agents.[4]

The primary aim of criminology is to determine the causes of crime. Cressey (1979: 457) defines **criminology** as

> the body of knowledge concerning crime as a social phenomenon. It is the product of systematic studies of the processes of making laws, breaking laws, and reacting to the breaking of laws. The objective of criminology is persistent progress in the development of valid information regarding this set of interactions.[5]

generality The breadth, depth, or limited nature of criminological theories

grand theories Criminological theories that are attempts to explain all types of criminal behavior

middle-range theories Theories more limited in their approach and scope and that are attempts to explain a specific area or type of crime

criminology Body of knowledge that represents attempts to determine the causes of crime

---

BOX 3.1 **ATTRIBUTES OF THEORY**

Generality   Classification of theories by their scope or level of generality.
Grand theories   Sweeping theories that attempt to explain all types of delinquency.
Middle-range theories   Theories that try to explain a certain type of crime (e.g., serial murder, white-collar crime).

Similarly, Lynch and Groves (1996: 89) list several desirable attributes of a "culturally and historically specific" criminological theory[6]:

1. Address multiple levels of causation

2. Demonstrate a connection between structural and subjective factors

3. Include a discussion of opportunity structure as an important (but not the only) dimension for understanding crime

4. Discuss the effects of enforcement policy, the context and construction of law as these elements bear upon the social construction of crime

5. Built theory from the bottom up (from the concrete), keeping in mind the cultural and historical limits of explanation

6. Construct explanations that are grounded in (but not a slave to) empirical research findings.

In short, **criminological theory** is an attempt to explain why crime exists, how it takes place, and what can be done about it.

criminological theory Attempts to explain why crime exists, how it takes place, and what can be done about it

Theories of delinquency are attempts to explain the causes of juvenile criminal behavior. The juvenile laws do not search for the underlying reasons for a person's actions but simply determine whether in fact that act took place and that the person did it. To understand juvenile delinquents better, however, we must continue to examine the relationship between the actors and the kinds of factors and variables that made them commit the deviant act in the first place. Theories are important for students to review to have a larger tool kit with which to work in the field of juvenile justice.

What is the cause of the condition called *delinquency*? Historically, the traditional literature on crime and delinquency has approached this question by examining behavior patterns, sociological influence, and economic factors that might lead a child to be labeled as delinquent.

In part, delinquency is caused by the social judgment process that defines it in the first place. This tenet is exacerbated when one considers that the outcome of most, if not all, delinquency research is predetermined by those whose values have been adopted for the purposes of distinguishing the comparable criterion groups of delinquents and nondelinquents.

The absence of a discriminating scheme for the prediction of who is or is not a delinquent can also lead to a tainting of the targeted delinquents in the treatment population. The use of inconsistent discriminators could result in *false positives* (juveniles labeled as probable delinquents who are not) and *false negatives* (juveniles labeled as nondelinquent who are actually serious delinquents). On the one hand, if juveniles in the false-positive category are given intervention strategies (e.g., *radical nonintervention,* wherein nothing is done to "fix" them), they will never become delinquents anyway and the effort will tell researchers nothing. On the other hand, juveniles in the false-negative category, in which serious intervention might be called for, will continue to be delinquent and will therefore also brand the effort a failure.

Students will find many studies that declare that there are observable and predictable differences between delinquents and nondelinquents. These books and articles contain theories from many disciplines, ranging from those based on the medical model to those embracing the "process model" and everything in between. The most valid observable difference between delinquents and nondelinquents is that one gets *caught and labeled,* and the other does not. Apart from this, as mentioned previously, we do not believe that there is any cut-and-dried difference between the two groups. If such a discernible difference did exist, it would make prediction much easier, help to eliminate false positives from target groups, and assist the juvenile justice system in achieving one of its most sought-after goals: the prevention of delinquency in the first place.[7]

This chapter examines some of the better-known definitions of delinquency and describes some of the theoretical bases of causality. We stress the linkage between theory, a serious issue, and the resulting practices that have been developed in the juvenile justice system.

DEFINING DELINQUENCY

Before attempting to discuss conditions or circumstances that seem to cause delinquency, it is important for us to define *juvenile delinquency,* a term that tends to conjure up a vision of a leather-jacketed thug. However, even the clearly identified delinquent is difficult to categorize. For example, suppose that there are two boys who have nothing in common but the fact that both have violated the law. One was caught engaging in an armed robbery and the other stealing soft drinks from a grocery store. Although they may both fit into the same legal pigeonhole, they do not necessarily share the same or even a common psychological category. In this case, the label *delinquent* cannot be used without qualification, as though it denoted a common set of facts or a specific kind of juvenile. We cannot simply assume that because a youth was in court, he was ipso facto a member of some subspecies of citizenry. To simplify the process of definition, juvenile delinquency can be divided into two separate areas: legal and social.

Legal Definition

Juveniles in the United States must obey and are subject to the same ordinances and criminal statutes that govern adults. In addition, they are

---

BOX 3.2 **STATUS OFFENDER**

A status offender is generally accepted as a juvenile who has come into contact with the juvenile authorities because of conduct that is an offense only when committed by a juvenile. A status offense is conduct that would not be defined as a criminal act when committed by an adult.

---

governed by a second set of rules that are applicable because they are specific to juveniles.

Most states continue to include status offenders in the category of delinquents. This is the case despite the major provisions of the Juvenile Justice Act amended in 1977 that called for the **deinstitutionalization** of status offenders and their eventual removal from the purview of the juvenile court. In fact, even today, according to some guesses, close to one-half of all youths brought before our juvenile courts are involved in acts that if committed by an adult, would not be a crime (see Box 3.2).

deinstitutionalization The act of removing nondelinquent juveniles from secure detention or institutions

For example, Substitute House Bill No. 371 of Washington State lists the following conditions that characterize a child as dependent and therefore subject to the jurisdiction of the juvenile courts. A dependent child is one who meets the following criteria:

1. He or she has been abandoned; that is, left by his or her parents, guardian, or other custodian without parental care and support.

2. He or she is abused or neglected or has no parent, guardian, or custodian.

3. He or she is in conflict with his or her parent, guardian, or custodian.

4. He or she refuses to remain in any nonsecure residential placement ordered by a court.

5. His or her conduct evidences a substantial likelihood of degenerating into serious behavior if not corrected.

6. He or she is in need of custodial treatment in a diagnostic and treatment facility.[8]

State codes vary on the legal definition of **juvenile delinquency**. Keeping this in mind, the following definition of delinquency is based on material developed in Title 11, U.S. Code and therefore facilitates general application at the federal and state level:

juvenile delinquency A violation of a law by a person considered a juvenile (by age) in the jurisdiction

Juvenile delinquency is a violation of a law of the United States or its several states committed by a person who is not yet 18, which would have been a crime if committed by an adult and which is liable to disposition through the juvenile justice system.

A juvenile, also based primarily on the U.S. Code (Title 11), is defined as follows:

> A person who is not yet 18; or, for the purposes of proceedings and disposition of such a person for an act of juvenile delinquency or a crime committed prior to his/her eighteenth birthday, a person who is not yet 21.

The 18-year-old limit is applied in approximately two-thirds of the jurisdictions in the United States. Some states include youths up to age 21 years in their delinquency statutes, and others allow children as young as 12 years to be bound over to adult courts and tried as adults. Finally, some states have no lower age limit for children to be waived to adult court.

Obviously, there are many legal definitions of delinquency. Depending on the source, whether federal statutes, state laws, social commentators, or textbooks, the definition will vary. A legal definition of delinquency, even when agreed on, provides only a partial insight into the delinquency problem. A knowledge of the sociological factors surrounding delinquency becomes equally important in the quest for a solution to the definition problem. In fact, the term *juvenile delinquency* was developed in conjunction with the rise of the juvenile court in Chicago, Illinois, in 1899.[9] The legal definition of delinquency is inadequate for the understanding of the juvenile's position in society, the public's approval or disapproval of that child, or understanding the factors contributing to the juvenile's becoming labeled as a delinquent. We now turn, therefore, to a discussion involving the social impact of delinquency.

Social Definition

The social definition of delinquency primarily involves the views of the family, friends, and community regarding a child's behavior. A child may, for example, be part of a subculture that could have as norms many behaviors that would be labeled delinquent if exhibited outside that subculture. Thus, an African American child from the ghetto who is bused to a predominantly all-white suburban school may elicit disapproval from his new temporary community and may be forced to associate with groups and persons who are less conducive to the transmitting of socially accepted norms.

The social definition of delinquency, therefore, is a subjective reflection of how the youth's parents, friends, neighbors, and community view him or her as a person. It is also a reflection of how well "they" feel that he or she is fitting into a socially sanctioned behavioral mold in keeping with community standards of accepted behavior. This reflection is often quite different from the way in which the members of officialdom (i.e., the courts, police, and parole and/or probation officers) might see the youth.

DELINQUENCY AMONG GIRLS

Studies that seek to assess the impact of the gender of the juvenile offender have had mixed results. Overall, juvenile boys have a higher rate of incarceration than girls. However, in some cases, girls are more likely to be incarcerated for status offenses and receive longer sentences for status offenses than boys.[10] Status offenses have been a major issue in the adjudication and institutionalization of female juveniles. In the early 1980s, studies found 75 percent of all juvenile girls who were arrested and incarcerated were arrested for status offenses.[11] This suggests that a double standard exists for the two gender groups. That is, girls are seen as more "vulnerable to abuse and exploitation" and so in need of greater protection. They are also expected to adhere to "stricter standards of acceptable behavior."[12] Consequently, girls who defy parental authority and/or violate sexual norms are more likely to be "retained in the system" for their own protection,[13] whereas boys who commit similar acts are filtered out.

Juvenile Girl Following Arrest

In a 2008 study commissioned by the Office of Juvenile Justice and Delinquency Prevention (OJJDP) to understand gender differences in juvenile offending, researchers determined through juvenile arrest, victimization, and self-report data that girls are no more violent today than in the previous two decades.[14] Furthermore, the authors determined no more of an increase in female offending relative to male offending. The following context is provided for female juvenile offending[15]:

- **Peer violence**. Girls fight with peers to gain status, to defend their sexual reputation, and in self-defense against sexual harassment.
- **Family violence**. Girls fight more frequently at home with parents than do boys, who engage more frequently in violence outside the household. Girls' violence against parents is multidimensional: For some, it represents striking back against what they view as an overly controlling structure; for others, it is a defense against or an expression of anger stemming from being sexually and or physically abused by members of the household.
- **Violence within schools**. When girls fight in schools, they may do so as a result of teacher labeling, in self-defense, or out of a general sense of hopelessness.
- **Violence within disadvantaged neighborhoods**. Girls in disadvantaged neighborhoods are more likely to perpetrate violence against others because of the increased risk of victimization (and the resulting violent self-defense against that victimization), parental

Video Profile: *Runaway–Status Offender*

Cesare Beccaria Founded the "classical" school of criminology

levels of deterrence Specific and general deterrence; both based on the idea that people act in ways that maximize pleasure and minimize pain

inability to counteract negative community influences, and lack of opportunities for success.

- **Girls in gangs**. Survey research has shown several factors associated with girls' involvement in gangs (e.g., attitudes toward school, peers, delinquency, drug use, and early sexual activity); qualitative research points to the role of disadvantaged neighborhoods and families with multiple problems (e.g., violence, drug and alcohol abuse, neglect). Girls associated with primarily male gangs exhibit more violence than those in all-female gangs. Girls in gangs are more violent than other girls but less violent than boys in gangs.

THE CLASSICAL SCHOOL OF CRIMINOLOGY

The "classical" school of criminology was founded in the 1700s by **Cesare Beccaria** (see Box 3.3). Its emphasis was on the crime committed by the person. Its basic tenet was that humans are rational beings who seek the good things in life (i.e., they are pleasure oriented) and avoid the bad (i.e., pain oriented). Assuming, therefore, that people prefer pleasure to pain, Beccaria contended that no one would commit a criminal act unless it could be anticipated that the pleasurable consequences would outweigh the painful ones. The purpose of society was to secure the happiness of the majority. Early laws were quite simple, with punishments administered publicly and aimed primarily at deterrence (see Boxes 3.4 and 3.5 for discussion of **levels of deterrence** and theory).

Beccaria and his contemporaries embraced the doctrine of free will and its correlative that each person is morally responsible for his or her own acts. In keeping with this doctrine, Beccaria's principles about punishment are summarized as follows:

> Beccaria put the problem of punishments on a new plane, stating that the purpose of penalties is not retribution, but prevention; justice requires a right proportion between crimes and punishments, but the purpose of penalties is to prevent a criminal from doing more harm and to deter others from doing similar damage. . . . Beccaria wanted a

---

BOX 3.3 CESARE BONESANA, MARCHESE DI BECCARIA (1738–1794)

Beccaria wrote *An Essay on Crimes and Punishment*—published anonymously in 1764—the most exciting essay on law of the eighteenth century. It proposed a reorientation of criminal law toward humanistic goals. Beccaria suggested that judges should not interpret the law but, rather, that the law should be made more specific, as he believed that the real measure of crime was its harm to society. He is regarded as the founder of the classical school of criminology.

BOX 3.4 LEVELS OF DETERRENCE

Deterrence is based on the idea that persons are free to choose a course of action in a rational manner. They will act in ways that maximize pleasure and minimize pain. It can take place on two **levels of deterrence** that have different effects:

- **Specific deterrence** focuses on the individual offender. It seeks to teach criminals a lesson so that they will learn from the experience and "go straight" in the future. **Incapacitation** is another feature of specific deterrence. For example, the result of the death penalty is that the executed inmate is prevented from ever committing murder again.

- **General deterrence** involves society as a whole. Punishment is a message aimed at everyone. The punishment of the offender demonstrates what will happen to them if they violate the law. Here, the death penalty is a negative example. Execution of an offender is meant to be a lesson to all.

incapacitation The action of holding an offender in secure detention or in jail or in prison so that the individual does not have the opportunity to commit any additional offenses against society

BOX 3.5 ELEMENTS OF DETERRENCE THEORY

The **elements of deterrence theory** outlines several aspects of punishment that are predicted to affect the future behavior of the offender or potential offender:

- The primary assumption behind deterrence theory is that individuals have free will and are rational.
- For punishments to have the maximum deterrent effect, they should guarantee that the anticipated benefits from a criminal act will not be enjoyed.
- Certainty of punishment (especially of apprehension) is more important that severity of punishment. The level of punishment should reflect the severity of the crime.
- Punishments should be uniform: All persons—regardless of their position, status, or power—convicted of the same crime should receive the same punishment.
- All penalties should be known to prevent the rational person from committing crime.

elements of deterrence theory Identifying the aspects of punishment that are predicted to affect the future behavior of an offender or potential offender

society of kind and civilized people and he believed that the abolition of cruel punishments, including the death penalty, would contribute to the formation of such a society.[16]

Beccaria believed that the function of law was to promote justice. In *On Crimes and Punishments* (1764), he formulated the following principles that were a departure from the criminal law:[17]

1. Prevention of crime is more important than punishment for the crime committed. Punishment is desirable only as it helps to prevent crime and does not conflict with the ends of justice.

2. Desirable criminal procedure calls for the open publication of all laws, speedy trials, human treatment of the accused, and the abolition of secret accusations and torture. Moreover, the accused must have every right and facility to bring forward evidence.

3. The purpose of punishment is to deter persons from the commission of crime, not to give society an opportunity for revenge. In addition, punishment must be certain and swift, with penalties determined strictly according to the social damage wrought by the crime. Therefore, celerity—the time span between the crime and punishment—is a key element in deterrence.[18]

Beccaria redefined criminality, prescribed fair treatment for individual persons, and temporarily removed revenge and retribution as rationales for punishment. Beccaria was a reformer who was interested in limiting the official abuse of power—both political and judicial. He believed that the primary concern of the judge was the determination of guilt or innocence. He also denounced the use of torture and the death penalty.[19]

Despite Beccaria's liberal views, deterrence has become the cornerstone of conservative policy in the fight against crime and delinquency. Foremost among the potential penalties has been the death penalty. It has been called for use against juveniles who commit murder.

Issue: Juvenile Homicides

As discussed previously in this text, a "Get Tough" movement, which fundamentally refocuses the sanctioning capacities of the juvenile justice system beyond child saving and rehabilitation to stress deterrence and incapacitation, has been adopted. Accordingly, policy changes have focused on trying serious juvenile offenders as adults and even sentencing juveniles convicted of murder to death. For example, Kentucky legislation was enacted in 1994 to send juveniles who use a gun to commit felonies to an adult institution.

But are things getting worse? Let's check the data on juvenile homicides. Statistics reveal that the 1999 juvenile murder arrest rate was the lowest in twenty years. Between 1980 and 1999:

1. Juvenile murder victims were predominantly male (83 percent) and white (51 percent).

2. Most of the juvenile murderers were male (93 percent) and more than half (56 percent) were African American.

3. Male juvenile murderers were most likely to kill someone they know (56 percent), but 37 percent killed a stranger.

4. Female juvenile murderers were most likely to kill a family member (39 percent); 21 percent of them killed young children.

5. For juvenile murderers, 82 percent murdered persons of their own race. This was especially true of female offenders.

6. Older juvenile offenders were more likely to commit murder with adults.[20]

7. In 1999, about 1,800 juveniles (a rate of about 3.0 per 100,000) were victims of homicide in the United States. This rate is higher than that of any other developed country.

8. Homicides of juveniles in the United States are unevenly distributed, both geographically and demographically. Rates are substantially higher for African American juveniles in certain jurisdictions. Yet, 85 percent of all U.S. counties had no homicides of juveniles in 1997.[21]

Studies of juvenile murderers reveal that most juvenile homicides are spontaneous, unpremeditated acts prompted by emotional stress, lack of experience, irresponsibility, volatility, brain damage, absence of calculation, and a lack of consideration for the consequences of their actions. Typically, the murders stemmed from another offense, and then the juvenile panicked and killed the victim, often in a most brutal and heinous manner.[22]

In summary, these studies question the effectiveness of deterrence to prevent juvenile homicide. Their roots do not run to the factors that deterrence can reach. Premeditation is markedly absent. In its place are factors that can only be affected by attention to treatment and social problems.

Application: The Death Penalty for Juveniles

According to the National Association for the Advancement of Colored Persons Legal Defense and Education Fund (2002), a total of 3,718 inmates were under a sentence of death in the United States as of July 1, 2002. Of this total, 83 inmates (all male, 2.23 percent of the total) were juveniles when they committed their offenses.

Since the reinstitution of capital punishment in the United States in 1976, there have been 784 persons executed for murder. Of this total, 20 inmates (2.6 percent) were juveniles at the time of the offense.[23] A list of these inmates is presented in Table 3.1.

Throughout American history, Hale presents five periods of time during which juveniles were susceptible to a sentence of death for their crimes. Period One (1642 to 1762) contains the first execution of a juvenile in the United States: In 1642, the first juvenile execution was conducted—Thomas Graunger, Plymouth Colony, Massachusetts. Social control was a paramount concern. Juveniles were treated no differently than adults during this period. In Period Two (1762 to 1842), Beccaria's call to abolish capital punishment was taken up by Benjamin Rush and William Bradford. Period Three (1842 to 1922) marked a transition in attitudes toward juveniles. Child labor laws and the juvenile court were established on the philosophy of *parens patriae*. Period Four (1922 to 1962) introduced the modern view of the juvenile. Juveniles were not executed. Period Five (1962 to the present) marks a return to the death penalty for juveniles.[24]

Table 3.1

U.S. INMATES EXECUTED FOR HOMICIDES COMMITTED AS JUVENILES, 1985–JULY 1, 2002

Year	State	Name
1985	Texas	Charles Rumbaugh
1986	South Carolina	James Terry Roach
1986	Texas	Jay Pinkerton
1990	Louisiana	Dalton Prejean
1992	Texas	Johnny Garrett
1993	Texas	Curtis Paul Harris
1993	Missouri	Frederick Lashley
1993	Missouri	Ruben Cantu
1993	Georgia	Christopher Burger
1998	Texas	Joseph Cannon
1998	Texas	Robert A. Carter
1998	Virginia	Dwayne Allen Wright
1999	Oklahoma	Sean Sellers
2000	Virginia	Douglas C. Thomas
2000	Virginia	Steve Edward Roach
2000	Texas	Glen McGinnis
2000	Texas	Gary Graham
2001	Texas	Gerald Mitchell
2001	Georgia	Jose High
2002	Texas	Napoleon Beazley

Since the Graunger execution, approximately 361 persons have been executed for juvenile crimes (1.8 percent of roughly 20,000 confirmed American executions since 1608). Of these executions, 18 have been imposed since the reinstatement of the death penalty in 1976.[25] Sixteen states and the federal government have an age minimum of 18 years for capital punishment.[26]

The United States Supreme Court has made several key rulings about the constitutionality of the death penalty for juveniles. Three major decisions have been issued to clarify the Court's position on this matter. In *Eddings v. Oklahoma* (1982), the juvenile defendant was charged with the murder of a state police officer. The Court deferred on the key issue of whether capital punishment for juveniles violated the Eighth Amendment prohibition against cruel and unusual punishment. Instead, it focused on age as a mitigating circumstance in a capital trial and noted that the trial court judge had failed to consider it.[27]

In a second decision on this matter (*Thompson v. Oklahoma*, 1988), the Court again avoided the Eighth Amendment question and ruled that the Oklahoma statute was unconstitutional because it failed to specify a minimum age for which the commission of a capital crime by a juvenile can lead to execution. Defense counsel made some standard arguments on behalf of their juvenile client—that juveniles lack the emotional and mental capacity of adults, that they have rehabilitative potential, and that they can be sentenced to death at an age when they cannot vote, drink, or drive.[28]

Thompson v. Oklahoma The U.S. Supreme Court ruled that Oklahoma's death penalty statute was unconstitutional because it failed to specify a minimum age for which the commission of a capital crime by a juvenile can lead to execution.

The Court finally addressed the Eighth Amendment question in a landmark decision, *Stanford v. Kentucky* (1989). Justice Scalia issued the majority opinion that juvenile executions do not constitute cruel and unusual punishment. The majority dismissed the arguments about the diminished capacity of juveniles and noted that no national consensus exists against the death penalty for juveniles. The decision allowed states to determine whether to impose the death penalty on juveniles and at what age.[29] Thus, the Court held that the practice of executing juveniles (aged 16 or 17 years at the time of the offense) did not violate the "evolving standards of decency" (ESD) of American society. Their determination was based on legislative authorization of juvenile executions.[30] In effect, the Court drew a line that bans the execution of offenders under the age of 16 years but permits execution for crimes committed at the age of 16 years or older.

Stanford v. Kentucky The U.S. Supreme Court ruled that juvenile executions do not constitute cruel and unusual punishment.

Beginning in the late 1980s, several studies indicated that the public sentiment in support of the death penalty for juveniles has begun to waver. Opinion surveys revealed that support for capital punishment wavers when the accused is a juvenile, even though they typically commit heinous offenses.[31] The desire to execute juveniles does not seem to be widespread and strong.

It also seems that juvenile cases have not been thoroughly decided in court. A review of 91 juvenile death penalty cases (from 1973 to 1991) documented the mitigating circumstances for each offender. They fell into the following categories: (1) "troubled" family history and social background, (2) psychological disturbance, (3) mental retardation, (4) indigence, and (5) substance abuse.[32] These factors were not always noted in the original trial or always fully considered on appeal.

There are more juvenile offenders on death row in the United States than in any other country known to Amnesty International. The imposition of death sentences on juvenile offenders is in clear contravention of international human rights standards contained in numerous international instruments. Since 1990, juvenile offenders are known to have been executed in only six countries: Iran, Pakistan, Yemen, Nigeria, Saudi Arabia, and the United States. Through 2000, the death penalty for juvenile offenders had become a uniquely American practice, in that it seems to have been abandoned by nations everywhere else in large part due to the express provisions of the United Nations Convention on the Rights of the Child and of several other international treaties and agreements.[33]

Thus, the U.S. Supreme Court revisited the Eighth Amendment issue in 2005 and declared the death penalty for juveniles unconstitutional. Specifically, in ***Roper v. Simmons***, the Court ruled that the death penalty for those who had committed their crimes when under 18 years of age was cruel and unusual punishment.[34] The ruling affected the sentences of 71 juveniles on death row across the United States in 2005, of which 28 were on death row in Texas and had their sentences commuted to life in prison by the Texas Governor.[35]

Roper v. Simmons Decision (2005) outlawed the death penalty for juveniles in the United States.

SOCIAL THEORIES OF DELINQUENCY

The social theories of juvenile delinquency are grounded in present-day sociological thought and focus strictly on the *collective* behavior of the person rather than the individual behavior. Discussion of social theories has caused sociologists to address themselves primarily to two basic questions: (1) How does the juvenile in society acquire criminality? and (2) How does society acquire or produce crime?

The process model, of which social theory is considered to be a part, is meaningful to a present-day discussion of causality. The process model is in direct conflict with the medical model, which contends that criminal behavior is the fault of the person, caused by some flaw in the

Juveniles in Joplin Youth Center, Orange County, California (Example of Group v. Individual Behaviors; Social and Behavioral Controls)

person's psychological, biological, or physiological makeup. The process model holds that criminal behavior is caused by factors external to the person: economic class, environmental surroundings, delinquent subcultures, lower-class structure, and so forth. The process model, therefore, contends that as the result of various cultural, economic, sociological, racial, and ethnic conditions or influences, criminal behavior is produced and that changes in these conditions have the potential to influence the incidence of criminal or delinquent behavior.

Social theories state that a child's individuality cannot be separated from his or her interactions in a group. Of special importance in group interaction is motivation. However, social theory concerns itself with those things that determine motivation in social interactions that are external to the juvenile. Internal or psychological motivation is not given as much emphasis. In *Explaining Crime,* Gwynn Nettler emphasizes this point:

> A strictly sociological explanation is concerned with how the structure of a society or its *institutional practices* or its *persisting cultural themes* affects the conduct of its members. Individual differences are denied or ignored, and the explanation of collective behavior is sought in the patterning of social arrangements that is considered to be both "outside" the actor and "prior" to him. That is, the social patterns of power or of institutions which are held to be determinative of human action are also seen as having been in existence before any particular actor came on the scene. They are "external" to him in the sense that they will persist with or without him. In lay language, *sociological explanations of crime place the blame on something social that is prior to, external, and compelling of a particular person.*[36] [emphasis in original]

Here, we will examine two explanations of delinquency: (1) subcultural and (2) social disorganization. Both theories relate to and offer explanations for gang behavior.

SUBCULTURAL THEORIES

Richard Cloward and Lloyd Ohlin expanded and applied the theory that delinquent behavior is more likely to be experienced among lower-class juveniles to explain urban gang behavior. Their hypothesis is stated as follows:

> The disparity between what lower-class youth are led to want and what is actually available to them is the source of a major problem of adjustment. Adolescents who form delinquent subcultures, we suggest, have internalized an emphasis upon conventional goals.

Faced with limitations on legitimate avenues of access to these goals, and unable to revise their aspirations downward, they experience intense frustrations; the exploration of nonconformist alternatives may be the result.[37]

This explanation characterizes delinquency as being both adaptive and reactive. It is adaptive insofar as it is instrumental in the attainment of goals that most youths generally share and reactive because it is partly prompted by the resentment of juveniles at being deprived of things that they either believe they should have or have been advised or told they should have.

"Subculture is a term devised by social scientists to refer conveniently to variations within a society on its cultural themes, patterns, artifacts, and traditional ideas, as these are incorporated and expressed within various groups."[38] It is the nature of a community's integration of legitimate and illegitimate means that will normally determine the nature of the subcultural accommodations to goal-achieving criteria. Cloward and Ohlin have identified three types of delinquent subculture: (1) the criminal subculture, (2) the conflict subculture, and (3) the retreatist subculture.

The *criminal subculture,* and criminal gangs, will develop where there is cross-age integration of offenders plus close relations between the carriers of criminal and conventional values. For example, a young boy who grows up in a family in which the father and brothers and their associates are all involved in criminal activities may himself be either intrigued or coerced into similar displays of delinquent or criminal behavior. The criminal subculture is composed of juveniles who are thought to have become delinquent as a result of associations or contacts with persons who are outside the law. Many parole and probation authorities state, as a condition of parole or probation, that the juvenile shall not associate with known felons or persons whose influence may have a negative potential.

Albert Cohen, in *Delinquent Boys,*[39] indicates that the basis of delinquency lies in the variables of social class structure. He theorizes that the delinquent from a lower-class environment lacks self-respect, and in his frustration with his class or social position, he strikes out against middle-class values (called a **reaction formation**) and adopts opposite values. As a result, a delinquent subculture is formed that emerges as a collective attempt to contend with and solve class-based frustrations and angers.

Within this subculture, the norms of the dominant culture are ridiculed, and the **norms of the delinquent subculture** are valued. Thus, for example, physical aggression, toughness, and hedonism are stressed. Members of these delinquent groups do not consider the future consequences of their behavior but instead focus on immediate gratification of

reaction formation Cohen's theory that a delinquent from a lower-class environment lacks self-respect and, in his or her frustration with class or social position, strikes out against middle-class values

norms of the delinquent subculture The resulting norms of the delinquent subculture that form and emerge from reaction formation

---

BOX 3.6 **NORMS OF THE DELINQUENT SUBCULTURE**

- **Nonutilitarianism:** Delinquents are not always rationally motivated and thus may break the law "for the hell of it."
- **Malice:** Delinquents often enjoy tormenting their victims and delight in violating the norms of society.
- **Negativism:** The norms of delinquents tend to be the mirror image or exact opposite of those of society.
- **Short-term hedonism:** The actions of delinquents reveal their emphasis on immediate pleasure. They live for the moment and do not calculate the consequences of their actions.

---

their desires. Gang members are openly hostile to the agents of conformity. Moreover, they oppose other delinquent groups and use force to ensure loyalty and conformity to their own group. In short, it is a culture all its own and of its own making. Box 3.6 discusses key characteristics of such delinquent subcultures.

Walter B. Miller,[40] a principal advocate of the *conflict subculture* explanation of delinquency, rejects Cohen's contention that delinquency is produced by lower-class conflict with or reaction formation to a larger, dominant society. Instead, he contends that the violation of middle-class norms "is a 'by-product of action' primarily oriented to the lower-class culture, and the standards of lower-class culture cannot be seen as merely a reverse function of middle-class culture—as middle-class standards turned upside down'; lower-class culture is a distinctive tradition many centuries old with an integrity of its own."

Miller uses the concept of focal concerns in explaining his interpretation of the conflict subculture approach. *Focal concerns* are areas or issues that command widespread and persistent attention and a high degree of emotional involvement and that Miller believes tend to characterize a lower-class culture—thus named the **six focal concerns of lower-class delinquents**. Some of these focal concerns are trouble, toughness, smartness, excitement, fate, and autonomy. Miller prefers to speak of these focal concerns within a conflict subculture rather than of values, because focal concerns can be observed and examined more readily in direct field investigation. These attributes are listed in Box 3.7.

Lower-class delinquency resulting from a conflict subculture cannot be classified as deviant or aberrant in Miller's view. Rather, it is part of the lower-class culture and, within the group, is highly functional and necessary in preparing youngsters for an adult life that will probably be lived within the confines of that subculture. Therefore, delinquent behavior among lower-class youths can be considered normal behavior within that class. What causes a lower-class youth's behavior to be

six focal concerns of lower-class delinquents Concerns identified by Miller include trouble, toughness, smartness, excitement, fate, and autonomy

BOX 3.7 **SIX FOCAL CONCERNS OF THE LOWER-CLASS DELINQUENTS**

- **Trouble:** The underlying goal; the street is where the action is.
- **Toughness:** The need to demonstrate that one can stand up to adversity and "take" whatever the street brings (e.g., run-ins with other gangs and the police).
- **Smartness:** The high value placed on "street smarts"; one must know how to handle oneself on the street.
- **Excitement:** The view of what "life" is all about; the thrill of engaging in conflict and ripping people off.
- **Fate:** The belief that what happens in life is beyond one's control; whatever happens is "meant to be."
- **Autonomy:** The intolerance of challenges to one's personal sphere; the need to stand up to anything or anyone.

considered delinquent is that the youth's focal concerns come in conflict with those roles and norms that constitute the traditional and institutional values of the middle class.

The final type of delinquent subculture to be discussed is the *retreatist subculture.* "A retreatist subculture, and retreatist gangs, will develop among boys locked out of the above two avenues [criminal and conflict subcultures] because of the lack of means for integration and because of 'internalized prohibitions' or 'socially structured barriers' to the use of violence. This 'double failure' leaves only retreat, most specifically through drugs and alcohol."

A retreatist subculture can occur, therefore, almost by default. Youths barred from participation in the criminal or conflict subcultural gangs often find themselves banding together out of commonality, and thus, as their numbers increase, a gang comes into being. Juveniles constituting a retreatist gang are often typified as being oddballs, misfits, or loners in relationship with the larger delinquent subculture around them. Because of rejection by their peers, parents, or others, they may seek out or simply happen to find themselves hanging around with other youth outsiders. They replace violent or criminal behavior with retreatist behavior, such as drinking, smoking pot, or other activities that, though they may cause trouble with the law, are generally either nonviolent or low key.

In general, these subcultural theories are attempts to explain why lower-class boys become delinquent. The gang offers them an opportunity to "be somebody" and achieve the status that has been denied them by society. One flaw of these theories, however, is that they ignore individual deviance. They assume that subcultural values are strong enough to determine individual behavior. However, this perspective does provide a framework to study and examine gang activity.

SOCIAL DISORGANIZATION THEORY

At the University of Chicago, a pioneering group of delinquency researchers emerged in the late 1930s. Robert E. Park, a former Chicago news reporter, believed that the city could be used as a laboratory to study crime. Influenced by prominent sociologists W. I. Thomas, George H. Mead, Erving Goffman, and Georg Simmel, Park saw a connection between how animals live in natural settings and how humans live in urban settings.[41]

Park considered the city a social organism within which neighborhoods survive, thrive, or fall apart. Why, he asked, is crime and delinquency widespread in certain areas and not in others? To answer this question, Park and his colleague, Ernest Burgess, organized 1920s Chicago into a series of concentric zones according to residential, occupational, and class characteristics. Specifically, they sought to understand how these urban zones changed over time and what effect this process had on rates of crime.

Park and Burgess identified the **zone in transition** as the major source of urban crime. This suggested that as businesses expand into this area from the central zone and as zoning laws change to accommodate them, those residents who can afford to leave do so. With the stable wage earners gone, housing deteriorates and the zone becomes an undesirable place to live. Those who are left have no economic or political power. They are the poor, the unemployed, and the disenfranchised. Social control mechanisms weaken, and ethnic and racial segregation become a way of life. Given the social disorganization caused by conflicting norms and competing values, the crime rate is bound to soar: Residents of this zone are in conflict and competing to survive.[42]

Park and Burgess found that these areas also have the highest rates of delinquency, disease, infant death, and other social problems. In addition, they found that the crime rate declines as one moves from the center of the city to the outer zones.

zone in transition Identified by Park and Burgess as the major source of urban crime due to the social disorganization caused by conflicting norms and competing values; residents of this zone are in conflict and competing to survive

---

BOX 3.8 FORMS OF DELINQUENT SUBCULTURES

- **Criminal subculture:** Follows the basic organized crime model. Areas where organized crime is firmly established provide a goal for delinquents. Inhabitants of this subculture rationally seek economic gain and view crime as a career.

- **Conflict subculture:** Places high premium on violence. This subculture often occurs in neighborhoods populated with new immigrants, where the delinquent pursues opportunities lacking elsewhere.

- **Retreatist subculture:** Emphasizes drug abuse or other forms of escape. This delinquent is a "double failure" who cannot achieve success in either the criminal or conflict subcultures.

Other theorists built on this research foundation. Perhaps the best known are Clifford Shaw and Henry McKay. Shaw and McKay focused their attention on four trends that have come to characterize urban life: crime, poverty, ethnic heterogeneity, and residential mobility. These trends, they contend, lead to the disruption of community social organization and thus to crime and delinquency.[43] In other words, the urban environment spawns criminality: The social conditions in transitional neighborhoods promote deviance.

To study this breakdown of social norms, Shaw and McKay conducted several studies on delinquency in Chicago over a 30-year period. Their studies confirmed Park's finding that delinquency is highest in the zone in transition. Furthermore, the farther one moved from this zone, the lower the rate of delinquency.

Other key findings include the following:

1. Stable communities have lower rates of delinquency;
2. Communities with higher rates of delinquency have social values that differ from those with lower rates of delinquency;
3. Lower-income areas with a high rate of frustration and deprivation have a higher level of delinquency;
4. Social conditions in a community (e.g., overcrowding, physical deterioration, concentrations of foreign-born and African American populations) are directly related to the rate of delinquency; and
5. In lower-class areas, no stable social values unify the community; therefore, delinquency is seen as a legitimate alternative to a law-abiding posture.[44]

Yablonsky also cites several key concepts about youth gangs that emerged from "Chicago School" research:

1. The youth begins his delinquent career on a thin line of malicious and mischievous play and then becomes more concretely involved in delinquent gang activity;
2. The natural conflict of a youth with the community and its conflicting set of norms and values drive him further into gang activity;
3. The gang emerges as a result of the failure of community forces, particularly the family, to integrate youths properly into the more constructive, law-abiding society;
4. Loyalty and esprit de corps are strong mobilizing forces in the delinquent gangs, and it becomes a cohesive entity;
5. The gang becomes a kind of street corner family for youth who are detached and disassociated from and in conflict with the law-abiding community;

6. The gang in this context becomes a school for crime that provides the opportunity, training, and motivation for a criminal career in association with others; and

7. A youth enmeshed in the delinquent gang as a primary group gets driven further into a delinquent career by the negative effect of society's institutionalized patterns for dealing with the gang youth and his problems.[45]

Thus, faced with the pressures of a community in decline, the youth enters the gang and is immersed in the delinquent subculture. Taken together, these theories explain the forces that lead to gang formation.

SOCIAL CONTROL THEORY

The central theme of social control theories is that all youths have the same potential for delinquency. Beyond the influence of personality, the forces in the social environment can pull, pressure, or push people toward a life of crime. Society has developed certain control mechanisms to maintain the social order, including values and behavioral norms. Delinquency results when the mechanisms of social control fail.

Standing other criminological theories on their heads, social control theorists ask, "Why aren't we all criminals? Why is it that only certain individuals living in a crime-promoting environment become criminals while others do not?"[46]

Reckless's Containment Theory

An early version of social control theory was developed by Walter Reckless (see Box 3.9). He believed that criminological theory had not explained why certain people who were exposed to criminal influences did not turn to crime. Noticing that some youngsters who lived in high-crime areas did not turn to delinquency, Reckless concluded that they were "insulated" (hence the term **insulation**) from crime. The primary insulator, he found, was self-concept. A favorable self-concept could lead a person, even one faced with a crime-promoting environment, away from a life of crime.[47] Thus, his **containment theory** explains both

insulation The term used by Reckless to describe why some juveniles living in high-crime areas did not turn to crime

containment theory Theory by Reckless that the tendency to commit unlawful acts is determined by the type, or quality, of the self-concept the person has and the person's ability to "contain" the act

---

BOX 3.9 **WALTER C. RECKLESS (1899–1989)**

A member of the "Chicago School" of criminology, Reckless developed *containment theory* as another way to explain criminal behavior. His theory stated that the tendency to commit unlawful acts is determined by the type, or quality, of the self-concept the person has and the person's ability to "contain" the act.

BOX 3.10 **INGREDIENTS OF CONTAINMENT**

Inner Containment

In addition to self-concept, Reckless outlined other forms of "inner containment," including

Self-control

Ego strength

Well-developed super ego (conscience)

High frustration tolerance

High resistance to diversions

High sense of responsibility

Goal orientation

Ability to find substitute satisfactions

Tension-reducing rationalizations

These inner forces enable the person to resist the lure of criminal behavior.

Outer Containment

These elements represent "the structural buffer in the person's immediate social world" that is able to restrain the person. They include

Presentation of a consistent moral front

Institutional reinforcement of norms, goals, and expectations

Existence of a reasonable set of social expectations

Alternatives and safety valves

Opportunity for acceptance

These social forces help the family and other groups contain the individual and prevent delinquency.

Source: Based on Walter C. Reckless' *The Crime Problem* (New York: Appleton-Century-Crofts, 1973).

conforming and criminal behavior. Box 3.10 lists his ingredients of inner and outer containment.

Reckless believed that internal containments were stronger, more important, and more effective crime control elements than outer containments. People lacking a high degree of inner containment, Reckless suggested, would be unlikely to be saved by external containment. For example, if unemployment or lack of educational opportunity pressures juveniles toward crime, the last line of defense is the self-concept. If it is strong, the juvenile can resist the lures of delinquency.

However, Reckless did not present containment theory in a causal framework. Rather, he described the forces of containment as buffers or insulators that block the social pressures bearing down on the person. If these buffers are not in place, the person confronted with crime-promoting conditions is more likely to deviate. Conversely, the presence of inner and outer forces of containment makes a person less likely to succumb to the temptations of a bad environment.

Reckless's research on self-concept showed that "bad" boys clearly had lower self-esteem than "good" boys.[48] Research showed that the "good" boys avoided delinquency and had a higher self-concept.[49] Yet, an intervention project designed to improve the self-concept of predelinquent boys in Columbus (Ohio) junior high schools had no significant impact.[50]

Moreover, follow-up research on self-concept and delinquency has failed to establish a firm link between the two,[51] although Jensen did discover that juveniles with high self-esteem were less likely to engage in delinquent acts.[52] But a positive family environment is viewed as potentially an inhibiting factor in criminal behavior.

In summary, inner containment is most important when aspects of external containment are absent. The self-concept can serve as a buffer when the influence of traditional structures like the family, church, and school is weak or ineffective. Resistance is especially great when people internalize law-abiding norms and values, making them a part of their self-concept. Containment theory explains why some people who live in high-crime areas do not turn to crime and why some juveniles do not become involved in gang activities. Therefore, it also indirectly prescribes treatment by citing its forces as insulators against crime and delinquency. Prevention efforts must include the traditional elements of society to establish a united front against crime.

Containment theory has been influential. Potential inadequacies of his theory notwithstanding, Reckless is cited as "one of the fathers of control theory laying the groundwork for the more sophisticated later versions of scholars like Travis Hirschi."[53]

Hirschi's Social Bond Theory

Travis Hirschi developed a social control theory that modified containment theory. Like Reckless, Hirschi believed that all youths are potential delinquents. The central issue is why some youths do not commit crimes at all.

According to Hirschi, **social controls** are the actual or potential rewards—positive or negative, internal or external—for conformity to social mores. These controls take the form of **social bonds**: the ties that people have to parents, school, peers, and others. When those bonds are weak, a person is freer to engage in criminal activity. Moreover, a person is more apt to learn to be delinquent or criminal when young, and juveniles are more likely to become delinquent when social bonds are weak. Thus, social bonds are essential to the prevention of crime and delinquency. People who strongly believe in conventional norms and values are unlikely to become involved in deviant behavior.

mycrimekit

Video Profile: *Mental Illness*

social controls The actual or potential rewards—either positive or negative; internal or external—for conforming to social mores

social bonds The form that social controls take; for example, the ties that people have to parents, school, peers, and others. When those bonds are weak, a person is freer to engage in criminal activity.

Hirschi's social bonds manifest themselves in conformity, involvement, and respect for social institutions. For example, a conformist has an investment in society. Conventional actions, such as taking a job and developing a social reputation, build prosocial ties and discourage criminal involvement. In addition, allegiances to norms and legitimate behavior block the formation of ties to deviant subcultures. Seeking success, the conformist will not risk the chance of advancement by committing crimes. Moreover, involvement is a time-consuming process. The more heavily one is involved in conventional activities, the less time is available to engage in deviant behavior. Finally, belief in the way the society operates engenders sensitivity to the rights of others and respect for the laws. Box 3.11 summarizes key elements of the social bond.

Hirschi stressed the importance of the family as a sponsor of conventional, conformist behavior. Parents can strongly contribute to conformity by providing supervision for, building a quality relationship with, and communicating with their children. The stronger the bonds the person has with the family, the greater his or her resistance to crime and delinquency.

In two major studies, Hirschi basically confirmed his control theory in two ways. In the first study, he showed that a strong attachment to, and good communication with, parents was a strong factor in nondelinquent behavior. In the second study, he found that the less the subjects of the study believed they should obey the laws, the more likely they were to break them. His theory has its detractors, as Hirschi himself acknowledged, and for which he gives some probable reasons.

> …the problem with social control as a concept is that it tends to expand until it becomes synonymous with sociology, and then it dies. It dies because there is nothing unique or distinct about it. This danger is present even when the concept is limited initially to delinquency.[54]

Despite the critics, the concept of social control is a basic theory for delinquent behavior.

BOX 3.11 ELEMENTS OF THE SOCIAL BOND

Attachment: The basic element for the internalization of norms and the values of a society. Attachment reflects effective ties to family, schools, and friends, and affection for and sensitivity to others.
Commitment: The stake a person has in society and what that person stands to lose by committing a crime.
Involvement: The extent to which one participates in the conventional activities of a society.
Belief: Respect for moral validity of the rules of a society. The extent to which people believe in the laws of a society and what that society stands for.

Boys Fighting

Issue: Juvenile Violence

Juvenile violence has become a serious problem. As both victims and perpetrators, certain youths are at risk for violent behavior. Research on juvenile violence in Washington, D.C., and South Carolina has identified the following **risk factors**.

For offending:

1. **Age:** Many juveniles involved in violent behavior (including homicide) begin their involvement by age 15 years.

2. **Race:** African Americans were somewhat overrepresented in the homicide and assault and battery groups compared with other serious offender groups in these studies. Including Hispanics in the analysis, studies in Denver, Colorado, and Rochester, New York, determined that violence prevalence rates were higher among minority groups than among Caucasians at each age and site (except for 18-year-olds in Rochester).

3. **Other Individual Factors:** Hyperactivity, risk taking behavior, aggressiveness, early initiation of violence (by age 12–13 years), and involvement in other forms of antisocial behavior.[55]

risk factors Demographic characteristics (e.g., involvement in violent behavior prior to age 15 years) that identify juveniles "at risk" for offending

As victims of homicide/violence:

1. Typically, juvenile homicide victims are of the same race and sex as their perpetrators.
2. The most likely victims of juvenile homicide are acquaintances, followed by strangers, and then family members.
3. Most juvenile homicide victims are male.
4. The majority age group for juvenile homicide victims was 16 to 17 years (69 percent).

In addition, these studies demonstrated that many violent juvenile offenders live in disruptive and disorganized families and communities.[56]

Application: The SafeFutures Initiative

The SafeFutures Initiative is an extension of the OJJDP's Comprehensive Strategy for Serious, Violent, and Chronic Juvenile Offenders. This strategy focuses on the following:

1. Youths who are at high risk of future delinquent behavior and
2. Youthful offenders who have already exhibited delinquent behavior and are at risk of, or already are, engaging in serious, violent, or chronic law breaking.[57]

social development model A comprehensive approach to preventing youth crime by addressing their risk factors and matching them to appropriate interventions at the correct stage of their lives

The initiative is based on the Hawkins and Catalano **social development model**. It is a comprehensive approach to preventing youth crime by addressing their risk factors and matching them to appropriate interventions at the correct stage of their lives.

The model is based on the premise that the most important units of socialization (family, schools, peers, and community) influence behavior in a sequential fashion. When youths have the opportunity to engage in conforming behavior within each of them, law-abiding behavior is the result. To accomplish this, youths must develop necessary skills and be rewarded for positive behavior. These conditions will sponsor the development of the social bonds that inhibit association with delinquent peers and prevent delinquent behavior.[58]

The social development model is based on such research findings. Hawkins and Catalano present data on risk factors associated with several problem behaviors, such as violence, drug abuse, teen pregnancy, and dropping out of school. In the social development model, these risk factors are conditions that increase the likelihood that a child will develop one or more behavior problems in adolescence: The greater the exposure to these factors, the greater the likelihood that juveniles will engage in these negative behaviors.

Community risk factors and the behaviors they engender include the following:

- Availability of drugs (substance abuse)
- Availability of firearms (delinquency, violence)
- Community laws and norms favorable toward drug use, firearms, and crime (substance abuse, delinquency, and violence)
- Media portrayals of violence (violence)
- Transitions and mobility (substance abuse, delinquency, and dropping out of school)
- Extreme economic deprivation (substance abuse, delinquency, violence, teen pregnancy, and dropping out of school).

Family risk factors and the behaviors they engender include the following:

- A family history of high-risk behavior (substance abuse, delinquency, violence, teen pregnancy, and dropping out of school).
- Family management problems (substance abuse, delinquency, violence, teen pregnancy, and dropping out of school).
- Family conflict (substance abuse, delinquency, violence, teen pregnancy, and dropping out of school).
- Favorable parental attitudes and involvement in the problem behavior (substance abuse, delinquency, and violence). Children whose parents engage in violent behavior inside or outside the home are at greater risk for exhibiting violent behavior.

School risk factors and the behaviors they engender include the following:

- Early and persistent antisocial behavior (substance abuse, delinquency, violence, teen pregnancy, and dropping out of school).
- Academic failure beginning in elementary school (substance abuse, delinquency, violence, teen pregnancy, and dropping out of school).
- Lack of commitment to school (substance abuse, delinquency, violence, teen pregnancy, and dropping out of school).

Individual/peer risk factors and their indicators consist of the following:

- Alienation and rebelliousness (substance abuse, delinquency, and dropping out of school). It may be a more significant risk for young people of color. Discrimination may cause these youths to reject the dominant culture and rebel against it.

- Friends who engage in the problem behavior (substance abuse, delinquency, violence, teen pregnancy, and dropping out of school). This factor has proven to be a consistent predictor of problem behaviors.

- Favorable attitudes toward the problem behavior (substance abuse, delinquency, teen pregnancy, and dropping out of school). Here, the middle school years are particularly significant. If youths are involved with peers who demonstrate favorable attitudes to these behaviors, they are more likely to engage in them.

- Early initiation of the problem behavior (substance abuse, delinquency, violence, teen pregnancy and dropping out of school). The research review demonstrates that youths who begin to use drugs before age 15 years are twice as likely to have drug problems as those who wait until after the age of 19 years.

- Constitutional factors (substance abuse, delinquency, and violence). These factors are biological or psychological in nature. Youths who have problems with sensation-seeking behavior, low harm avoidance, and lack of impulse control are more likely to engage in these problem behaviors.[59]

Hawkins and Catalano assert that these risks occur in multiple domains. Therefore, the most effective way to combat them is a multifaceted approach across the community. Neighborhood residents and community agencies of all types should join together to deal with these problems. The aim is to provide protection against the sponsorship of risk factors and the spread to problem behaviors that result from them. The goal is to use the public health model to prevent crime. Awareness of these factors is the first step in the development of plans and programs to deal with them in an effective manner.

Within demonstration communities, SafeFutures is based on nine components:

1. Afterschool programs (Pathways to Success)
2. Juvenile mentoring programs (JUMP)
3. Family strengthening and support services
4. Mental health services for at-risk and adjudicated youth
5. Delinquency prevention programs
6. Comprehensive communitywide approaches to gang-free schools and communities
7. Community-based day treatment programs (Bethesda Day Treatment Center model)
8. Continuum-of-care services for at-risk and delinquent girls and
9. Serious, violent, and chronic juvenile offender programs (with an emphasis on enhancing graduated sanctions).[60]

This program is presently in the implementation stage; it has not reached the stage of national evaluation.[61] However, it offers great promise by incorporating the principles of social control theory and bringing them into operation.

LABELING THEORY

Labeling theory emphasizes the influence of powerful groups in society to both define and react to deviant behavior. The general position is that no act is inherently criminal. Rather, the law defines certain acts as criminal. For example, Erickson (1962) claims that deviance is not inherent in all socially defined deviant acts but depends on (1) when the act is committed, (2) who commits the act and who is the victim, and (3) what the consequences of the act are.[62] In labeling theory, the crucial dimension is the societal reaction to the act, not the act itself. It is an attempt to explain all forms of deviant behavior, not just crime and delinquency.

labeling theory No act is inherently criminal; it is the law that defines certain acts as criminal

According to Tannenbaum, labeling can be defined as "the process of making the criminal [by] tagging, defining, segregating, describing, emphasizing, making conscious and self-conscious.... The person becomes the thing he is described as being."[63] Thus, labeling theory focuses on the process of labeling and on the reasons some persons can commit deviant acts and avoid the consequences and others cannot. In terms of delinquency, labeling theory is especially applicable to status offenses and offenders.

Juveniles and Secondary Deviance

Edwin Lemert developed the theory of **secondary deviation** to explain further how the legal process can make the crime problem worse through intervention. Box 3.12 lists the steps in this process.[64]

secondary deviation Theory developed by Lemert to explain how the legal process can make the crime problem worse through the official reaction to the act

---

BOX 3.12 **FROM PRIMARY TO SECONDARY DEVIANCE**

Phase 1	A person commits a deviant act.
Phase 2	Society reacts by instituting repressive measures against the person.
Phase 3	The person responds with more deviation, (secondary deviation), which draws more penalties, which draws still more deviation, in a continuous cycle.
Phase 4	The labeled person develops hostilities and resentments toward law enforcers.
Phase 5	Society reacts by further labeling and stigmatizing the offender.
Phase 6	The person's options become so restricted that the deviant status is accepted by both sides and the deviance is strengthened.
Phase 7	The person accepts deviant social status.

Lemert is not concerned with the motivation behind the initial deviant act. Instead, he focuses on the official reaction to the act and the way in which it causes more damage than the act itself. For example, Schur condemns the sanctioning by juvenile courts of status offenses—acts (e.g., running away, truancy) committed by juveniles that would be considered crimes if committed by adults. Schur maintains that these are moral judgments that make a bad situation worse. A runaway (primary deviation), placed in a juvenile institution, can become a burglar (secondary deviation) because of the labeling process. Like Tannenbaum and Lemert, Schur suggests a policy of **radical nonintervention**: *Leave kids alone whenever possible.*[65]

radical nonintervention Schur's policy suggestion to leave kids alone whenever possible

In summary, Lemert argues that the stigma that society places on the deviant causes more (and possibly worse) criminal behavior. As a result, the stigmatized, labeled deviant organizes his or her self-concept around deviance. Box 3.13 outlines this process.

If labeling theory is accurate, status offenders will eventually engage in secondary deviance as a result of this process. However, research on status offenders does not seem to support this idea. For example, Murray cites several studies that show that status offenders do not "escalate." In other words, they do not engage in secondary deviance and go on to commit more serious offenses.[66]

Issue: Status Offenders in Juvenile Court

We have examined this issue in several other chapters. We revisit it to determine the nature of the problem and its linkage to theory and practice. Again, labeling theory asserts that labeling juveniles as status offenders will make the problem worse by tagging them and causing secondary deviance.

In 1974, the U.S. Congress passed the Juvenile Justice and Delinquency Prevention Act. The act provided for the removal of all status offenders from juvenile detention and correctional facilities. States were required to comply with this mandate and report on their progress in achieving it or face the loss of federal funding. There have been several amendments to the act in passing years that have continued to address

---

BOX 3.13 **KEY PROCESSES OF LABELING**

Phase 1: Stereotyping.

Phase 2: Retrospective Interpretation: Once a person is identified as deviant, he or she is seen in a totally new light. Reconstituted, they are what they were "all along."

Phase 3: Negotiation: Depending on the social status of the person, the stigma attached to the label can be negotiated and even avoided.

Phase 4: Official Reaction: The person is labeled by others as evil, abnormal people, not to be trusted by law-abiding people.

this issue. In 1990, judges were permitted to confine status offenders in secure detention for a limited time if they had violated a valid court order. A related problem involves the "chronic status offender"—runaways or juveniles with emotional and behavioral problems who often flood the juvenile justice system. When is it appropriate to intervene and for what purpose? These are the key issues on status offenders.

Application: Decriminalization, Diversion, and Deinstitutionalization of Status Offenses

Calls to eliminate juvenile justice system involvement in status offenses have specifically called for the decriminalization, diversion, and deinstitutionalization of status offenses (known in short as DSO). Sponsored by the Juvenile Justice and Delinquency Prevention Act, these actions are undertaken with the belief that the juvenile justice system has been ineffective in solving the problems of status offenders, unjust in its treatment of these offenders, and has, through labeling and stigmatization, caused more harm than good.[67] The DSO requirements caused states to examine current practices, abandon the use of detention as the dominant method to deal with status offenders, and to pursue legal, administrative, and physical remedies to achieve the goal of this policy.

Studies demonstrate that the DSO mandate has been effective. Although implementation was difficult, most states have achieved either full or minimal compliance with the requirements of the Juvenile Justice and Delinquency Prevention Act. They have reformed their laws, policies, and practices for handling status offenders, particularly dependency and neglect cases. In addition, noninstitutional programs and community-based services have been developed for these youths.[68] Of course, the ultimate goal is to act in the best interests of the youth. Treatment of status offenders requires a careful approach that will alleviate, rather than aggravate, harm.

SUMMARY

There are other theories regarding delinquency causation that are not covered in this chapter. Our selections were guided by their application within the juvenile justice system. They have resulted in action programs designed combat delinquency. Theory without practice based on sound research does little but add to the already voluminous rhetoric regarding the causes of delinquency. Great strides are being made in this area.

Sound policy must be based on theory. Theory serves to guide programs and policies, rather than reliance on rhetoric and guesswork. Of course, these policies and programs must be thoroughly researched and evaluated to determine if they are being properly implemented and effectively executed.

The practices highlighted in this chapter are based on sound theory. They have several common themes. First is the importance of a community-based approach to delinquency. It cannot be handled by governmental officials alone. The factors that prevent delinquency are centered on the community and its institutions: schools, the family, the neighborhood, and churches. They must sponsor the foundations of self-control and the development of a sound self-concept. Second, treatment does not exclude punishment. Juveniles must be held accountable for their actions, but punishments must truly fit both the crime and the offender. Delinquency will not be conquered by treatment or punishment alone or by the community or government officials acting alone. A balanced, cooperative approach is what these various theories promote. The programs that build on them offer hope for the future.

KEY TERMS

Cesare Beccaria
containment theory
criminological theory
criminology
deinstitutionalization
elements of deterrence theory
generality
grand theories
incapacitation
insulation
juvenile delinquency
labeling theory
levels of deterrence
middle-range theories

norms of the delinquent subculture
radical nonintervention
reaction formation
risk factors
Roper v. Simmons
secondary deviation
six focal concerns of lower-class delinquents
social bonds
social controls
social development model
Stanford v. Kentucky
Thompson v. Oklahoma
zone in transition

DISCUSSION AND REVIEW QUESTIONS

1. What are the elements of a criminological theory? What is their purpose?
2. The delinquent subculture has many attributes. Choose one and give an example of how it is present in American culture.
3. How does containment insulate against delinquency? Why are you a college student instead of a criminal in prison or jail?
4. How does labeling contribute to delinquency?
5. What are the key features of the social development model? Does it look like an effective way to combat delinquency?
6. Do you think the deinstitutionalization of status offenders is a good policy? Why or why not?
7. Explain why someone you either know personally or know of may have committed a delinquent act.

VIDEO PROFILES

The *Mental Illness* video profile in MyCrimeKit highlights issues associated with dealing with abnormal behaviors with juveniles, including self-mutilation and anger. Discuss how the superintendent and the staff address Jacob's behavior. Identify the structure/program issues that may assist Jacob in learning how to follow directions; which programming issues may hinder his progress in this area? Finally, identify the theory/theories that may be associated with the behavior(s) Jacob demonstrates.

The *Runaway—Status Offender* video profile in MyCrimeKit shows how the court balances what is in the best interest of the juvenile (and her baby) with public safety. Discuss the options for Melissa after the initial arrest, as well as the role of the public defender, state attorney, and guardian ad litem in the detention hearing. What criminological theory/theories are associated with the court's reasoning and decision making? Does the court's decision address the risk factors posed in applying such theory/theories? Why or why not?

MYCRIMEKIT

mycrimekit™   Go to MyCrimeKit.com to explore the following study tools and resources specific to this chapter:

- Practice Quiz: Test your knowledge with multiple-choice, true-false, fill-in-the-blank, and essay questions.
- Flashcards: 20 flashcards to test your knowledge of the chapter's key terms.
- Web Quest: Review the Web sites highlighting the criminologists presented in this chapter.
- Web Links: Check out sites related to crime theory and determine whether any juvenile delinquents in your region exemplify such theories.

ENDNOTES

1. Abraham Kaplan, *The Conduct of Inquiry: Methodology for Behavioral Science* (San Francisco: Chandler, 1964), p. 295.
2. Charles R. Tittle, "The Assumption That General Theories Are Not Possible." In Richard C. Monk, ed., *Taking Sides: Clashing Views on Controversial Issues in Crime and Criminology* (Guilford, CT: Dushkin, 1996), pp. 76–81.
3. Robert K. Merton, *On Theoretical Sociology* (New York: Free Press, 1967).
4. Clayton A. Hartjen, C. A. *Crime and Criminalization* (New York: Holt, Rinehart & Winston, 1978), pp. 51–53.

5. Donald R. Cressey, "Fifty Years of Criminology: From Sociological Theory to Political Control," *Pacific Sociological Review,* Vol. 22 (1979), p. 457.

6. Michael J. Lynch and W. Byron Groves, "In Defense of Comparative Criminology: A Critique of General Theory and the Rational Man." In Richard C. Monk, ed., *Taking Sides: Clashing Views on Controversial Issues in Crime and Criminology* (Guilford, CT: Dushkin, 1996), p. 89.

7. See the thirty-five-year study of delinquency by Sheldon and Eleanor Glueck, *Unraveling Juvenile Delinquency* (New York: Commonwealth Fund, 1950).

8. Engrossed Third Substitute House Bill No. 371, State of Washington, 45th Legislature, 1st Extraordinary Session, April 11, 1977, the Committee on Institutions, pp. 18–19.

9. Donald J. Shoemaker, *Theories of Delinquency* (New York: Oxford University Press, 2000), p. 3.

10. Studies include P. Lerman, "Order Offenses and Juvenile Delinquency," in L. T. Empey, ed., *Juvenile Justice: The Progressive Legacy and Current Reforms* (Charlottesville: University Press of Virginia, 1979), pp. 150–80; M. Chesney-Lind, "Guilty by Reason of Sex: Young Women and the Juvenile Justice System," in B. R. Price and N. J. Sokoloff, eds., *The Criminal Justice System and Women* (New York: Clark Boardman, 1982), pp. 77–113; J. F. Huntington, "Powerless and Vulnerable: The Social Experiences of Imprisoned Girls." *Juvenile and Family Court Journal,* 33 (2, 1982): 33–44; and C. Grimes, *Girls and the Law* (Washington, DC: Institute for Educational Leadership, 1983).

11. Huntington, "Powerless and Vulnerable."

12. Grimes, *Girls and the Law.*

13. Chesney-Lind, "Guilty by Reason of Sex."

14. Margaret A. Zahn, Susan Brumbaugh, Darrell Steffensmeier, Barry C. Feld, Merry Morash, Meda Chesney-Lind, Jody Miller, Allison Ann Payne, Denise C. Gottfredson, and Candace Kruttschnitt. "Violence by Teenage Girls: Trends and Context." *Girls Study Group, Understanding and Responding to Girls' Delinquency* (Washington, DC: OJJDP, 2008).

15. Ibid.

16. Marcello Maestro, *Cesare Beccaria and the Origins of Penal Reform* (Philadelphia: Temple University Press, 1973), pp. 158–159.

17. George B. Vold, *Theoretical Criminology* (New York: Oxford University Press, 1970), pp. 18–22.

18. Ernest van den Haag, "The Neoclassical Theory of Crime Control," *Criminal Justice Policy Review,* Vol. 1 (1986), p. 100.

19. Elio Monachesi, "Cesare Beccaria," in Hermann Mannheim, ed., *Pioneers in Criminology* (Montclair, NJ: Patterson-Smith, 1960), pp. 36–50.

20. James A. Fox, *Uniform Crime Report: Supplementary Homicide Reports, 1976–1997* (Boston, MA: Northeastern University, College of Criminal Justice [producer], 1999).

21. David Finckelhor and Richard Ormrod, *Homicides of Children and Youth—OJJDP Juvenile Justice Bulletin* (Washington DC: Office of Juvenile Justice and Delinquency Prevention, October 2001), p. 1.

22. Studies of juvenile homicide offenders include Dewey G. Cornell, "Juvenile Homicide: A Growing National Problem," *Behavioral Sciences & the Law,* Vol. 11 (1993), pp. 389–396; Dewey G. Cornell, D. G., E. P. Benedek, and D. M. Benedek, "Characteristics of Adolescents Charged with Homicide: Review of 72 Cases," *Behavioral Sciences & the Law,* Vol. 5 (1987), pp. 11–23; Joel P. Eigen, "Punishing Youth Homicide Offenders in Philadelphia," *Journal of Criminal Law and Criminology,* Vol. 1079 (1981), pp. 867–1924; Dorothy O. Lewis, "Intrinsic and Environmental Characteristics of Juvenile Murderers," *Journal of the American Academy of Child & Adolescent Psychology,* Vol. 27 (1988), pp. 582–587; J.R.P. Ogloff, "The Juvenile Death Penalty: A Frustrated Society's Attempt at Control," *Behavioral Sciences & the Law,* Vol. 5 (1987), pp. 447–455; J. C. Rowley, C. P. Ewing, and S. I. Singer, "Juvenile Homicide: The Need for an Interdisciplinary Approach," *Behavioral Sciences & the Law,* Vol. 5 (1987), pp. 1–10; and Victor L. Streib, *Death Penalty for Juveniles* (Bloomington, IN: Indiana University Press, 1987).

23. NAACP Legal Defense and Education Fund, *Death Row U.S.A.—Summer 2002.* http://www.deathpenaltyinfo.org/

24. Robert L. Hale, *A Review of Juvenile Executions in America* (Lewiston, NY: Edwin Mellen Press, 1997).

25. Death Penalty Information Center, "Executions of Juvenile Offenders," http://www.deathpenaltyinfo.org/juvexec.html

26. The states are California, Colorado, Connecticut, Illinois, Indiana, Kansas, Maryland, Montana, Nebraska, New Jersey, New Mexico, New York, Ohio, Oregon, Tennessee, and Washington. Death Penalty Information Center, "Juveniles and the Death Penalty," http://www.deathpenaltyinfo.org/juveniles-and-death-penalty

27. *Eddings v. Oklahoma,* 455 U.S. 104 (1982).

28. *Thompson v. Oklahoma,* 101 L Ed 702 (1988).

29. *Stanford v. Kentucky,* 45 CrL 3202 (1989). Kevin Stanford has been pardoned by Kentucky Governor Paul Patton. His sentence was commuted to life in prison.

30. Mark C. Seis and Kenneth L. Elbe, "The Death Penalty for Juveniles: Bridging the Gap Between an Evolving Standard of Decency and Legislative Policy," *Justice Quarterly,* Vol. 8 (1991), pp. 465–487.

31. N. J. Finkel, K. C. Hughes, S. Smith, et al., "Killing Kids: The Juvenile Death Penalty and Community Sentiment," *Behavioral Sciences and the Law,* Vol. 12 (1994), pp. 5–20; Mark S. Hamm, "Legislator Ideology and Capital Punishment: The Special Case for Indiana Juveniles," *Justice Quarterly,* Vol. 6 (1989), pp. 219–232; M. Sandys and E. McGarrell, "Attitudes Toward Capital Punishment: Preference for the Penalty or Mere Acceptance," *Journal of Research in Crime and Delinquency,* Vol. 32 (1995), pp. 191–213; Gennaro F. Vito and Thomas J. Keil, "Selecting Juveniles for Death: The Kentucky Experience," 1976–86," *Journal of Contemporary Criminal Justice,* Vol. 5 (1988), pp. 181–198.

32. Dinah A. Robinson and Otis H. Stephens, "Patterns of Mitigating Factors in Juvenile Death Penalty Cases," *Criminal Law Bulletin,* Vol. 28 (1992), pp. 246–275.

33. Death Penalty Information Center, "Juvenile Death Penalty in Other Countries," http://www.deathpenaltyinfo.org/juvintl.html

34. Death Penalty Information Center, "Juveniles and the Death Penalty," http://www.deathpenaltyinfo.org/juveniles-and-death-penalty

35. Death Penalty Information Center, "Juveniles News and Development: 2005," http://www.deathpenaltyinfo.org/juveniles-news-and-developments-2005

36. Gwynn Nettler, *Explaining Crime* (New York: McGraw-Hill, 1974), p. 138.

37. Richard A. Cloward and Lloyd E. Ohlin, *Delinquency and Opportunity* (Glencoe, IL: The Free Press, 1960), p. 86.

38. Cloward and Ohlin, *Delinquency and Opportunity,* p. 86.

39. Albert A. Cohen, *Delinquent Boys* (New York: The Free Press, 1955).

40. Walter B. Miller, "Lower Class Structure and Generating Milieu of Gang Delinquency," *Journal of Social Issues,* Vol. 14 (1958), p. 19.

41. Robert Park, *Human Communities* (Glencoe, IL: The Free Press, 1952); Robert Park, *The Criminal Area* (New York: Humanities Press, 1966).

42. Randy Martin, Robert Mutchnick and Tim Austin, *Criminological Thought: Pioneers Past and Present* (New York: Macmillan, 1990), p. 103.

43. Robert Bursik, "Social Disorganization and Theories of Crime and Delinquency," *Criminology,* Vol. 26 (1988), pp. 519–551.

44. Rodney Stark, "Deviant Places: A Theory of the Ecology of Crime," *Criminology,* Vol. 25 (1987), pp. 893–909.

45. Lewis Yablonsky, *Gangsters: Fifty Years of Madness, Drugs, and Death on the Streets of America* (New York: New York University Press, 1997), pp. 37–38.

46. Martin, Mutchnick, and Austin, *Criminological Thought,* p. 183.

47. Walter C. Reckless, *The Crime Problem* (New York: Appleton Century Crofts, 1973), pp. 55–59.

48. Walter C. Reckless, Simon Dinitz, and E. Murray, "Self Concept as an Insulator against Delinquency," *American Sociological Review,* Vol. 21 (1956), pp. 744–756.

49. Frank R. Scarpitti, E. Murray, Simon Dinitz, and Walter C. Reckless, (1960). "The 'Good Boy' in a High Delinquency Area: Four Years Later, *American Sociological Review,* Vol. 25 (1960), pp. 555–558.

50. Walter C. Reckless and Simon Dinitz, *The Prevention of Juvenile Delinquency* (Columbus, OH: The Ohio State University Press, 1972).

51. Walter C. Reckless and Thomas G. Enyon, "Companionship at Delinquency Outset," *British Journal of Criminology,* Vol. 2 (1961), pp. 162–170; M. Schwartz and S. S. Taangri, "A Note on Self-Concept as an Insulator against Delinquency," *American Sociological Review,* Vol. 30 (1965), pp. 922–926; M. Schwartz and S. S. Tangri, "Delinquency Research and the Self-Concept Variable," *Journal of Criminal Law, Criminology, and Police Science,* Vol. 18 (1967), pp. 182–190.

52. Gary F. Jensen, "Inner Containment and Delinquency," *Criminology,* Vol. 64 (1973), pp. 464–470.

53. Martin, Mutchnick, and Austin, *Criminological Thought,* pp. 185–186.

54. Travis Hirschi, *Causes of Delinquency* (Berkeley, CA: University of California, 1969), p. 26.

55. OJJDP, *Report to Congress on Juvenile Violence Research* (Washington, DC: OJJDP), pp. 5–6.

56. Ibid., pp. 7–9.

57. Elaine Morley, Shelli B. Rossman, Mary Kopczynski, Janeen Buck, and Caterina Gouvis, *Comprehensive Responses to Youth at Risk: Interim Findings From the SafeFutures Initiative* (Washington, DC: Office of Juvenile Justice and Delinquency Prevention, 2000), p. 3.

58. J. David Hawkins and Joseph Weis, "The Social Development Model: An Integrated Approach to Delinquency Prevention," *Journal of Primary Prevention,* Vol. 6 (1985), pp. 73–97.

59. J. David Hawkins and Richard F. Catalano, *Communities That Care* (San Francisco: Jossey-Bass, 1990). See also J. David Hawkins, "Controlling Crime before It Happens: Risk-Focused Prevention," *National Institute of Justice Journal* (August 1995), pp. 10–18. In addition, see the SafeFutures web site at http://www.sfyc.net/

60. Morley, Rossman, Kopczynski, Buck, and Gouvis, *Comprehensive Responses to Youth at Risk,* p. x.

61. Kathleen Coolbaugh and Cynthia J. Hansel, *The Comprehensive Strategy: Lessons Learned from the Pilot Sites* (Washington, DC: Office of Juvenile Justice and Delinquency Prevention, 92000).

62. Kai Erickson, (1962). "Notes on the Sociology of Deviance," *Social Problems,* Vol. 9 (1962), pp. 397–414; Harold K. Becker, *The Outsiders—Studies in the Sociology of Deviancy* (New York: Free Press, 1963).

63. Frank Tannenbaum, *Crime and the Community* (Boston: Ginn, 1938).

64. Edwin M. Lemert, *Human Deviance, Social Problems, and Social Control* (Englewood Cliffs, NJ: Prentice-Hall, 1967).

65. Edwin M. Schur, *Radical Non-Intervention.* (Englewood Cliffs, NJ: Prentice Hall, 1973).

66. John P. Murray, "Status Offenders: Roles, Rules, and Reactions," in Ralph A. Weisheit and Robert G. Culbertson, eds., *Juvenile Delinquency: A Justice Perspective* (Prospect Heights, IL: Waveland Press, 1990), pp. 17–26.

67. Edward J. Latessa, Lawrence F. Travis, and George P. Wilson, "Juvenile Diversion: Factors Related to Decision Making and Outcome," in Scott H. Decker, ed., *Juvenile Justice Policy: Analyzing Trends and Outcomes* (Beverly Hills, CA: Sage Publications, 1984), pp. 145–165.

68. Gwen A. Holden and Robert A. Kapler, "Deinstitutionalizing Status Offenders: A Record of Progress," *Juvenile Justice,* Vol. 2 (1995), pp. 3–10; National Criminal Justice Association, *Unlocking the Doors for Status Offenders: The State of the States* (Washington, DC: National Criminal Justice Association, 1995).

PART II

The Juvenile Justice System

4

The Juvenile Justice Process

According to the labeling and stigmatization process, at least part of the responsibility for the development of an identity and subsequent career as a "juvenile delinquent" appears to rest with the handling of the juvenile by the police and the courts. Ambiguity in the laws governing juvenile conduct places a great deal of emphasis upon the exercise of discretionary powers.

HAROLD J. VETTER

LEARNING OBJECTIVES

1. Discuss how a juvenile enters and is processed through the juvenile justice system.
2. Describe law enforcement and juvenile interactions.
3. Describe courts and juvenile interactions.
4. Describe correctional and juvenile interactions.
5. Discuss the various methods for which juvenile court will give up its jurisdiction.

CHAPTER OVERVIEW

This chapter highlights the three components of the juvenile justice system: police, courts, and corrections. One of the major problems faced by the administrators of these components is lack of control resulting from the fragmentation of the juvenile justice "system." Like the adult criminal justice system, the actual coordination between the components of the juvenile justice system does not automatically operate in an integrated fashion. Each has developed special ways for dealing with children and young people in trouble. However, because of the need to protect information regarding juveniles and because of conflicting purposes and missions within these subsystems, the fragmentation problem is even more exacerbated in the juvenile justice system than in the adult system.

Police departments have responded to the problems of juvenile crime in several different ways, sometimes through specialized units for juvenile control. The juvenile courts have also developed special philosophies and procedures to deal with juveniles, but the recent movement away from the philosophy of *parens patriae* to one that stresses due process and constitutional safeguards for juveniles has indicated that the courts are in need of change. The same movement away from *parens patriae* has happened in juvenile corrections. In juvenile corrections, there is a move to more formal processing (i.e., adjudicated to detention) and toward due process.

The basic problem with the juvenile justice process is the clear presence of **goal conflict**.[1] This conflict operates at two levels. First, the juvenile justice system deals with juveniles who have committed crimes—the delinquents. Under the doctrine of *parens patriae,* the juvenile justice system (especially juvenile court) was designed to exist and act in the best interests of the child. The focus was that of redemption and rehabilitation, and not that of punishment. Second, the juvenile justice system is structured for **dual beneficiaries**[2]—it is designed to serve both delinquents and **children in need of services (CHINS)**—the abused and neglected. These often are different populations. Sometimes, however, delinquency can be the result of unmet needs and adverse environmental influences (e.g., broken homes, drugs, sexual and/or physical abuse). This is an issue of one system accommodating both juvenile delinquents and juvenile victims.

Thus, the conflict is between guardianship (under *parens patriae*) and accountability (notably, punishment). The balance between the two ideals is moving toward punishment. Since the late 1990s, most states have abandoned rehabilitation and *parens patriae* in favor of holding delinquents responsible, punishing them as if they were adults. Years earlier, the Supreme Court began departing from *parens patriae* by providing procedural safeguards to protect the rights of juveniles. This chapter examines some of the problems in the juvenile justice system that have resulted from the movement away from *parens patriae* and from the conflict of dealing with both juvenile delinquents and juvenile victims.

goal conflict The goals of the juvenile justice system include working with juveniles who have committed offenses as well as juveniles who are in need of services

dual beneficiaries Due to the goal conflict in the juvenile justice system, it serves both delinquents and children in need of services

children in need of services (CHINS) Abused, neglected, abandoned, and other victimized children

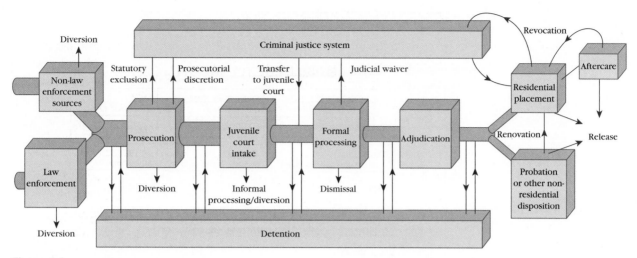

Figure 4.1
The Juvenile Justice Process

Figure 4.1 presents a case flow diagram of the juvenile justice process from the Office of Juvenile Justice and Delinquency Prevention (OJJDP). Because case processing varies from state to state and jurisdiction to jurisdiction, this chart provides a general overview of juvenile practices and outlines a series of decision points. Refer to this chart as we review the various decision points in the juvenile justice process.

THE POLICE

Historically, the restrictive procedures by which the law protects juveniles tended to create many administrative problems for the police in their enforcement of the law. A youth's age, for example, is a major factor in determining criminal responsibility. In some states, statutes use the age of 7 years for declaration that a child is free of criminal responsibility. Between the ages of 7 and 16 or 18 years (depending on the jurisdiction), the juvenile is sometimes considered a juvenile delinquent rather than criminal. The problem is clouded further by the fact that about one-half of all juveniles who come in contact with the police are status offenders, whose conduct would violate no criminal statute if they were adults (e.g., runaways, dependent children).

A police officer has much discretion in his or her contact with an alleged juvenile offender. The officer may ignore the delinquent behavior altogether. The contact could be very casual, with light conversation and inquiry to identify participants in the alleged offense. The police officer may conduct a search, an order for dispersal, or other more official action. Even after deciding to intervene, the officer may still decide to take the juvenile home (no action), warn the juvenile or his or her parents, or decide on some other informal action. Only when informal

MOBILE COUNTY SHERIFF'S OFFICE

STANDING OPERATING PROCEDURE	FILE INDEX NUMBER: SOP# 27	PAGE: 1 OF 13
EFFECTIVE DATE: 06-14-99	DATE OF ISSUE: 06-01-99	RESCINDS:
SUBJECT: Youth and Juvenile Procedures	AMENDS: SOP# 27, Issued 10-01-96	DISTRIBUTION: All Personnel

PURPOSE:

The purpose of this Standing Operating Procedure is to establish guidelines for the handling of juvenile offenders, neglected, abused, missing, or runaway children, and for the identification, investigation, processing, referral, and custody of minors.

DISCUSSION:

It is the policy of the Mobile County Sheriff's Office (MCSO) to promote public safety and reduce juvenile delinquency by maintaining the integrity of the substantive laws prohibiting certain socially unacceptable behavior and by developing individual responsibility for lawful conduct. This policy shall be pursued through means that are fair and just, that recognize the unique characteristics and needs of children, and that give children access to opportunities for personal and social growth.

DEFINITIONS:

A Adult. Anyone eighteen (18) years of age or older.

B. Age of Criminal Culpability. The age at which a person becomes subject to prosecution for violation of state laws. In the State of Alabama, this is seven (7) years of age.

C. Age of Consent. The age at which a person may legally consent to have sexual relations. In the State of Alabama, this is sixteen (16) years of age.

D Child in Need of Supervision (CHINS).

1. A child who, being subject to compulsory school attendance, is habitually truant from school.

2. A child who disobeys the reasonable and lawful demands of his/her parents, guardian or other custodian, and whose behavior is beyond their control.

Figure 4.2

Example of Police Standard Operating Procedures for Juveniles (pp. 1, 5–6)

alternatives seem to be inadequate will an officer take formal and official action that will bring the juvenile into the juvenile justice system.

Oftentimes departmental policy determines the action taken by officers in response to juveniles. For example, some departments may have standard operating procedures (SOPs) for dealing with juveniles. Figure 4.2 highlights the SOP for the Mobile County, Alabama, Sheriff's Office. Notice the purpose of the SOP on page 1 to "establish guidelines for the handling of juvenile offenders, neglected, abused, missing, or runaway children. . . ." This highlights the juvenile system's conflict between

Page 2   MCSO SOP   Youth and Juvenile Procedures - 27

    E. <u>Competent Adult</u>.

        1. A parent.

        2. A legal guardian or custodian.

        3. Another relative, neighbors or adult whom the detaining Deputy may reasonably believe will notify the juvenile's parent or custodian of the offense and detention, and who will assume responsibility for, and custody of, the juvenile.

    F. <u>Dependent</u>. Title 12-15-1 (Juvenile Proceedings) of The Code of Alabama defines a dependent child as a child:

        1. Who is destitute, homeless or dependent upon the public for support.

        2. Who is without a parent or guardian who is able to provide support, training and education.

        3. Whose custody is the subject of controversy.

        4. Whose home, or in whose care the child may be, is an unfit and improper place for him/her.

        5. Whose parent (s), guardian, or custodian neglects the care necessary for the child's health and well-being.

        6. Whose condition or surroundings endangers the child's morals, health or general welfare.

        7. Who has no proper parental care nor guardianship.

        8. Whose parent (s), guardian or custodian fails, refuses or neglects to send such child to school.

        9. Who has been abandoned by his/her parents, guardian, or other custodian.

       10. Who has been physically, mentally or emotionally abused by parent (s), guardian or other custodian, or who is without proper care and control because of the faults of his/her parent (s), guardian or custodian, and they are unable to discharge their responsibilities to, and for, the child.

Figure 4.2
(Continued)

guardianship and accountability. The effect of policy varies greatly among departments. Of course, officer response is also determined by the seriousness of the offense.

    Beginning with arrest, the police decide between formally bringing the juvenile into the juvenile justice system (through arrest) and diverting the juvenile into some type of alternative program. Typically, the decision is made after the police officer talks to the victim, the juvenile, and the parents. The record of the juvenile's prior contacts with the system is also routinely reviewed. According to federal regulations, juveniles

Form must be signed by a responsible adult. A copy of the Missing Persons Documentation Form shall be sent or FAXed to the NCIC.

2. <u>Child in Need of Supervision</u>. When parents advise that their children are misbehaving or refusing to obey at home, and they wish the child to be transported to the Youth Center, the Deputy should tactfully advise the parents that they can transport the child themselves, since they are best able to convey the true nature of the problem (s) to Youth Center counselors. Should Deputies find it necessary to initiate a CHINS complaint, a report shall be prepared, a juvenile petition signed and the juvenile placed in the Youth Center.

3. <u>Truancy</u>. All truancy complaints must be initiated by school authorities.

C. <u>Juvenile Miranda Warnings</u>.

1. Rule 11 (B) of the *Alabama Rules of Juvenile Procedures (ARJP)* establishes the rights of a child before being questioned while in custody. Before the juvenile is questioned about anything concerning the charge on which the juvenile is arrested, the person asking the questions must inform the juvenile of the following rights (see enclosure):

   a. The juvenile has the right to counsel.

   b. If the juvenile is unable to pay for a lawyer, and if the juvenile's parent (s) or guardian have not provided a lawyer, one can be provided.

   c. The juvenile is not required to say anything and anything the juvenile may say, may be used against the juvenile.

   d. If the juvenile's counsel, parent (s), or guardian is not present, then the juvenile has the right to communicate with them, and that, if necessary, reasonable means will be provided for the juvenile to do so.

2. Any statement the juvenile gives, without being advised of the above *Juvenile Miranda Warnings*, will not be admissible in court.

3. A juvenile under the age of 18 years arrested for a class "A" felony, or any offense requiring the juvenile to be placed in the Mobile County Metro Jail, <u>must</u> be advised of their Juvenile Miranda rights in order for any statements given to be admissible in court.

Figure 4.2
(Continued)

should not be held in jail or adult lockups following an arrest. If they are detained in adult facilities, it is only temporary; juveniles must not be held for longer than six hours and in an area that is not within the sight and sound of adult inmates.[3]

Juvenile crime should concern all personnel in a modern police department. Although it is important for all officers to deal with juveniles effectively, separate juvenile units are sometimes set up if a demonstrated need has been established. For example, separate juvenile units are used to provide special investigation techniques for the processing of juveniles, disposition requirements, and coordination with family and community. Specifically, special interrogation skills and handling techniques are sometimes needed with juvenile offenders. Officers in the juvenile unit are attuned to the community and the needs of the juvenile in a way that "regular" police officers usually are not.

Several names have been used in the past for juvenile units in police organizations: Crime Prevention Bureau, Juvenile Bureau, Youth Aid Bureau, or Juvenile Control Bureau. Logically, the functions of a juvenile unit seem to be as follows:

1. Discovery of delinquents, potential delinquents, and conditions including delinquency;
2. Investigation of delinquency and causes of delinquency;
3. Disposition or referral of cases;
4. Protection of children and youth; and
5. Community organization.

Although these functions are general in nature, they provide the basis for the operation of the juvenile unit. When viewed in terms of overall departmental objectives for juvenile control, as discussed in Chapter 5, they provide the basis for the juvenile control unit's operation.[4]

In smaller departments (i.e., agencies with one to fifteen officers), every officer must be prepared to assume all police functions; specialization for juvenile cases would be an impractical and expensive use of limited resources. One officer in the department may be assigned as the juvenile case coordinator. Because the juvenile problem often affects the community in a different manner from adult crime in small communities, the chief, in an attempt to follow juvenile crime closely, may be the person assigned to the juvenile cases. In departments larger than fifteen officers, the assignment of a juvenile bureau, even if it is composed of only one officer, seems to be the most common practice. This bureau is often assigned several duties, such as bicycle patrol, school safety patrol, "Officer Friendly" programs, and other initiatives aimed at the juvenile population.

As police organizations adjust to meet the changes in the mission of the juvenile justice system, the police role is magnified. Law enforcement, working in an environment that is changing its views of juveniles from protective to punitive, must continuously train officers to work with juveniles more effectively, while cracking down on juvenile crime. Police agencies must justify some of the progressive changes in the police sector while juvenile crime legislation is hardening. Protecting the rights of juveniles and protecting the juveniles themselves continues to be a top priority for police agencies. To this end, care must be exercised to ensure that the rights of juveniles are protected during investigations.

INTAKE AND THE JUVENILE COURT

Returning to Figure 4.1, the intake function is the responsibility of the juvenile probation department or the prosecutor's office. Following arrest, police will take the juvenile to a local detention facility or juvenile assessment center for intake. At this time, juvenile probation officers will review the current charges and both legal and extralegal factors related to the juvenile's case. If applicable, a detention hearing will be occur within 24 hours of intake.

Serious cases involving juveniles may be filed or **waived** to the adult criminal justice system. Here, the legislature has determined that juvenile offender should be treated as an adult. A growing number of states have decided that both the juvenile and adult courts have original jurisdiction over these cases. The prosecutor selects the court that will handle the matter. The growth of **prosecutorial discretion** in juvenile cases reflects the shift toward punishment as a key element in the juvenile process. The general belief is that juveniles should be treated as adults when they commit serious crimes such as murder. Such cases, although they involve juvenile offenders have been **statutorily excluded** from the juvenile justice system.[5]

Juvenile Court Intake

At juvenile court intake, the decision is made to (1) dismiss the case, (2) handle the matter informally, or (3) send it on to juvenile court. The intake officer makes this decision by reviewing the facts of the case to determine if there is sufficient evidence to prove the allegation.

> About one-half of all cases referred to juvenile court intake are handled informally and most of these cases are dismissed. If an informal case is processed, then usually the juvenile will voluntarily agree to specific conditions in a written agreement. Such conditions may be drug or alcohol treatment, attendance at school or after-school functions, and/or restitution. In some jurisdictions an informal disposition is an option only if the juvenile admits to committing an offense. If the juvenile successfully complies with the conditions outlined in the informal disposition, the case will be dismissed. If the conditions are not met, then the case may be referred for an adjudicatory hearing.[6]

If the juvenile court judge believes that it is in the best interests of the child, juveniles can be held in a secure detention facility. Then either juvenile probation officers or detention workers review the case to determine whether the juvenile should be held pending a judicial hearing. In every state, the detention hearing must be held within the time period

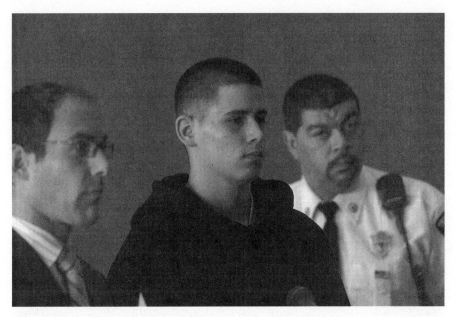

Juvenile in Court

defined by statute (usually 24 hours). At this hearing, the judge reviews the case and determines if the youth should be released or continue to be detained. Detention may extend beyond the adjudicatory and dispositional hearings.[7]

Formal Processing

If the case is handled in juvenile court, two types of petitions may be filed: **delinquency petition** or **waiver petition**. The delinquency petition states the charges against the juvenile. It seeks to have the juvenile **adjudicated** delinquent. The juvenile then becomes a ward of the court. Note the difference in tone from the adult criminal justice system, where the offender is convicted and sentenced.

In response to the delinquency petition, an **adjudicatory hearing** is scheduled. During the hearing, witnesses are called and facts of the case are presented. Typically, a judge makes the final decision about the case.

If the prosecutor or the intake officer believes that the case belongs in the adult rather than juvenile justice system, a waiver petition is filed. Here, the juvenile court judge determines if there is probable cause that the juvenile in question committed the act. If this determination is positive, then the court decides whether the case should be waived to adult court. The judge's final decision typically centers on whether the juvenile is amenable to treatment in the juvenile justice system. In its arguments, the prosecution may present the previous record of the juvenile and note that past treatment failed to prevent recidivism. The prosecutor may also argue that the crime is so serious that the court cannot meet the time period necessary to rehabilitate the youth.

mycrimekit™

Video Profile: *The Hearing Process*

delinquency petition Formal petition seeking to adjudicate the juvenile delinquent that states the charges against the juvenile

waiver petition Formal petition seeking to adjudicate the juvenile as an adult

adjudicated Term used in juvenile court that means the same as *convicted* in the adult court

adjudicatory hearing Hearing that includes witnesses and all facts of the case. Typically, the judge makes the final decision about the case.

If the judge transfers the case to adult criminal court, juvenile jurisdiction is waived. The case is filed in adult court. If the waiver is not approved, the case remains in juvenile court and an adjudicatory hearing is scheduled.[8]

The Disposition Hearing

If adjudicated delinquent, a disposition plan is developed for the juvenile. Probation staff develops the plan, examining the background of the youth, family, school, church, and other relevant social support systems. Recommendations are made following a detailed assessment of the juvenile; psychological examinations and other diagnoses (e.g., drug tests, IQ tests) can be ordered by the court.

These recommendations are presented at the hearing. The prosecutor and the juvenile can make other dispositional recommendations. The judge considers all this information and orders a final disposition for the case. It can include the following:

- A probation order with special conditions like drug counseling, weekend confinement in local juvenile detention center, community and/or victim restitution.

- A period of probation that is either specified (limited) or open-ended. Review hearings are conducted to monitor the performance of the juvenile client. If the conditions of probation are successfully met, the judge terminates the case.

- Residential commitment for a specific or indeterminate specified time period.[9] Juvenile facilities are operated by private corporations as well as the government.

Some facilities have secure environments, whereas others have an open setting. If sent to the state department of juvenile corrections, department officials determine the placement of the juvenile and when the youth will be released. Review hearings are held to assess the progress of the juveniles in custody.

Juvenile Aftercare

Like the adult system of parole, juveniles released from an institution are often ordered to follow a period of aftercare. During this period, the youth is under the supervision of the court or the department of juvenile corrections. If the conditions of release are not followed, the youth can be recommitted to a juvenile facility.

Status Offense Cases

Status offenses are acts committed by juveniles that would not be considered crimes if committed by adults. They include such offenses as running away from home, truancy, juveniles who are beyond the control of their parents or guardians ("ungovernable" or "incorrigible"), curfew violations, and underage drinking. The issue with status offenders is how to treat them—like delinquents or dependents? Some experts believe that treating status offenders like delinquents will lead them to become delinquent and/or criminal in the future. In effect, juvenile justice processing will make them worse. For example, Schur condemns status offenses as moral judgments that make a bad situation worse. A runaway placed in a juvenile institution can become a serious criminal as a result of incarceration. Schur advocates a policy of radical nonintervention: Leave the kids alone whenever possible.[10]

Three procedures involve removing juveniles from formal processing. Decriminalization makes the act committed by the juvenile no longer a crime that is subject to sanction. Its primary aim is to remove certain types of behaviors from the scope of law that are not dangerous to society. Typically, these acts are seen as deviant rather than illegal and are "not the law's business."[11] To handle such things as status offenses, deinstitutionalization has been implemented. For example, the Institute of Juvenile Administration of the American Bar Association recommended the following:

1. A juvenile's acts of misbehavior, ungovernability, or unruliness, which do not violate the criminal law, should not constitute a ground for asserting juvenile court jurisdiction over the juvenile committing them.

2. Any law enforcement officer who reasonably determines that a juvenile is in circumstances that constitute a substantial and immediate danger to the juvenile's physical safety requires such action, should take the juvenile into limited custody (subject to the limitations of this part).[12]

Finally, **decarceration** removes as many juveniles as possible from custody and treats them in an open environment. Given the violent nature of many of the incarcerated juveniles, this option has been questioned. It seems more appropriate for the juveniles who should be diverted from the system because they have committed either status or nondangerous offenses.

decarceration Removing as many juveniles as possible from custody and treating them in an open environment

Due Process Rights of Juveniles

The protections for juveniles against unjustified punishment were established as a result of several well-known cases. *In re Gault* [387 U.S. 1 (1967)] established that proceedings that determine delinquency "must measure up to the essentials of due process and fair hearing." Juveniles must be given adequate notice of the specific charges against them, the assistance of counsel, the right to confront and cross-examine witnesses against them, and the privilege against self-incrimination. *In re Winship*

[397 U.S. 358 (1970)] stated that the Supreme Court held that due process required that every fact presented to prove delinquency must meet the "beyond a reasonable doubt" standard.

However, it is clear that the U.S. Constitution does not require that all aspects of adult criminal procedure be applied in juvenile court. In *McKeiver v. Pennsylvania*, 403 U.S. 528 (1971), the court held that due process did not require that an alleged delinquent be extended the right to trial by jury. The court's language indicated that it retained hope for the preservation of the juvenile court as a separate and distinguishable process:

> The juvenile concept held high promise. We are reluctant to say that despite disappointments of grave dimensions, it still does not hold promise, and we are particularly reluctant to say . . . that the system cannot accomplish its rehabilitative goals. So much depends on the availability of resources, on the interest and commitment of the public, on willingness to learn, and on understanding as to cause and effect and cure.[13]

After all screening or diversionary actions have been taken or all nonjudicial alternatives exhausted, the juvenile who is still a problem will finally be referred to the juvenile court for disposition.

When considering the nature and future of juvenile court, there are two central concerns that persist. The first is the place of the juvenile court in the criminal justice system, including the breadth of its jurisdiction over juveniles, its location within the judicial system to hear such cases, and its relationship to other agencies. The second area of concern is its procedures, including those used during the formal hearing as well as the methods by which the decision is made to detain a juvenile prior to the formal hearing itself.

The appropriate administrative approach to the processing of delinquency cases is the formal court procedure. It should vary little from that of adult criminal prosecutions. The processing of juvenile cases should differ from that of adult cases primarily in a greater willingness to use informal, nonpunitive measures. If, however, formal court action is sought and the juvenile contests the facts on which court jurisdiction is sought, the procedure for resolving the dispute should not differ substantially from that used in adult cases. Such an approach can preserve the value of the juvenile justice process as a means of dealing with young offenders without unduly sacrificing the right of alleged offenders to a full and fair determination of whether official action is justified.

The juvenile court judge is in a position of conflict in today's justice environment. He or she is pressed from one sector for more humane sentencing practices, more diversion, and differential decision making despite limited information. From another sector, there is pressure to "get tough"—to inflict more punishment, impose longer institutional confinement, and exhibit less interest in the juvenile's rights. Not surprisingly, the juvenile justice process as a means of dealing with young offenders is not without the problems of overcrowding and repeat offenders.

JUVENILE CORRECTIONS

Juvenile corrections seem to be at a crossroads. Partly because of the emphasis on juvenile rights and partly because of the failure of past models, juvenile correctional administrators are looking for new answers to old questions. Obstacles to juvenile corrections reform are the fragmentation of corrections, the variety of governmental authorities involved, and, most of all, a lack of overall correctional planning that assigns each segment of the system specific involvement and accountability. Detention and incarceration may be overused for some crimes. An additional obstacle is the ambivalence of community members: They want treatment, but they also want punishment; they want good programs, but they do not want to pay the price for them; they want offenders incarcerated, but they do not want juvenile delinquents back in the community after release. Lack of sufficient information on which to base good planning is one more serious deficiency.

The focus on diversion, particularly for status offenders, often causes some legal problems. For example, if a child referred to a social agency has caused social but not legal problems, should he or she be processed through the courts for the same offense? If so, a case could be made for double jeopardy.[14] Status offender cases—for example, drunkenness, truancy, incorrigibility—might well be treated in a separate system. However, most jurisdictions cannot afford even one juvenile correctional system. There is little probability of setting up a separate status offender system. Another major issue is the amount of discretion that exists in the system. Juvenile court judges, the police, the correctional programs, and the district attorney have wide discretion in the decisions they make. The system lacks consistent standards to govern this discretion.

In corrections, treatment and justice are intertwined and almost inseparable. Corrections is committed to both. The juvenile correctional administrator has no choice about whom the court commits to his or her care but has had the choice of determining how long they are kept. the correctional administrator's ability to alter or change the direction of juvenile justice is difficult to determine. He or she has little choice but to continue to follow the direction of court decisions and legislatures.

The juvenile justice administrator comes in several different forms: police officers with great discretion, probation officers who must respond to several constituencies, and judges faced with many problems in protecting both the juvenile and the public. The juvenile correctional administrator has the most clearly defined role, but even it suffers from fragmentation of jurisdictional control among cities, counties, and states. Only a few states have seen fit to consolidate juvenile and adult corrections under a single authority. The lingering fear of the "terrible" adult institutions still inhibits the majority from taking that difficult but seemingly logical step. The management muddle of the U.S. juvenile justice "nonsystem" can be cleared up only when society decides whether it wants to punish, protect, or treat its miscreant youth. That prospect seems dim, so we struggle on, trying to make programs work in an environment of administrative uncertainty whose by-product is uncertain administrators.

THE DIRECTION OF JUVENILE JUSTICE

Disenchantment with and criticisms of the juvenile court and its *parens patriae* procedures have been voiced across the board. Here, we introduce several problems facing the juvenile justice system that will be closely examined in subsequent chapters.

diversion Process of limiting the amount of involvement a juvenile has with the formal organization and procedures of the criminal and juvenile justice systems.

transfer of juveniles to adult court When the seriousness of the behavior and the nature of the acts committed warrant, juveniles are transferred to adult courts.

For example, criticisms have led to alterations in the juvenile justice funnel and in the handling of juveniles; specifically, both **diversion** and the **transfer of juveniles to adult court** have been introduced. Although these alternatives share the goal of getting juveniles out of the system, they do so for remarkably different reasons. Whereas diversion looks to the welfare of the juvenile and to use the system only when necessary, transfer to adult court holds that the seriousness of the behavior of delinquents and the nature of the acts they commit merit more severe punishment than the juvenile justice system is designed to mete out.

Diversion

The due process model for juveniles was derived from the *Gault, Winship,* and *Kent* decisions. They defined the constitutionally guaranteed rights that must be accorded to every citizen, both adults and juveniles. The diversion of juveniles involves the official halting or suspension of formal juvenile justice proceedings against an alleged offender at any legally prescribed processing point after a recorded justice system entry, and referral of that person to a treatment program (administered by a public or private agency)—or to no program at all.

Diversion programs are designed to take youths (especially status offenders) out of the juvenile justice system. Diversion can occur at any point in the system. The aim is to avoid formal contact with the court

Diversion Counseling Session

and correctional agencies. Instead, it encourages the use of alternative programs including remedial education programs, foster homes, group homes, and local counseling facilities and centers.

Diversion has several different policy aims. First, it can be designed to relieve pressure and the caseload burden on the juvenile justice system—especially in court and in detention facilities. When less serious and more promising juveniles are diverted, the system can concentrate on the more serious offenses and offenders.

It is also hoped that diversion will alleviate issues of discrimination throughout the juvenile justice system. Minorities are far more likely to face serious outcomes throughout the juvenile justice process. For example, minorities are more likely to be detained and sentenced to a detention facility than Caucasians regardless of the seriousness of the charge against them.[15] Diversion could help reduce bias in processing by removing minorities from the system when it is appropriate to do so.

Another expectation with diversion is that rehabilitation is more likely to occur outside of the formal system. Juveniles and their families are matched with services that meet their needs and reduce the risk of delinquency. However, the effectiveness of such programs has been questioned. In particular, studies of diversion programs have found that they often result in a **widening of the net**. This means that diversion has extended the jurisdiction of the juvenile justice system. Instead of taking juveniles out of the system, diversion programs often bring in juveniles that were normally not subject to the system. Then, the programs divert these formerly untargeted youths, rather than taking out juveniles who were in the system. In this way, the scope and power of the juvenile

widening of the net Utilization of diversion has extended the jurisdiction of the juvenile justice system, thereby brining in juveniles who may not normally have entered the system.

justice system is expanded and strengthened. The previously listed benefits of diversion are wiped out. Diversion is an example of an idea gone haywire.

To prevent such problems, Ezell has recommended that diversion programs should feature the following elements:

- More sound criteria to determine which youth are diverted so that net-widening is prevented;
- Greater attention to due process rights to juveniles accused of delinquent acts that are considered for diversion;
- Improved ability to match diverted youth to appropriate interventions and services; and
- Avoidance of stigmatization of youths who are diverted.[16]

One example of a diversion program designed to accomplish such objectives is the Detention Diversion Advocacy Program (DDAP).

The DDAP features a case management system that is designed to integrate services provided to the juvenile by several different agencies and service providers and to develop the skills of the client. It also features the use of laypersons acting on behalf of offenders at disposition hearings. The case management system coordinates the provision of services for both the client and his or her family. The focus is on "high-risk" juveniles whose personal circumstances make them ripe for delinquency. Research on DDAP found that it was effective in providing services and in reducing recidivism (referral to juvenile court for a new offense) among its clients. The recidivism rate for the DDAP group was almost twice as low (34 percent) as that of the comparison group (60 percent) that was not treated. In addition, the members of the comparison group were more likely to engage in serious crime and have more than two referrals. The lower recidivism rate for DDAP clients was also true among juveniles classified as high risk" On the basis of this evidence, it seems that programs that divert juveniles and provide needed social services can affect delinquency rates.[17]

The Transfer of Juveniles to Adult Court

As indicated previously, the juvenile court was designed to prevent juvenile offenders from being treated and tried in the same courts as adult offenders. It was established to "save children" from the adult system. Recent criticisms sponsored by the "Get Tough" movement have called for severe punishments for juvenile offenders who commit serious crimes. From this point of view, juvenile offenders escaping just punishment for their crimes and the aims of deterrence and incapacitation of serious delinquents were not being met in juvenile court. In the 1990s, most state legislatures introduced punitive measures in response to rising rates of youth crime. One particular measure was the transfer of an increasing number and range of adolescents to adult criminal courts for prosecution. This procedure, known as **remanding**, waives juvenile court jurisdiction over a youth and sends the case to the adult criminal court.

An option in some states since 1920, a juvenile case can be transferred to adult criminal court in one of three ways (see also Chapter 7)[18]:

- Judicial waiver,
- Prosecutorial discretion, or
- Statutory exclusion.

In any state, one, two, or all three methods may be in place. Of the three, judicial waiver is the most common transfer provision. Most statutes are limited to juveniles who are no longer amenable to treatment. The factors leading to this determination typically include previous offense history and dispositional outcomes. Statutes typically instruct the juvenile court to consider the availability of dispositional outcomes for treating the juvenile, the time available for sanctions, public safety, and the best interests of the child. A reverse transfer is also possible with adult criminal courts returning a case to juvenile court. Until 1966, transfers of juveniles were made without full benefit of due process of law. In the *Kent* decision, the U.S. Supreme Court ruled that juveniles facing a waiver to adult court had a right to a hearing, representation by counsel, access to records, and a right to a written statement of the reasons for the decision made by the court.[19]

During a waiver hearing, a juvenile court judge is asked to waive jurisdiction over a matter and transfer the case to criminal court so the juvenile can be tried as though he or she were an adult. Waiver decisions are often based on several factors, including the following:

- The seriousness of the offense,
- The juvenile's prior record, and
- The youth's amenability to treatment.

The waiver procedure has grown in popularity in recent years. In 1998, juvenile court judges waived 8,100 delinquency cases. The number of cases waived in 1998 was 1 percent more than in 1989, 9 percent less than in 1997, and 33 percent less than in 1994, the peak year. Of the cases waived in 1998, 36 percent (2,900) were for personal offenses, 40 percent (3,200) were property offenses, 16 percent (1,300) involved a drug law violation, and 8 percent (700) involved a public order offense as the most serious charge.[20] For the period 1988 to 1997, it was estimated that only 8 out of 1,000 formally handled delinquency cases were waived to adult criminal court.[21]

The trend toward more punitive responses to delinquency is most evident in new laws that facilitate the transfer of young offenders to criminal court without the traditional waiver hearing. The most highly controversial of these streamlined transfer methods is prosecutorial waiver. It allows prosecutors to choose whether to initiate proceedings in juvenile or criminal court.

Several criticisms have been raised about the transfer decision. Specifically, transfer policies have been called into question for sending many minor and nonthreatening juvenile offenders to the adult system, aggravating racial disparities, and moving special needs adolescents into adult correctional systems that are ill prepared to handle them. Also, the evidence that transfer results in more severe penalties for some juvenile offenders and achieves a deterrent effect is questionable.[22]

SUMMARY

The administration of the juvenile justice system is in some ways more difficult than its adult counterpart. In other ways, it is much easier. The problem of whether the police, courts, and corrections agencies should develop complete and separate apparatus for juveniles or absorb them into the existing adult criminal justice system is one of long standing. The separate subsystems have had varying degrees of success in seeking autonomy for juveniles. The most successful of these has been the juvenile courts, which have had almost absolute power over the juvenile offender under the doctrine of *parens patriae.*

The trend in administration seems to be heading toward a more selective jurisdiction over offenders, focusing on the seriousness of the offense instead of the status of the offender. As attitudes change toward making juveniles more accountable for their actions, the adult and juvenile justice systems will become less distinguishable. As a result, the administration of juvenile justice will become more and more formalized. The traditional *parens patriae* approach will give way to a more legalistic one. Administration officials, who want and need rules as guidelines, will favor this process, but its impact on the youth is yet to be determined.

KEY TERMS

adjudicated
adjudicatory hearing
children in need of services
   (CHINS)
decarceration

delinquency petition
diversion
dual beneficiaries
goal conflict
prosecutorial discretion

remanding   waived
statutorily excluded   waiver petition
transfer of juveniles to adult court   widening of the net

DISCUSSION AND REVIEW QUESTIONS

1. Why has the concept of *parens patriae* become difficult to maintain in the present juvenile justice environment?
2. What alternatives are usually used by the police in juvenile incidents?
3. What is the role of the prosecutor in the juvenile justice process?
4. What takes place at a dispositional hearing?
5. Analyze the goals of diversion. What are the benefits and problems associated with this process?
6. How can a juvenile be transferred to adult court? How do these processes differ?
7. Can the juvenile justice system meet the goals of treatment and punishment?

VIDEO PROFILES

Entering the Juvenile Justice System video profile in MyCrimeKit shows the intake process for Morris, a juvenile who has previous arrests. Discuss the intake process of juveniles who arrive at intake under the influence of alcohol or drugs. List some of the questions asked of Morris by the intake officer. Why is it important for the officer to ask Morris these questions during the intake process?

The Hearing Process video profile in MyCrimeKit shows two brothers entering and moving through the initial steps of the juvenile justice system. Each has previously come into contact with the system. What are the brothers charged with? Discuss the differences between the brothers and whether the differences affect the state's attorney and judge. Describe the judge's comments as they relate to Kenneth and Kentrell and how she sees the juvenile system working (or not) for each of them.

MYCRIMEKIT

 Go to MyCrimeKit.com to explore the following study tools and resources specific to this chapter:

- Practice Quiz: Test your knowledge with multiple-choice, true-false, fill-in-the-blank, and essay questions.
- Flashcards: 20 flashcards to test your knowledge of the chapter's key terms.

- Web Quest: Review the Web site of your state's Juvenile Justice agency and its mission statement.
- Web Links: Check out sites related to the content presented in this chapter.

ENDNOTES

1. Kevin N. Wright, "The Desirability of Goal Conflict in the Criminal Justice System," *Journal of Criminal Justice,* Vol. 9 (1981), pp. 209–218.

2. Peter M. Blau and W. Richard Scott, *Formal Organizations: A Comparative Approach* (San Francisco: Chandler, 1962).

3. "Juvenile Justice Facts & Figures," Office of Juvenile Justice and Delinquency Prevention Web site: http://ojjdp.ncjrs.org/facts/caseflowexplan.html, p.1.

4. John P. Kenney and Dan Pursuit, *Police Work with Juveniles and the Administration of Juvenile Justice* (Springfield, IL: Charles W. Thomas, 1989), pp. 104–107.

5. "Juvenile Justice Facts & Figures," p. 3.

6. Ibid, p. 2.

7. Ibid.

8. Ibid, p. 3.

9. Ibid, p. 4.

10. Edwin Schur, *Radical Non-intervention: Rethinking the Delinquency Problem* (Englewood Cliffs, NJ: Prentice Hall, 1973).

11. Robert Meier and Gilbert Geis, *Victimless Crime?* (Los Angeles: Roxbury Publishing, 1997).

12. Institute of Judicial Administration, American Bar Association, *Standards Relating to Interim Status: Release, Control and Detention of Accused Juvenile Offenders between Arrest and Disposition* (Cambridge, MA: Ballinger, 1980).

13. *McKeiver v. Pennsylvania,* 403 U.S. 541 (1971).

14. *Breed v. Jones,* 421 U.S. 519 (1975).

15. M. A. Bortner, M. L. Sunderland, and R. Winn, "Race and the Impact of Juvenile Deinstitutionalization," *Crime and Delinquency,* Vol. 31 (1985), pp. 35–46. See also J. E. Fagan, E. Slaughter, and E. Hartstone, "Blind Justice? The Impact of Race on the Juvenile Justice Process," *Crime and Delinquency,* Vol. 33 (1987), pp. 224–258.

16. M. Ezell, "Juvenile Diversion: The Ongoing Search for Alternatives," in Ira M. Schwartz, ed., *Juvenile Justice and Public Policy: Toward a National Agenda* (New York: Macmillan, 1992), pp. 45–58.

17. Randall G. Shelden, *Detention Diversion Advocacy: An Evaluation* (Washington, DC: U.S. Department of Justice, Office of Juvenile Justice and Delinquency Prevention, 1999).

18. Howard N. Synder and Melissa Sickmund, *Juvenile Offenders and Victims: A National Report* (Washington, DC: Office of Juvenile Justice and Delinquency Prevention, 1995), p. 26.

19. Barry C. Feld, "Delinquency Careers and Criminal Policy: Just Desserts and the Waiver Decision," *Criminology,* Vol. 21 (1983), pp. 195–212.

20. Anne L. Stahl, *Delinquency Cases in Juvenile Court, 1998* (Washington, DC: Office of Juvenile Justice and Delinquency Prevention, 2001).

21. Charles M. Puzzanchera, *Delinquency Cases Waived to Criminal Court, 1988–1997* (Washington, DC: Office of Juvenile Justice and Delinquency Prevention, 2000).

22. Donna M. Bishop, "Juvenile Offenders in the Adult Criminal Justice System," in Michael Tonry, ed., *Crime and Justice: A Review of Research,* Volume 27 (Chicago: University of Chicago Press, 2000), pp. 81–167.

5

Juveniles and the Police: Where the System Starts

As the initial gatekeeper to the juvenile justice system, police are granted perhaps the most critical discretion of any decision maker in the response to juvenile crime: whether or not to arrest and pursue formal processing. The role of the police in determining the type and level of diversion has also long been recognized.

GORDON SIZEMORE AND SCOTT SENJO

LEARNING OBJECTIVES

1. Identify how the police deal with juveniles and how these procedures differ from their handling of adults.

2. Identify the elements and effectiveness of the D.A.R.E. program.

3. Identify how the juvenile interrogation process operates under the requirements of the *Miranda* decision.

4. Identify the discretionary powers of the police with juveniles and the limitations of these powers.

5. Identify the elements and effectiveness of juvenile curfews.

6. Identify how the police handle neglected and abused children.

7. Identify how community and problem oriented policing methods are used with juveniles.

CHAPTER OVERVIEW

The quote at the beginning of the chapter reveals the central role of the police as an entry point for the entire justice system, whether for adults or juveniles. The police are typically the first social agency on the scene, and they respond often without knowing or caring whether the juvenile is the offender or the victim. Their powers are varied, from arrest to diversion, but they usually fit into the *parens patriae* style of the juvenile justice system. The desire to help is paramount, yet the power to arrest and the ability to help often conflict. But, with the advent of **community policing** and problem solving, the police have become more proactive in their involvement with juveniles. In recent years, police officers have directly offered services to youth to prevent their involvement with both drugs (D.A.R.E.) and gangs (G.R.E.A.T; see Chapter 12).

In this country, people are hired, appointed, or elected to wear uniforms, carry badges and guns, and be, as President Grover Cleveland put it, "servants of the *people* to execute the laws which *people* have made." These public servants include town constables, city police, county sheriffs and deputies, state patrol officers, warehouse guards, institutional guards, and truant officers. Every one of these control and law enforcement agents could and often do have contact with America's children. In this chapter, we review the use of the powers and responsibilities these myriad agencies have and their involvement in the juvenile justice system. By virtue of their position on the "leading edge" of the system, the role of the police is significant.

community policing Partnership between the police, neighborhoods, and the people they serve

THE POLICE AND JUVENILES: AN OVERVIEW

Until the late 1800s and the early 1900s, juveniles were subject to the same laws and punishments and the same treatment by the police as adults. There were no separate juvenile courts or juvenile laws to regulate the treatment and protection of children. Early courts and correctional systems followed English common law in cases involving juveniles.

Until the problems of the big city slums began to affect the lives of the "refined" citizenry, not much thought was given as to what should done to, or for, youths in trouble. At the turn of the century, citizens started urging the police to protect them from delinquents and youthful beggars. The police approach at that time, however, was to act only as guardians of the peace, not as social workers. The concept of special juvenile police units patrolling neighborhoods and helping to stop delinquency before it started had not been adopted, and the somewhat brutal police methods of the time were applied to youthful criminals as well as adults.

Protests favoring differential treatment of juveniles eventually caught the public fancy, creating a general clamor for change throughout the nation. As a result of the efforts of the Society for the Prevention of Cruelty to Children (composed mostly of women), in 1877 the New York state legislature passed the first law in this country that dealt specifically with police treatment of juveniles.[1]

Additional laws to protect and separate juveniles from adult criminals were passed in the ensuing years. One of the most important, and the cornerstone of the present system, was an act designed "to regulate the treatment and control of dependent, neglected, and delinquent children," signed into law in Illinois in April 1899. This was the first act in the United States that included a definition of juvenile delinquency: "Any child under the age of 16 who violates any law of this state or any city or village ordinance" was held to be a juvenile delinquent. The law was designed to avoid treating the child as a criminal, placing emphasis on rehabilitation of juvenile offenders rather than on punishment.[2]

With the passage of the Illinois act, a policing authority was introduced with a specific duty to work with delinquents. This authority was to be known as the juvenile probation officer, an official position even to this day. Many modern metropolitan police departments have special units to deal with juveniles exclusively; other police forces cooperate with county probation workers. In smaller communities, the same police who sometimes shoot it out with major criminals also investigate vandalism by roving gangs of youths. Wolcott indicates that the police regulated delinquency in the streets through their arrest powers and discretion to bring juveniles in the system for a 50-year period (1890–1940) in Chicago, Detroit and Los Angeles.[3]

Some analysts would suggest that this discretionary authority still exists. For example, the Midvale (Utah) Police Department has established the following policy for officers dealing with juveniles in enforcement and custody situations:

> This agency's interests concerning juvenile offenders reflect the interest of the community to prevent juvenile delinquency. This agency expects all members to handle juveniles consistent with state laws and common sense. The best interest of the community may dictate a limited application of arrest powers regarding juveniles and officers may handle errant juveniles informally in certain instances.[4]

Here, the broad powers and authority that the police bring to the situation are apparent. Flexibility and discretion are also highlighted. The officer must assess the situation and use the method that is most appropriate to the individual case.

POLICE: THE FIRST CONTACT WITH THE SYSTEM

A youth's first contact with the police is the most important contact they may ever have with the juvenile justice system. The way in which the police treat them initially will have a decided influence on their perception and impression of both the juvenile and adult justice systems.

The police determine whether youths become further involved with the juvenile justice system. In many cases, police make what is referred to as "on-the-spot" adjustments, also known as **street corner justice**. These adjustments may take the form of a warning to the youth, a ride home in the police cruiser, or possibly a meeting with parents or guardians. Some readers of this text may have experienced on-the-spot adjustments firsthand when growing up. Consider for a moment whether your life would have been different had the police decided to refer the case to court for an adjudicatory hearing. Such police discretion is a valuable tool when used properly, but it can be open to abuse if not carefully monitored and supervised.

Generally, the first role of the police in dealing with juveniles is the *control function* of detection, investigation, and arrest.[5] However, we will also see that police departments have become increasingly concerned about their *prevention function*: involving the community in the solving problems and improving conditions that can lead to crime and delinquency.[6] Box 5.1 presents information on the effectiveness of one well-known police drug prevention program, (D.A.R.E.).

street corner justice When police make "on-the-spot" adjustments when interacting with youth on the street

---

BOX 5.1 **DRUG ABUSE RESISTANCE EDUCATION**

Police departments have focused on prevention methods as well as diversion to combat delinquency and the problems that promote it. In 1983, the Los Angeles Police Department and the Los Angeles Unified School District created a substance abuse prevention program for grades kindergarten through twelve. The Drug Abuse Resistance Education (D.A.R.E.) program features a core curriculum of seventeen hour-long lessons that were offered once a week to fifth and sixth graders. The curriculum emphasizes the following:

- Acquiring the knowledge and skills to recognize and resist peer pressure to experiment with tobacco, alcohol, and other drugs;
- Enhancing self-esteem;
- Learning assertiveness techniques;
- Learning about positive alternatives to substance abuse;
- Learning anger management and conflict resolution skills;
- Developing risk assessment and decision-making skills;
- Reducing violence;
- Building interpersonal and communication skills; and
- Resisting gang involvement.

Typically, the program specifically featured the use of a uniformed law enforcement officer as well as a certified teacher in the classroom. The officers were trained in the use of the D.A.R.E. curriculum. Their presence also provided a positive role model for students. From its California roots, the program became a national sensation. More than 75 percent of America's school districts have adopted the program.

Initially, official assessments of the program were positive. In July 1993, a Gallup poll of more than 2,000 D.A.R.E. students revealed that 90 percent of them believed that the program helped them avoid drug and alcohol abuse, and increase their self-esteem and ability to deal with peer group pressure. They also reported that they had used one or two of the avoidance techniques taught by their D.A.R.E. officers. Another survey sponsored by the National Institute of Justice highlighted positive attitudes held by D.A.R.E. graduates and school officials. Program support, user satisfaction, and teacher involvement were reported as strong. These results cut across racial lines, and respondents believed that D.A.R.E. was better than other substance abuse programs that they had encountered.

However, as noted in the Maryland study, scientific assessments of the program reported mostly negative results. Harmon evaluated the impact of a South Carolina D.A.R.E. program. She compared the beliefs, commitments, and attitudes and reported drug use of 341 D.A.R.E. fifth graders with that of 367 non- D.A.R.E. students and reported positive results. Program participation was associated with lower alcohol use in the last year of the program, higher beliefs in prosocial norms, less association with drug-using peers, more positive peer associations, increased attitudes against substance abuse, and greater assertiveness to peer pressure. However, there were no significant differences between the groups for cigarette, tobacco, or marijuana use; frequency of any drug use during the past month; attitudes about the police; coping strategies; attachment and commitment to school; rebellious behavior; and self-esteem.

Similarly, Rosenbaum and Harmon conducted a sophisticated study of the D.A.R.E. program in Los Angeles. A sample of 1,584 students completed questionnaires in February 1991 and 1992. The researchers determined that D.A.R.E. had no statistically significant overall impact on students' use of alcohol or cigarettes approximately one year after completion of the program. It did register a positive effect on student susceptibility to media portrayals of beer drinking. However, interaction effects between D.A.R.E. participation and other factors (e.g., metropolitan status) did suggest that program effectiveness varied across subgroups of the targeted population. However, the results of this study indicate that the effect of D.A.R.E. was minor and limited to certain groups of students.

A study based in Kokomo, Indiana, found that D.A.R.E. failed to register significant differences in drug-use behaviors or attitudes between 288 high school seniors who participated in the program as seventh graders and 335 nonparticipating seniors. Focus group interviews with six seniors confirmed these findings. The authors concluded that D.A.R.E. is a form of "symbolic politics," supported by direct and indirect stakeholders, embedded in a complex and potent organizational support structure that accounts for its continued popularity, despite negative evaluation results.

A review of eight methodologically sound D.A.R.E. program evaluations determined that the effect of the program was substantially smaller than that for other programs that featured social and general competencies and interactive teaching strategies. The conclusion was that the short-term effectiveness of D.A.R.E. in reducing or preventing drug abuse is small and less than that registered by interactive prevention programs.

Kochis examined the impact of D.A.R.E. in a suburban New Jersey township. She tracked the behavior of fifty students, including those who did and did not take part in the program. She found that a total of twelve criminal offenses were officially recorded by either group. Eleven of these offenses were committed by five males in the experimental

(continued)

group. Most of the offenses were property crimes. Thirteen of the experimental subjects and fifteen members of the control group experienced some form of school discipline. The results indicate that programs like D.A.R.E. must be specifically targeted for appropriate juveniles.

Another D.A.R.E. evaluation used a complex design to study 10,000 students from 440 classrooms across the nation and determined that participation led to increased self-esteem, stronger institutional bonds, and less endorsement of risky behavior. Lower self-esteem and weaker institutional bonds weakened the effects of D.A.R.E.

Sigler and Talley examined data from a 1990 field experiment of the D.A.R.E. program in Los Alamos, New Mexico. The program consisted of seventeen lessons in the sixth-grade curriculum. Half of the schools in the district initiated D.A.R.E., and a survey was administered to all seventh graders. The attitudinal findings were positive. Students who completed D.A.R.E. had stronger drug-use avoidance attributes than students who did not complete the program. This impact was retained by the D.A.R.E. graduates one year after program completion. However, the D.A.R.E. graduates did not have lower rates of self-reported drug abuse than the members of two control groups.

Dukes, Ullman and Stein also examined the long-term effectiveness of the program. They surveyed ninth grade students who participated in the program in the sixth grade as well as others who had not participated. They found no differences between these two groups regarding concepts promoted by the program (including self-esteem, resistance to peer pressure, delay of experimentation with drugs and drug use).

Overall, the research has considered several different goals of the D.A.R.E. program (positive attitudes toward police, increasing attitudes toward drug abuse) as well as drug and alcohol use. The majority of it concludes that the D.A.R.E. programs in different states have failed to register long-term impact on youths. In fact, one juvenile expert, Richard J. Lundman, recommends that D.A.R.E. be abandoned because it produces only short-term effects that disappear with the passage of time and fails to address the known causes of delinquency. Still, the D.A.R.E. program is immensely popular and its reputation is intact. In fact, some studies indicate that D.A.R.E. is more effective when combined with other prevention activities (Just Say No Clubs, Red Ribbon Week) and with community policing in general.

Sources: Richard J. Lundman, *Prevention and Control of Juvenile Delinquency* (New York: Oxford University Press, 2001), p. 67; Bureau of Justice Assistance, *Fact Sheet: Drug Abuse Resistance Education (D.A.R.E.)* (Washington, D.C.: U.S. Department of Justice, 1995), p. 1; D.A.R.E. America Web site, D.A.R.E. Scientific Advisory Board—FAQs, "Background," www.dare.com; Harold K. Becker, Michael W. Agopian, and Sandy Yeh, "Impact Evaluation of Drug Abuse Resistance Education (DARE)," *Journal of Drug Education,* Vol. 24 (1992), pp. 293–291; M. A. Harmon, "Reducing the Risk of Drug Involvement among Early Adolescents: An Evaluation of Drug Abuse Resistance Education (D.A.R.E.)," *Evaluation Review,* Vol. 17 (1993), pp. 221–239; E. Wysong, R. Aniskiewicz, and D. Wright, "Truth and D.A.R.E.: Tracking Drug Education to Graduation and as Symbolic Politics," *Social Problems,* Vol. 41 (1994), pp. 448–472; R. L. Dukes, J. B. Ullman, and J. A. Stein, "An Evaluation of D.A.R.E. (Drug Abuse Resistance Education) Using a Solomon Four-Group Design with Latent Variables," *Evaluation Review,* Vol. 19 (1995), pp. 409–435; Richard T. Sigler and G. B. Talley, "Drug Abuse Resistance Education Program Effectiveness," *American Journal of Police,* Vol. 14 (1995), pp. 111–121; D. S. Kochis, "The Effectiveness of Project D.A.R.E.: Does It Work?" *Journal of Alcohol and Drug Education,* Vol. 40 (1995), pp. 40–47; Dennis P. Rosenbaum and Gail S. Hanson, "Assessing the Effects of School-Based Drug Education: A Six-Year Multilevel Analysis of Project D.A.R.E.," *Journal of Research in Crime and Delinquency,* Vol. 35 (1998), pp. 381–412; Donald R. Lynam, Richard Milich, Rick Zimmerman, et al., "Project DARE: No Effects at a 10-year Follow Up," *Journal of Consulting and Clinical Psychology,* Vol. 67 (1999), pp. 590–593; Joseph F. Donnemeyer and Russell R. Davis, "Cumulative Effects of Prevention Education on Substance Use among 11th Grade Students in Ohio," *Journal of School Health,* Vol. 68 (1998), pp. 151–158; David L. Carter, *Community Policing and DARE: A Practitioner's Perspective* (Washington, DC: Bureau of Justice Assistance, 1995).

Detection

Detection of a crime or response to a complaint will usually lead to an investigation by the police and may result in an arrest. Detection is often left to persons or agencies outside the police department. Even today, only the larger or more sophisticated forces have juvenile officers out on the streets. When police are assigned to a specific neighborhood and know that neighborhood, its people, its problems, and its resources, they become effective forces in the detection and deterrence of delinquency or abuse. When police officers are aware that a delinquent act may have been committed, they find themselves in the role of investigators.

Investigation

During the investigation of a delinquent act the suspects, if any, may be held in detention, released to parents, or some other disposition. It is therefore extremely important that the police investigate the act as thoroughly as possible so that the youth might not be falsely labeled as a delinquent.

In the course of interviewing the suspect, witnesses, and other parties who are involved, the police face a crucial test of their effectiveness in the community. Often they come into a hostile situation in which all concerned distrust the police. This attitude is especially prevalent in traditionally high-crime and low-income areas.

The officer must learn as much about the alleged offense or abuse as possible in the shortest time possible. Interviewing is more art than

Police Officer Talking to a Group of Gang Members

science and often must be learned only by experience. The officer must be flexible. For example, interviewing a 16-year-old girl picked up for countless crimes and prostitution and who is wanted on a drug charge will not be, and should not be, the same as interviewing a 10-year-old girl who got caught stealing candy bars.

In questioning suspects in criminal cases, several restrictions have been placed on the police. Whether these restrictions provide safeguards against overzealousness or whether they are well meaning but unrealistic erosion of necessary police authority is open to debate. Nonetheless, the practical result is that the effectiveness of interrogations as a police technique is seriously curtailed in many cases, especially with suspects who are, in fact, guilty. These few suspects have learned to rely on these restrictions for protection from punishment, knowing full well that if they cannot be interviewed adequately, this manner of proving guilt is denied the police. Moreover, the innocent are denied opportunity to prove their innocence without being formally charged. The people, not the police are the ultimate victims of these restrictions. In general, the police do not seek the privilege of denying suspects their rights, but they do believe that some balance between rights and cooperative responsibilities must be achieved in the public interest.

If the interview is successful, the police will usually have sufficient proof of a suspect's guilt or innocence. If there was no clear suspect at the onset of the investigation, well-conducted interviews will often provide one. Interviewing may not be the most important cog in the investigatory wheel; furthermore, it is not always feasible or successful. Many delinquent acts have no witnesses at all, or at least none that will cooperate. In such cases, investigatory techniques (piecing together clues, fingerprints, and physical evidence) must come into play.

The police may take juveniles into custody if probable cause is present. The requirement of probable cause exists for both arrests and warrants. Although many states permit juveniles to be taken into custody for their own protection and well-being, such arrests are intended to be a protective, rather than punitive, form of detention. They are also not intended to avoid the traditional limits placed on arrest powers by the U.S. Constitution.[7] The Supreme Court has held that isolation of a juvenile for prolonged periods may lead to confessions that are inadmissible in court.[8]

One example is how status offenders (such as runaways) should be handled. The courts have emphasized that the broad jurisdictional power enjoyed by the police should neither be abused nor be used as a method to circumvent constitutional rights when a youth is taken into custody for what amounts to a criminal offense.[9] Typically, state statutes require that juveniles be treated in a special manner. For example, parents, a probation officer, or the juvenile court should be notified at the apprehension of the juvenile. In Alabama, the state court ruled that a juvenile's request to have his grandmother present during questioning was the same as a request to have a lawyer present.[10]

Questioning and arresting juveniles presents special problems to the police. In *Haley v. Ohio*, the courts stated, in considering whether a juvenile's statements are voluntary, that the length of questioning, the child's age, the time of day or night of questioning, whether the child was fed and allowed to rest, and whether the child was allowed child's rights are all extremely important factors.[11]

One of the best tests of a child's rights is whether the child has been treated with "**fundamental fairness**." Factors to be considered by the police in making this decision . . . in addition to the age of the child . . . are: apparent intelligence and all-around maturity, experience or lack of experience in such situations involving the police, the seriousness of the violation suspected of having been committed, and the extent of continuing danger to society in the situation. Even when the police decide that the child is mature enough to make these decisions every effort should be made to notify parents at the earliest possible moment so that they can furnish their support and advice.[12]

fundamental fairness The test of a juvenile's rights when considering whether the juvenile's statements were voluntary

The concept of fundamental fairness varies in significance and definition according to different jurisdictions. Police administrators should seek the counsel of legal advisors on what the law is and how it is interpreted in the local jurisdiction before a youth is questioned, searched, or arrested.[13]

Arrest

Assuming that the investigation does turn up a suspect, the next step is confrontation and/or arresting the suspected offender. Here, too, the conduct of the police weighs heavily on the attitudes of the youth, his or her peer group, and the community. Citizen cooperation is extremely important to the police in all their dealings with the young. Many times the police, with citizen cooperation and consent, are able to waive legal guidelines, such as search warrants. Citizen cooperation saves time and money and should be encouraged. As adults, these citizens have the right to waive legal proceedings on the behalf of juveniles because they are considered mature persons and to understand what they are doing. However, research on the role of parents and guardians in juvenile custodial interrogations suggests that attorneys have more ability to determine when a youth's waiver to testify is knowing, voluntary, and intelligent.[14]

One aspect of the arrest process is the search of the alleged offender and the seizure of evidence pursuant to arrest. Basically, the courts have ruled that the Fourth Amendment is applicable to juvenile arrest proceedings and that the exclusionary rule (prohibiting the government's use of illegally obtained evidence) is applicable.[15] Basically, a "warrantless" search is justified only when (1) the search is incident to lawful arrest, (2) an on-the-street "stop and frisk" occurs, (3) the officer obtains the consent of the person searched, and (4) it is necessary to prevent the destruction or removal of vital evidence.[16]

On-the-street stops of persons by the police can involve a restricted privilege to search without a warrant provided that there is a "reasonable suspicion" linking this person to a crime. Such searches are justified by the need to protect the arresting officer and the public from any weapons involved in the crime. This right is an extension of *Terry v. Ohio*.[17] It has been extended in juvenile cases to cover situations in which the police have a reasonable suspicion that the youth has committed a crime. However, the police cannot stop and frisk a juvenile suspect simply because he or she is in an area where crime has been committed.[18] Here again, the police must consider the "totality of circumstances" to detain juveniles when they suspect that a crime has occurred.[19]

Searches and seizures involving juveniles and school officials enjoy a certain freedom from the legal restrictions placed upon the police. The courts have often ruled that a school official (as a private person, not an officer of the government and not subject to the Fourth Amendment)

Students Arrested Outside of School

usually acts *in loco parentis* and has a special duty to maintain conditions of safety and discipline—a standard that is much broader than the one applied to the police.[20] In 1985, the U.S. Supreme Court ruled that school authorities need only a "reasonable suspicion" that their search will disclose evidence that a student broke the law or violated school rules. The Court held that such searches must be reasonably related to their objectives and not excessively intrusive in light of the age and sex of the student and the nature of the infraction.[21]

In *Miranda v. Arizona* (384 U.S. 436), the court ruled that a suspect must be advised of his or her rights (e.g., the right to remain silent) when in any way deprived of freedom of movement. California incorporated these requirements into its juvenile rules for arresting youths. Several other states have followed suit since then (see Box 5.2).

However, even the *Miranda* ruling does not guarantee that, when read his or her rights, a juvenile knows what they mean. Because many authorities consider a child's problem to be a family problem, one of the best safeguards of a child's rights is to have the parents present at all police proceedings.

Must officers administer Miranda warnings to juveniles? Should they be modified for juveniles? How? Holtz tested a simplified version of the Miranda warning with 25 juveniles taken into custody at the Atlantic City, New Jersey, Police Juvenile Bureau. He compiled a "Youth Rights Form" that he then sent to twenty law enforcement agencies. Their responses noted that the use of such a form would bolster the admissibility of a juvenile confession.[22]

Lawrence interviewed forty-five youths in a juvenile court, forty of their parents, thirty-six attorneys, and twenty-eight probation officers. He reported that probation officers believed that they were the primary legal advisors for juveniles. The juveniles acknowledged that they had a poor understanding of their legal rights. More than one-fourth did not remember

---

BOX 5.2 **MIRANDA WARNINGS**

1. You have the right to remain silent.
2. Any statements you make may be used as evidence against you in a criminal trial.
3. You have the right to consult with counsel and to have counsel present with you during questioning. You may retain counsel at your own expense or counsel will be appointed for you at no expense to you.

Even if you decide to answer questions now without having counsel present, you may stop answering questions at any time. Also, you may request counsel at any time during the questioning.

or did not understand the police Miranda warning. As a result, their ability to make an intelligent, informed waiver of their rights is questionable.[23]

This is a crucial issue. Can a juvenile make a knowing waiver of his or her rights without aid of some kind? The general rule established by the courts is that a minor has the capacity to make a voluntary confession without the presence or consent of counsel or other responsible adult and that the "totality of circumstances" surrounding the admission including the following:[24]

- Age of the accused,
- Education of the accused,
- Knowledge of the accused of both the substance of the charge and the nature of his or her rights to consult with an attorney and remain silent,
- Whether the juvenile was held incommunicado or was allowed to consult with relatives,
- Whether interrogation was held before or after the filing of formal charges,
- Methods of interrogation,
- Length of the interrogation, and
- Whether the accused had repudiated an extrajudicial statement given at a later date.[25]

Thus, a juvenile is legally capable of waiving his or her rights under the Fourth, Fifth, or Sixth Amendments if these conditions are met and the youth is able to comprehend the meaning and possible effect of any statements given to the police.

Some other requirements should be followed to ensure the admissibility of juvenile statements and confessions. First, due to the "special vulnerability of children in the hands of the police," a statement made by a juvenile may not be used in juvenile court if it has been involuntarily given. Second, in some jurisdictions, confessions are inadmissible if the arresting officer fails to follow the statutory directives for making a special disposition of a juvenile case. Third, the custodial confession of a juvenile produced from an interrogation may not be used in juvenile court unless the required Miranda warnings have been given. The Miranda warnings should also be given to the parents of the juvenile, so that they may also protect the juvenile's Fifth Amendment rights. It may be that a youth is able to waive the protection against self-incrimination only after a parent or guardian has offered some guidance on the subject.[26] Scott-Hayward suggests that police procedures for interrogating juveniles be changed to include videotaping of all interrogations to ensure that juveniles fully understand their rights under *Miranda*.[27]

The U.S. Supreme Court decision in the case of *Fare v. Michael C.* gives us some indication of the ability of a juvenile to waive his or her rights. This case involved a murder in which the juvenile suspect, a person with a long juvenile history (he had been on probation since 12 years of age), made incriminating statements after asking to meet with his probation officer. Therefore, the central issue in the case was this: Is a juvenile's request, made while undergoing custodial interrogation, to see his probation officer per se an invocation of the juvenile's Fifth Amendment rights under *Miranda*? The Court ruled that a probation officer is not necessary for the protection of the legal rights of the accused and that such an extension would impose burdens associated with the rule of *Miranda* on the juvenile justice system and the police without serving the interests that the rule was simultaneously designed to protect. In addition, the Court ruled that the request by the juvenile to speak with his probation officer did not constitute a request to remain silent, directing the police officers to stop the interrogation process. Therefore, the Court ruled that the statements made by the accused were admissible in court.[28]

Lower court rulings have also addressed *Miranda* issues with juveniles. In *United States v. Bernard S.*, the court ruled that despite language difficulties, statements made by a juvenile are admissible as long as a waiver of rights is given by the juvenile.[29] The same standard has been applied to statements made by juveniles in the absence of their parents.[30] However, it is clear that police interrogation must cease when a juvenile invokes the right to remain silent.[31] Research by Feld indicates that the police used the same interrogation tactics on juveniles that they did on adults. The majority of the juveniles (about 80 percent of the subjects) that he observed waived their Miranda rights and provided incriminating evidence to the police.[32]

Finally, juveniles possess some specific protections with regard to pretrial identification and prehearing detention and release. In lineups, juveniles have the same right to counsel as adults.[33] In many states, the fingerprinting and photographing of juveniles during the booking process are subject to stringent restrictions because juveniles are viewed with care and are thought to need protection against a criminal record. Moreover, juveniles have the same rights as adults regarding bail and "the statutory duty to notify the child's parents that he (or she) has been taken into custody is fairly typical."[34]

It is clear that juveniles possess the same rights as adults in the police process and that they enjoy some additional protections. Again, we see that the police are expected to treat and handle juveniles in a special manner, giving specific attention to their problems in an attempt to protect them from harm—from either their environment or the juvenile justice system itself.

GUIDELINES FOR POLICE DISPOSITION: THE POWER OF DISCRETION

Regardless of whether a child is arrested or taken into custody, another role of the police is brought into play: They act as judge, jury, and executioner. As pointed out previously, many youthful offenders never enter the juvenile justice system. They are released, reprimanded, or punished before the court ever enters into their lives. The old story of a child picked up in a rich neighborhood, driven home to parents, and given a stern weekend in detention is not at all unrealistic. Different police practices in different neighborhoods are undeniable and often necessary. Large inner-city police forces often do not have the personnel to deal with youths in any other way than to arrest them and get them off the streets. In smaller or well-to-do communities where crime rates are lower, the police are often more understanding and lenient toward disruptive or delinquent youths. Thus, there is a developing and serious need for clear and realistic guidelines for police dispositions.

In any situation, the course of action the police may choose may vary considerably among departments and among individual officers. It is governed to some extent by departmental practice, either explicitly enunciated or tacitly understood. Some well-thought-out and recommended guidelines follow:

- Police should exercise, whenever practical, every alternative at their disposal before applying for a petition to the court. To do this they must know agencies other than the court to which they can and should make referrals.

- If on-the-spot adjustments are used, they should be used equally, regardless of the juvenile's skin color, which part of town he or she comes from, or who the parents are.

- Although diversion from formal court procedures is desired, police should not withhold evidence or other relevant facts involving a case from the courts.

- Police should be trained and educated so as to judge the juveniles they are confronting more effectively. They should be able to evaluate the effect of their disposition decisions. A sad-eyed girl running a long con story may require something stronger than a warning, whereas a boy who ran away from home because his father beat him continuously may not benefit from being driven back to the source of his problem.

- Police should make periodic checks on those they have diverted. Continuous warnings do the youth no more good than do continuous harassment and arrest. The power of helpful discretion must be brought to bear.

These guidelines are presented to give the student an idea of the specific areas that should be considered. For every police administrator, flexibility in applying guidelines and policies used by officers are necessary in dealing with juveniles in their specific environment.

Again, the Midvale, Utah, Police Department provides some specific examples of police procedures regarding juvenile matters. For example, they provide for taking a child into custody if the following conditions exist:

- There is a legal detention order.
- Custody is necessary for the safety of the child or if the child seriously endangers others.
- Custody is necessary to ensure the child's appearance in court.
- The child has committed a felony.
- The child had committed a misdemeanor in the officer's presence.
- The child is a runaway.
- The child is a truant.[35]

Such policies are difficult to evolve; indeed, in many instances, policies cannot be made specific enough to be helpful without being too rigid to accommodate the vast variety of street situations. Nevertheless, it is important that, wherever possible, guidelines be formulated for the police in their dealings with juveniles. Without specific, standardized, and universal guidelines, it is extremely difficult for both the police and the citizenry to know when an adequate job is being done. What may be more reasonable, practical, and of course more helpful is that practices be at least standard within each precinct or department.

Guidelines, when they are formulated, must meet the local needs and be flexible enough to allow for individual treatment of each case. In most cases, all laws that local police departments become involved with are bound to guidelines made by the state legislature or the federal courts. This does not necessarily mean that any nice, neat, clear, and understandable guidelines actually exist. For this very reason, police departments have or should develop their own practices and guidelines for dealing with juveniles.

The Decision to Arrest

As the gatekeepers of the juvenile justice system, the police control access of juveniles. They determine whether the juvenile will enter the system at all and at what point or if they will be diverted. Of course, these decisions are significant. If they are racially biased in any way, minority youth may be more at risk later during the correctional processing stages.[36]

Studies of police arrests of juveniles reveal the following factors (either alone or in combination) that affect decision making:

- Demeanor: Police view demeanor as a predictor of future behavior. Hostile or fawningly respectful behavior arouses both action and suspicion.
- Seriousness of the offense: Incidents of minor legal significance are more likely to be diverted.
- Group offenses: Group offenses are treated as an obvious indicator of gang activity. This factor is known as "the group hazard hypothesis."[37]
- Victim priorities: If the victim calls for action, the police are more likely to oblige them.
- Race and socioeconomic status.
- Sex: In general, males are more likely to be arrested for violent and drug offenses, and females for status offenses.[38] As female involvement in more serious offenses changes, so will the arrest rate.[39]

Furthermore, these variables are likely to be correlated. For example, juveniles in a group may be more likely to "act out" and talk back to the police. Here, the group action and demeanor may combine to make arrest more likely. Minority groups are overrepresented among the poor. The poor are more likely to be arrested. Poor, minority-group victims are more likely to complain and demand action from the police. Thus, evidence of racial discrimination is difficult to determine absolutely, but several studies of police arrest practices have documented its existence.[40] There is little question that the police encounters with juvenile suspects are treated differently from those with adults. Factors such as disrespect for officers and adolescent males who are out late at night acting "suspicious" have been determined to influence the decision to arrest.[41]

BOX 5.3 **JUVENILE CURFEW PROGRAMS**

Curfews for juveniles have been touted as a method of controlling juvenile crime and preventing juvenile victimization. It is not a new or novel idea. In the United States, curfews have been imposed for more than a century. From the 1890s to during World War II, curfews were used in large cities to decrease crime among immigrant youth and to help parents busily engaged in the war effort. As a result of a perceived increase in juvenile crime, they have recently been proposed in several cities. For example, Charlottesville, Virginia, adopted a curfew ordinance in 1996 that had the following goals:

- To promote the general welfare and protect the general public through the reduction of juvenile violence and crime within the city;

- To promote the safety and well-being of the city's youngest citizens, persons under the age of 17 years, whose inexperience renders them particularly vulnerable to becoming participants in unlawful activities, especially unlawful drug activities, and to being victimized by older perpetrators of crime; and

- To foster and strengthen parental responsibility for children.

To generate support for this program, the Charlottesville Police Department used its school resource officers to inform students and school personnel about its operations.

Citing this program, Ward offers the following suggestions on how juvenile curfews should be implemented:

- Create a dedicated curfew center or using recreation centers and churches to house curfew violators;

- Staff these centers with social service professionals and community volunteers;

- Offer referrals to social service providers and counseling classes for juvenile violators and their families;

- Establish procedures such as fines, counseling, or community service for repeat offenders;

- Develop recreation, employment, anti-drug, and anti-gang programs; and

- Provide hotlines for follow-up services and crisis intervention.

He also recommends that the police develop consistent curfew enforcement policies that are known to parents and juveniles. It should include an accurate record-keeping information system that will facilitate follow-up with affected citizens. Ward also noted that the program led to a dramatic decrease in the number of juveniles on the street and that all parties associated with the program believed that the curfew was implemented properly. However, the research evidence regarding the effectiveness of juvenile curfews in reducing crime is mixed.

- In Vernon, Connecticut, researchers noted that the pattern of curfew stops, arrests, and the timing of Part I (Index) crime changes could not be attributed to enforcement of the nighttime curfew.

- In New Orleans, Louisiana, victimizations of both adults and juveniles and juvenile arrests during curfew hours did not decrease significantly following program implementation. There was some evidence of displacement by time. During noncurfew hours, some victimization increased significantly. Yet, interviews with juveniles revealed that although they did not know the full extent of the curfew law, they disobeyed it. Although they complained about unfair police practices, juveniles supported the curfew because they believed it would promote safety—something they desire from both the police and their parents.

- An early study of the impact of a curfew on crime in Detroit, Michigan (1976), also reported evidence of displacement. Although the curfew suppressed juvenile crime, some juvenile criminal activity simply moved to earlier hours of the day.

- A study of the impact of a curfew on crime in Washington, D.C. (Cole, 2003), found no difference in the total juvenile arrests before and after implementation of the ordinance.

- On a more positive note, a study of fifty-seven major American cities considered the impact of curfew laws on homicides (from 1976 to 1995) and juvenile arrests for other crimes (from 1985 to 1995). Following the passage of curfew laws, county (or rural) areas registered decreases in burglary, larceny, and simple assault. Homicide and other crime rates and did not change.

- The use of a curfew and police saturation patrol had an effect on juvenile crime in Dallas and Corpus Christi, Texas.

(continued)

Overall, this experience with curfews again confirms the conclusion that juvenile crime is immune to a quick-fix approach.

Consistent with the community policing model, police may wish to assume a partnership role with other agencies. The long-term effect of a Chicago-based program that stressed preschool involvement and dropout prevention was particularly promising. Preschool participation was linked to lower rates of juvenile arrests (including violent crimes) and lower rates of school dropout. Acting in conjunction with other agencies, police in San Diego, California, helped reduce rearrest rates for juveniles involved in a program that stressed graduated sanctions ranging from informal handling to probation and restitution.

Sources: Janice Ahmad, Katherine Bennett and Jim Ruiz, "Juvenile Curfews." In Craig Hemmens (ed.), *Current Legal Issues in Criminal Justice* pp. 223–238 (Belmont, CA: Roxbury, 2007); A. J. Bannister, D. L. Carter, and J. Schafer, "A National Police Survey on the Use of Juvenile Curfews," *Journal of Criminal Justice*, Vol. 29 (2003), pp. 233–240; D. Cole, "The Effect of a Curfew Law on Juvenile Crime in Washington, DC," *American Journal of Criminal Justice*, Vol. 27 (2003), pp. 217–232; E. J. Fritsch, T. J. Caeti, and R. W. Taylor, "Gang Suppression through Saturation Patrol and Aggressive Curfew and Truancy Enforcement: A Quasi-Experimental Test of the Dallas Anti-Gang Initiative." In S. H. Decker (ed.), *Policing Gangs and Youth Violence*, pp. 267–284 (Belmont, CA: Thomson Wadsworth, 2003); J. Richard Ward, Jr., "Implementing Juvenile Curfew Programs," *FBI Law Enforcement Bulletin* www.fbi.gov.; Mike A. Males, "Vernon, Connecticut's Juvenile Curfew: The Circumstances of Youths Cited and Effects on Crime," *Criminal Justice Policy Review*, Vol. 11 (2000), pp. 254–267; K. Michael Reynolds, Ruth Seydlitz, and Pamela Jenkins, "Do Juvenile Curfew Laws Work? A Time-Series Analysis of the New Orleans Law," *Justice Quarterly*, Vol. 17 (2000), pp. 205–230; K. Michael Reynolds, William Ruefle, Pamela Jenkins, et al., "Contradictions and Consensus: Youths Speak Out about Juvenile Curfews," *Journal of Crime and Justice*, Vol. 22 (1999), pp. 171–192; A. Lee Hunt and Ken Weiner, "The Impact of a Juvenile Curfew: Suppression and Displacement in Patterns of Juvenile Offenses," *Journal of Police Science and Administration*, Vol. 5 (1977), pp. 407–412; David McDowall, Colin Loftin, and Brian Wiersema, "The Impact of Youth Curfew Laws on Juvenile Crime Rates," *Crime and Delinquency*, Vol. 46 (2000), pp. 76–91; Arthur J. Reynolds, Judy A. Temple, Dylan L. Robertson, et al., "Long-Term Effects of an Early Childhood Intervention on Educational Achievement and Juvenile Arrest: A 15-Year Follow-Up of Low-Income Children in Public Schools." *Journal of the American Medical Association*, Vol. 285 (2001), pp. 2339–2346; Susan Pennell, Christine Curtis, and Dennis C. Scheck, "Controlling Juvenile Delinquency: An Evaluation of an Interagency Strategy," *Crime and Delinquency*, Vol. 36 (1990), pp. 257–275.

POLICE AND THE NEGLECTED OR ABUSED CHILD

Thus far, this discussion has focused mainly between police and delinquent youths. However, there are several types of children/juveniles who come under the purview of the police.

Childhood is a reasonably happy and secure time for most children; they have parents or relatives who love them, provide for them, protect them, and give them a sense of security. But there are many children whose childhood has been lost or scarred by parents who fail them altogether or who inadequately meet their basic needs. These children are called **neglected**. They come from all kinds of homes and income strata. Rich children can be as easily considered neglected as those who are poor.

Typically, police become involved in neglect or abuse cases when a report is filed. Then, an immediate investigation is in order, for the

neglected Children whose parents fail them or whose parents inadequately meet their basic needs

protection and safety of the youth(s) in question. The following guidelines are helpful:

- The investigating officer shall make all attempts to locate and conduct an interview with the abused child or juvenile as soon as possible.
- In cases involving severe injuries to a child, medical attention should be sought for the child immediately.
- Attempts shall be made by the investigating officer to identify and locate all additional victims, witnesses, and suspects in abuse cases.
- The investigating officer shall attempt to identify and secure any physical evidence.[42]

Police must make sure that the alleged neglect or abuse actually does exist when handling a case of this nature. Their methods of investigation and interview should be much the same as when responding to delinquency cases. An additional tool useful to police is the photograph or videotape; it will help to substantiate the condition of the child or his or her home at the time contact is made.

In dependent neglect cases it is usually persons other than the parents who make the complaint. As a result, it can often be difficult for the police to gain the cooperation of the parents in their investigation. The investigating officer must be certain to find out if the reported neglect or abuse is an isolated incident or only one event in a history of such occurrences.

The officer should make an immediate assessment of the situation and determine if action to protect the child must be taken. Many answers to complaints from interested parties, schoolteachers, social workers, and so forth can be handled with a warning or reprimand to the parents. The officer may choose simply to inform the parents that any further complaints regarding the treatment of their children may result in a court appearance.

For example, the Cicero, Illinois, Police Department defines an *abused minor* as "any minor under 18 years of age whose parent or immediate family member, person responsible for the minor's welfare, or any person residing in the same home or a paramour of the minor's parent

- Inflicts, causes or allows to be inflicted upon such minor physical injury which causes death, disfigurement, impairment or physical or emotional health, or loss or impairment of any bodily function;
- Creates a substantial risk of physical injury to such minor;
- Commits or allows to be committed an act or acts of torture;
- Inflicts excessive corporal punishment; or
- Whose environment is injurious to his or her welfare."[43]

On the basis of the officer's judgment, recommending professional counseling for the family may be advisable. Here, the officer's knowledge of community resources is vital. With the parent's cooperation and a referral to the appropriate source, the child may be saved the agony of further moral, mental, emotional, or physical punishment at his or her parent's hands.

Factors in Police Action

The following are factors that either alone or in combination require immediate police intervention:

battered child syndrome A disease that impacts children due to persistent physical abuse

- Evidence of the **battered child syndrome** and fear of recurring abuse by parents;
- Lack of appropriate adult supervision, discipline, and/or guidance;
- Lack of adequate physical care and/or protection from potentially harmful things or events;
- A parent's sexual exploitation of children, whether incestuous or for money (i.e., child pornography); and
- Failure to provide for the child's basic needs of food, clothing, and shelter appropriate to the climate in which the child lives.

Rumors and actual accounts of abuse of children at the hands of their parents or others are numerous. Police departments, courts, and social agencies have records and photographs on file that would turn anyone's stomach. The ways in which children are abused stand as an indictment of the inventiveness of humankind, ranging from boiling an infant alive on the stove to locking a 6-year-old in a box or closet for several years.

Alternatives in Police Action

Assuming that the situation warrants punishment of the parents or removal of the child from the home, what are the alternatives available to the police?

minors requiring authoritative intervention (MRAI) Juveniles who, depending on jurisdiction, meet criteria to be taken into custody until they can be served by a mandated crisis intervention agency

Just as laws dealing with delinquency varies from state to state, so, too, do laws and police procedures. For example, in Illinois, **minors requiring authoritative intervention (MRAI)** are defined as follows: Any minor under 18 years of age who

- is taken into limited custody;
- is absent from home without the consent of the minor's parent or guardian;
- is beyond the control of his or her parent, guardian, or custodian and in circumstances that constitute a substantial or immediate danger; or
- refuses to return home and whose parents cannot agree to placement after crisis intervention services have been tried.

Such juveniles may be taken into custody for up to six hours until they can be served by mandated crisis intervention agencies (including family preservation and family reunification). Officers must inform the juvenile of the reason for such custody and must make a good faith attempt to notify the parents or guardian(s) before the crisis intervention agency is contacted.[44]

Police are usually the ones who will take the child from his or her home. For example, procedures for the Cicero, Illinois. Police Department state that officers may (without a warrant) take into temporary custody a minor who (with **reasonable cause**) is believed to be neglected, abused, or dependent (adjudicated as a ward of the court); or suffering from any sickness or injury that requires care, medical treatment, or hospitalization when found on any street or public place. Police officers have the legal responsibility and authority to place an abused or neglected child in protective custody and remove the child from parents (or a harmful situation) only when the child's safety is endangered.[45]

reasonable cause Evidence that would lead a reasonable person to believe that action is needed (e.g., evidence of abuse that would allow for a juvenile to be taken into temporary custody)

Whenever possible, the police should consult with community social agencies when custody is required. Many communities have "shelters for kids," foster homes, and group homes. All too often, however, a neglected child will spend days or even months in a county jail cell. Such a situation stems from inadequate planning and coordination of community resources on the part of the community leaders.

Many parents are unaware that they may be financially liable for all or part of the costs incurred for housing, feeding, and clothing their children while they are in protective custody. In some cases, parents are liable in cases involving both delinquent and dependent neglected children, but the amount assessed is usually based on the parent's ability to pay.

The question of the police role in the handling of neglected or abused children is an old and complex one. The police and the child are usually part of the same community (except in the case of runaways), and the problems of kids in need of help are the problems of the community. Consequently, only when everyone becomes aware of this community problem and understands its nature will the thousands of abused and battered kids have a hope of being found, heard, and eventually helped. The police are the crucial first step in this process. Given the money, resources, and training, they can become, as an extension of those they serve in the communities, a more effective force.

THE PROMISE OF COMMUNITY POLICING

Community policing has become the dominant reform movement within policing. More of a theory than a specific plan of action, the idea of community policing is difficult to define. As a result, community policing has become mistakenly synonymous with certain tactics and

Police Officer with a Group of Children

methods. It is more than beat, foot, or bicycle patrols. It is and should be viewed as a philosophy and organizational strategy. It has specific applications to juveniles.[46]

Defining Community Policing

By its very title, community policing infers a partnership between the police, the neighborhoods, and the people they serve. This partnership is designed to improve the quality of life in the community through the introduction of strategies designed to enhance neighborhood solidarity and safety.[47] Under this model, the police and the community work together to offer solutions to serious social problems they face. This bond between the police and the community is encouraged, and officers are usually given time and authorization by their department to get to know the community's habits, wishes, and customs. The assumption and belief is that when the police can truly relate to a community, they can be in the position to offer creative responses to local problems.

Community policing is different from the traditional/professional model of policing, essentially because it demands that officers and their departments adopt proactive strategies and tactics to repress crime, fear, and disorder within local neighborhoods. In turn, community members are also expected take a proactive stance in helping the police and other government entities set policy. Through this exchange process, the citizens receive tangible input into setting organizational goals, objectives, and departmental values.

2. **Collaborate with social service agencies.**

3. **Develop joint protocols with foster care providers and group homes.** These facilities can provide shelter and permanent placement for juveniles, whereas the police typically cannot.

4. **Cross-train staff from multiple agencies.** It makes all providers more aware of the services available across the board for juvenile runaways as well as provides a clear understanding of the problems that runaways face.

5. **Share information.** Across agencies, information should be made available to all relevant parties.

6. **Assess risk.** A careful determination of the problems faced by each individual runaway will facilitate successful placement and treatment options.

Before They Run:

7. **Provide prevention materials when responding to calls for service.**

8. **Use respite care.** A temporary facility can provide a "cooling off" period for the runaway rather than use detention facilities.

9. **Use "Missing from Care" Forms.** These forms can provide the police with information to identify and help locate juveniles as well as determine the risk factors that they face.

10. **Determine whether absences are voluntary or involuntary.** This assessment will allow the police to respond to cases appropriately.

11. **Divert cases to a community-based organization.**

While They Are Absent from Home or Care:

12. **Refer Juveniles to Appropriate Social Service Providers.**

13. **Implement a Specialized Patrol to Deal with Runaways.**

14. **Provide safe locations for juveniles.**

15. **Use secure placement when appropriate.**

When or If They Return:

16. **Use transportation aides or free transportation services.** This will help the juveniles return home regardless of their ability to pay.

17. **Refer juveniles to aftercare services when needed.**

18. **Interview juveniles on their return.** This should be done by other persons to determine family problems and prevent future episodes.

Responses with Limited Effectiveness:

19. **Handling problems over the telephone.** Runaway cases are best dealt with in person.

20. **Confining juveniles in secure detention facilities.** These spots should be reserved for delinquents, rather than status offenders.

21. **Forcing juveniles to return home.**   It may expose them to the situation and risks that they fled to escape and avoid.

22. **Restricting privileges on return.**   Harsh punishment may make the problem worse. New and appropriate sanctions should be developed and proposed.

This listing considers the options available and appropriate responses to deal with juvenile runaways under the POP framework.

Community policing has the following implications for police work with juveniles:

1. The frequency of contact and level of intimacy should increase as a result of efforts to prevent and reduce opportunities for crime by greater presence in neighborhoods.

2. The already wide discretion exercised by police is expected to increase under POP as police are encouraged to place increased emphasis on solving underlying problems believed to cause crime, increase the proportion of officer activity directed at order maintenance, and work with neighborhoods in "community building" efforts.

3. Both problem solving and order maintenance activities are expected to result in more proactive efforts to engage citizens and more opportunities for police to participate in community life than has been the case under the professional model of policing.[53]

Thus, under community policing, the relationship between juveniles and the police should change considerably.

JUVENILE POLICE OPERATIONS

A national standard bearer, The Commission on Accreditation for Law Enforcement Agencies, sets the following standard for juvenile police operations:

When dealing with juveniles, law enforcement officers should always make use of the least coercive among reasonable alternatives, consistent with preserving public safety, order, and individual liberty. Generally speaking, law enforcement agencies have four sets of alternatives from which to choose when dealing with juveniles: they may release the offender and take no further action; they may divert the offender to any of a number of social service agencies; they may dispose of the case themselves; or they may (in the case of serious offenders) refer the youth to juvenile court (intake). Because a range of alternatives exists, agencies should establish guidelines and criteria for the use of each.[54]

Accordingly, Kenney and his colleagues have offered this list of the standard ways that a juvenile police unit can handle a case:

1. **Application for petition.**   A petition is filed when the circumstances of the case are such that only the juvenile court can reasonably be expected to safeguard the interests and welfare of society and the juvenile concerned. A petition means that the youth is subject to its jurisdiction and may be brought before the juvenile court.

2. **Transfer of case.**   Juvenile cases are transferred when another agency has jurisdiction, such as a probation department, state training school, or other law enforcement agency.

3. **Referral to other agencies.**   A referral is made when it is believed that the case in question should be investigated further and some rehabilitative program set in motion for the guidance and adjustment of the juvenile.

4. **Action suspended.**   In cases in which it seems that the parents and juvenile, alone and unaided, can effect a satisfactory adjustment, no further action need be taken.

5. **Insufficient evidence.**   When there is conflict in evidence or reasonable doubt as to the responsibility of the juvenile and the evidence is of such a nature as to preclude a determination of involvement, the juvenile should be released and no further action taken.

6. **Exoneration.**   When the investigation clearly indicates that a juvenile is not responsible for the delinquency charged, he or she should be released and exonerated, or cleared of all involvement.

7. **Voluntary police supervision.**   This form of disposition is employed when it is believed that the parents unaided are incapable of affecting the child's rehabilitation, but that the officer and the parent working cooperatively can assist the child to self-adjustment without the help of the juvenile court or probation department or other agency. This disposition consists of furnishing guidance and counsel to the juvenile with the consent and full cooperation of the parents. Without such acquiescence it is valueless.

8. **Proves to be adult.**   When investigation discloses that the true age of the person arrested as a juvenile to be over the juvenile court age limit, the charges shall be suspended and prosecution of the charge or charges handled as with an adult.

9. **Declared unfit.**   The juvenile officer may recommend in the application for petition to the juvenile court that the juvenile be

declared unfit for further consideration by the juvenile court and be remanded for trial under the general laws in the criminal court.

10. **Detention.**   Although at times detention may form a part of the treatment process, it is presumed to be protective in nature, never punitive. All detention not under the order of the courts is temporary in nature. A child must be held no longer than is reasonably necessary for effective placement or for being brought to the attention of the court.[55]

One of these standard methods, diversion, is particularly significant. Nationwide, police diversion programs vary regarding goals, screening, and services provided. One innovative example of diversion involving the police is the community conferencing program in Woodbury, Minnesota. Here, the police refer cases to the program. Again stressing the potential of community policing, this program emphasizes community involvement to hold offenders accountable and provide benefits directly to victims of juvenile crime.

family group conferencing
Model that many police diversion programs follow. The conference is aimed at resolving conflicts between all concerned parties (e.g., juveniles, parents, victims, community members).

The program follows the **family group conferencing** model from Australia. A specially trained person (either police officers or community volunteers) coordinates the program. They contact offenders, their parents, victims, and affected community members to explain the process and seek their voluntary participation. The conference is aimed at resolving the conflict between all concerned parties. They must decided who is the victim and how the harm caused can be set right, and attempt to prevent future victimization. Agreements are reached by a consensus of the participants and the community.

Offenders must complete agreements to complete the program successfully. Until then, prosecution is always an option. If they are successful, further involvement in the system and the creation of a juvenile record are avoided. The program is based on the beliefs that people most affected by a crime should resolve cases. It benefits the community by setting, maintaining, and enforcing norms of behavior and conduct through a partnership with the police. Moreover, the offender avoids stigma and is able to make amends constructively.

Through the year 2000, this program had conducted approximately fifty conferences per year. Approximately 82 percent of the cases assigned to conferencing are successfully completed. In the remaining cases, about half were settled in preconference stages, and half were sent to juvenile court. Only two cases resulted in a failed agreement. This program runs a restitution payment success rate of more than 95 percent compared with the court system rate of just over 50 percent. The overwhelming majority of persons involved in the process (more than 90 percent) were satisfied with the outcome of their case.[56] Overall, this program represents the potential of police–community partnerships to solve the problems of juvenile delinquency.

SUMMARY

Juveniles are neither exempt from the law nor immune from the enforcement of the law. They must answer for their deeds just like anyone else. Immaturity and youth are not excuses for theft, rape, murder, or vandalism. Just as police are not always permitted to use force when arresting someone just because he or she is an adult, police may not use force when arresting someone simply because he or she is a child.

Basically, there are no significant differences in police philosophy toward adults or juveniles. There are, however, various differences in the adaptations and application of that philosophy. These differences do not change basic police objectives, but they do affect the procedural methods used in handling a juvenile.

The similarity of police philosophy toward an adult criminal and juvenile criminal should not be misunderstood or misinterpreted. Police departments are genuinely concerned about rehabilitating juveniles who get into trouble with the law. Because of their acceptance of this growing public policy, police departments are more than ready and anxious to co-operate with other community agencies.

In the following chapter, we will go on to the juvenile court to examine how youths are processed through the system.

KEY TERMS

battered child syndrome	neglected
community policing	problem-oriented
family group conferencing	policing (POP)
fundamental fairness	reasonable cause
minors requiring authoritative intervention (MRAI)	street corner justice

DISCUSSION AND REVIEW QUESTIONS

1. What should a police officer do with a juvenile that he or she has taken into custody for committing a delinquent act?
2. How should an officer handle a child abuse or neglect case?
3. What role should the police officer have in a community program to prevent and control juvenile delinquency?

4. How do Dedel's POP suggestions deal with the problem of juvenile runaways?
5. What are the goals of juvenile curfews? What are the questions surrounding implementation and effectiveness?
6. What do the research results on the D.A.R.E. program mean for the continuation of this police prevention program?
7. What are the problems for the police in coping with juvenile crime? What suggestions can you make to help the police cope with this task more effectively?

VIDEO PROFILES

Calling the Police video profile in MyCrimeKit highlights formal and informal interactions between juveniles and officers. Discuss how these formal and informal interactions may or may not influence a juvenile's behavior. According to the officers, why are they called to deal with juveniles? What difficulties do parents face that lead them to call the police? Finally, describe the aims of these officers when they deal with juveniles.

Police Perspective video profile in MyCrimeKit shows interaction between law enforcement and juveniles. According to these officers, how are juveniles handled in comparison with adults? Do their answers correspond with the research on arrest decisions contained in this chapter? How do these officers decide how and when to give a juvenile a "break"? Finally, describe the goals of these officers when dealing with juveniles.

MYCRIMEKIT

mycrimekit™   Go to MyCrimeKit.com to explore the following study tools and resources specific to this chapter:

- Practice Quiz: Test your knowledge with multiple-choice, true-false, fill-in-the-blank, and essay questions.
- Flashcards: 20 flashcards to test your knowledge of the chapter's key terms.
- Web Quest: Review the Web sites of federal, state, and local law enforcement agencies to see if they have juvenile-related policies or jurisdiction.
- Web Links: Check out sites related to the content presented in this chapter.

ENDNOTES

1. Richard W. Kobetz, *The Police Role and Juvenile Delinquency* (Gaithersburg, MD: International Association of Chiefs of Police, 1971), p. 147.

2. Kobetz, *The Police Role and Juvenile Delinquency*, p. 148.

3. David Wolcott, "'The Cop Will Get You': The Police and Discretionary Juvenile Justice, 1890–1940," *Journal of Social History*, Vol. 35 (2001), pp. 349–371.

4. International Association of Chiefs of Police net, Document Display, Document #559103, "Juvenile Offenders," Midvale Police Department (2/11/2002) www.iacpnet.com

5. John P. Kenney, Donald E. Fuller, and Robert J. Barry, *Police Work with Juveniles and the Administration of Juvenile Justice* (Springfield, IL: C. C. Thomas, 1995), p. 57.

6. Ibid., pp. 57–58.

7. S. M. Davis, *The Rights of Juveniles: The Juvenile Justice System* (New York: Clark Boardman, 1974), p. 43.

8. Rolando del Carmen, Mary Parker, and Frances P. Reddington, *Briefs of Leading Cases in Juvenile Justice* (Cincinnati, OH: Anderson, 1998), pp. 21–22.

9. Davis, *Rights*, p. 45.

10. *Smith v. State* (1992) 623 So. 2d 369; del Carmen, Parker, and Reddington, *Leading Cases*, pp. 38–40.

11. *Haley v. Ohio*, 332 U.S. 596 (1948).

12. Kenney, Fuller, and Barry, *Police Work with Juveniles*, p. 24.

13. Ibid.

14. H. B. Farber, "The Role of the Parent/Guardian in Juvenile Custodial Interrogations: Friend or Foe?" *American Criminal Law Review*, Vol. 41 (2004), pp. 1277–1312.

15. Davis, *Rights*, pp. 54–55.

16. M. G. Paulsen and C. H. Whitebread, *Juvenile Law and Procedure* (Reno, NV: National Council of Juvenile Court Judges, 1974), pp. 80–81.

17. *Terry v. Ohio* (1968) 392 U.S. 1.

18. *In the Interest of J.L., A Child* (1993) 623 So.2d 860 Fla. App. del Carmen, Parker and Reddington, *Leading Cases*, pp. 40–41.

19. *In the Interest of S.A.W.* (1993) 499 N.W. 2d. 739 Iowa App. del Carmen, Parker and Reddington, *Leading Cases*, pp. 40–41.

20. Paulsen and Whitebread, *Law and Procedure*, pp. 87–88. W. Wadlington, C. H. Whitebread, and S. M. Davis, *Cases and Materials on Children in the Legal System* (Mineola, NY: The Foundation Press, 1983), pp. 271–273.

21. *New Jersey v. T.L.O.* (1985) 105 S.Ct. 733.

22. L. E. Holtz, "*Miranda* in a Juvenile Setting: A Child's Right to Silence," *Journal of Criminal Law and Criminology*, Vol. 78 (1987), pp. 534–556.

23. Richard A. Lawrence, "The Role of Legal Counsel in Juveniles' Understanding of Their Rights," *Juvenile and Family Court Journal*, Vol. 34 (1983), pp. 49–58.

24. *West v. United States* (1968) 399 F.2d 467.

25. Davis, *Rights*, p. 93.

26. Paulsen and Whitebread, *Law and Procedure*, pp. 89–94.

27. C. S. Scott-Hayward, "Explaining Juvenile False Confessions: Adolescent Development and Police Interrogation," *Law & Psychology Review*, Vol. 31 (2007), pp. 53–76.

28. *Fare v. Michael C.* (1974) 99 S.Ct. 2560. Wadlington, Whitebread and Davis, *Children in the Legal System*, pp. 326–330. See also *California v. Prysock* (1981) 453 U.S. 355; *Yarborough, Warden v. Alvarado* (2004) 541 U.S. 652.

29. *United States v. Bernard S.* (1986). del Carmen, Parker, and Reddington, *Leading Cases*, pp. 35–36.

30. *State v. Sugg* (1995) 623 So. 2d 369. del Carmen, Parker, and Reddington, *Leading Cases*, pp. 47–48.

31. *In re Gilbert E.* (1995) 39 Cal. Rptr. 2d 866 Cal. App. del Carmen, Parker and Reddington, *Leading Cases*, pp. 45–46.

32. Barry C. Feld, "Juveniles' Competence to Exercise Miranda Rights: An Empirical Study of Policy and Practice," *Minnesota Law Review*, Vol. 91 (2006), pp. 26–100; Barry C. Feld, "Police Interrogation of Juveniles: An Empirical Study of Policy and Practice," *Journal of Criminal Law & Criminology*, Vol. 97 (2006), pp. 219–316; see also J. R. Meyer and N. D. Raspucci, "Police Practices and Perceptions Regarding Juvenile Interrogation and Interrogative Suggestibility," *Behavioral Sciences & the Law*, Vol. 25 (2007), pp. 757–780.

33. Paulsen and Whitebread, *Law and Procedure*, pp. 96–97. Davis, *Rights*, pp. 96–100.

34. Davis, *Rights*, pp. 71–73.

35. International Association of Chiefs of Police, Midvale Police Department.

36. Carl E. Pope and William Feyerherm, *Minorities and the Juvenile Justice System: Research Summary* (Washington, DC: U.S. Department of Justice, Office of Juvenile Justice and Delinquency Prevention, 1993), p. 10.

37. Maynard Erickson, "Group Violations and Official Delinquency: The Group Hazard Hypothesis," *Criminology*, Vol. 11 (1973), pp. 127–160; Michael J. Hindelang, "With a Little Help from Their Friends: Group Participation in Reported Delinquent Behavior," *British Journal of Criminology*, Vol. 16 (1976), pp. 109–125; William Feyerherm, "The Group Hazard Hypothesis: A Re-examination," *Journal of Research in Crime and Delinquency*, Vol. 17 (1980), pp. 56–58; Mary Morash, "Establishment of a Juvenile Record: The Influence of Individual and Peer Group Characteristics," *Criminology*, Vol. 22 (1984), pp. 97–112.

38. Christy A. Visher, "Gender, Police Arrest Decisions, and Notions of Chivalry," *Criminology*, Vol. 21 (1983), pp. 5–28; Ruth Horowitz and Anne E. Pottieger, "Gender Bias in Juvenile Justice Handling of Seriously Crime-Involved Youths," *Journal of Research in Crime and Delinquency*, Vol. 28 (1991), pp. 75–100; Jean E. Rhodes and Karla Fischer, "Spanning the Gender Gap: Gender Differences in Delinquency among Inner-City Adolescents," *Adolescence*, Vol. 28 (1993), pp. 879–889.

39. Meda Chesney-Lind and Vickie V. Paramore, "Are Girls Getting More Violent? Exploring Juvenile Robbery Trends," *Journal of Contemporary Criminal Justice,* Vol. 17 (2001), pp. 142–166.

40. Irving Piliavin and Scott Briar, "Police Encounters with Juveniles," *American Journal of Sociology*, Vol. 70 (1964), pp. 206–214; William F. Hohenstein, "Factors Influencing the Police Disposition of Juvenile Offenders," in Thorsten Sellin and Marvin E. Wolfgang, eds., *Delinquency: Selected Readings* (New York: John Wiley & Sons, 1969), pp. 138–149; Neal L. Weiner and Charles V. Willie, "Decisions by Juvenile Officers," *American Journal of Sociology*, Vol. 77 (1971), pp. 199–210; David Black and Albert J. Reiss, Jr., "Police Control of Juveniles," *American Sociological Review*, Vol. 35 (1970), pp. 63–77; Richard J. Lundman, Richard E. Sykes, and John P. Clark, "Police Control of Juveniles: A Replication," in Richard J. Lundman, ed., *Police Behavior: A Sociological Perspective* (New York: Oxford University Press, 1980), pp. 130–151; M. Wordes and T. S. Bynum, "Policing Juveniles: Is There a Bias against Youths of Color?" in K. K. Leonard, C. E. Pope, and W. F. Feyerherm, eds., *Minorities in Juvenile Justice* (Thousand Oaks, CA: Sage Publications, 1995), pp. 47–65.

41. T. T. Allen, "Taking a Juvenile into Custody: Situational Factors that Influence Police Officers' Decisions," *Journal of Sociology & Social Welfare*, Vol. 32 (2005), pp. 121–129; R. A. Brown, K. J. Novak and J. Frank, "Identifying Variation in Police Officer Behavior between Juveniles and Adults," *Journal of Criminal Justice*, Vol. 37 (2009), pp. 200–208.

42. International Association of Chiefs of Police net, Document Display, Document #557880, "Child Abuse—Physical/Sexual/Neglect," Craig (CO) Police Department (12/06/2001) www.iacpnet.com

43. International Association of Chiefs of Police net, Document Display, Document #546802, "Juvenile Processing Handbook," Cicero (IL) Police Department (08/12/1999) www.iacpnet.com

44. Ibid.

45. Ibid.

46. Jeffrey T. Walker and Louie C. Caudell, "Community Policing and Patrol Cars: Oil and Water or Well Oiled Machine?" *Police Forum*, Vol. 3 (July 1993), pp.1–9.

47. Robert Trojanowicz and Bonnie Bucqueroux, *Community Policing: A Contemporary Perspective.* (Cincinnati, OH: Anderson, 1990), p. xii.

48. Albert J. Reiss, Jr., "Police Organizations in the Twentieth Century," in Michael Tonry and Norval Morris, eds., *Modern Policing* (Chicago: University of Chicago Press, 1992), pp. 91–94.

49. Jerald R. Vaughn, "Community-Oriented Policing. . . You Can Make It Happen," *Law and Order* (June 1991), pp. 35–39.

50. George E. Capowich and Janice A. Roehl, "Problem-Oriented Policing: Actions and Effectiveness in San Diego," in Dennis P. Rosenbaum, ed., *The Challenge of Community Policing: Testing the Promises* (Thousand Oaks, CA: Sage Publications, 1994), pp. 127–128.

51. Gordon Bazemore and Scott Sanjo, "Police Encounters with Juveniles Revisited: An Exploratory Study of Themes and Styles in Community Policing," *Policing: An International Journal of Police Strategies & Management*, Vol. 20 (1997), p. 62.

52. Kelly Dedel, *Juvenile Runaways* (Washington, DC: U.S. Department of Justice, Office of Community Policing Services, 2006), pp. 23–38.

53. Ibid., p. 64.

54. Commission on Accreditation for Law Enforcement Agencies, Inc. *Standards for Law Enforcement Agencies: The Standards Manual of the Law Enforcement Agency Accreditation Program* (Fairfax, VA: Fourth Edition, 1999), Standard 44.

55. Kenney, Fuller, and Barry, *Police Work with Juveniles*, pp. 107–108.

56. Innovations in American Government, "Restorative Community Conferencing," www.innovations.harvard.edu

6

Juvenile Assessment and Classification[1]

Classification refers either to the arrangement or division of entities into groups according to some system or principle or to the placement of entities into groups according to rules already determined.... The aim is to develop groups whose members are similar to one another and who differ from members of other groups.

DON GOTTFREDSON

LEARNING OBJECTIVES

1. Discuss the pros and cons of the Community Assessment Center model in terms of classifying and assessing juveniles.
2. Describe the intake process.
3. Define what is meant by classification.
4. Identify and apply the different types of assessment instruments.

CHAPTER OVERVIEW

What happens between the time a juvenile comes in contact with law enforcement and the time he or she moves (or does not move) into the court system? This chapter provides an overview of how juveniles "enter" the juvenile justice system and the processes of assessment and classification as they enter the system. In Chapter 5, we review the powers and responsibilities of the police and their involvement in the juvenile justice system, including the different management styles and their potential influence on the police–juvenile relationship. This chapter begins at the time following the police officer's arrest of the juvenile and then moves through the booking process, assessment process, preliminary hearing, and "entry" of the juvenile into juvenile probation through formal or informal processing.

We discuss the history of classification and its role in the juvenile justice system, as well as the different types of assessments juveniles will face during the intake and classification processes. Juvenile assessment and classification are components of the process of sorting youths into various groups fro the purpose of custody, supervision, and treatment. The chapter continues the use of case examples, through narrative and video, to demonstrate what happens following the arrest of a juvenile—in other words, the process in action.

THE INTAKE PROCESS

The Decision to Arrest

intake The point at which the juvenile is "booked" into the juvenile justice system

The **intake** process begins when a juvenile is arrested by a law enforcement officer and is taken into custody. The officer must determine whether youths become formally involved with the system as a result of arrest or whether the juvenile may be handled informally. Officers must assess the situation and use the method (e.g., arrest, warning) that is most appropriate to the individual case. As mentioned in Chapter 5, the first role of the police in dealing with juveniles is the control function of detection, investigation, and arrest.[2] As the gatekeepers of the juvenile justice system, the police control access of juveniles. They determine whether the juvenile will enter the system at all and at what point, or if they will be diverted. As pointed out previously, many youthful offenders never enter the juvenile justice system. However, when a juvenile is arrested, the next step for the law enforcement officer is to take the juvenile to a Community Assessment Center for processing. See Figure 6.1[3] for an example arrest report from Florida, in which a 13-year-old juvenile was arrested and charged with two counts of Battery on a Detention Staff Member, a third-degree felony in Florida.

```
ARREST REPORT
REPORT NO:                            Printed On: 01/22/            Page: 1

Jail Booking No      Offense No          Other No          OBTS


[ DEFENDANT ]    [ MNI              ]  [ SSN :              ]  [ OCA :            ]
   * JUVENILE ON DATE OF OCCURRENCE *
Last                First              Middle       Title  H R S  DOB        Age
                                                          N B M              13
Hgt  Wgt   Eyes  Hair  SSN        I.D. No.         St      Type
5'00 90    BRO  BL
Birth Location:
Addresses (Current/Last Known is Listed First)
                                              Entered:   /21/20
Occupations (Current/Last Known is Listed First)
   Business:              MIDDLE, Job Title: STUDENT, Entered:   /21/20

Aliases (Last, First Middle Title DOB)
   * none found in MNI *
Street Names
   * none found in MNI *


[ CHARGES ]
FSS:  784.075 .          COUNTS : 1                UCR : 130B    NCIC :

    AOL2    BATTERY
    DESC    ON DETENTION STAFF MEMBER
    GENERAL OFFENSE CODE... (GOC) :    N    Not Applicable
    ARREST CHARGE LEVEL......(ACL) :    F    Felony
    ARREST CHARGE DEGREE...(ACD) :      T    Third Degree
    ARREST OFFENSE NUMBER.(AON) :      1319
[ CHARGES ]
FSS:  784.075 .          COUNTS : 1                UCR : 130B    NCIC :

    AOL2    BATTERY
    DESC    ON DETENTION STAFF MEMBER
    GENERAL OFFENSE CODE... (GOC) :    N    Not Applicable
    ARREST CHARGE LEVEL......(ACL) :    F    Felony
    ARREST CHARGE DEGREE...(ACD) :      T    Third Degree
    ARREST OFFENSE NUMBER.(AON) :      1319
```

Figure 6.1
Arrest Report

Taking the Juvenile into Custody: Community Assessment Centers

As part of the Comprehensive Strategy for Serious, Violent, and Chronic Juvenile Offenders, the Office of Juvenile Justice and Delinquency Prevention developed **Community Assessment Centers (CACs)**. Local CACs were established to assist agencies in identifying, assessing, and classifying juvenile offenders. The CAC model is based on four key elements:

Community Assessment Centers (CACs) The intake point for the juvenile following arrest

1. **Single point of entry.** CACs provide a twenty-four-hour centralized point of intake and assessment for juveniles who have come into contact with the juvenile justice system.

```
ARREST REPORT
REPORT NO:                    CONTINUED FROM PREVIOUS PAGE. .              Page: 2
=====================================================================================
[PHYSICAL EVIDENCE ]
[NO PHYSICAL EVIDENCE LISTED]
```

```
[ ARREST INFORMATION ]
Arrested            Resist?          Weapon?         Drinking?        Drugs?
/22/20              N = No Resist    N               N=No             N=No
No.       Di    Street              A/L    City              ST    Zip

Arresting Officer                            Unit                (GEO)
```

```
[ INCIDENT INFORMATION ]
Occurred Date Range:   /22/20              to    /22/20
No.       Di    Street              A/L    City              ST    Zip

                                                          (GEO)
```

```
[ STATEMENT OF PROBABLE CAUSE
         ON      AT          COUNTY,          DID AT
INTENTIONALLY STRIKE VICTIM, AGAINST SAID PERSONS WILL.

         I WAS DISPATCHED TO,              IN REFERENCE TO A POSSIBLE BATTERY.  ON
ARRIVAL I MADE CONTACT WITH V/           STATED HE HAD BEEN STRUCK TWICE BY
    . V'        STATED THAT WHILE SEARCHING PRISONERS, THAT WERE COMING
FROM COURT,          REPEATEDLY KEPT GOING TO THE FEMALES AND TALKING TO
THEM, AFTER BEING TOLD SEVERAL TIMES TO STAY WITH THE MALES.          AGAIN
WENT BACK TO THE FEMALES TO TALK TO THEM  AND THEN V/     ATTEMPTED TO PUT
         BACK TO THE MALES, WHEN        PULLED AWAY.          THEN
CHARGED V/      WHERE HE BROKE AWAY, AT WHICH TIME        CHARGED
V/.     AGAIN AND SWINGING AT HIM WHERE HE STRUCK HIM IN THE LEFT EAR. WHILE
         WAS SWINGING AT V/            STATED, "I'M GOING TO KILL YOU."
WHEN V/      ALONG WITH WA/     WERE FINALLY ABLE TO GET
SUBDUED AND IN A HOLDING CELL. V/      ADVISED THAT WHILE THEY HAD
UNDER CONTROL       STATED, "I'LL HIT YOU AGAIN IF YOU LET ME GO."  V/
WAS STANDING BY WHILE OTHER OFFICERS DEALT WITH          AT WHICH TIME
         BEGAN SWINGING AT V/     AGAIN AND STRUCK HIM ON THE RIGHT SIDE OF
HIS MOUTH.

         I MADE CONTACT  WITH WA/     , WHO STATED THAT SHE WAS DEALING WITH
OTHER PRISONERS WHEN SHE LOOKED UP AND SAW V/      BACKED UP INTO THE
LOCKERS AND          SWING AND STRIKE V/     IN THE LEFT EAR. WA/
STATED THAT DURING THIS INCIDENT          WAS YELLING 'I'M GOING TO KILL YOU."

         I MADE CONTACT WITH          AND I ASKED HIM,  WHAT I WAS DOING HERE.
"HE STATED MY MOMMA TOLD ME NOT TO TALK TO STRANGERS AND I AM NOT YOU
CRACKERS SLAVE."

              WAS TAKEN INTO CUSTODY TRANSPORTED TO RAPID INTAKE FOR
FINGER PRINTS AND BACK TO DYS FOR PROCESSING.
```

Figure 6.1
(Continued)

2. **Immediate and comprehensive assessment.** Juvenile justice practitioners and community-based youth service providers affiliated with the CAC make initial, broad-based, and, if necessary later, more in-depth assessments of juveniles' circumstances and treatment needs.

3. **Management information system (MIS).** Through the use of an MIS, CACs manage and monitor youth, ensuring the provision of appropriate treatment and rehabilitation services and avoiding duplication of services.

4. **Integrated case management.** CAC staff use information from the assessment process and MIS to develop recommendations,

facilitate access to services, conduct follow-ups, and periodically reassess cases.

In fiscal year 1996, CAC "planning sites" were established in Denver, Colorado, and Lee County, Florida. "Enhancement sites" (Juvenile Assessment Centers) were developed in Jefferson County, Colorado, and Orlando, Florida.[4] The following list highlights the purpose of these assessment centers and their goals to better coordinate juvenile services.

- Reduce law enforcement time devoted to juveniles,
- Create a central booking and receiving facility specifically for juvenile offenders,
- Collect good, clear information about juveniles' needs,
- Accelerate access to treatment for juveniles,
- Pool resources from different agencies,
- Provide referrals to parents and children,
- Develop a facility to hold dependent juveniles who are awaiting placement,
- Expedite court proceedings by providing better information to defense attorneys and prosecutors,
- Provide early intervention services for troubled juveniles,
- Develop a single point of entry for assessing and referring juveniles,
- Facilitate cooperation and communication among the agencies,
- Expedite processing of juveniles through the system,
- Streamline the current fragmented service delivery system, and
- Provide courts with better tools and information.[5]

Clearly, Community or Juvenile Assessment Centers are designed to do more than simple assessment. They are structured to serve as "one-stop shopping" for juvenile services beginning with transfer of the juvenile from law enforcement following arrest. The Escambia, Florida, Juvenile Assessment Center includes the following as part of its mission[6]:

to prevent and reduce juvenile delinquency. We are committed to a balanced approach that increases public safety, promotes accountability, and provides quality, comprehensive assessments which focus on the youth's risk to public safety and specific needs requiring individualized interventions and sanctions.

Juvenile Female Being Taken into Custody

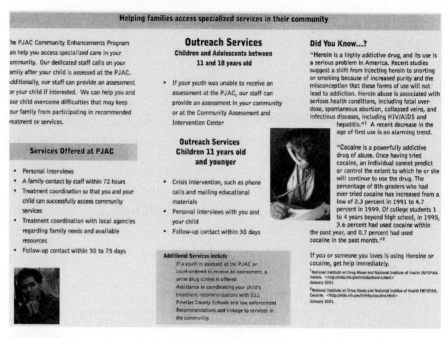

Figure 6.2
Pinellas, Florida, Juvenile Assessment Center Brochure

screener The probation officer
or intake officer who assesses the
juvenile

The Pinellas, Florida, Juvenile Assessment Center (JAC) created
a brochure to highlight its major functions and services, including its
Community Enhancement Program, which makes contact with a juvenile's family after he or she has been assessed and offers extending
outreach services for juveniles. See their brochure in Figure 6.2.[7]
Research on the Hillsborough, Florida, JAC has noted that the center
has improved efficiency in the processing of youths who have been
arrested.[8]

As mentioned previously, the CACs offer a centralized point of intake for juveniles who have been arrested by police. Most large metropolitan areas will have one CAC, whereas rural locations or smaller cities
may share a "regional" CAC. In such cases, the CAC might serve a 1,200
square mile area.

Upon arrival to the CAC, the law enforcement officer will bring
the shackled juvenile into the center. Custody of the juvenile is transferred to the CAC worker, either an assessment center **screener** or a
probation/intake officer unless the juvenile is under the influence of alcohol or drugs. If this is the case, then some state statutes do not allow
for the transfer of jurisdiction; instead, the law enforcement will transport the juvenile to a hospital or shelter. In addition, if a juvenile states
that he or she is suicidal, then the police officer must take the juvenile
to the hospital for an evaluation prior to the screening process. The law
enforcement officer completes a questionnaire or notification as part of

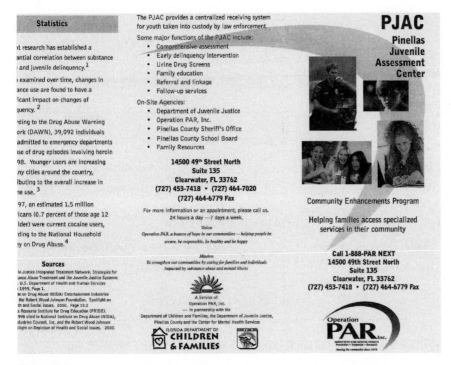

Figure 6.2
(Continued)

the transfer. Figure 6.3[9] highlights a sample notification. The police officer's comments on the notification are used during the screening process and are also included in the recommendation to the State Attorney.

Screening, Assessment, and Classification

Community Assessment Centers streamline services and prevent gaps in the system. They also are an attempt to provide services for all the types of cases that the juvenile justice system receives and prevent the problems that lead to both delinquency and dependency. The primary function of intake and screening is to determine whether the juvenile falls under the jurisdiction of the juvenile justice system. Most states have statutes that define what kind of cases may be handled by the juvenile system. Thus, each juvenile brought to the CAC is first screened.

The screening process includes a review of the arrest report, input of offender demographics into the state's offender information system database, a mug shot, and an interview with the juvenile at which time the juvenile is advised of his or her legal rights. Prior to any questioning, a juvenile version of the **Miranda** warning is read and explained to the juvenile. The juvenile Miranda warning may vary between local jurisdictions; for example, Figure 6.4 shows the juvenile Miranda warning for Escambia County, Florida.[10] Look at the Miranda warning.

Miranda Prior to any questioning, the juvenile is notified of his or her rights

Escambia County Juvenile Assessment Center
1800 St. Mary's Avenue, Box 8
Pensacola, Florida 32501

LAW ENFORCEMENT QUESTIONNAIRE/NOTIFICATION

Juvenile's Name: _____
(Last, First, Middle)   (Date of Birth)

ARREST AGENCY INFORMATION

Officer's Name: _____ ID#: _____ Unit: _____ Report/Case No: _____

Agency Address: _____ Phone Number: _____

OFFENSE INFORMATION

Number of Charges this arrest: _____   Most Serious Level is a: Felony / Misdemeanor

Offense Address: _____ Date/Time: _____

CO-DEFENDANT INFORMATION

_____
(Last, First, Middle)   (Date of Birth)

PLEASE RESPOND TO THE FOLLOWING QUESTIONS WITH EITHER "YES" OR "NO"

Is the youth wearing Gang Colors? _____

Is the youth a member of a GANG or SATANIC CULT? _____

Is the youth a suicide risk? _____

Does the youth appear to be intoxicated or under the influence of drugs? _____

Does the youth appear to have need of medical attention at this time? _____

Has the youth been searched for contraband? _____

Has the youth's guardian been contacted to come to the Assessment Center? _____

Do you recommend a DIVERSION program? Such a program provides immediate Consequences. If successful there will be no further judicial action. _____

As the arresting officer, we will insure your comments are included in the recommendation to the State Attorney. Please provide any comments below. If none, so indicate.

_____
_____

Signature of Arresting Officer: _____

Figure 6.3
Law Enforcement Notification

Do you think a 13-year-old arrestee would understand it? What about an 8-year-old? The **grievance procedure** that a juvenile or his or her family may take when they think they are being treated unjustly while in supervision is also explained at this time. During the initial screening process, the intake officer also contacts the juvenile's parents or guardians to inform them that the youth has been arrested and is at the CAC, and to ask them questions about the juvenile's emotional health.

grievance procedure Policy in place for a family to utilize when they think they are being treated unjustly or unfairly while in supervision

Juvenile's Notification of Rights

Issued to: _____   Date of Complaint: _____

Complaint(s): _____

Notification of Rights

1. You have the right to a lawyer.

2. If you are unable to pay a lawyer and your parents or guardians have not provided a lawyer, one can be provided. You or your parents may be required to pay up to $750 for the lawyer services (Ch 27.F.S.).

3. You are not required to say anything, anything may be used against you, and

4. If your parent, custodian, or lawyer is not present, you have the right to talk with them, and reasonable means will be provided for you to do so.

The child wants to be represented by counsel and has been/will be placed in communication with:

| Public Defender | ☐ | Private Attorney | ☐ | Lawyer Referral Service | ☐ |

Check one of the above, if the child wishes an attorney.

_____   _____   _____
DATE   SCREENER/JPO   CHILD

Waiver of Counsel

I, the undersigned childe, _____ years of age, understand:

1. That a complaint of delinquency / ungovernability alleging that I did:

_____
_____

    has been made against me.

2. That I have a right to and offer of a lawyer, and being aware of the effect of this waiver, I knowingly, intelligently, understandingly, and of my own free will, now choose to and, by the signing of this waiver, do hereby waive my right to a lawyer, and elect to proceed in this case without the benefit of a lawyer.

_____   _____
DATE   CHILD

This waiver of counsel was signed in the presence of the undersigned witness who, by their signature, attest to its voluntary execution by this child.

_____
WITNESS

Statement of Parent or Responsible Adult

This waiver of counsel was read by me and explained fully to this child in my presence. I understand the right of this child to an attorney and as the _____ of this child; I consent to a waiver of this right.

_____   _____
DATE   SIGNATURE

Figure 6.4
Example of a Juvenile Miranda Warning

In addition to the screening process, the intake officer also completes several assessments and uses a mandated "point system" to determine the appropriate classification of the juvenile. Classification at this stage relates to the detention decision—that is, whether the juvenile will remain in detention or is released under the supervision of the parents or guardians. The intake process may take from one hour to many hours to complete, depending on the number of juveniles at intake, behavior of the juvenile(s) in intake, time of day, alleged offense, or whether it is the juvenile's first offense. Most states require that the intake process be completed and the juvenile either transferred to detention or to the parents or guardians within a limited number of hours. For example, in Florida, the intake period may last no longer than six hours.

SCREENING

The screening process is an interview with the juvenile and entering of the juvenile's information, current offense and offense history, as well as personal information, in a statewide database. This is similar to the booking process with adult arrestees. In Florida, the Juvenile Justice Information System (JJIS) is a statewide information system that houses information about any juvenile that has had contact with any juvenile intake and assessment center, juvenile intensive probation agency, community case management agencies, or juvenile correctional facilities. Box 6.1 describes an example of the type of information that may be included in the JJIS or other state systems.

One problem with some state databases is that it is not possible to view information about delinquent youths from other states. Thus, unless the juvenile discloses that he or she has previously been delinquent,

---

BOX 6.1 INFORMATION ON THE STATE JUVENILE JUSTICE SYSTEM DATABASE

Face sheet. Record of the juvenile's demographics and entire history with the Department of Juvenile Justice. The face sheet shows every offense for which the juvenile has been arrested and whether there are any special "alerts" related to prior offenses. It also shows if a youth is on a conditional supervision status, and if so for what and when they were placed. The legal or disposition history is also included.

Current offense information. The arrest report or warrant is used to identify the charges and victim, in addition to checking whether the youth meets any aggravating factors.

Detention risk assessment (DRAI). Using, the DRAI the screener can determine whether a youth is released, placed on home detention, or transferred to secure detention.

Mental health risk assessment. An instrument used when interviewing the juvenile to identify potential mental health or substance abuse issues.

Suicide risk screening. An instrument used when interviewing the juvenile to determine the level of supervision related to the possibility of the juvenile committing suicide.

Supervision risk classification instrument. Used in conjunction with the State Attorney Recommendation with the purpose of recommending a proper level of supervision for the youth based on many factors, including prior referrals to the juvenile system, current supervision status, age at time of current charge, drug or alcohol use, parental control, school status (e.g., expulsions, tardiness), peer relationships, abuse or neglect by custodians, mental health diagnosis, and employment.

State Attorney Recommendation. Reports information collected from the DRAI to the State Attorney. It also includes a recommendation to either file a petition or handle the matter outside the court.

Juvenile Being Screened/Interviewed

there may be no way the screener could know this. Next we discuss what kind of issues may occur because of this, especially as it relates to the DRAI.

Figure 6.5 is an example of a **face sheet** from the Florida Department of Juvenile Justice. Notice the information recorded on the report. The information is gleaned from the arrest report for the current offense and through the interview process. Note also that this example is for a juvenile with no current charge but a pickup order for "Failure to Appear." However, the juvenile has had prior institutional placements in the juvenile justice system for both new charges and court and noncourt interventions. The "special alerts" section highlights behaviors or offenses that are important for supervisory staff to know and may include domestic violence, sex offenses, use of firearm during offense, gang involvement, special medical needs, drug use, and mental health needs.

face sheet Data recorded about the juvenile (e.g., prior arrests, current charges) during the intake process

ASSESSMENT

After the juvenile's initial information is added into the computerized state database system, several assessments are completed.

Suicide Risk Screening

The **Suicide Risk Screening Instrument (SRSI)** is used to identify the level of supervision the youth may need as it relates to his or her risk of suicide. Both the juvenile and the parent or guardian are interviewed. A sample

Suicide Risk Screening Instrument (SRSI) Assessment of the juvenile's risk for suicide

FLORIDA DEPARTMENT OF JUVENILE JUSTICE
EXPANDED FACE SHEET

Date: Sunday, _____ 15, 20 ____

YOUTH INFORMATION

DJJID _____

Last Name _____ First Name _____ Middle Name _____
DOB _____ Age _____ Sex _____
Race _____ Eye Color _____ Hair Color _____
Weight _____ Height _____ CIS ID # _____
Address _____
City/State/Zip _____
Phone Number _____
Residence County _____ Circuit _____

PHOTO
OF
YOUTH

Aliases
Type _____ Name _____

Special Alerts
Description _____ Begin Date _____ County _____
Description _____ Begin Date _____ County _____

Member Information
Name _____ Relationship _____
Name _____ Relationship _____

Charges

Offense Date	Description	Ref ID	Court Docket	Unit, JPO	Disp Date	Adj	Disposition
	MARIJUANA-DISTRIB-SCHEDULE I (Closed)						Other Non/Jud Disposition (Del/Non Jud) (1st)

Pick-Up Orders and Court Dates

Offense Date	Description	Ref ID	Court Docket	Unit, JPO	Disp Date	Adj	Disposition
	Pick-Up Order – Pick-up Order Failure to Appear (Open)						
	Court Order – Prosecution Previously Deferred-Case Reopened (Open)						

Expanded Face Sheet Information for _____   Page 1 of ____
Report Date: _____

Figure 6.5
Face Sheet from the Florida Department of Juvenile Justice

SRSI form is presented in Figure 6.6.[11] In the form shown, suicide risk is assessed by asking the juvenile three questions: (1) Have you ever tried to commit suicide within the past 6 months; (2) Are you thinking about killing yourself now? and (3) Have you ever tried to kill yourself?[12] If the juvenile answers yes to question 1, then he or she is placed on constant sight and sound. Meanwhile, if the juvenile answers yes to questions 2 or 3, then he or she is placed on close watch.

The juvenile's parents or guardians are asked additional questions related to the juvenile's suicide risk. The parents are asked if there have been any major life changes in the juvenile's life recently, including someone he or

FLORIDA DEPARTMENT OF JUVENILE JUSTICE
EXPANDED FACE SHEET

Current Location

Program Name	Program Type	Location Begin Date	Admit Reason
_____ Detention	Detention – Secure Detention		Court Order
Youth is at Home - ___ Circuit	Intervention – Intake		Prosecution Previously Deferred – Case Reopened

Youth Placement

Ref ID	Status	Custody Unit	Admit Date	Admit Reason	Release Date	Release Reason	Released To
	Detention – Secure	___ Detention		Court Order			
	Intervention – JAC	_____ JAC		Court Order		Detained	
	Intervention – In-Transit	In-Transit – Detention		Order to take into custody		Admitted to Facility/Program	
	Intervention – Intake	Youth is at Home		Prosecution Previously Deferred – Case Reopened			
	Diversion – Diversion	Diversion – ___ Circuit		Non-judicial		Non-Compliance – Referred to State Attorney	
	Intervention – JAC	_____ JAC		New Charges		Released	
	Intervention – Intake	Youth is at Home		New Charges		Non-judicial handling	

Law Enforcement Information

Arrest Date	Referral ID	Circuit	Agency Name	Officer's Name	Badge #
__/22/20__					
__/22/20__					

Youth's Current School Information

School Name _____

Street _____

City/State/Zip _____

School Phone _____

Grade Level _____   Last Grade Completed _____

Last Date Attended _____

Scheduled Hours _____ to _____

Expanded Face Sheet Information for _____   Page 2 of _____
Report Date: _____

Figure 6.5
(Continued)

she knows that has committed suicide. They are also asked if the juvenile has ever threatened to commit suicide in the past or has exhibited suicidal behaviors (e.g., giving away treasured items). Even if the parent or guardian states that the juvenile is not exhibiting suicidal behaviors, if the juvenile's answers suggest otherwise, the juvenile is placed under appropriate supervision.

Detention Risk Assessment

The **Detention Risk Assessment Instrument (DRAI)** assesses whether the juvenile is released, placed on home detention, or held in secure detention. The DRAI is based on a point system; in general, if a youth scores six

Detention Risk Assessment Instrument (DRAI) Assessment of the juvenile's risk to the community

DEPARTMENT OF JUVENILE JUSTICE
SUICIDE RISK SCREENING INSTRUMENT

Identifying Data: DJJID: _____   Referral#: _____

Youth's Name		Date of Birth	14 Age
Aliases			
Parent/Guardian			
Address/Telephone			
01/29/20 Date/Time Detained			

Statute Number/Offense(s)

812.13 2a ROBBERY- WITH FIREARM

Interview of Arresting/Transporting Officer
(To be completed by Juvenile Probation Officer before the officer leaves)

Officer's Name: _____   Badge/ID#: _____

Agency: _____

If Yes, Place youth on sight and sound supervision. Refer youth for immediate Suicide Risk Assessment	YES	NO
Do you have any reason to think this youth will try to kill himself?	☐	☒

Explain: _____
Other Comments: _____

Juvenile Probation Officer Interview Of Child
(Juvenile Probation Officer shall ask the youth the following questions)

If Yes for questions 1 or 2, place youth on sight and sound supervision. Refer youth for immediate Suicide Risk Assessment	YES	NO
1. Have you tried to kill yourself in the past 6 months?	☐	☒

When? _____
How? _____

If Yes for question 3, place youth on close watch. Refer youth for Suicide Risk Assessment within 24 hours		
2. Are you thinking about killing yourself now?	☐	☒

Explain: _____

| 3. Have you ever tried to kill yourself? | ☐ | ☒ |

When? _____
How? _____
Other Comments: _____

Figure 6.6
Suicide Risk Assessment Instrument from the Florida Department of Juvenile Justice

points or less, then he or she is released to go home. If a juvenile scores seven to ten points, he or she is placed on home detention; and with twelve or more points, the juvenile is placed in secure detention. To be placed on either home or secure detention, however, the juvenile may also need to meet additional criteria. For example, the juvenile may have:

(1) absconded from a commitment or conditional supervision program; (2) legal counsel provide a written request for detention; (3) been charged with at least a 3rd degree felony crime of violence or a 2nd degree non-drug felony; or (4) possessed a firearm during the commission of the alleged offense.[13]

Youth's Current DJJ or C& F Involvement: (Check all that apply)

- [ ] Delinquency Intake
- [X] Probation
- [ ] Delinquency Commitment
- [ ] Conditional Release
- [ ] Child Protective Investigation
- [ ] PS
- [ ] Foster Care
- [ ] Adoptions
- [ ] None

Counselor(s): _____

Juvenile Probation Officer Interview of Parent/Guardian or Relative and Assigned Counselor:
(To be completed by Juvenile Probation Officer during the intake process. Interview the assigned counselor. If unavailable, proceed with screening and contact the next day per circuit operating procedures.)

Parent/Guardian or Relative Name: _____

Relationship: Mother   Contacted Date/Time 01/29/20   pm

Assigned Counselor _____   Contacted Date/Time 01/29/20 -   pm

	Parent/ Gaurdian or Relative		Assigned Counselor	
If Yes for question 1, place youth on sight and sound supervision. Refer youth for immediate Suicide Risk Assessment	YES	NO	YES	NO
1. Has the child tried to kill himself in the past six months?	[ ]	[X]	[ ]	[X]

When? _____

How? _____

If one or more Yes for questions 2 through 8, place youth on close watch and refer youth for immediate suicide Risk Assessment within 24 hours				
2. Has the child threatened to kill himself in the past six months?	[ ]	[X]	[ ]	[X]

Explain: _____

Has the child ever tried to kill himself?	[ ]	[X]	[ ]	[X]

When? _____

How? _____

4. Have you noticed the child having any of the following behaviors: Giving away his favorite things, dropping close friends, drastic changes in eating or sleeping habits, saying that things are hopeless?	[ ]	[X]	[ ]	[X]
5. Other than being arrested and detained, has the child had a major change or loss in the past six months, such as a death, divorce of parents, breaking up with (girlfriend, boyfriend, etc?)	[ ]	[X]	[ ]	[X]

Explain: _____

6. Does the child have any serious mental health problems (e.g. depression, withdrawn, hears voices, etc.)?	[ ]	[X]	[ ]	[X]

Explain: _____

7. Has someone this child knows well committed suicide?	[ ]	[X]	[ ]	[X]

Who? _____

When? _____

How? _____

8. Is there any other information that will help us in caring for this child?	[ ]	[X]	[ ]	[X]

Explain: _____

Other Comments: _____

Figure 6.6
(Continued)

If the juvenile has previously failed to appear for a court hearing, he or she may also be placed on either home or secure detention.[14] Moreover, juveniles who possess a firearm may also be detained regardless of the total number of points they score on the assessment. The DRAI used in Florida is presented in Figure 6.7.[15] Additional circumstances, such as "special alerts," also may be considered. For example, if a juvenile is charged with a domestic violence offense, then the alleged victim is called. If the victim states that he or she fears for his or her own safety, then the screener will attempt to place the youth in a local shelter. If the shelter refuses the youth for any reason, the youth may be placed in secure detention. Juveniles who are under conditional supervision (e.g., probation) may also be scored on their underlying offense; in cases in

Juvenile Probation Officer & Detention Worker Observations
(These are not interview questions. DO NOT ASK THE YOUTH THESE QUESTIONS but observe the youth during the intake process and record the observations.)

you observed any of the following:

	Intake Counselor		Detention Care Worker	
If one or more Yes for questions 1 through 3, place youth on sight and sound supervision. Refer youth for immediate Suicide Risk Assessment	YES	NO	YES	NO
1. Threatening to kill self/preoccupied with suicide.	☐	X	☐	☐
2. Fresh wounds/injuries that appear to be self-inflicted.	☐	X	☐	☐

Describe: _____

| 3. Do you have any other reason to think that the youth will try to kill himself? | ☐ | X | ☐ | ☐ |

Explain: _____

If one or more Yes for questions 4 through 6, place youth on close watch & refer youth for Suicide Risk Assessment within 24 hours.				
4. Symptoms of alcohol/drug withdrawal (depression, anxiety, jittery).	☐	X	☐	☐
5. Dramatic mood changes (e.g., from crying to laughing in a short period of time).	☐	X	☐	☐

Describe: _____

| 6. Indications of self-mutilating behavior (e.g., marks/scars or cigarette burns observed). | ☐ | X | ☐ | ☐ |

Describe: _____

Other Comments: _____

Juvenile Probation Officer Name:
Observation Complete: Date/Time: __./29/20 _____

>tention Care Worker Name:
Observation Complete: Date/Time: _____
                         Shift: _____

Juvenile Probation Officer Screening Results

[X] No referral necessary based on available information.

_____
Juvenile Probation Officer Signature

☐ Telephone consultation with assessor: ☐ Assessor will see child immediately
                                            ☐ Assessor will see child within 24 hours
                                            ☐ Assessor will not need to see the child

Referred to: _____
Referred by: _____
Date/Time: _____

Intake Counselor's Signature

Suicide Risk Assessment Results

Assessed by: _____
                                            Date/Time

Results: ☐ High Risk   ☐ Low Risk _____
                                            Assessor's Signature

Recommended:
Supervision: Intervention:
  ☐ Sight and Sound Supervision   Describe: _____
  ☐ Close Watch
  ☐ Standard Supervision
  ☐ Other (specify):

Figure 6.6
(Continued)

which the offense is a nondrug felony, this may mean that every time the juvenile is rearrested, they will be automatically detained.

Though the DRAI scores are based on specific criteria, a screener also has some discretion on whether to influence the DRAI "decision." Consider, for example, a juvenile who repeatedly suggests that he will "skip court" or "harm someone" if released. In such cases, the screener may communicate the situation to the State Attorney, who is able to release or detain a juvenile regardless of the total number of points.

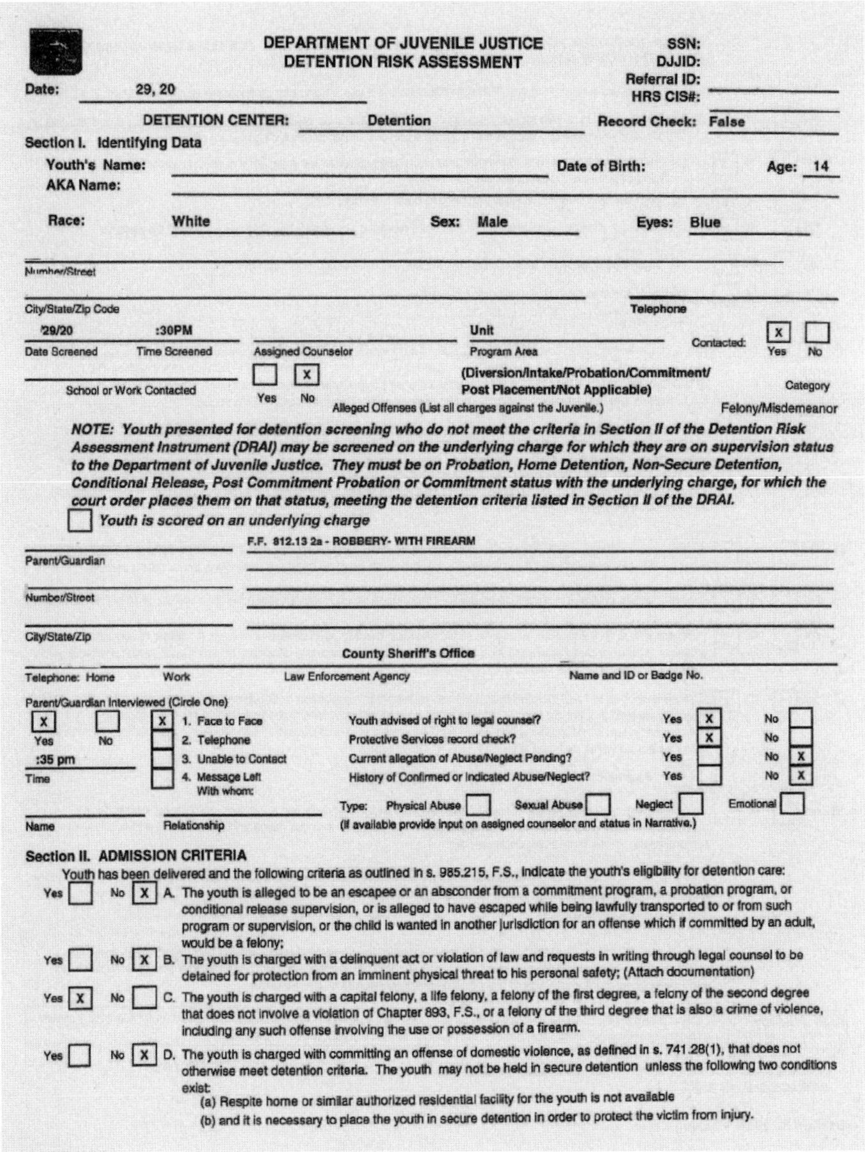

DEPARTMENT OF JUVENILE JUSTICE
DETENTION RISK ASSESSMENT

SSN:
DJJID:
Referral ID:
HRS CIS#:

Date: 29, 20

DETENTION CENTER: Detention

Record Check: False

Section I. Identifying Data

Youth's Name:

Date of Birth:

Age: 14

AKA Name:

Race: White

Sex: Male

Eyes: Blue

Number/Street

City/State/Zip Code

Telephone

'29/20 — Date Screened

:30PM — Time Screened

Assigned Counselor

Unit — Program Area

Contacted: [X] Yes [ ] No

School or Work Contacted [ ] Yes [X] No

(Diversion/Intake/Probation/Commitment/Post Placement/Not Applicable)

Category

Alleged Offenses (List all charges against the Juvenile.)

Felony/Misdemeanor

NOTE: Youth presented for detention screening who do not meet the criteria in Section II of the Detention Risk Assessment Instrument (DRAI) may be screened on the underlying charge for which they are on supervision status to the Department of Juvenile Justice. They must be on Probation, Home Detention, Non-Secure Detention, Conditional Release, Post Commitment Probation or Commitment status with the underlying charge, for which the court order places them on that status, meeting the detention criteria listed in Section II of the DRAI.

[ ] *Youth is scored on an underlying charge*

F.F. 812.13 2a - ROBBERY- WITH FIREARM

Parent/Guardian

Number/Street

City/State/Zip

Telephone: Home — Work

County Sheriff's Office — Law Enforcement Agency

Name and ID or Badge No.

Parent/Guardian Interviewed (Circle One)

[X] Yes [ ] No

[X] 1. Face to Face
[ ] 2. Telephone
[ ] 3. Unable to Contact
[ ] 4. Message Left With whom:

:35 pm — Time

Youth advised of right to legal counsel?	Yes	[X]	No	[ ]
Protective Services record check?	Yes	[X]	No	[ ]
Current allegation of Abuse/Neglect Pending?	Yes	[ ]	No	[X]
History of Confirmed or Indicated Abuse/Neglect?	Yes	[ ]	No	[X]

Type: Physical Abuse [ ] Sexual Abuse [ ] Neglect [ ] Emotional [ ]

Name — Relationship

(If available provide input on assigned counselor and status in Narrative.)

Section II. ADMISSION CRITERIA

Youth has been delivered and the following criteria as outlined in s. 985.215, F.S., indicate the youth's eligibility for detention care:

Yes [ ] No [X] A. The youth is alleged to be an escapee or an absconder from a commitment program, a probation program, or conditional release supervision, or is alleged to have escaped while being lawfully transported to or from such program or supervision, or the child is wanted in another jurisdiction for an offense which if committed by an adult, would be a felony;

Yes [ ] No [X] B. The youth is charged with a delinquent act or violation of law and requests in writing through legal counsel to be detained for protection from an imminent physical threat to his personal safety; (Attach documentation)

Yes [X] No [ ] C. The youth is charged with a capital felony, a life felony, a felony of the first degree, a felony of the second degree that does not involve a violation of Chapter 893, F.S., or a felony of the third degree that is also a crime of violence, including any such offense involving the use or possession of a firearm.

Yes [ ] No [X] D. The youth is charged with committing an offense of domestic violence, as defined in s. 741.28(1), that does not otherwise meet detention criteria. The youth may not be held in secure detention unless the following two conditions exist:
(a) Respite home or similar authorized residential facility for the youth is not available
(b) and it is necessary to place the youth in secure detention in order to protect the victim from injury.

Figure 6.7
Detention Risk Assessment Instrument from the Florida Department of Juvenile Justice

Supervision Risk Classification

supervision risk Assesses the immediate level of supervision for the juvenile

The **supervision risk** instrument is used to assess the immediate level of supervision for the juvenile. The "risk" is measured using several factors including prior offense history, current supervision status, age at current charge, drug or alcohol use, and peer relationships. In addition, the juvenile's most serious charge and his or her risk to recidivate are also considered. Figure 6.8 provides an example supervision

NOTE TO COURT: THE YOUTH MAY NOT BE HELD IN "DETENTION CARE" FOR MORE THAN 48 HOURS, UNLESS THE COURT MAKES SPECIFIC WRITTEN FINDINGS OF (a) and (b).

Factor #E requires an affirmative answer to at least one of the qualifiers before a yes answer can be recorded (s. 985.215(2)(g), F.S.).

Yes [X] No [ ]   E. The youth is charged with any second-degree or third-degree felony involving a violation of Chapter 893, F.S., (Felony Drugs), any third-degree felony that is also not a crime of violence (excluding firearm offenses) and the:

Yes [ ] No [X]   (1) Youth has a record of failure to appear at court hearings after being properly notified in accordance With the Rules of Juvenile Procedure;

Yes [ ] No [X]   (2) Youth has a record of law violations prior to court hearings;

Yes [ ] No [X]   (3) Youth has already been detained or has been released and is awaiting final disposition of the case; or

Yes [X] No [ ]   (4) Youth has a record of violent conduct resulting in physical injury to others;

Yes [X] No [ ]   (5) Youth found to be in possession of a firearm.

F. Yes [X] No [ ]   Not withstanding s.985.213 or s. 985.215(1), F.S., if a minor under 18 years of age is charged with an offense that involves the use or possession of a firearm, as defined in s 790.001, F.S., including a violation of subsection 790.22(3), or is charged for any offense during the commission of which the minor possessed a firearm, the minor SHALL BE DETAINED in secure detention unless the state attorney authorizes the release of the minor.

NOTE TO COURT: WITHIN 24 HOURS THE COURT MUST HAVE A HEARING. AT THE HEARING THE COURT MAY ORDER THAT THE YOUTH CONTINUE TO BE HELD IN SECURE DETENTION IN ACCORDANCE WITH THE APPLICABLE TIME PERIODS SPECIFIED IN 985.215(5), IF THE COURT FINDS THAT THE MINOR MEETS THE CRITERIA SPECIFIED IN S. 985.215(2), OR IF THE COURT MAKES WRITTEN FINDINGS BY CLEAR AND CONVINCING EVIDENCE THAT THE YOUTH IS A CLEAR AND PRESENT DANGER TO HIMSELF OR HERSELF OR THE COMMUNITY.

G. Yes [ ] No [X]   A youth delivered with a judicial order requiring detention care must be detained. The risk assessment instrument still must be completed for informational purposes, but the youth must be detained regardless of the points scored.

A. Yes [ ] No [X]   A youth may be placed into detention status for contempt of court, however, this requires a written court order.

I. Yes [ ] No [X]   Pursuant with s. 316.635, F.S., a juvenile traffic offender found to be in contempt of court for failure to appear or not performing court-ordered sanctions for traffic violations, must be securely detained, unless a staff secure shelter is available, if ordered by the court.

J. Yes [ ] No [X]   A youth is alleged to have violated the conditions of the youth's probation or conditional release supervision. The youth may only be held in a consequence unit if one has been designated and is made available by the Department. If a consequence unit is not available, the youth shall be placed on home detention with electronic monitoring and shall be given a hearing within 24 hours after being taken into custody.

[ ] Consequence Unit   [ ] Home Detention

K. Yes [ ] No [X]   The youth is detained for failure to appear and has previously willfully failed to appear, after proper notice, for an adjudicatory hearing on the same case regardless of the score on the risk assessment instrument and is scheduled for a hearing within 72 hours of being detained, or

The youth is detained for failure to appear and has previously willfully failed to appear, after proper notice, at two or more court hearings of any nature on the same case regardless of the results of the risk assessment instrument and is scheduled for a hearing within 72 hours of being detained.

Note to court: The youth's failure to keep the clerk of court and defense counsel informed of a current and valid mailing address where the child will receive notice to appear at court proceedings does not provide an adequate grounds for excusal of the youth's nonappearance at the hearing.

If any of the above (A-E) are answered yes, proceed to Section III, unless youth is charged solely with an act of misdemeanor domestic violence (D). If each of the above (A-E) are answered no the youth must be released, unless F through K is answered yes.

The responsibility of law enforcement and juvenile probation officers for releasing a youth from custody will be discharged in accordance with s. 985.211

Section III. RISK ASSESSMENT

Figure 6.7
(*Continued*)

risk scoring instrument and related supervision recommendations for juveniles.[16]

In general, if a juvenile is placed on home detention or in secure detention, he or she is required to see a judge within 24 hours for a detention hearing. The detention hearing is not a hearing of guilt or innocence but rather one to determine if there is probable cause for the charges. At the detention hearing, the judge will also issue an arraignment date. Furthermore, the judge will determine whether the youth was placed on the appropriate level of supervision or whether there is a need for a higher or lower level of supervision.

A. Most serious current offense

1. All capital, life, and first degree felony PBL	15	15
2. All other first degree felonies, vehicular homicide, violent second degree felonies, youth is wanted by another jurisdiction for a felony offense	12	0
3. Second degree felony drug charges, escape or absconding, any third degree felony involving the use or possession of a firearm, burglary of an occupied residential structure, or possession of a firearm or concealed weapon by a youth previously adjudicated or with adjudication withheld for a crime that would be a felony if committed by an adult	10	0
4. Violent third degree felonies	9	0
5. All other second degree felonies (except dealing stolen property)	8	0
6. Dealing in stolen property, other third degree felonies that qualify for detention in s. 985.215(2)(g) (See factor #5 above)	7	0

B. Other current offenses and pending charges (separate, non-related events)

1. Each felony	Points Per Felony 2 #	0	0
2. Each misdemeanor	Points Per Misdemeanor 1 #	0	0
3. Prior felony arrest within last 7 days		6	0

C. Prior History

1. 3 felony adjudications or adjudications withheld last 12 months, or	4	0
2. 2 felony adjudications or adjudications withheld last 12 months, or	2	0
3. 1 felony adjudication or adjudication withheld or misdemeanor adjudications or adjudications withheld	1	0

D. Legal Status

1. Committed or detention	8	0
2. Active probation cases with last adjudication or adjudication withheld within 90 days	6	6
3. Active probation cases with last adjudication or adjudication withheld more than 90 days ago	2	0

E. Aggravating or Mitigating Circumstances

1. Aggravating factors (add to score)	1-3	0
2. Mitigating factors (subtract from score)	1-3	0
The juvenile probation officer must fully document the reason for scoring aggravating or mitigating points.		

F. Mandatory Aggravating Circumstance: Illegal possession of a firearm.   3   0

G. Detain/Release Decision

0 - 6 points = release
7 - 11 points = non-secure or home detention
12 or more points = secure detention

TOTAL (Sum A-F)   21

Section IV. STATE ATTORNEY REVIEW/DECISION (COMPLETE BASED UPON ITEM #1 BEING APPROPRIATE)

1. If the juvenile probation officer believes that a youth who is eligible for detention based upon the results of the risk assessment instrument should be released, the state attorney must be contacted to approve release. The state attorney also may approve home or non-secure detention for a youth who scores eligible for secure detention. The juvenile probation officer must document the reasons for the recommendation in the narrative section.

2. (a) State Attorney contacted?   Yes ☐   No ☐
   Name _____
   (b) State Attorney decision   Detain ☐   Release ☐

Section V. SCREENING DECISION

Detention: Yes ☒   No ☐   Notification of Hearing: Hearing Date: /30/20   Time:

Placement: Secure ☒   Home ☐   Non-secure ☐   Staff-Secure ☐   Respite ☐   Release ☐

Criminal Background Check done? _____

Results: _____

Figure 6.7
(*Continued*)

Assessment for Mental Health

State laws require that each juvenile entering a state juvenile justice system be screened for substance abuse, mental health problems, and suicide risk. When the juvenile is under the jurisdiction of the Department of Juvenile Justice, the department is responsible for the safety and security of the juvenile. Therefore, during the intake process, juveniles are assessed using instruments that may alert the screener and other juvenile justice officials to the juvenile's potential need for additional screening or mental health and substance abuse treatment services. One mental health and substance abuse screening instrument that may be used at intake is called the **Massachusetts Youth Screening Instrument (MAYSI)**. The MAYSI consists of a list of

Massachusetts Youth Screening Instrument (MAYSI) Assesses substance abuse and mental health at intake

SUPERVISION RISK CLASSIFICATION INSTRUMENT

Juvenile Name: ______________________

DJJID: __________ JPO Name: __________ Unit: ____

Date Completed: __________ Referral ID: ______

1. [2] **Prior Referrals** 5 = 7 or More 3 = 5 or 6 2 = 3 or 4 1 = 1 or 2 0 = None	6. [1] **Peer Relationships** 2 = Gang involvement or peers are gang members 1 = Primarily negative peers/ no peers 0 = Primarily positive peers
2. [1] **Higher Level of Prior Disposition or Current Status** 2 = Committed 1 = Probation 0 = None of the Above	7. [1] **Parental Control** 2 = No control or supervision 1 = Limited control or supervision 0 = Effective control or supervision
3. [0] **Age at Time of Current Arrest** 4 = 13 or under 2 = 14 or 15 years old 0 = 16 or over	8. [1] **History of Abuse/Neglect** 2 = History of physical or sexual abuse of youth 1 = History of neglect of youth 0 = None
4. [1] **Drug or Alcohol Use** 2 = Chronic use w/serious disruption of functioning 1 = Occasional use w/some disruption of functioning 0 = No use or no interference	9. [1] **Mental Health** 2 = Current Diagnosis, in treatment or prescribed medication 1 = Mental health assessment needed 0 = None
5. [1] **School Adjustment** 2 = Suspended, Expelled, Dropped Out, (or history of) 1 = Chronic Tardiness or Truancy 0 = Regular attendance, GED, H.S. Diploma	10. [2] **Employment** 2 = 16 or over, not employed, and not pursuing education 0 = All others
Total Score: 11 0-5 Low Risk; 6-10 Moderate Risk; 11-15 High Risk; 16+ Very High Risk	Override Category: Diversion Juvenile Supervision Category: Intensive Probation

Figure 6.8

Supervision Risk Classification Instrument from the Florida Department of Juvenile Justice

fifty-two yes-no items that identify "potential mental health and substance use needs of youth" (Grisso and Underwood 1999, 49). More specifically, the MAYSI measures (1) alcohol and drug use, (2) angry or irritable behaviors, (3) depressed and anxious behavior, (4) somatic complaints, (5) suicide ideation, (6) thought disturbance (boys), and (7) traumatic experiences (boys and girls).[17] It usually takes less than thirty minutes to administer and can be scored and interpreted electronically. Figure 6.9 shows a report generated from one juvenile's answers on the 52-item MAYSI-2 questionnaire[18]

SUPERVISION RISK CLASSIFICATION INSTRUMENT

MATRIX

MOST SERIOUS CURRENT CHARGE	LOW RISK (0 – 5)	MODERATE RISK (6 – 10)	HIGH RISK (11 – 15)	VERY HIGH RISK (16 +)
1ST Degree Felony OR 2nd Degree Violent Felony	Recommend Commitment OR Intensive Probation	Recommend Commitment OR Intensive Probation	Recommend Commitment	Recommend Commitment
2nd Degree Felony OR 3rd Degree Violent Felony	Intensive Probation OR General Probation	Intensive Probation OR General Probation	Recommend Commitment OR Intensive Probation	Recommend Commitment
3rd Degree Felony OR 1st Degree Violent Misdemeanor	Diversion OR Minimum Probation	General Probation OR Minimum Probation	Recommend Commitment OR Intensive Probation	Recommend Commitment OR Intensive Probation
1st Degree Misdemeanor OR 2nd Degree Misdemeanor	Diversion	Diversion	General Probation OR Minimum Probation	Recommend Commitment OR Intensive Probation

*Staff should use professional judgment to choose the most appropriate level of supervision when a cell offers more than one choice.

Figure 6.8
(Continued)

and indicates which statements from the questionnaire contribute to measurement of each of the seven subgroups (e.g., alcohol and drug use).

The results from the MAYSI screening are incorporated into the report for the State Attorney. One purpose of the screening is to determine if there are extralegal variables influencing the juvenile's delinquent behavior.[19] If the screening results in the need for a referral, state statute requires that a follow-up be completed within a certain amount of time, usually within ten to fourteen days.[20] However, when the suicide ideation measure indicates the immediate attention to suicide risk, the juvenile should be referred immediately or at least within twenty-four hours.[21] How is the need for a referral made? A "scoring summary" for the juvenile assessed (see Figure 6.9) is provided in Figure 6.10.[22] Note the bold vertical line starting between the "2" and "3" in row 1 and ending between "0" and "1" on the last row; if a juvenile scores to the right of the line, then he or she will be issued a referral. There are other assessment instruments that may be used instead of the MAYSI. One is the **Positive Achievement Change Tool (PACT)**, which the Florida Department of Juvenile Justice approved as its

Positive Achievement Change Tool (PACT) Screening instrument at intake which uses a series of risk factors to assess whether a juvenile has a substance abuse or mental health problem

DEPARTMENT OF JUVENILE JUSTICE
SUBSTANCE ABUSE AND MENTAL HEALTH
PRELIMINARY SCREENING
EXPANDED M.A.Y.S.I.

Client's Name: _____ SSN: _____ DJJID# _____

Date of Birth: _____ Age: **14** Race: **White** _____ Sex: **Male** Referral ID: _____

Client's Address/Phone: _____

Parent/Guardian: _____ Relationship to Client: **Mother**

Parent/Guardian's Address: _____

Home Phone: _____ Work Phone: _____

Circuit of Residence: **Circuit** _____ Court Docket #: _____

Current Charge(s): **812.13 2a ROBBERY- WITH FIREARM**

If Suicide Risk, Screening Instrument Administered   Date: **/29/20**

If currently in SA or MH Treatment: _____
                                    Provider's Name   Type of Treatment

Date of Screening: **/29/20**   Time: **:30 pm**   Location: **JAC**

Screening Completed by: _____
                        DJJ Worker   Phone   Unit

Case Assigned to: _____   Unit
                  DJJ Worker   Phone   Unit

Respondent: _____
            Name   Relationship to Client

Referred to:
[X] a) for assessment   In Detention? Yes [X] No [ ]

[ ] b) for referral to crisis intervention/treatment   Date Assessment Recommendation due to DJJ Worker

[ ] c) no referral necessary based upon available information

Alcohol/Drug Use   0/8

[ ] 10. Have you done anything you wish you hadn't, when you were drunk or high?

[ ] 19. Have your parents or friends thought you drink too much?

[ ] 23. Have you gotten in trouble when you've been high or have been drinking?

[ ] 24. If yes[to #23], has the trouble been fighting?

[ ] 33. Have you used alcohol or drugs to help you feel better?

[ ] 37. Have you been drunk or high at school?

[ ] 40. Have you used alcohol and drugs at the same time?

[ ] 45. Have you been so drunk or high that you couldn't remember what happened?

Figure 6.9
MAYSI Mental Health and Substance Abuse Screening Report Example

Video Profile: The Intake
Process II

screening instrument in 2007. The PACT uses a series of risk factors to assess whether a juvenile has a substance abuse or mental health problem.[23]

CLASSIFICATION

Classification is an arrangement according to some systematic division into classes or groups. In classifying individual people, one separates a group of people into smaller groups, each with something in common. The possibilities of classification are almost limitless. For example, in the intake process classifications are made by sex, age, and offense committed. Think about the benefits of first classifying juveniles who come into contact with the

Angry/Irritable   4/9

[X] 2. Have you lost your temper easily, or had a "short fuse"?

[X] 6. Have you been easily upset?

[X] 7. Have you thought a lot about getting back at someone you have been angry at?

[ ] 8. Have you been really jumpy or hyper?

[ ] 13. Have you had too many bad moods?

[ ] 35. Have you felt angry a lot?

[ ] 39. Have you gotten frustrated easily?

[ ] 42. When you have been mad, have you stayed mad for a long time?

[X] 44. Have you hurt or broken something on purpose, just because you were mad?

Depressed-Anxious   0/9

[ ] 3. Have nervous or worried feelings kept you from doing things you wanted to do?

[ ] 14. Have you had nightmares that are bad enough to make you afraid to go to sleep?

[ ] 17. Have you felt lonely too much of the time?

[ ] 21. Has it seemed like some part of your body always hurts you?

[ ] 34. Have you felt that you don't have fun with your friends anymore?

[ ] 35. Have you felt angry a lot?

[ ] 41. Has it been hard for you to feel close to people outside your family?

[ ] 47. Have you given up hope for your life?

[ ] 51. Have you had a lot of bad thoughts or dreams about a bad or scary event that happened to you?

Somatic Complaints   0/6

When you feel nervous or anxious ......

[ ] 27. Have you felt shaky?

[ ] 28. Has your heart beat very fast?

[ ] 29. Have you felt short of breath?

[ ] 30. Have your hands felt sweaty?

[ ] 31. Has your stomach been upset?

[ ] 43. Have you had bad headaches?

Figure 6.9
(*Continued*)

juvenile justice system; what variables would be best for classifying juveniles? Remember, when people are classified, they are invariably defined or described by their classification. Thus, classifications resulting in observations of differences must be used cautiously. The classifications must be both accurate and objective.

History of Classification

Previous attempts at classifying offenders were mostly devoted to adult groups, with some recognition given to the fact that children, because of their age, constituted a separate group. Common correctional practices separated adult and juvenile offenders, and there was some limited experimentation with reeducation or retraining of youthful offenders. By separating and assigning prison populations by age, sex, and potential for salvation, correctional administrators in the past were initiating a system

Suicide Ideation __0/5__

☐ 11. Have you wished you were dead?
☐ 16. Have you felt like life was not worth living?
☐ 18. Have you felt like hurting yourself?
☐ 22. Have you felt like killing yourself?
☐ 47. Have you given up hope for your life?

Thought Disturbance - Boys __0/5__

☐ 9. Have you seen things other people say are not really there?
☐ 20. Have you heard voices other people can't hear?
☐ 25. Have other people been able to control your brain or your thoughts?
☐ 26. Have you had a bad feeling that things don't seem real, like you're in a dream?
☐ 32. Have you been able to make other people do things just by thinking about it?

Traumatic Experience - Girls __0/5__

☐ 48. Have you EVER IN YOUR WHOLE LIFE had something very bad or terrifying happen to you?
☐ 49. Have you ever been badly hurt or been in danger of getting badly hurt or killed?
☐ 50. Have you ever been raped, or been in danger of getting raped?
☐ 51. Have you had a lot of bad thoughts or dreams about a bad or scary event that happen to you?
☐ 52. Have you ever seen someone severely injured or killed (in person - not in movies or on TV)?

Traumatic Experience - Boys __0/5__

☐ 46. Have people talked about you a lot when you're not there?
☐ 48. Have you EVER IN YOUR WHOLE LIFE had something very bad or terrifying happen to you?
☐ 49. Have you ever been badly hurt or been in danger of getting badly hurt or killed?
☐ 51. Have you had a lot of bad thoughts or dreams about a bad or scary event that happen to you?
☐ 52. Have you ever seen someone severely injured or killed (in person - not in movies or on TV)?

☐ **Invalid Instrument**

Figure 6.9
(*Continued*)

of classification that has remained, in large part, with us today. Ever since the practice of putting people into prisons or jails has existed, there have been various means of separating one type of prisoner from another. Thus, the practice of separation (i.e., simply physically isolating one offender group from another) has become identified with classification.

Most early forms of classification were based primarily on superficial characteristics. For example, men were housed separately from women in Spanish prisons as early as 1518. In the early eighteenth century, the Society of St. Vincent de Paul, which cared for orphans and the poor, realized the necessity of segregating children from adults and instituted separate so-called houses of refuge for children. One of the first houses of refuge for delinquent children was started in Germany in 1824, and a similar refuge was established in New York in 1825. In the Walnut Street

DEPARTMENT OF JUVENILE JUSTICE
SUBSTANCE ABUSE AND MENTAL HEALTH
PRELIMINARY SCREENING
M.A.Y.S.I.

Client's Name: SSN: DJJID#
Date of Birth: Age: 14 Race: White Sex: Male Referral ID:

Client's Address/Phone:

Parent/Guardian: Relationship to Client: Mother
Parent/Guardian's Address:
Home Phone: Work Phone:
Circuit of Residence: Circuit Court Docket #:
Current Charge(s): 812.13 2a ROBBERY- WITH FIREARM

If Suicide Risk, Screening Instrument Administered Date: /29/20
If currently in SA or MH Treatment:
Provider's Name Type of Treatment

Date of Screening: /29/20 Time: :30 pm Location: JAC
Screening Completed by:
DJJ Worker Phone Unit
Case Assigned to: Unit
DJJ Worker Phone Unit
Respondent:
Name Relationship to Client

Referred to:
[X] a) for assessment In Detention? Yes [X] No [ ]
[ ] b) for referral to crisis intervention/treatment Date Assessment Recommendation due to DJJ Worker
[ ] c) no referral necessary based upon available information

MAYSI-2 SCORING SUMMARY

ASSESSMENT ZONE

AD	ALCOHOL/DRUG USE	0	1	2	3	4	5	6	7	8	
AI	ANGRY-IRRITABLE	0	1	2	3	4	5	6	7	8	9
DA	DEPRESSED-ANXIOUS	0	1	2	3	4	5	6	7	8	9
SC	SOMATIC COMPLAINTS	0	1	2	3	4	5	6			
SI	SUICIDE IDEATION	0	1	2	3	4	5				
TD	THOUGHT DISTURB. (BOYS)	0	1	2	3	4	5				
TE	TRAUMATIC EXPERIENCES (BOYS)	0	1	2	3	4	5				
TE	TRAUMATIC EXPERIENCES (GIRLS)	0	1	2	3	4	5				

If any area is highlighted to the right of the cut-off line an assessment recommendation must be made in accordance with the attached procedures.

Figure 6.10
MAYSI Scoring Summary Example

jail, which opened in Philadelphia in 1790, a rudimentary classification of prisoners was practiced. Men were separated from women, and children from adults. In 1797, "the management of the Walnut Street jail actually began a classification that may be regarded as the first attempt to separate prisoners by type."[24]

The first major correctional institution specifically for juveniles was the **New York Reformatory at Elmira** (1876). The founders of the New York Reformatory and others patterned after it reasoned that the separation of young offenders from adult criminals would enable the correctional personnel to facilitate the treatment of their young charges more

New York Reformatory at Elmira The first major correctional institution specifically for juveniles

effectively. These juvenile institutions offered educational programs for their young offenders, as opposed to the industrial programs offered in the adult prisons.

The notion that a system of classification of offenders might lead to better, more effective treatment programs spread to other institutions, juvenile and adult alike. Warden Cassidy of the Eastern Penitentiary (1833) remarked on this type of prison administration called classification:

> After hearing so much of herding and grading, congregation and classification, I am the more fully convinced that the individual treatment for the people that have to be cared for in prisons for punishment of crime, is the simplest and most philosophical and is productive of better results.[25]

During the latter part of the nineteenth century, a slow but discernible trend toward treatment programs was evident. These programs affected both classification and administrative systems.

In the twentieth century, classification of prisoners moved from the obvious differences among prisoners, such as age and sex, to those related to personality characteristics and various types of crime. In 1917, for example, New Jersey implemented the first formalized prison classification system in the United States, a system that was the result of the Prison Inquiry Commission of the same year. The commission, among other things, brought clinical experts inside the prison walls to prepare and implement classification systems. Classification in New Jersey prisons was identified as follows:

- The difficult class who are hostile to society and require close custody,
- The better class who are good prisoners with reasonably good prognosis but are serving for long terms and require close custody,
- The simple feeble-minded whose condition is not complicated by psychopathic traits,
- The senile and incapacitated class,
- The psychotic and epileptic class who should be transferred to the hospitals for the mentally ill, and
- The defective delinquent class whose low intelligence is combined with high emotional instability and may need long periods of custody and training under an indeterminate sentence.[26]

A congressional act of 1930 provided a program for the classification of federal prisoners. The federal system was similar to New Jersey's and was adopted quickly by other Eastern metropolitan states.[27] Vernon Fox, who examined the influence of the advent of classification schemes as they relate to the treatment needs of prisoners, concluded that

> Classification, in its modern sense, is an administrative vehicle by which treatment resources get to an inmate. Conversely, classification, in its older sense, was a way of getting inmates to the program that would benefit them most and/or hurt them least. A modern classification system serves both functions.[28]

Classification of Juveniles

There are three simple ways that youth can be channeled through the juvenile justice system:

- They could all be handled in the same manner, receiving the same dispositions and services (impractical).
- They could be dealt with randomly, depending on the personal beliefs, skills, and interests of the juvenile justice personnel with whom they come into conflict (often used).
- They could be assessed, classified, and directed to the programs and services that are most appropriate for them and will provide the level of supervision needed to ensure public safety (most desirable).[29]

As discussed previously, juvenile assessment and classification are components of the process of sorting youths into various groups for the purpose of custody, supervision, and treatment. In some states, juveniles are assigned to an institution on the basis of their potential risk of re-offending, supervision risk, or the need for treatment.

One of the shortcomings of the assessment instruments discussed previously is that juveniles, regardless of diagnostic evaluations, are required to fit the institution's needs and limited treatment capabilities and not the other way around. For example, although classification by management needs has had some good effects at juvenile institutions, it has been implemented at the risk of tailoring the treatment needs of juveniles to fit the institutions, regardless of whether those needs are in concert with the institution's treatment philosophy. Diagnostic practitioners are often frustrated by this course of events. They see their treatment recommendations being accommodated to a managerial classification system and wonder why they should bother with the diagnostic process in the first place.

The development of an accurate method to identify juvenile offenders with a high potential of recidivism or who might be dangerous to themselves or others would be of great benefit today. Such a system could be of help at the time of disposition or sentencing in making the right choice in each case, increasing the cost-effectiveness of correctional programs, and looking after the potential safety to the community. Worth mentioning, however, is the fact that sentencing decisions are not based on risk factors alone or even the desire to protect others from the offender. Courts are also expected to maintain civil liberties, act as deterrent forces to others, maintain a sense of fair play, and punish those who transgress the law, and many of these goals are not altogether compatible with protecting the interests of society and reducing recidivism.

In assessing the utility of classification as it relates to our current juvenile justice system, three major judgment calls by members of officialdom must be considered. First is the **classification of the actor**—the juvenile delinquent himself or herself. There are several schemes, some of which are examined subsequently in this chapter, that are attempts to classify juveniles in some meaningful and useful way. However, it is generally conceded that no valid and applicable system of classification of delinquents now exists. There is agreement within the juvenile correctional field that such a system is desirable, and several serious and dedicated social scientist researchers have long sought the development of "treatment-relevant typologies" of delinquents. There is even a possibility that they might reach a consensus regarding the basic components of a classification system and types of delinquents at some future point.

The second major judgment call required of the classifiers is the **classification of the act**—the delinquent behavior. Judging the seriousness of the crime is aimed at accurately assessing the harm caused by the juvenile and what punishment is in order.

The third judgment call is perhaps the most important: It answers the question, "For what purpose?" Most juvenile classification schemes in use today are referred to as **classification systems for treatment** purposes. However, even a cursory analysis of these schemes and the ways in which they are used reveals that they could be called more accurately **classification systems for management** purposes. When those making the decisions determine why a juvenile is to be classified, it will make the "how to do it" become more logical and self-evident. As mentioned previously, there are two major purposes for the development of juvenile offender typologies: classification for management purposes and classification for treatment purposes. With some variations, the methods of accomplishing these purposes interface quite frequently. Box 6.2 lists goals and applications juvenile justice officers may employ in analyzing and classifying juveniles.

Most management classification systems have taken on a new responsibility today: the accurate assessment of the offender's potential risk in terms of danger to both self and the community, and the subsequent placement of the offender in a facility capable of assuming that risk and protecting the offender from both himself or herself and other inmates, and the community from the offender. Thus, the placement decision involves the determination of restrictiveness that fits the severity of the juvenile's offense balanced by the desire to protect the community. The aim is to decide whether the juvenile should be placed in an institution or under

classification of the actor
Classification of the juvenile

classification of the act
Classification of the delinquent behavior

classification systems for treatment Assessing the juvenile for treatment needs

classification systems for management Assessing the juvenile to determine classifications

BOX 6.2 **GOALS AND APPLICATIONS FOR ASSESSMENT AND CLASSIFICATION**

Goal	Possible Applications
1. To determine case plans for individual youth	• Conduct an individualized assessment of each youth • Assess the risk of recidivism • Channel youth to programs and/or levels of supervision that best meet their needs and control risks • Ensure youth are receiving equitable and consistent treatment compared with others with similar risks and needs • Match identified needs with available resources • Ensure that certain types of problems are considered for all cases • Provide data for future monitoring of cases • Identify youth for whom further in-depth assessments are needed
2. To allocate resources appropriately and implement effective supervision policies	• Direct the most intensive interventions to the most serious, violent, and chronic offenders • Set priorities for case plans • Organize staff and other agency resources • Determine workloads
3. To provide justification and accountability for case decisions	• Reassess and evaluate effectiveness of case plans and program strategies • Provide equal, nondiscriminatory treatment
4. To enhance other parts of the juvenile justice system	• Develop formalized procedures, such as sentencing guidelines • Provide recommendations to juvenile court (i.e., through presentence reports)
5. To gather program data and evaluate programs	• Collect uniform statistical data on results of assessments and provision of services • Use data to plan, monitor, and evaluate programs
6. To conduct research on programs and juveniles	• Test hypotheses about programs and youth

Source: Ann Crowe, *Jurisdictional Technical Assistance Package for Juvenile Corrections* (Washington, DC: OJJDP National Training and Technical Assistance Center, December 2000), pp. 4–5.

community supervision. Balancing the risk to the community and the potential for rehabilitation are the aims of this process. Accordingly, and as discussed previously, the classification and assessment instruments combine items that assess the seriousness of current and past offenses plus the youth's potential for recidivism. Thus, they place great emphasis on **risk assessment.** These instruments are research based and reflect the probability that a youth

risk assessment The juvenile's potential for recidivism

with certain characteristics are more likely to re-offend. An example of a placement instrument from Louisiana is presented in Figure 6.11; compare it with the one from Florida presented previously in the chapter (see Figures 6.7 and 6.8). The Louisiana instrument is geared toward making a decision on whether to institutionalize the offender or place him or her in a community-based program. After the decision on institutionalization is made, a **custody assessment** (i.e., supervision risk) comes into play. This is an instrument meant to gauge the juvenile's potential for disruption in the institution, affecting both him- or herself or others. Here, common concerns include assaults on staff or peers, escapes, and suicides.[30]

custody assessment Assessment of the juvenile's supervision risk

	Score
1. Severity of Present Adjudicated Offense	___
Level 0 felony	10
Level 1 felony	7
Level 2 felony	5
Level 3 felony	3
Level 4 felony	1
All other	0
2. If Present Adjudication Involves	___
Possession/use of firearm	2
Multiple felonies	2
3. Number of Prior Adjudications	___
Two or more felony adjudications	2
One felony or two+ misdemeanors	2
None	0
4. Most Serious Prior Adjudication	___
Level 0 or Level 1 felony	5
Level 2 felony	3
Level 3 or below	0
5. For Offenders With Prior Adjudications	___
Age at first adjudication	
Age 13 or younger	2
Age 14	1
Age 15 or older	0
6. History of Probation/Parole Supervision	___
Offender currently on probation/parole	2
Offender with probation/parole revocation	2
7. History of In-Home/Nonsecure Residential Intervention	___
Three or more prior failures	3
One or two prior failures	1
None	0
8. In the Offender Had a Prior Placement in the OJS	2 ___
9. Prior Escapes or Runaways	___
From secure more than once	3
From secure once or nonsecure 2+	2
From nonsecure once	0
Total Score	___
Recommended Action	
0–6 = Consider nonsecure placement	
7–8 = Consider short-term placement	
9+ = Consider secure placement	

Figure 6.11
Louisiana Office of Juvenile Services Secure Custody Screening Document

Source: *Crowe, Jurisdictional Technical Assistance, p.150*

Classification was devised to serve particular purposes. Sometimes classification has direct application to the management of the juvenile offender population; other times it has direct application to their treatment; and still other times classification is useful in testing new management methods. Classification systems are needed for the control of delinquents, for demonstrating treatment effectiveness, and for enumerating possible etiologies.[31]

classification Administrative controls utilized to manage delinquents for treatment

SUMMARY

As noted, a good assessment and classification system should answer three questions:

1. What caused the juvenile to become a delinquent?
2. What kind of help does the offender need to prevent further law violations? and
3. Where can the juvenile obtain the help needed?

This chapter examines assessment classification in a general way beginning with the intake process—its definition, the physical settings of classification systems, and its purposes: for risk assessment, supervision assessment, and treatment. In addition, the Community Assessment Center model is described.

KEY TERMS

classification
classification systems for
    management
classification systems for
    treatment
classification of the act
classification of the actor
Community Assessment
    Centers (CACs)
custody assessment
Detention Risk Assessment
    Instrument (DRAI)
face sheet

grievance procedure
Massachusetts Youth Screening
    Instrument (MAYSI)
Miranda
intake
New York Reformatory at Elmira
Positive Achievement Change
    Tool (PACT)
risk assessment
screener
Suicide Risk Screening Instrument
    (SRSI)
supervision risk

DISCUSSION AND REVIEW QUESTIONS

1. Discuss the pros and cons of the CAC model in terms of classifying and assessing juveniles.
2. Define what is meant by classification. Give examples of how you personally have seen a classification system used.

3. Discuss the different types of assessment instruments.

4. Using the various scales presented in this chapter, classify the following cases using the most appropriate scale for the case.

   a. Kyle is 13 years old and was brought to the detention center with several peers after they were arrested for vandalism. They had defaced signs in a park and deliberately scratched and broken mirrors on vehicles. Kyle has had no previous contact with the juvenile justice system. The school reports that until this year his grades were average, but his work declined in recent months. A urinalysis indicated chemicals in his system, and one of the peers involved in the incident said they sniff paint on occasion. Kyle's mother reported that she and her husband divorced a year ago, and as a single mother, she has had increasing difficulties managing Kyle and her other children. Kyle was released to his mother pending further processing of the case to determine the best disposition.

   b. Jennifer is 15 years old and was arrested for prostitution. There is a record at protective services of involvement with the family because a relative sexually abused Jennifer and a sister. During intake at the local detention center, Jennifer's urine screen tested positive for marijuana. She reported that she began smoking cigarettes and using drugs and alcohol around age 11. When her family was contacted, they said Jennifer frequently runs away and had not been home for several days. Although Jennifer is enrolled in school, she is often truant and makes very poor grades. Jennifer has never been arrested before, but her parents did arrange for her to spend six months in a private treatment center. She claims her best friend is a 21-year-old male who is homeless and has a record of drug-related offenses. Jennifer's parents believed it was not best for her to return home, and she was placed in a nonsecure emergency shelter until her case is arraigned.

   c. Brad is 17 years old and was arrested for armed robbery. He was with two other males, ages 19 and 20 years, when they robbed a gas station attendant at gunpoint. Brad tested positive for amphetamines. His records indicate a lengthy list of juvenile crimes, beginning with status offenses at age 11. His first arrest for a delinquent offense was at age 13 years. Brad quit school at age 16 years but had only completed about half the credits needed for ninth-grade work. School reports also indicate frequent disciplinary problems, including fights with other students and one incident in which he hit a teacher. His mother has had recurring hospitalizations for a mental illness. Brad was placed on probation, but his record of compliance with court orders was poor.

Source: Ann Crowe, *Jurisdictional Technical Assistance Package for Juvenile Corrections* (Washington, DC: OJJDP National Training and Technical Assistance Center, December 2000), p. 1.

VIDEO PROFILES

The Intake Process 1 video profile in MyCrimeKit shows the interactions between Rodrick, a juvenile offender, and the intake/probation officer. The officer is familiar with Rodrick's delinquent history and talks about his successes/potential problems that face him given this new arrest. The video also shows Rodrick entering detention. Compare and contrast this intake environment with that of the adult system. What charges have brought Rodrick to intake this time? Finally, describe the detention intake process.

The Intake Process 2 video profile in MyCrimeKit shows the intake process for Kenneth and Kentrell with the intake/probation officer. What is Kentrell's criminal history? Given this and his most immediate charge, what do you think is an appropriate action/decision by the juvenile justice system? The brothers are held in detention until their hearing. Utilizing one of the sample forms in this chapter and either Kenneth's or Kentrell's criminal history and current charges, identify why each was detained prior to the initial hearing.

MYCRIMEKIT

mycrimekit™ Go to MyCrimeKit.com to explore the following study tools and resources specific to this chapter:

- Practice Quiz: Test your knowledge with multiple-choice, true-false, fill-in-the-blank, and essay questions.
- Flashcards: 20 flashcards to test your knowledge of the chapter's key terms.
- Web Quest: Review the Web site of your local Juvenile Assessment Center and compare it with the Pinellas County, Florida, Juvenile Assessment Center; What are the similarities and differences?
- Web Links: Check out sites related to the content presented in this chapter.

ENDNOTES

1. Laura Manis, Juvenile Assessment Officer, coauthored this chapter.
2. John P. Kenney, Donald E. Fuller, and Robert J. Barry, *Police Work with Juveniles and the Administration of Juvenile Justice* (Springfield, IL: C. C. Thomas, 1995): p. 57.
3. Law Enforcement Arrest Report from the State of Florida, 2002.
4. Debra Oldenettel and Madeline Wordes, *The Community Assessment Center Concept* (Washington, DC: Office of Juvenile Justice and Delinquency Prevention, 2000), pp. 1–2.

5. Ibid, p. 4.

6. Escambia County, Florida, Juvenile Assessment Center. *Mission Statement.* Retrieved November 20, 2006, http://uwf.edu/ojs/Programs/jac.htm

7. Pinellas County, Florida, Juvenile Assessment Center Brochure.

8. Richard Dembo, G. Turner, J. Schmeidler, C. C. Sue, P. Borden, and D. Manning, "Development and Evaluation of a Classification of High Risk Youths Entering a Juvenile Assessment Center," *Substance Abuse and Misuse,* Vol. 31 (1996), pp. 303–322; Richard Dembo, J. Schmeidler, B. Nini-Gough, and D. Manning, "Sociodemographic, Delinquency-Abuse History, and Psychosocial Functioning Differences Among Juvenile Offenders of Various Ages," *Journal of Child and Adolescent Substance Abuse,* Vol. 8 (1998), pp. 63–78; James E. Rivers, Richard Dembo, and Robert S. Anwyl, "The Hillsborough County, Florida Juvenile Assessment Center: A Prototype," *The Prison Journal,* Vol. 78 (1998), pp. 439–450.

9. Escambia County, Florida, Juvenile Assessment Center Law Enforcement Notification, 2002.

10. Escambia County, Florida, Juvenile Miranda Warning or Notification of Rights, 2002.

11. Florida Department of Juvenile Justice Suicide Risk Screening Instrument, 2002.

12. Ibid.

13. Florida Bureau of Intervention Services. (June 1996). *Florida Department of Juvenile Justice Intervention Services Manual.* (Tallahassee, FL: Bureau of Intervention Services): Chapter 1 Detention Screening.

14. Ibid.

15. Florida Department of Juvenile Justice Detention Risk Assessment Instrument, 2002.

16. Florida Department of Juvenile Justice Example Supervision Risk Classification Instrument, 2002.

17. T. Grisso, R. Barnum, R. Famulare, and R. Kinsehem (2000) Massachusetts Youth Screening Instrument (MAYSI-2).

18. Florida Department of Juvenile Justice Example MAYSI Report, 2002.

19. Florida Department of Juvenile Justice, Probation and Parole. *Form 35*: page 2.

20. Ibid.

21. Florida Department of Juvenile Justice. *Rules for Probation Intake* 63D-1.001 - .005. Retrieved online February 11, 2008, http://www.djj.state.fl.us/rules/Probation-Intake_63D-1_001-005.pdf

22. Probation and Parole. *Form 35*: page 1.

23. *Rules for Probation Intake.*

24. Harry E. Barnes and Negley K. Teeters, *New Horizons in Criminology* (Englewood Cliffs, NJ: Prentice Hall, 1959), p. 466.

25. *Annual Report of the Eastern Penitentiary,* 1968, p. 80.

26. W. J. Ellis, "Classification as the Basis for Rehabilitation of Prisoners," *News Bulletin of the National Society for Penal Information* (February 1931).

27. Congressional Act of 1930 (C, 339, Section 7, 46 Stat. 390).

28. Vernon B. Fox, "Changing Classification Organizational Patterns: 1870-1900," *Correctional Classification and Treatment* (Cincinnati, OH: Anderson Press, 1975), p. 9.

29. Ann Crowe, *Jurisdictional Technical Assistance Package for Juvenile Corrections* (Washington, DC: OJJDP National Training and Technical Assistance Center, December 2000), p. 3; http://www.ncjrs.org/html/ojjdp/juris_tap_report/ch5.html

30. Ibid., pp. 10–11.

31. See Richard D. Hoge and Donald A. Andrews, *Assessing the Youthful Offender: Issues and Techniques* (New York: Plenum Press, 1996).

7
Legal Rights of Juveniles

*J*uvenile Court history has again demonstrated that
unbridled discretion, however benevolently motivated,
is frequently a poor substitute for principle and procedure.
. . . The absence of substantive standards has not necessarily
meant that children receive careful, compassionate, individualized treatment. The absence of procedural rules based upon
constitutional principles has not always produced fair, efficient,
and effective procedures. Departures from established principles
of due process have frequently resulted not in enlightened
procedures, but in arbitrariness.

IN RE GAULT 387 U.S. 1 (1967)

LEARNING OBJECTIVES

1. Determine the significance of the landmark cases involving the rights of juveniles in court.
2. Determine the significance of the landmark cases involving the rights of incarcerated juveniles.
3. Identify the elements of a juvenile's right to treatment.
4. Identify the reasons the death penalty no longer applies to juveniles in the United States.
5. Identify the substantive rights of juveniles.

CHAPTER OVERVIEW

Since the late 1960s, decisions laid down by the U.S. Supreme Court have led to changes in juvenile court operations that have turned the system away from its original rehabilitative posture. The "criminalization" of the juvenile court has changed it to what Feld refers to as a second-rate criminal court that provides neither therapy nor justice.[1] Despite these rulings, the rights of juveniles have not been extended past the situation cited by the Court in the *Kent* decision, with juveniles getting "neither the protection accorded to adults nor the solicitous care and regenerative treatment postulated for children."[2]

Justice for the child in trouble is touted as an official goal for a modern society. However, in practice, children are often dealt with in ways that would be unacceptable if used for adults. The constitutional rights of juveniles are often violated, and there is little regard for their integrity, human dignity, and privacy.

Television, which attempts to reflect the realities of our society, has many popular series involving the police. But seldom does one see a juvenile being informed of his or her constitutional rights (Miranda warnings) before being taken into custody by the police. In reality, children are not constitutionally guaranteed the privilege of being informed of their rights.

Police must have probable cause for stopping, detaining, or even questioning an adult suspect. If the police handle an arrest incorrectly, it is quite possible that the adult offender cannot be found guilty at trial because of a technicality. However, it is not uncommon practice for police to stop, detain, and question a juvenile for little or no cause. Seldom do the police release a juvenile offender from custody because of a legal technicality resulting from improper arrest procedures (see Chapter 5).

This chapter explores juvenile rights. Emphasis is placed on what has been done and what seems to remain to be done to ensure juveniles equal protection under the law.

A BRIEF HISTORY

Duke of Beaufort v. Berty
Court decision (England, 1721) that children should be treated differently than adults

The earliest precedent related to the development of a modern-day juvenile code is the case of the ***Duke of Beaufort v. Berty*** (England, 1721). The basic principle of that case was that children should be treated differently than adults, primarily for the purpose of prevention rather than punishment. The principle flowing from this case did not receive immediate acceptance, but it is considered fundamental to juvenile law.

The principle of individualized justice for youth came with the decision *Rex v. Delaval* (England, 1763). The concept of *parens patriae*, which allows the state, through the courts, to assume parental responsibility for any child under its purview, evolved from *Ellesley v. Ellesley* (England, 1828).

Early American practices did not reflect a strong feeling for children, as evidenced by their treatment in the New England colonies. In fact, children who committed crimes in colonial times were often punished more severely than were adults.

By the nineteenth century, however, several champions had surfaced to lead the crusade for children's rights. More Americans were becoming aware that children might not be as responsible for their criminal acts as adults. By 1858, in California, a youth industrial school was established as an institution for children under the age of 18 years who were leading "idle or immoral" lives. Moreover, in 1887, California held that it was unlawful to confine persons under the age of 16 years in jails.

The nation's first juvenile court was established in Cook County, Chicago, in 1899. *Mill v. Brown* (Utah, 1907) states the importance of the laws establishing early juvenile courts:

> The juvenile court law is of such vast importance to the state and society that, it seems to us, it should be administered by those who are learned in the law and versed in the roles of procedure, effective and individual rights respected. Care must be exercised in both the selection of a judge and in the administration of the law.[3]

In 1923, the National Probation Association's Annual Conference proposed a Standard Juvenile Court Act. The last state to adopt this act

Juvenile Courtroom Door

was Wyoming, in 1945. Between 1925 and 1945, various states defined their own juvenile code.

The "new" court system, which was more than 100 years in coming, defined all procedures of the juvenile courts as civil rather than criminal. (Civil suits relate to and affect only individual wrongs, whereas criminal prosecutions involve public wrongs.) It is evident, therefore, that the greatest effort in the juvenile justice system has been aimed at creating a separate court system for youths and delinquents. This separate system and the perpetuation of the doctrine of *parens patriae* have resulted in a system that has largely chosen to ignore the legal rights of juveniles. Those rights accorded adults—such as the right to a speedy trial, trial by jury, bail, confrontation of one's accusers, and protection from self-incrimination—were deemed unnecessary for juveniles.

However, as the rights of adults were being pursued, as in *Miranda v. Arizona*, some court decisions did have a bearing on juvenile rights. The decision in **Gideon v. Wainwright**, 372 U.S. 335 (1963), set the stage for legislation regarding due process. Although this case involves the right to legal counsel in adult, noncapital felony cases, several states have required that indigent children who request counsel be so provided and at public expense. *Gault* established this as a right for juveniles.

Gideon v. Wainwright Court decision (1963) allowing right to legal counsel in adult felony cases

Some Landmark Cases

Kent v. United States, *383 U.S. 541 (1966).* In the landmark opinion of *Kent v. United States*, the Supreme Court evaluated juvenile court proceedings and juveniles' constitutionally guaranteed rights. As previously mentioned, due to its rehabilitative origins, juvenile court proceedings were regarded as civil rather than criminal. In *Kent*, the Court noted that the child involved in certain juvenile court proceedings was deprived of constitutional rights and at the same time not given the rehabilitation promised under earlier juvenile court philosophy and statutes. It pointed out that "there may be grounds for concern that the child receives the worst of both worlds."[4]

Kent v. United States (1966) Provided due process rights to juveniles

The Court attempted to institute due process requirements in juvenile court with this decision. Waiver to adult court was recognized as a serious proposition for juveniles. Accordingly, the Court ruled that juveniles had rights in such proceedings in accordance with the due process clause of the Fourteenth Amendment. Because waiver to adult court is a "critically important" stage in the juvenile court, juveniles are entitled to the following:

1. A hearing,
2. To be represented by counsel at such a hearing,
3. To be given access to records considered by the juvenile court, and
4. A statement of the reasons in support of the waiver order.

The bottom line of this decision is that "a juvenile must be given due process before being transferred from a juvenile court to an adult court."[5]

The *Kent* decision upheld a juvenile's **right to a judicial hearing**. The Supreme Court ruled that the lower court decision on the waiver of this right was unconstitutional. In making this ruling, the Court emphasized that although juvenile court procedures were still civil and, consequently, juveniles were not entitled to all the protections given to adult criminals, waiver hearings must still provide all the protections implied in the Fourteenth Amendment's due process clause.

Kent was 21 when the Court issued its opinion, so he could not be remanded to juvenile court. The Supreme Court sent his case to the U.S. District Court of the District of Columbia with instructions to hold a waiver hearing. This court held that "the waiver of Morris A. Kent was, on the merits, appropriate and entirely consistent with the purpose of the Juvenile Court Act." This act called for the waiver of juveniles charged with certain crimes to be sent to adult criminal court. Kent was then found guilty of six counts of housebreaking and robbery but not guilty by reason of insanity on two counts of rape.[6]

In the *Kent* decision, the court also addressed the factors the judge should consider in the transfer decision process: the seriousness of the offense, violence demonstrated, maturity and sophistication of the child, and rehabilitative resources available to the court.[7] In a subsequent related decision *(Breed v. Jones)*, the Court held that a juvenile who had been adjudicated delinquent in juvenile court could not be convicted of the same crime in adult court due to the constitutional provision against double jeopardy.[8]

In re Gault, *387 U.S. 1 (1967)*.   On May 15, 1967, the Supreme Court rendered its first decision in the area of juvenile delinquency procedure (*In re Gault*). Gerald Gault allegedly made a telephone call to a woman living in his neighborhood, during which he used some obscene words and phrases. The use of a telephone for such purpose violated an Arizona statute and, therefore, Gerald, age 16 years, was subject to adjudication as a juvenile delinquent. The adjudication was in fact made after a proceeding in which he was not offered the basic procedural protections to which he would have been entitled had he been charged in a criminal court. In this decision, Justice Abraham Fortas ruled that a child alleged to be a juvenile delinquent had at least the following rights:

1. Notice must be given in advance of proceedings against a juvenile so that he or she has reasonable time to prepare a defense.
2. If the proceedings may result in the institutionalization of the juvenile, then both the juvenile and the parents must be informed of

right to a judicial hearing
Juveniles' right upheld by the *Kent* decision

In re Gault (1967) Extended due process rights to juveniles, specifically right to a notice of charges, right to counsel, right to confront and cross-examine witnesses, and right of privilege against self-incrimination

their right to have counsel and be provided with one if they cannot afford to obtain one on their own.

3. Juveniles have protection against self-incrimination. The juvenile, parents, or guardians must be advised of the right to remain silent.

4. Juveniles have the right to hear sworn testimony and to confront the witnesses against them for cross-examination.[9]

The *Gault* decision ended the presumption that the juvenile courts were beyond the scope or purview of due process protection. The primary outcome of this case is that juvenile courts would have to become courts of law and follow standard procedures regarding the constitutional rights of those on whom they passed judgment. Juveniles have basic constitutional rights when they face an adjudication hearing that could result in incarceration in a juvenile facility.[10]

The following subsections present a review of the basic procedural due process rights that were granted to juveniles through the *Gault* decision.

Right of Notice of Charges.   The *Gault* case established that a juvenile has a constitutional right to be given a timely notice of the charges against him or her. The right to a notice of charges is required to give the juvenile's defense counsel adequate time to prepare for the trial.[11] To provide this timely notice, most states use a summons. A summons is the legal instrument to give notice to the accused of the proceedings against him or her. *Gault* held that the due process requirements of notice in juvenile court proceedings were to be the same as in other criminal or civil proceedings.

Right to Counsel.   In *Gault*, the Court held that the accused juvenile has the **right to counsel**. Counsel may be of the person's own choosing or appointed by the court for financial or other reasons. By the time the *Gault* decision was made, several states had already taken steps to provide legal counsel for juveniles. Since *Gault*, however, the regular participation of defense counsel in juvenile court has become commonplace. However, whether the juvenile uses private or assigned counsel, such defense counsels are likely to be unfamiliar with the proceedings of a juvenile court, because many will have had only civil court experience. Notice of the juvenile's right to counsel must be clearly understood by both the child and the family and should be given both in writing and orally. This notice contains two important elements: (1) The child and/or parents may be represented by counsel, and (2) If they cannot afford and therefore cannot employ counsel, the child and parents are, in the absence of a competent waiver, entitled to be represented by counsel at public expense.

right to counsel Accused juveniles' right to legal counsel established by *In re Gault*

Juvenile with the Right to Counsel

Procedures direct that notice of the right to counsel shall be given to the child and parents at the first intake interview or when the child is admitted to a detention center or shelter-care facility. Counsel should be given to children whenever possible. No simple action holds more potential for achieving procedural justice for the juvenile in court than legal representation.

Rights of Confrontation and Cross-Examination.   The juvenile's **rights of confrontation and cross-examination** of hostile witnesses was upheld in *In re Gault*. Most states apply this ruling to only the first phase of the criminal court proceedings—that is, to that part dealing with the determination of one's guilt or innocence. However, many statutes and cases allow the juvenile the right of confrontation and cross-examination at dispositional hearings at which the second phase of criminal court proceedings is carried out, designed to determine appropriate sentencing. For example, in *Strode v. Brorby*,[12] a commitment order that would have sent a boy to an industrial school rather than place him on probation was reserved. The court ruled that the juvenile had been refused the opportunity to present witnesses in his favor that would have testified that he deserved probation rather than institutionalization.

rights of confrontation and cross-examination Accused juveniles' right to confront and cross-examine witnesses was upheld in *In re Gault*

Right of Privilege against Self-Incrimination.   The Fifth Amendment right to remain silent (i.e., the **right of privilege against self-incrimination**) is the last entitlement conferred on juveniles by the *Gault* decision. The Court concluded that the constitutional privilege against self-incrimination is as applicable in juvenile cases as it is in adult cases.

right of privilege against self-incrimination Accused juveniles' entitlement of the constitutional privilege against self-incrimination, the Fifth Amendment, established by *In re Gault*

If the juvenile court judge in the *Gault* case had reached a decision on Gerald Gault's guilt, based on Gault's own admissions, it would have been based on admissions obtained without regard to his privilege against self-incrimination. In ruling on the *Gault* decision, Justice Abraham Fortas believed that juvenile court judges should not be influenced by confessions, admissions, and like acts that may have been obtained under dubious circumstances and without regard to the provisions of the Fifth Amendment. Court decisions since *Gault* have extended the privilege against self-incrimination during judicially required examinations (i.e., psychological evaluation) as part of a transfer proceeding.[13]

However, *In re Gault* failed to answer one question: whether a juvenile must be advised of his or her rights at some point in the prejudicial stage. When serious offenses are involved and the juvenile might be transferred to an adult criminal court, some police forces are giving such warnings.

In re Winship, 397 U.S. 358 (1970). Some states, such as California, apply *Miranda* restrictions as a rule to juvenile interrogation. In the landmark case **In re Winship**, the Supreme Court held that to justify a court finding of delinquency against a juvenile, there must be **proof beyond a reasonable doubt** that the juvenile committed the alleged delinquent act.[14]

In re Winship (1970) To justify the finding of delinquency against a juvenile, there must be proof beyond a reasonable doubt

proof beyond a reasonable doubt Adjudication of delinquency burden of proof established by *In re Winship*

Twelve-year-old Samuel Winship was adjudicated delinquent as the result of a theft of $112 from a woman's purse. Consequently, he was committed to a training school for one and one-half years, subject to annual extensions of commitment, until his eighteenth birthday. The case was appealed to the New York Court of Appeals and was upheld by that court. The Supreme Court, however, later reversed that decision. The Supreme Court contended that the loss of liberty is no less significant for a juvenile than for an adult. Therefore, no juvenile may be deprived of his or her individual liberty on evidence less precise than that required depriving an adult of his or her individual liberty. With this ruling, the Court mandated that the criminal law burden—rather than the traditionally less stringent civil law burden of the mere preponderance of all evidence—is applicable in juvenile cases.

Before this case, the requirement seemed to be that the judge be influenced only by a preponderance of evidence against the accused delinquent. As in *Gault*, the implications of this decision were limited to cases in which juveniles were charged with crimes, not status offenses or cases of neglect or dependency. They are faced with the possibility of incarceration and curtailment of freedom.[15]

McKeiver v. Pennsylvania, 403 U.S. 528 (1971). In 1971, the Supreme Court agreed to hear arguments about whether juveniles had a constitutional **right to a jury trial**. In the *McKeiver v. Pennsylvania* decision, the Court implied that the due process standard of "fundamental fairness" applied to juveniles, but the Court rejected the concept of trial by jury for juvenile cases. The Court contended that the "juvenile proceeding has not yet been held to be a 'criminal prosecution' within the meaning and reach of the Sixth Amendment."[16] The Supreme Court stated that it was as yet unwilling to "remake the juvenile proceeding into a full adversary process" and put "an effective end to what has been the idealistic prospect of an intimate, informal protective proceeding."[17] The Court concluded by encouraging the states to "seek in new and different ways the elusive answers to the young."[18] However, the Supreme Court was careful to note that there "is nothing to prevent a juvenile court judge in a particular case where he feels the need, or when the need is demonstrated, from using an advisory jury."[19]

Jury trials for juveniles in most cases, however, are the exception rather than the rule, unless a motion specifically requesting the statutory provision of a trial by jury is made in the court jurisdiction in which the case is to be heard.[20] Sanborn asserts that several structural changes would be required to grant the right to trial by jury in juvenile court. They would include making delinquency records and probation officer treatment plans unavailable to judges. Such changes would completely alter the *parens patriae* nature of the proceedings and duplicate procedures of adult criminal court.[21]

Thus, the right to trial by jury is one of the few constitutional rights not provided to juveniles. The other constitutional rights not extended to juveniles are the right to a public trial, the right to bail, and the right to a grand jury indictment.[22]

Legislative Changes

The Supreme Court has not been the only source of change in the area of juvenile rights. Federal acts and legislation have also played an important role. For example, until the Uniform Juvenile Court Act of 1968, police or others could still take a child into custody in a situation in which the Fourth Amendment would have exempted an adult. The Uniform Juvenile Court Act set some limits on nondiscriminatory home removals of children. It provides for the removal of a child from his or her home only if there are reasonable grounds to believe that the child is suffering from illness or injury or is in immediate danger from the environment and that removal from that environment, therefore, is necessary.

In 1974, the U.S. Congress passed the Juvenile Justice and Delinquency Prevention Act (Public Law 93-415). The legal impact of this legislation and its amendments are presented in Box 7.1.

It seems, then, that the courts and the legislative bodies (state and federal) are still reluctant to allow children to be treated as the legal

right to a jury trial One of the few constitutional rights that are not provided to juveniles. Jury trials for juveniles in most cases are the exception rather than the rule, unless a motion specifically requesting the statutory provision of a trial by jury is made in the court jurisdiction.

McKeiver v. Pennsylvania Court decision (1971) about whether juveniles have a constitutional right to a jury trial. The Court implied that the due process standard of "fundamental fairness" applied to juveniles, but the Court rejected the concept of trial by jury for juvenile cases.

BOX 7.1 THE CORE REQUIREMENTS OF THE JUVENILE JUSTICE AND DELINQUENCY PREVENTION ACT

The Juvenile Justice and Delinquency Prevention Act of 1974, as amended, establishes four custody-related requirements for juveniles:

1. The "deinstitutionalization of status offenders and non-offenders" requirement (1974) specifies that juveniles not charged with acts that would be crimes for adults "shall not be placed in secure detention facilities."

2. The "sight and sound separation" requirement (1974) specifies that "juveniles alleged to be or found to be delinquent and [status offenders and non-offenders] shall not be detained or confined in any institution in which they have contact with adult persons incarcerated because they have been convicted of a crime or are awaiting trial on criminal charges." This requires that juvenile and adult inmates cannot see each other and no conversation between them is possible.

3. The "jail and lockup removal" requirement (1980) states that juveniles shall not be detained or confined in adult jails or lockups. There are, however, several exceptions to this requirement. Regulations implementing the Act exempt juveniles held in secure detention facilities if the juvenile is being tried as a criminal for a felony or has been convicted as a criminal felon. In addition, there is a six-hour grace period that allows adult jails and lockups to hold delinquents temporarily until other arrangements can be made. Jails and lockups in rural areas may hold delinquents up to twenty-four hours under certain conditions. Some jurisdictions have obtained approval for separate juvenile detention centers that are collocated with an adult jail or lockup facility.

4. The "disproportionate confinement of minority youth" requirement (1992) specifies that states determine the existence and extent of the problem in their state and demonstrate efforts to reduce it where it exists.

Regulations effective December 10, 1996, modify the Act's requirements in several ways:

• Clarify the sight and sound separation requirement: In nonresidential areas brief, accidental contact is not a reportable violation.

• Permit time-phased use of nonresidential areas for both juveniles and adults in collocated facilities.

• Expand the six-hour grace period to include six hours both before and after court appearances.

• Allow adjudicated delinquents to be transferred to adult institutions when they have reached the state's age of criminal responsibility, where state law expressly authorizes such transfer.

The revised regulations offer flexibility to states in carrying out the Act's requirements. States must agree to comply with each requirement to receive funding in the Formula Grant program under the Act's provisions. The Formula Grant program supports prevention and intervention initiatives at the state and local levels of government. States must submit plans outlining their strategy for meeting the requirements and other statutory plan requirements. Noncompliance with core requirements of the Act and other statutory plan requirements results in the loss of 25 percent of the state's annual Formula Grants program allocation.

In 2008, OJJDP reported 1,775 subgrants across more than 900 separate organizations. This represents more than $98 million in funded activities serving more than 518,000 youth.[24]

Sources: Office of Juvenile Justice and Delinquency Prevention, *1999 National Report Series, Juvenile Justice Bulletin—Juvenile Justice: A Century of Change* (Washington, DC: U.S. Department of Justice, 1999), p. 4; Office of Juvenile Justice and Delinquency Prevention, Formula Grants Program, *In Focus* (2009). Retrieved from: http://www.ncjrs.gov/pdffiles1/ojjdp/227470.pdf, p. 4.

equals of adults. As a doctrine, *parens patriae* is as firmly entrenched as was the earlier doctrine to treat delinquent children by having them whipped and put to bed without supper.

As noted, these decisions extended due process rights to juveniles when they are faced with significant sanctions: waiver to adult court and incarceration. Compared to adults, juveniles do not have full protection under the law. When facing the bars or being sentenced as an adult, juveniles charged with delinquency have equal protection under the law.[23] Blending the philosophy of *parens patriae* with criminal responsibility again presents significant difficulties for the juvenile court and its charges. The original goal was to give the juvenile court unlimited ability to extend benefits to juveniles in trouble. When their behavior is serious, the nature of the proceedings and the protections afforded juveniles change accordingly.

Other Procedural Rights

As a result of the Supreme Court cases mentioned previously, procedural guarantees are extended to juveniles through the due process provisions of the Fourteenth Amendment of the Constitution. **Procedural rights** are rights pertaining to statutory laws and are accorded to juveniles during the fact-finding process of a juvenile case.[25]

procedural rights Rights pertaining to statutory laws and are accorded to juveniles during the fact-finding process of a juvenile case

To date, the procedural rights guaranteed to juveniles in court proceedings are (1) the right to adequate notice of charges against him or her; (2) the right to counsel and to have counsel provided if the child is indigent; (3) the right to confrontation and cross-examination of witnesses; (4) the right to refuse to do anything that would be self-incriminatory; (5) the right to a judicial hearing, with counsel, prior to the transfer of a juvenile to an adult court;[26] and (6) the right to be considered innocent until proven guilty beyond a reasonable doubt. In addition to procedural rights in court, juveniles do have certain other procedural rights within the various stages of the juvenile justice system.

Arrest.   Many states, though they do not consider the taking of a child into custody by police an arrest, do require that this act be legal under the state and federal constitutions. Since the *Gault* decision, many courts have required that the police have **probable cause** before taking a child into custody as a suspect in a criminal act. "In the near future, courts will have to decide whether the taking of a juvenile into custody for noncriminal misbehavior, or ungovernability is subject to these or other standards. Certainly, there are some constitutional limitations on how the police handle problem children."[27]

probable cause Evidence that would lead a reasonable person to believe that the accused juvenile may have committed a delinquent act

Though laws applicable to the arrest of adults may be applicable to the arrest (or taking into custody) of juveniles, provisions found in juvenile acts relating to detention, custody, and interrogation may differ

bail Money or property presented to the court for release of the accused from custody; The U.S. Supreme Court has not determined if juveniles have a constitutional right to bail.

U.S. Supreme Court has not determined if juveniles have a constitutional right to **bail**.[42] However, with the increasing attention to waiver to adult court, the right to bail may become a significant issue.

There are many factors to be considered in regard to bail for juveniles. For example, where does a 14-year-old teenager get the money for bail, especially when his or her parents cannot pay it? Would the right to bail simply widen the gap between justice for the rich and justice for the poor? Bail is a constitutional guarantee in most adult cases, and the disparity between rich and poor exists there. The adult who posts bail usually suffers if he or she skips bail, especially if the bail money was his or her own or a friend's or a relative's. Would a juvenile feel any responsibility to the person who put up the money to ensure the child's temporary freedom? Would bail bond agents be willing to provide bail money for indigent juveniles, especially those who receive no financial support from their parents?

These and other questions will have to be considered in devising a system of bail for juveniles accused of criminal acts, especially if the courts rule in favor of this provision as a constitutional right for juveniles.

Rights of Incarcerated Juveniles

The last of the procedural rights of juveniles at other stages of the juvenile justice system involves the rights of incarcerated juveniles. Concern for incarcerated or institutionalized juveniles comes from a similar concern in adult cases. The primary issues are prisoner rights and the right to treatment.

In its examination of the causes of the Attica prison riot of 1971, a tragedy in which more than forty people died, the McKay Commission cited a long record of disregard of legitimate grievances arising from inadequate medical care, bad food, and the absence of recreational facilities; obstacles to any form of communication with the outside world; rules that were "poorly communicated, often petty, senseless, or repressive and... selectively enforced," and a "relationship between most correctional officers and inmates that was characterized by fear, hostility, mistrust, nurtured by racism."[43]

If the proper grievance practices had existed at the time, the riots at Attica and the New Mexico prison might never have happened. The need for just grievance procedures is as real in juvenile institutions as in adult prisons. As yet there have been no juvenile equivalents of either the New York or New Mexico riots. However, this should not be taken to mean that injustices do not take place within juvenile institutions. The basic aim is to establish fairness in institutional proceedings. Grievance procedures can be set up to guide operations.

Grievance procedures enable a child to grieve daily life issues that do not involve discipline (e.g., food quantity or quality). The basic elements of adequate grievance procedures are (1) notice to the children of the availability of grievances, (2) a clear and simple procedure for children to present their grievances to staff, (3) prompt investigation of grievances (usually 3 days), (4) opportunity for children to present grievances to an impartial person, (5) notice to children of the decision of the impartial person, and (6) the taking a final action.[44]

Although this section is limited to a brief overview, there are other issues related to the rights of incarcerated juveniles. They are mail and censorship; dress codes; personal appearance; visitations; religious freedom; notice of rules; searches; work assignments; right to care and treatment (expanded on in the following section); the use of corporal punishment; the use of physical, mechanical, and/or medical restraints; room confinement; loss of privileges; disciplinary procedures; and transfers.

The Right to Treatment

The issue of a person's **right to treatment** has been the subject of several court rulings over the past two decades. The majority of these rulings involved the involuntary confinement of adults in mental institutions or similar treatment facilities, and it has been just recently that their application was considered for persons confined to prisons or correctional facilities, adult or juvenile. Birnbaum (1960) was perhaps the first to articulate the right to treatment:

right to treatment The U.S. Supreme Court has not addressed the constitutional right to treatment for juveniles. However, in *Morales v. Truman*, the court ruled that juveniles housed in detention had a constitutional right to treatment.

> The courts, under their traditional powers to protect the constitutional rights of our clients should begin to consider the problem of whether or not a person who has been institutionalized solely because he is sufficiently mentally ill to require institutionalization for care and treatment actually does receive adequate medical treatment so that he may regain his health, and therefore, his liberty, as soon as possible; that the courts do this by means of recognizing and enforcing the right to treatment; and that the courts do this, independent of any action by the legislature, as a necessary and overdue development of our present concept of due process.[45]

Since this beginning, the right to treatment has been established in two key cases that apply to the rights of adult mentally ill persons: *Wyatt v. Stickney* (1971) and *Donaldson v. O'Connor* (1975). In *Wyatt*, the Court ruled that the due process clause of the Fourteenth Amendment guarantees mental patients a right to receive treatment, given a reasonable opportunity to be improved or cured.[46]

Because the inmates of training schools and juvenile institutions are confined against their wills, the right-to-treatment issue regarding juveniles was inevitable. As such, many courts have held that an institutionalized child must receive appropriate treatment or be released. Some states, therefore, require periodic progress reports on the juvenile, and cases have been brought before the courts to require juvenile correctional systems to improve institutional services and to release children when these services are inadequate or in violation of the juvenile's right to an "acceptable home substitute" as his or her place of detention.[47]

In *Creek v. Stone*, the Court of Appeals for the District of Columbia interpreted the local juvenile court act to mean that a juvenile has a statutory right to treatment.

> The purpose stated in the 16 D.C. Code § 2316(3)—to give the juvenile the care "as nearly as possible" equivalent to that which should have been given by his parents—establishes not only an important policy objective, but an appropriate case, a legal right to a custody that is not in conflict with the parens patriae premise of the law.[48]

Certainly, the recognition of a juvenile's legal right to treatment would be consistent with the ideal of *parens patriae*.

In the courts, this right became entwined with conditions of confinement in juvenile institutions. In *Nelson v. Heyne*, a federal court coupled a right to treatment under the due process clause of the Fourteenth Amendment with the right to be free from cruel and unusual punishment (Eighth Amendment). Held at the Indiana Boys School, the plaintiffs asked for a restraining order to protect them against the use of corporal punishment and psychotropic drugs. The court stated:

> In our view, the "right to treatment" includes the right to minimum acceptable standards of care and treatment for juveniles and the right to individualized care and treatment. Because children differ in their need for rehabilitation, the individual need for treatment will differ. When a state assumes the place of a juvenile's parents, it assumes as well the parental duties, and its treatment of its juveniles should, as far as can be reasonably required, be what proper parental care would provide. Without a program of individualized treatment, the result may be that the juvenile will not be rehabilitated, but warehoused, and that at termination of detention they will likely be incapable of taking their proper places in free society, their interests and those of the state and the school thereby being defeated.[49]

Morales v. Turman Court decision providing juveniles housed in institutions the right to treatment

Although the U.S. Supreme Court has never established a juvenile's right to treatment, this concept was also strengthened in another lower court ruling. In **Morales v. Turman**, the court ruled that juveniles housed in the facilities of the Texas Youth Council had a constitutional right to treatment. As in *Nelson*, the conditions of confinement at these institutions were held as violations of the Eighth Amendment prohibition against cruel and unusual punishment.[50]

Two rights are related tangentially to the right-to-treatment issue that are not widely discussed or generally examined in a text on juvenile delinquency: (1) the right to refuse treatment and (2) the right to punishment. Normally the right to refuse treatment is claimed in cases involving mental patients, but an inmate of a correctional facility can use it. The acceptance or rejection of treatment seems at first to be the individual person's prerogative. However, if a patient or inmate is allowed to refuse treatment, he or she would more than likely remain a burden on society.

One could hypothesize that the increasingly high rate of recidivism among juveniles released from institutions may be a result of their refusal to accept treatment; this is, however, doubtful. One would have to prove that treatment had been offered in the first place before one could conjecture that it had been refused.

The right to refuse treatment is closely related to, but not the same as, the right to choose punishment rather than treatment. Both these proposed rights are alternative and theoretical companions to the right to treatment. The courts have both supported and refuted the right to refuse treatment, but they have yet to decide a case involving the issue of "right to punishment."

The right to choose punishment may seem absurd at first, but it is plausible when looked at in the following manner. Just as the right to treatment is based on statutory law, the right to punishment under the law is supportable under the same concept. This concept is applicable to the offender who is criminally responsible for his or her crime. The delinquent could object to conventional treatment by citing the First Amendment right to privacy and then demand a statutory right to punishment based on a state criminal code designating a specific length of imprisonment as punishment for the crime for which he or she was convicted or committed.

The theoretical approach to a right to punishment is clarified further by the following argument. Treatment often takes place in confinement. Confinement itself has been defined as punishment.[51] Therefore, treatment, when it takes place in confinement, can be punishment. If the inmate has the right to accept or refuse treatment and possibly even choose what kind of treatment, then it would seem that the inmate may, therefore, have the right to choose punishment (confinement) as his or her treatment. This may seem somewhat oblique, but such an interpretation is theoretically correct and could be put into practice. Courts have not decided such a case, but people sentenced in criminal or juvenile court who are classified as psychopaths and receive indeterminate sentences may be expected to raise this issue in the near future.

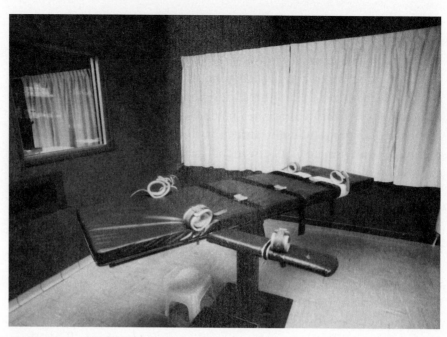

Lethal Injection Chair

The Death Penalty for Juveniles

Stanford v. Kentucky Decision by the Court that juvenile executions do not constitute cruel and unusual punishment (1989)

Two major decisions finally outlawed the death penalty for juveniles. In the first—***Stanford v. Kentucky*** (1989)—the Court finally addressed whether capital punishment of juveniles violated the Eighth Amendment. Justice Scalia issued the majority opinion that juvenile executions do not constitute cruel and unusual punishment. The majority dismissed the arguments about the diminished capacity of juveniles and noted that no national consensus exists against the death penalty for juveniles. The decision allowed states to determine whether to impose the death penalty on juveniles and at what age.[52] Thus, the Court held that the practice of executing juveniles (aged 16 or 17 years at the time of the offense) did not violate the evolving standards of decency of American society. Their determination was based on legislative authorization of juvenile executions.[53] In effect, the Court banned the execution of offenders under the age of 16 years but permitted their execution for crimes committed at the age of 16 years or older.

However, in *Roper v. Simmons* (2005), the U.S. Supreme Court revisited the issue of whether the death penalty for juveniles violated the Eighth and Fourteenth Amendments to the U.S. Constitution.[54] Simmons and his codefendant broke into a woman's house, kidnapped her, bound her with duct tape and threw her off a bridge and into a river to drown. As permitted under Missouri law, the prosecution tried Simmons as an adult because he was 17 years of age at the time of crime and sought the death penalty because the murder was committed for financial gain, to prevent the apprehension of the defendant, and was outrageously and wantonly vile, horrible, and inhuman. Defense counsel cited Simmons' juvenile status as a mitigating factor in the crime. Simmons was found guilty and sentenced to death, but the sentence was overturned on appeal to the Missouri Supreme Court.

On review, the U.S. Supreme Court affirmed the lower courts' decision. Writing for the majority, Justice Kennedy cited several reasons why the court was finally declaring the death penalty for juveniles unconstitutional. First, some thirty states had outlawed the death penalty for juveniles following the *Stanford* decision.[55] Justice Kennedy noted three general differences between juvenile and adult offenders: (1) a lack of maturity and underdeveloped sense of responsibility, which has led state prohibitions against juveniles voting, serving on juries, and marrying without parental consent; (2) juvenile vulnerability to negative influences such as peer pressure; and (3) the fact that the character of a juvenile is not as well formed as an adult. The lesser culpability of juveniles made them less susceptible to the "distinct purposes of the death penalty": retribution and deterrence. Finally, he acknowledged that the United States stood alone "in a world that has turned its face against the juvenile death penalty."

As a result of the *Roper v. Simmons* decision, the death penalty for juveniles in the United States is now defunct. The execution of juvenile murderers will no longer take place. The U.S. Supreme Court has also agreed to hear the case of Joe Sullivan. Sullivan was sentenced to life without parole in Florida for the rape of a 72-year-old woman when he was 13 years of age. The Court will consider whether a life without parole sentence is also a violation of the Eighth Amendment against cruel and unusual punishment.[56] A summary of landmark case decisions is presented in Table 7.1.

Table 7.1
LANDMARK JUVENILE CASE DECISIONS

Case	Year	Significance
Kent v. United States	1966	This case upheld the rights of juveniles to a judicial hearing.
In re Gault	1967	Juveniles have the right to the same basic due process procedures as adults.
In re Winship	1970	Proof beyond reasonable doubt is required to justify a court finding of delinquency against a juvenile.
McKeiver v. Pennsylvania	1971	Juveniles do not have the right to trial by jury.
Schall v. Martin	1984	Preventive detention of juveniles awaiting adjudication is constitutional.
Creek v. Stone	1967	Recognition of a juvenile's legal right to treatment.
Nelson v. Heyne	1967	
Morales v. Turman	1974	
Roper v. Simmons	2005	This case declared the death penalty unconstitutional (cruel and unusual punishment) for juveniles.

PROCEDURAL RIGHTS OUTSIDE THE JUSTICE SYSTEM

Do juveniles, both delinquent and nondelinquent, have rights other than those associated specifically with the juvenile justice system? If so, what are they? To a limited extent, juveniles do have the same rights as other citizens. The term **limited extent** is used because these rights are not always acknowledged or honored. One of the major reasons for this lack of acknowledgment is that a juvenile's age of majority (adulthood) is adult defined, and until this age is attained, a juvenile is considered a child, or a second-class citizen. These limited-extent rights include rights under laws governing employment and employment practices; driving; contracts and legal agreements; voting; drinking; taking drugs; marriage, sex, and abortion; operating a business; rights in educational institutions; rights with regard to parents and home; and the right to the means to maintain an adequate standard of living.

The two most important institutions that hold almost totalitarian control over the life of the juvenile are the school and the family. These institutions have the greatest amount of contact with and both formal and informal control over juveniles.

The number of children receiving public assistance in the form of Temporary Assistance for Needy Families reflects the right to an adequate standard of living. In addition, the Social Security system and the Veterans Administration provide assistance to qualified families, regardless of income level. There is also Child Development Head Start, Child Development–Child Welfare Research and Demonstration Grants, public assistance–social services, work incentive programs, and community service training grants. Although some people may decry "welfare cheaters" and claim that most persons on welfare are not willing to work, it is generally accepted that children, at least, should receive public assistance.

Another right of juveniles is the right to employment and protection against employer abuses.[57] The labor market experience of juveniles has been discussed in national juvenile justice administration policy sessions for many years. Initially, there was concern because of the high rate of unemployment, but later the emphasis shifted to poor job preparation and insufficient occupational training for youths who enter the labor market with less than a college degree.

SUBSTANTIVE RIGHTS OF MINORS

Substantive rights are the basic rights of a human being—such as life, liberty, and the pursuit of happiness—that are not dependent on laws made by humankind. Although there has been some resolution in the area of procedural rights for juveniles, the issue of the **substantive rights of minors** has remained virtually unexamined.

limited extent The notion that juveniles' rights are not always recognized, acknowledged, or honored in society

substantive rights of minors Basic human rights such as life, liberty, and the pursuit of happiness

Substantive rights are especially important when discussing children who present no real threat to either themselves or society. Laws, regulations, and rules that would make an adult's lifestyle unbearable often control these children.

Substantive rights used to be expressed in terms of protection and welfare. The new substantive rights are a decidedly different breed; they include the right to refuse an unwanted service, the right to make or participate in choices that affect one's life, and the right to be free from unnecessary restrictions in individual development. "Underlying all efforts to define these new rights is the question of whether children, as well as adults, have a fundamental interest in privacy that might be expressed as the '**right to be left alone**.'"[58]

right to be left alone Juveniles' fundamental interest in privacy as expressed through substantive rights of all persons

For example, the courts have ruled on the juvenile's right to confidentiality. Juvenile court was designed to be a confidential process. Protecting the privacy of the juvenile would also prevent harm to youths. However, this right conflicts with the desire to protect the public from further delinquent or criminal acts at the hands of juveniles. To address such issues, the courts have established the following principles:

1. The legal status of a juvenile witness can be brought out on cross-examination in court.[59]

2. Under prescribed circumstances and their rights under the First Amendment, the press may report the results of juvenile court proceedings.[60]

3. The Federal Juvenile Delinquency Act does not violate the First Amendment by mandating the closure of juvenile court proceedings.[61]

4. Juveniles can be legally required to register as sex offenders.[62] However, the Kentucky appellate court has ruled that a juvenile cannot be required to give a blood sample to be compiled in the state's centralized DNA database. In that case, although adjudicated delinquent for sex offense, the juvenile in question was not convicted of a felony, as required by state law.[63]

As these decisions demonstrate, it is difficult to balance the rights of society and those of juvenile offenders.

SUMMARY

This chapter discusses the procedural rights of juveniles within the court system and how this relates to their substantive rights. What the eventual impact of the recent "revolution" in juvenile rights will be on the juvenile justice system has yet to be determined. However, as juveniles gain equal rights and protections under the law, they are losing the sometimes useful and heretofore "protective" cover of *parens patriae*.

If juveniles are eventually treated as equals with adults, will they then be also exposed to the potential dangers that might befall adults? If an adult attempts an escape from prison, he or she may be shot, even killed, in the process. Thousands upon thousands of youths "run" (abscond) or escape from training schools and juvenile institutions each year. What would be the public reaction if several of them were wounded or killed in their attempts? Adult correctional facilities, staffed with armed guards, are places where security and control are guiding considerations. Should relatively insecure youth camps be turned into likenesses of these facilities?

Currently, juveniles are protected from being identified in newspapers and from being fingerprinted until 16 years of age. Should governments change these practices and ensure exacting equality between juveniles and adults?

One thing is relatively clear: The juvenile offender of today is often the adult offender of tomorrow. How the system treats and reacts to these juveniles now may have great bearing on whether society will have to deal with them later, as adults, when they are at least guaranteed their full constitutional rights.

KEY TERMS

bail
detention
Duke of Beaufort v. Berty
exclusionary rule
Gideon v. Wainwright
In re Gault
In re Winship
limited extent
Kent v. United States
McKeiver v. Pennsylvania
Morales v. Turman
probable cause
procedural rights

proof beyond a reasonable
   doubt
right of privilege against
   self-incrimination
right to counsel
right to a judicial hearing
right to a jury trial
right to be left alone
right to treatment
rights of confrontation and
   cross-examination
Stanford v. Kentucky
substantive rights of minors

DISCUSSION AND REVIEW QUESTIONS

1. Define the following terms:
   a. Procedural rights
   b. Substantive rights
   c. Due process
2. Discuss the major court cases on which the procedural rights of juveniles within the court are based.

3. What ramifications would the right to trial by jury have on the juvenile justice system? Explain.

4. What are the advantages and disadvantages of juveniles receiving the same protection and constitutional rights as adults?

5. What is meant by the terms *right to treatment* and *right to punishment*? How do these rights apply to the juvenile justice system? Explain.

6. Discuss the potential psychological impact that due process rights might exert on children.

VIDEO PROFILES

The *Forgery Charges* video profile in MyCrimeKit shows the initial hearing for Delena who is charged with forgery and other offenses. The victim in this case is Delena's foster mother. What rights were listed by the judge in this case? What was the role of the lawyer in this case? How did the foster mother in this case react to the crime committed by the juvenile? What sentence was recommended in this case? What sentence did the judge impose? How do you account for the difference? Were the juveniles' rights protected under the requirements of the decisions in this chapter?

The *In Juvenile Court at Eighteen!* video profile in MyCrimeKit shows Devon arrested for a bench warrant for failure to appear. He is 18 years of age and has a history of delinquent behavior. The video shows him at intake and in the detention hearing. What was the nature of his prior record? What were the conditions of living in his home? What was the nature of this offense? How did his status as an adult affect the final decision? Were the defendants' rights protected under the requirements of the decisions in this chapter?

MYCRIMEKIT

mycrimekit™ Go to MyCrimeKit.com to explore the following study tools and resources specific to this chapter:

- Practice Quiz: Test your knowledge with multiple-choice, true-false, fill-in-the-blank, and essay questions.
- Flashcards: 20 flashcards to test your knowledge of the chapter's key terms.
- Web Quest: Review the Web site of the U.S. Supreme Court for any updates on the legal rights of juveniles.
- Web Links: Check out sites related to the content presented in this chapter.

ENDNOTES

1. Barry C. Feld, *Bad Kids: Race and the Transformation of the Juvenile Court* (New York: Oxford University Press, 1999).

2. *Kent v. United States* 383 U.S. 541 (1966); F. A. Orlando and G. L. Crippen, "Rights of Children and the Juvenile Court," in Ira M. Schwartz, ed., *Juvenile Justice and Public Policy: Toward a National Agenda* (New York: Macmillan, 1992).

3. Mill v. Brown, 31 Utah 473, 88 P. 609, 613 (1907).

4. *Kent v. United States.*

5. Rolando V. del Carmen, Mary Parker, and Frances P. Reddington, *Briefs of Leading Cases in Juvenile Justice* (Cincinnati, OH: Anderson, 1998), p. 137.

6. O. W. Ketcham, "*Kent* Revisited," *Juvenile Justice Update*, Vol. 2 (1996), pp. 1–2, 11–12.

7. *In re Marven C.,* 39 Cal. Rptr. 2d 354 (Cal. App. 1995); del Carmen, et al., *Briefs of Leading Cases in Juvenile Justice*, p. 134.

8. *Breed v. Jones* 421 U.S. 517 (1975).

9. *In re Gault,* 387 U.S. 1 (1967); A. Neigher, "*Gault* Decision: Due Process and the Juvenile Courts," in Barry W. Hancock and Paul M. Sharp, eds., *Criminal Justice in America: Theory, Practice, and Policy* (Upper Saddle River, NJ: Prentice Hall, 1996), pp. 305–320.

10. del Carmen, Parker, and Reddington, *Briefs of Leading Cases in Juvenile Justice*, p. 173.

11. For example, see *M. v. Superior Court,* 4 Cal. App. 3d 370, 482 P.2d 664, 93 Ca. Rptr. 752 (1971).

12. In Tennessee, a juvenile is entitled to a jury trial on an appeal de novo from a juvenile court decision. (A trial de novo is a trial that is held for the second time, as if there had been no former decision.)

13. *United States v. J.D.* 517 F.Supp. 69 (S.D.N.Y. 1981); *R.H. v. State* 777 P.2d 204 (Alaska App. 1989); del Carmen, Parker, and Reddington, *Briefs of Leading Cases in Juvenile Justice*, pp. 153–155; 160–162.

14. *In re Winship,* 397 U.S. 358, 365–66 (1970). See also *Debacher v. Bainard,* 396 U.S. 28, 6 Crl 3001 (1970).

15. del Carmen, Parker, and Reddington, *Briefs of Leading Cases in Juvenile Justice*, p. 179.

16. See, for example, *In re Richard S.,* 27 N.Y. 2d 802, 264 N.E. 2d 353, 315 N.Y.S. 2d 861 (1970).

17. See, for example, *In re Richard S.,* 27 N.Y. 2d 802, 264 N.E. 2d 353, 315 N.Y.S. 2d 861 (1970).

18. Larry Siegel and Paul E. Tracy, *Juvenile Law: A Collection of U.S. Supreme Court Cases* (Upper Saddle River, NJ: Pearson Prentice Hall, 2008), p. 64.

19. Douglas J. Basharov, *Juvenile Justice Advocacy: Practice in a Unique Court* (New York: Practicing Law Institute, 1974), p. 287.

20. Children's Bureau, U.S. Department of Health, Education, and Welfare, *Legislative Guide for Drafting Family and Juvenile Court Acts* (Washington, DC: U.S. Government Printing Office, 1973), p. 20.

21. Joseph B. Sanborn, "Remnants of *Parens Patriae* in the Adjudicatory Hearing: Is A Fair Trial Possible in Juvenile Court," *Crime and Delinquency*, Vol. 40 (1994), pp. 599–615.

22. del Carmen, Parker, and Reddington, *Briefs of Leading Cases in Juvenile Justice*, p. 181.

23. *Boyd v. State* 853 S.W.2d 263 (Ark. 1993).

24. Office of Juvenile Justice and Delinquency Prevention, Formula Grants Program, *In Focus* (2009). Retrieved from: http://www.ncjrs.gov/pdffiles1/ojjdp/227470.pdf

25. The requirements of due process were also extended to cover short-term school suspension cases in *Goss v. Lopez* 419 U.S. 565 (1975). del Carmen, Parker, and Reddington, *Briefs of Leading Cases in Juvenile Justice*, p. 183.

26. *Ex parte State ex rel.* Simpson, 288 Ala., 535, 263, So. 2d. 137 (1972).

27. U.S. Department of Justice, Law Enforcement Assistance Administration, *Standards for the Administration of Juvenile Justice* (Washington, DC: U.S. Government Printing Office, July 1980), p. 190.

28. Rush defines probable cause as "A set of facts and circumstances that would induce a reasonably intelligent and prudent person to believe that a particular person had committed a specific crime; reasonable grounds to make or believe an accusation." George E. Rush, *The Dictionary of Criminal Justice* (Guilford, CT: Dushkin/McGraw-Hill, 2000) p. 268.

29. Ibid., p. 129. See *Mapp v. Ohio* 367 U.S. 643, 6 L.Ed. 2d 1081, 81 S.Ct. 1684 (1961).

30. *Terry v. Ohio* 392 U.S. 1, 20 L.Ed. 2d 889, 88 S.Ct. 1868 (1968).

31. del Carmen, Parker, and Reddington, *Briefs of Leading Cases in Juvenile Justice*, pp. 40–41.

32. *United States v. Leon* 468 U.S. 897, 82 L.Ed. 2d 677, 104 S.Ct. 3380 (1984); *Massachusetts v. Shepard* 468 U.S. 981, 82 L.Ed. 2d. 737, 104 S.Ct. 3405 (1984).

33. *New Jersey v. T.L.O.* 469 U.S. 325 (1985); *Cason v. Cook* 810 F.2d. 188 (8th Cir. 1987); del Carmen, Parker, and Reddington, *Briefs of Leading Cases in Juvenile Justice*, pp. 24–26; 36–38.

34. *Haley v. State of Ohio* 68 S.Ct. 302 (1984); del Carmen, Parker, and Reddington, *Briefs of Leading Cases in Juvenile Justice*, pp.19–20.

35. *Gallegos v. Colorado* 370 U.S. 49 (1962); del Carmen, Parker, and Reddington, *Briefs of Leading Cases in Juvenile Justice*, pp.21–22.

36. *Fare v. Michael C.* 442 U.S. 707 (1979); *Smith v. State* 623 So. 2d 369 (Ala. Cr. App. 1992); *In re Gilbert E.* 38 Cal. Rptr. 2d. 866 (Cal. App. 1994); del Carmen, Parker, and Reddington, *Briefs of Leading Cases in Juvenile Justice*, pp. 22–24, 38–40, 44–45.

37. *State v. Sugg* 456 S.E. 2d 469 (W. Va. 1995); del Carmen, et al., *Briefs of Leading Cases in Juvenile Justice*, pp. 47–48.

38. *Schall v. Martin* 104 S. Ct. 2403 (1984); del Carmen, Parker, and Reddington, Briefs of Leading Cases in Juvenile Justice, pp. 88–89.

39. *Baldwin v. Lewis* 300 F. Supp. 1220 (E.D. Wis. 1969); del Carmen, Parker, and Reddington, *Briefs of Leading Cases in Juvenile Justice*, pp.90–92.

40. *D. B. v. Tewksbury* 545 F. Supp. 896 (D. Or. 1982); del Carmen, Parker, and Reddington, *Briefs of Leading Cases in Juvenile Justice*, pp. 98–100.

41. Gennaro F. Vito, Deborah G. Wilson, Richard Tewksbury, *The Juvenile Justice System: Concepts & Issues* (Prospect Heights, IL: Waveland Press, 1998) p. 93.

42. del Carmen, Parker, and Reddington, *Briefs of Leading Cases in Juvenile Justice*, pp. 85–86.

43. J. Michael Keating et al., *Grievance Mechanisms in Correctional Institutions* (Washington, DC: U.S. Government Printing Office, September 1975).

44. David W. Roush, *Desktop Guide to Good Juvenile Detention Practice* (Washington, DC: Office of Juvenile Justice and Delinquency Prevention, 1996), p. 141.

45. M. Birnbaum, "The Right to Treatment," *American Bar Association Journal*, Vol. 46 (1960), pp. 449–503.

46. *Wyatt v. Stickney* 325 F. Supp. 781 (M.D. Ala. 1971); *Donaldson v. O'Connor* 422 U.S. 563 (1975).

47. Juvenile Court of the District of Columbia, *In the Matter of Joseph Franklin Savoy and Tony Hazel*, p. 16.

48. *Creek v. Stone* 379 F.2d 106, 111 (D.C. Cir. 1967).

49. *Nelson v. Heyne* 491 F.2d 352 (7th Cir. 1974).

50. *Morales v. Turman* 383 F.Supp. 53 (E.D. Tex. 1974): del Carmen, Parker, and Reddington, *Briefs of Leading Cases in Juvenile Justice*, pp. 234–236.

51. *Cross v. Harris* 418 F.2d 1095.

52. *Stanford v. Kentucky*, 45 CrL 3202 (1989). Kevin Stanford has been pardoned by Kentucky Governor Paul Patton. His sentence was commuted to life in prison

53. Mark C. Seis and Kenneth L. Elbe, "The Death Penalty for Juveniles: Bridging the Gap Between an Evolving Standard of Decency and Legislative Policy," *Justice Quarterly*, Vol. 8 (1991), pp. 465–487.

54. *Roper v. Simmons* 543 U.S. 551.

55. The Governor of Kentucky, Paul Patton, commuted Kevin Stanford's death sentence to life without parole. He cited his status as a juvenile as the reason for his decision (http://www.ccadp.org/kevinstanford-news2003.htm).

56. http://www.nytimes.com/2009/05/05/us/05scotus.html

57. See Frances Fox Piven and Richard A. Cloward, *Regulating the Poor* (New York: Pantheon, 1971).

58. Ibid., p. 77.

59. *Davis v. Alaska* 415 U.S. 308 (1974); del Carmen, Parker, and Reddington, *Briefs of Leading Cases in Juvenile Justice*, pp. 274–275.

60. *Smith v. Daily Mail Publishing Co.* 443 U.S. 97 (1979); del Carmen, Parker, and Reddington, *Briefs of Leading Cases in Juvenile Justice*, pp. 276–277; *Oklahoma Publishing Company v. District Court in and for Oklahoma City* 480 U.S. 308, 97 S.Ct. 1045 (1977).

61. *United States v. Three Juveniles* 862 F. Supp. 651 (D. Mass. 1994); del Carmen, Parker, and Reddington, *Briefs of Leading Cases in Juvenile Justice*, pp. 281–283.

62. *State v. Acheson* 877 P.2d 217 (Wash. App. 1994); del Carmen, Parker, and Reddington, *Briefs of Leading Cases in Juvenile Justice*, pp. 283–284.

63. *J.D.K., a Juvenile, Appellant, v. Commonwealth of Kentucky, Appellee* 2001 WL 92996 (Ky. App).

8

Juvenile Probation and Diversion

I bailed nineteen boys, from 7 to 15 years of age, and in bailing them it was understood, and agreed by the court that their cases should be continued from term to term for several months, as a season of probation; thus each month at the calling of the court docket, I would appear in court, make my report, and thus the cases would pass on for 5 or 6 months. At the expiration of this term, twelve of the boys were brought into court at one time, and the scene formed a striking and highly pleasing contrast with their appearance when first arraigned. The judge expressed much pleasure as well as surprise at their appearance, and remarked, that the object of the law had been accomplished and expressed his cordial approval of my plan to save and reform.

JOHN AUGUSTUS[1]

LEARNING OBJECTIVES

1. Define and explain the terms *probation*, *formal probation*, and *informal probation*.
2. Identify the functions of probation today and discuss how they are administered.
3. Describe what a petition is and how and why it is filed.
4. Describe the current trends in juvenile probation.
5. Discuss the application process for juvenile probation officers, including the skills important to success.
6. Identify, describe, and analyze forms of supervision.

CHAPTER OVERVIEW

Diversion is the process of limiting the amount of involvement a juvenile has with the formal organization and procedures of the criminal and juvenile justice systems. Diversion is and has been a central objective of juvenile justice. Diversion is based on the belief that if a juvenile is labeled as "delinquent" or "bad," he or she will be permanently stigmatized. To avoid long-term negative consequences for juveniles, diversion programs are designed to avoid labeling and work with juveniles to rehabilitate them.

Today, with continuing emphasis on community-based services for juveniles, it is recognized that not all juveniles who are adjudicated delinquent belong in institutions. Probation (Box 8.1) is one method of court disposition that the juvenile justice system may impose when the youth is determined to be delinquent. In fact, probation is the most frequently used juvenile court disposition at the present time. Nationwide, in 2002, approximately 62 percent of the "most serious" cases in juvenile court proceedings resulted in probation.[2] This figure represents more than a 55 percent increase in the number of juvenile probationers in a three year period.[3]

The most recent statistics reveal more patterns in juvenile probation. In 2002, nearly 40 percent of the more than 1.6 million delinquency cases adjudicated resulted in probation. This is a 44 percent increase from 1985. Of the total number of cases adjudicated probation, 74 percent were male and 26 percent were female. By racial category, approximately 70 percent of the probationers were white, 27 percent were black, and 3 percent from other groups; this matches the percentages under probation supervision in 1999. There was no change in the percentage of the juvenile probation caseload aged 14–16 years between 1999 and 2002 (62 percent). In 2002, by referral offense, most persons placed on formal probation committed a property offense (38 percent), followed by offenses against public order (25 percent), person offenses (24 percent), and drug crimes (13 percent). This differs from adjudicated offenses in 2005, in which person, drug, and public order cases were ordered to formal probation in greater proportions.[4]

As it relates to juvenile offenders, probation is the "workhorse" of the Juvenile Justice System: "Juvenile probation is the oldest and most widely used vehicle through which a wide range of court-ordered services

probation A sentence not involving confinement that imposes conditions

---

BOX 8.1 **PROBATION**

Probation is a sentence not involving confinement that imposes conditions. The sentencing court retains authority to supervise, modify the conditions, and resentence the offender if conditions are violated. Probation is increasingly being linked with a short sentence to jail, followed by a period of probation.

as rendered. Probation may be used at the 'front end' of the juvenile justice system for first-time, low-risk offenders or at the 'back end' as an alternative confinement for serious offenders."[5]

Ordinarily, juveniles on probation submit to a set of conditions established by the court that are related to the offense committed. The "basic set" of juvenile probation functions includes intake screening of cases referred to juvenile and family courts, predisposition or presentence investigation of juveniles, and court-ordered supervision of juvenile offenders.[6]

Video Profile: Diversion 1

HISTORICAL BACKGROUND OF PROBATION

Basically, the history and development of modern probation for juveniles follows the same lines as that for adults. The antecedents of the present concept of probation started when those who dispensed the law tried to be both fair and compassionate to the convicted or accused offender by giving him or her an opportunity to avoid punishment under certain conditions. Typically, probation is a suspended sentence. The right to sanctuary, a predecessor of probation or the suspended sentence, permitted a convicted criminal freedom from arrest so long as the person remained in the sanctuary. There are several examples of the right to sanctuary cited in the Bible; in fact, holy places were often set aside for this purpose.[7] This early practice, abandoned in England in the seventh century, was a far cry from probation practices. But it did provide a criminal with a form of reprieve or stay of punishment.

In the Middle Ages, secular punishment could be avoided through a practice called **benefit of clergy**. Persons could use this device to escape the sanguine, often capital, punishments of English common law. Although benefit of clergy first applied only to members of the clergy, it eventually was extended to any person who could quote Psalm 51 from the Bible and thus beg personally for mercy. Benefit of clergy may be seen as an early form of suspended sentence. As it became available to more classes of accused persons, it lost its original intent and clerical meaning and became "a clumsy set of rules which operated in favor of all criminals to mitigate in certain cases the severity of the criminal law."[8] Gradually, the state acquired total jurisdiction from the church and benefit of clergy was eventually abolished. By 1827, it could no longer be claimed by commoners, and in 1841 it was no longer available to English peers. Benefit of clergy survived in the American colonies until only shortly after the Revolution.

benefit of clergy An early form of suspended sentence

Another early form of suspended sentence was **judicial reprieve**, the temporary suspension of the imposition or sentence by the court. The granting of such reprieve usually allowed the defendant to go free pending final disposition of the case. Its purpose was to allow the defendant to

judicial reprieve Temporary suspension of the imposition or sentence by the court

have time to appeal a case to the Crown or to apply for a pardon. It was also granted when the judge was not satisfied with the evidence presented against the accused. Although judicial reprieve did offer a form of suspended sentence, sometimes indefinite suspension, it did not set forth any conditions by which the accused was to be governed during this reprieve. This form of suspended sentence was not probation, which by earlier definition must carry with it some degree of supervision.

recognizance The obligation to appear in court

Recognizance (the obligation to appear in court), with or without bail, is deeply embedded in English law. Originally, it was used as a method for ensuring that a defendant would appear at trial. It was also used as a form of provisional suspension until the final disposition of a case. Today, it is used for only the first purpose. Recognizance originated as a form of preventive justice. It "consists of obliging those persons, whom there is a probable ground to suspect of future misbehavior, to stipulate with and to give full assurance to the public, that such offense as is apprehended shall not happen.... This 'assurance to the public' is given by entering into a recognizance or bond (with or without sureties) creating a debt to the state that becomes enforceable, however, only when the specified conditions are not observed. The recognizance is entered into for a specified period of time."[9] Recognizance and provisional release on bail were the first rudimentary stage in the development of probation.

EARLY PROBATION IN THE UNITED STATES

The Warwickshire Quarter Sessions, an English criminal court, practiced the conditional release of youthful offenders to the supervision of their masters or parents in England as early as 1820. But a Boston cobbler by the name of John Augustus (Box 8.2) deserves the title of the "father of probation," for he was the world's first probation officer.

Augustus spent a great deal of time observing the proceedings of the Boston police court. He became interested in the common drunks in jail.

John Augustus The father of probation

BOX 8.2 **JOHN AUGUSTUS (1785–1859)**

John Augustus, the "father of probation," was a Boston shoemaker interested particularly in the temperance crusade in the 1840s. As a member of the Washington Total Abstinence Society, he worked at getting men to give up alcohol. Part of his voluntary service in Boston was to visit courts and request temporary suspensions or postponements of sentence for those whom he judged were ready to quit liquor. During the next brief few weeks, Augustus would work with the bailed person and return to court to encourage a fine (usually one penny and court costs) for the men he believed would remain sober and law abiding. He bailed almost 2,000 men, women, and children, and of the first 1,100, only one forfeited a bond. He died almost penniless, after having established a new way of dealing with offenders: probation.

Because they could not pay their fines, he often paid them himself. In fact, by 1858 he had bailed out more than 1,152 men and boys as well as 794 women and girls. In addition to this, he would offer to help young girls and women who had either no place to go or no one to care for them.

Augustus undertook the task of supervising and guiding the behavior of those he bailed out during the period prior to the court's final disposition. The courts encouraged Augustus in his endeavors by not sentencing the convicted criminals to the usual stay in the House of Corrections. Instead, if they had shown signs of good behavior and reform during the period between their release on bail and their final court date, the judge would impose only a nominal fine and order the defendant to pay court costs.

Augustus' work resulted in the establishment of a visiting probation agent system in Massachusetts, in 1869. This system was devised primarily to assist delinquent children; the method of supervision employed was described as follows:

> If the offense of the convicted one appears exceptional to his general good conduct, and his appearance and surroundings are such as to give promise of future correct behavior, and if it be the first offense, the child is put on probation, with the injunction, "Go and sin no more," and becomes one of the wards of the state by adoption, over whom we exercise such guardianship as we may. If there is hope without strong promise that the offender may do well if released on probation, he is formally and legally committed to the agent of the Board of State Charities, and comes under his control independent of the parents, except as the agent permits; but he is allowed to return to the parents, and remain with them so long as he does well; although he may remain with his parents or friends, he becomes a ward of the State by due process of law, and a subject of visitation.[10]

Because of the humanitarianism of this one man, the nation's first probation law was passed in Massachusetts in 1878. In 1891, a second Massachusetts law required the criminal courts to appoint probation officers and to extend the provisions of the first law generally. By 1900, there were only four other states that recognized and used this new approach for the disposition of criminal cases: Missouri, beginning in 1897; Rhode Island, in 1899; New Jersey, in 1900; and Vermont, in 1900. Not until the creation of the first juvenile court in Chicago in 1899 was the idea of probation or suspended sentence with proper supervision considered in regard to juveniles.

By 1927, all but two states had passed laws similar to that in Illinois to establish juvenile courts, and all but one of those had established juvenile probation systems. The link between juvenile courts and the provision of probation services for juveniles so prevalent in the system today may be said to have originated at the very beginnings of the juvenile court movement.

Although probation sources have expanded greatly, there remains a valid challenge to practitioners in the juvenile justice system, particularly to the juvenile courts and probation officers, to see that the system does indeed work as intended.

PROBATION TODAY

Probation has become a major part of the juvenile justice system as well as a complex social institution that touches the lives of literally hundreds of thousands of young people each year. Underlying the practice of probation is the basic belief that there are juvenile delinquents who pose neither a threat nor a risk to society. Placing such juveniles in institutions would be in neither the youths' nor society's best interests. This is especially true if one accepts Gluecks' premise that most juvenile delinquency is self-correcting: The youth usually outgrows it regardless of whether there is official intervention by the juvenile justice system.[11] Indeed, placing juveniles in more than the "least restrictive environment" required for society's protection can lead to further law violations and more dangerous forms of delinquency. Putting a probation-eligible youth in an institution is also not cost-effective to the state. It costs significantly more to maintain a juvenile in an institution, camp, or ranch than it does to supervise that same youth on probation in the community. For example, a 2007 Texas study determined that the cost of juvenile incarceration was $153.24 per day compared with $8.44 per day for community supervision in 1998. In addition, a RAND Corporation study estimated that community supervision could prevent 70 serious crimes per every $1 million expenditure.[12] A very important task for probation personnel, therefore, is to identify those youths who pose no threat to the community. If the adjudicated delinquent poses no jeopardy to the community and demonstrates law-abiding behavior to the court, it is in the best interests of all concerned to consider placing the youth on probation.

Why Probation?

The primary goal of probation is to provide services designed to help youthful offenders in dealing with their problems and their environments. If the probation is successful, the factors that brought the youths into contact with the law should be resolved, and at the same time, a reintegration process for the youths into the community should be carried out. Probation is to be preferred over institutionalization for several reasons:

1. Probation allows the juvenile to function at a fairly normal level in the community while affording protection for the community against further law violations.

Juvenile Court Probation Department

2. Probation helps the juvenile to avoid the negative effects of institutionalization, which often hinder the progress of rehabilitation and the return to law-abiding behavior.

3. The verbal description of the offense in a probation case is often worded in a less severe manner than is that for other dispositions. For example, instead of a case description of "grand larceny," the words "bicycle theft" may be used. This decreases the impact of the labeling process on the juvenile.

4. The youth's rehabilitation program is greatly facilitated by keeping the youth in the community, living at home, and, if feasible, attending school, participating in extracurricular activities, working, and so forth.

5. Probation is much less expensive than incarceration. In fact, figures indicate that probation costs only one-sixth as much as incarceration.[13]

It is important to note that probation is not a suitable or desirable disposition in all cases. In some states statutes define certain offenses as ineligible for probation. All offenders convicted of these offenses must be incarcerated, regardless of circumstances. In these cases, the court must accept the questionable assumption that dispositional decisions for such offenders can be based on the offense alone and that other conditions such as personality, attitude, and life circumstances are inconsequential factors in the dispositional decision for the offender.

Even if an offense is probation eligible, the community may be so outraged by the crime committed by the youth that pressure is applied on the court to place the youth in an institution. It may also be clear from the youth's past behavior or attitude that there is a predictable risk to the community and that probation would be inappropriate. In most cases, however, probation is feasible if given a chance. A great deal depends on the training and attitude of the probation staff and the level of their commitment to making it work.

Granting Probation

How, then, is the judge to decide between placing a juvenile offender on probation and sending him or her to an institution? In 1973, the International Association of Chiefs of Police Delinquency Prevention/ Juvenile Justice Conference devised criteria to guide the juvenile court judge in such a decision. The factors to be considered are still valid today:

1. Does the court have a probation department? If so, is it adequately staffed to ensure maximum supervision of and counseling assistance to clients?

2. What is the nature and circumstances of the offense? How serious is the offense, both to the victim and to the public? What amount of criminal sophistication was evidenced in the planning and commission of the offense?

3. What is the history and character of the offender. Is he currently on probation for another offense? Was he previously incarcerated? Did she admit her guilt or involvement? What are his attitudes toward the offense, society, and juvenile justice officials?

4. What is the offender's family situation? Would placing her back in an unstable family jeopardize chances for rehabilitation? Are the parents willing to assist their child, or do they want to "get him off their hands"?

5. What is the availability of community resources? The juvenile court judge must establish excellent liaison procedures with community juvenile justice service agencies so he or she can refer the probationer to these agencies for assistance with the problem. The child's school must be willing to readmit him or her and assist him or her in making a satisfactory readjustment.[14]

We supplement these original guidelines with new provisos developed by the Office of Juvenile Justice and Delinquency Prevention. In their revised *Desktop Guide to Good Juvenile Probation Practice*, they envision the role of probation as a catalyst to develop safe communities and healthy youth and families. This role can be fulfilled by the following:

1. **Holding offenders accountable.** By exercising their proper function, probation officers protect the community through aggressive

enforcement of conditions (e.g., curfews, drug testing), effective communications with families of offenders, or providing timely help in a time of crisis.

2. **Building and maintaining community-based partnerships.** Ties should be developed and maintained between probation officers and the police, community members, schools, churches, and other community agencies.

3. **Implementing results-based and outcome-driven services and practices.** Because the juvenile offender is accountable to victims, juvenile probation offices must have clear and firm expectations of performance. Goals like fairness and consistency are paramount.

4. **Advocating for and addressing the needs of victims, offenders, families, and communities.**

5. **Obtaining and sustaining sufficient resources.**

6. **Promoting growth and development of all juvenile probation professionals.**[15]

This statement of principles stresses that juvenile probation is a catalyst. To accomplish its mission, entities and persons other than the probation officer must be involved in the prevention of delinquency.

FORMAL AND INFORMAL PROBATION

Put simply, formal probation occurs when the child's petition for probation is brought before the court and the court in turn decides that a formal hearing is necessary. A youth must usually be an adjudicated delinquent, dependent, or incorrigible before being placed on formal probation. If a juvenile is given formal probation, he or she is placed under direct supervision of an assigned probation officer and must abide by the conditions tailored to fit that situation.

A majority of cases never reach the formal court hearing stage. Informal or "vest pocket" probation may occur for several reasons. One of the most common is an overcrowded juvenile court calendar. To place a juvenile on informal probation, a petition must be filed with the court. This petition may be filed by just about anybody, but it is usually handled by the police, the probation office, a social service agency, or in some cases the juvenile court's intake service.

The juvenile court, in conference with those involved with the case (e.g., the probation officer, court intake officer), reviews the juvenile's case and determines if the offense, behavior, or life circumstances warrant a formal court hearing. If not, the juvenile can be placed on informal probation and is, therefore, technically under the supervision of the probation office.

> Informal dispositions are not always in the youth's best interests, however: The rationale for pre-judicial handlings rests on the greater flexibility, efficiency, and humanity it brings to a formal system operating within legislative and other definitive policies. But pre-judicial methods that seek to place the juvenile under substantial control in his pattern of living without anyone's consent are not permissible. The difficult task is to discriminate between the undesirable use of informality, benevolent as well as punitive, and tolerable, desirable modes of guidance.[16]

"Pre-judicial" means that the case does not reach the formal hearing stage, not that the court has not been involved. Most juvenile courts have juvenile probation departments that are defined and legitimized under statute and are part of the court.

FILING A PETITION

Generally, a petition is filed when the legal authority of the juvenile court is needed to ensure either the welfare of the child or the safety of the community (see Figure 8.1). Anyone who has firsthand knowledge of the case can file a petition with the court. The petition must, however, be reviewed and found to be justifiable by a juvenile probation officer or a juvenile court intake officer. If there is no charge in the petition, they will not be required to offer a defense. Although a petition may be amended to include all charges, such an amendment should not be necessary if special attention is paid to completeness and accuracy in the first place.

A completed petition should contain the following sections, if possible:

1. A positive identification of the child, including both true name and alias (if any), date of birth, place of birth, sex, and current address and telephone number. If the petitioner does not know any of this information, he or she should so state.
2. A positive identification of the parent or guardian, including true names and aliases (if any), marital status, current address and phone, specific relationship to the youth (this should state whether this relationship is natural, legal, putative, adoptive, or deceased), and the name and address of the persons with whom the youth is presently living.
3. A specific statement of the facts of the case. This statement should enable the court to determine its jurisdiction over the juvenile and the subject matter of the proceedings, and should be phrased in plain language and with a reasonable definiteness and particularity.

IN RE THE WELFARE OF B.D.   LEGAL NO

                                                           PETITION

_____
I represent to the Court as follows
Name of child
Place of residence
Name of person child resides with and relationship
Name of father   Residence
Name of mother   Residence
Marital status of parents
        That the child is
        That the child is within or residing within County and is in need of care and
        planning by the court.
        Wherefore your petitioner prays that the Court inquire into conditions and enter
s such an order as shall be for the child's welfare, pursuant to Chapter 13.04 of the
Revised Code of _____.

                                          _____
                                          Petitioner
STATE OF _____
COUNTY OF _____

                                          _____
                                          Petitioner

                                          _____
                                          Agency or Relationship
                                          or Residence

_____ being first duly sworn on oath, deposes and says:
        That with (s)he is the petitioner herein, that (she has read the foregoing
petition, knows the contents thereof.

                                          _____
                                          _____

SUBSCRIBED AND SWORN TO before me this _____day _____of 20____.

                                          SUPERIOR COURT CLERK by Deputy

                          or   _____

                                          Notary Public in and for the
                                          State of _____, residing at

                                          _____

_____

                  NOTICE TO CHILD AND PARENTS OR CUSTODIAN
                                READ CAREFULLY
The Court after appropriate hearings in open court may:

1. Commit a delinquent or incorrigible child to the Department of Social and
    Health Services, Division of Institutions or
2. Decline or waive jurisdiction in delinquency cases, to treat a child as an adult by
    referral to an appropriate adult court or prosecuting authority, or
3. Place a delinquent, incorrigible or dependent child in the parents custody
    subject to a probation plan or
4. Place a delinquent incorrigible or dependent child in the temporary custody of a
    group home or foster home or
5. Make any social plan for the best welfare of a delinquent incorrigible or
    dependent child

Hearing set for:
N & S to
Officer:

Figure 8.1
Sample Petition

4. A request for an inquiry into the case by the court, that is, that the court look into the welfare of the child and make such order as the court shall find to be in the best interests of the juvenile and the community.

5. A copy of or statement regarding previous court orders regarding the youth in question; this should include dates of the orders and the current legal status of the juvenile.

The initial investigation required to enable a person to file a petition is not enough. When the petition is accepted, the juvenile court intake worker, the probation officer, or any other party who filed the petition must conduct a further investigation. Witnesses (if applicable) must be found and interviewed, evidence must be compiled, and a case must be composed that will convince the judge that the court must intercede to either protect the child or safeguard the community.

FUNCTIONS OF JUVENILE PROBATION

The contemporary juvenile probation department serves three major functions: (1) intake and screening, (2) investigation, and (3) supervision.

Intake and Screening

The primary function of intake and screening is to determine whether those juveniles for whom petitions have been made fall under the jurisdiction of the court. Most states have statutes that define what kinds of cases may be handled by the probation department. Thus, each case sent to the department must be screened thoroughly to make sure it is an appropriate referral.

Many referral sources do not have the time, money, or staff to explore each case they refer properly. Often, the probation officer must confer with the child, family, and referral source to find out whether the probation office should handle the case directly or by referral to other community resources.

In addition to statutory deferment, other circumstances may prevent the involvement of the probation department. For example, most probation offices cannot offer services for the psychotic, mentally challenged, or severely handicapped child. The preliminary investigation at intake should include an interview with the juvenile, at which time the juvenile should be advised of his or her legal rights. The probation department should also contact the youth's parents or guardians to inform them of the status of the case and their right to contact an attorney.

It is possible that the case may be resolved at this early screening stage by what has been called previously an informal disposition. This occurs if it is decided that the juvenile need not go to court but may instead be supervised by the probation department with the consent of the parents or guardian.

A crucial part of the intake and screening process is to decide whether the child should be admitted to, continued in, or removed from detention prior to the final disposition of the case. Removal from the home may constitute a major threat to the child and/or family and may deal a severe psychological blow to the youth. Although removal may be necessary and even helpful for some, it may be damaging and inappropriate for others. The problem is rendered even more complex by the fact that in the 1960s and 1970s, many juvenile detention facilities degraded and brutalized their inmates rather than rehabilitated them. The importance of doing a good job during the intake and screening process must be emphasized. Inappropriate referrals and wrong decisions can do a great deal of harm to the youths involved.

Investigation

In addition to the preliminary investigation in regard to filing a petition, the probation department must develop a comprehensive social history on each youth who is scheduled for a hearing in juvenile court.

The juvenile court can be a dominant power in the life of a juvenile in trouble. Because the juvenile delinquent may be returned home, placed in an alternative living situation, or removed from society entirely for several years, depending on the action of the court, the social study or diagnostic study is extremely important to the future of the child.

> Such a study involves the awesome task of predicting human behavior. The focal concern is the probable nature of the child's response to the necessary demands of society. Will he or will he not be able to refrain from offending again if permitted to continue to reside in the free community? An even more complicated question is: What will be his adjustment under the various possible conditions of treatment, i.e., if he is returned home without further intervention, or if he is provided differing sorts of community supervision and service, or if he is confined in an institution? Only by illuminating such questions can the social study be of value to the court's dispositional decision.[17]

The probation department staff is charged with a major responsibility. The crucial and difficult task of pretrial investigation requires hard work, dedication, intelligence, and the ability to describe human behavior. Effective interview techniques and the ability to coordinate resources and knowledge represented by other disciplines such as law, medicine, and psychiatry must be used as backup to the investigator's own personal skills.

It is not always immediately possible to delineate a child's problems and formulate a precise treatment for those problems after the social diagnosis.

The treatment process is often a gradual one in which a continuing relationship between the child and the probation staff is involved. Starting with the problem as defined by the juvenile, and determining what that juvenile wishes to do about it, many other areas of difficulty are uncovered. It is not possible or even desirable for the probation officer to contend with everything that surfaces diagnostically. For example, many fatherless boys are in need of a strong father figure. Casework training (Box 8.3) may give the probation officer the flexibility to provide such a figure. But time, caseload size, or the danger of the youth's becoming overly dependent on the probation officer may make this option unrealistic.

Supervision

The overall picture of juvenile probation is muddied by the total lack of standardization. This problem exists in state jurisdictions and in the courts within a single state. This is true with regard to the provisions of probation in general and supervision in particular.

There seem to be no standardized procedures regarding the conditions of probation, the training of probation officers, the organization of the probation staff, or the provision of services. Probation procedures, in fact, seem to be determined by individual courts and by individual cases. This multiplicity of procedures requires that probation supervision be discussed in generalities rather than in specifics. Probation supervision involves three major factors: (1) surveillance, (2) casework service, and (3) counseling or guidance.

1. **Surveillance.**   The officer must keep in touch with the juvenile, the parents, the school, and other persons or agencies involved with the case. The degree of this surveillance depends on the amount of

---

BOX 8.3 **CASEWORK**

Casework generally refers to the social-work model of offering services to the client based on an analysis of the case, diagnosis of client needs and problems, and designing a treatment plan to rehabilitate the offender. This approach reflects a "medical model" of corrections that raises two questions: Who are offenders? and What shall we do with them? The answers are as follows: They are sick, and corrections should heal them and make them well.

Faced with the realities that most federal probation officers are not well prepared to provide casework and that most clients do not require this approach, the Federal Probation Service has shifted emphases to a Community Resource Management Team model. Basically, this approach indicates that the offender should be reintegrated in the community, using existing community resources. Team members, usually specializing in one aspect of client needs (e.g., employment, drug abuse problems, emotional counseling), serve as "brokers," referring clients to local facilities and services. This team approach is believed to be a more effective reintegration approach than an officer would provide through conducting classical casework therapy.

time the officer must spend on routine paperwork, the size of the caseload, and the individual philosophy of the court. Surveillance is intended to keep the probation officer informed about the child's progress, attitude, and reactions to the treatment plan; the parents' relationship with the child; and other aspects that would indicate the child's progress or lack thereof toward reintegration into the community. Surveillance should not be used as a threat to the child. If conducted properly, it can point out the responsibilities and the demands that life and society can make on each member of a community. By acting only as a monitor and reminder of failures, it can be a strong negative force.

2. **Casework.**   The probation officer is expected to utilize social casework methods to diagnose, treat, and generally deal with a juvenile. The officer makes home visits, conducts interviews, has discussions with the juvenile and parents, arranges for referrals to service agencies, works with the school, and engages in other tasks that are required in effective casework. The officer must determine to what extent the problems confronting the youth may be alleviated by involvement in community services or his or her own personal intervention. The officer must then coordinate such services and present them in an organized program aimed at helping the child and the parents to make effective use of them.

3. **Counseling or guidance.**   Guidance in supervision works hand in hand with the other two aspects and makes them both possible to perform.

Juvenile Meeting with his Probation Officer

Auxiliary Functions

Depending on the jurisdiction, the probation department provides several other services aside from surveillance, casework service, and counseling. Large probation departments often administer their own treatment or diagnostic services. These programs may include such things as foster care, group homes, drug treatment centers, and forestry camps. They may also be involved in organizing and planning community resources, and some may even operate delinquency prevention programs. In summary, the supervision of juveniles by the probation department depends on several factors. Some of the more significant are the size and staffing of the department and available financial resources.

The amount of success that the probation department experiences in carrying out its supervisory tasks depends in large measure on the ratio of probation officers to juveniles To emphasize this point, Douglas Besharov offers the following observation regarding juvenile probation supervision:

> The realities of probation supervision do not live up to those hopes of the theory. Few communities are blessed with sufficiently staffed probation services. Many probation departments are so completely overwhelmed that they provide almost no supervision or follow-up. Individuals on probation may be seen as infrequently as once every two months during a perfunctory office interview.... It is reasonable to assume that the effect... on a troubled youth is worse than no supervision at all. He sees that the end of court process was a sham and he loses further confidence, or fear in the system.[18]

Supervision Styles of Probation Officers

Supervision styles are framed by the manner in which officers view the job. This worldview defines the primary role that they follow. These roles revolve around the classic treatment (help the offender) and surveillance (protect the public) dichotomy.:

1. **The punitive officer** perceives his or her role as the guardian of middle class morality. He or she attempts to coerce the offender into conforming by a means of threats and punishment, and emphasizes control, the protection of the community against the offender, and the systematic suspicion of those under supervision. Typically, they view themselves as law enforcers.

2. **The protective officer** vacillates literally between protecting the offender and protecting the community. The tools are direct assistance, lecturing, and, alternatively, praise and blame. He or she is perceived as ambivalent in his or her emotional involvement with the offender and others in the community as the officer shifts back

and forth in taking sides with one against the other. The protective officer views him- or herself as a therapist trying to blend treatment and surveillance.

3. **The welfare officer** has as an ultimate goal the improved welfare of the clients, achieved by aiding them in their individual adjustment within limits imposed by the client's capacity. Such an officer believes that the only genuine guarantee of community protection lies in the client's personal adjustment, because external conformity will only be temporary and, in the long run, may make a successful adjustment more difficult. Emotional neutrality permeates relationships. The diagnostic categories and treatment skills that are employed from an objective and theoretically based assessment of the client's needs and capacities.

4. **The passive officer** sees the job as a sinecure requiring only minimum effort. They "fake it" and "never have enough time" to manage their "trouble-free caseload." They are marking time until retirement.[19]

Research on probation officer attitudes reveals that juvenile probation officers are likely to express strong support for the rehabilitation and caseworker type (treatment) of supervision strategy.[20] However, they also express a high degree of cynicism about the ability of the system to achieve the goal of offender rehabilitation.[21]

Probation officers thus have a broad range of supervision styles. They must blend the need for control with the need for treatment. Their choice of style also depends on the nature of the client and the demands of the situation.[22] Treatment and enforcement are two sides of the same correctional coin.

CONDITIONS OF PROBATION

At the present time, the conditions under which probation is granted are not standardized. Some courts dictate these conditions on an individual basis, whereas other courts follow state statutes.

The conditions of probation that do exist range from vague, general directives (e.g., "Stay out of trouble") to specific stipulations, which may include attending school regularly; being home by a certain hour (curfew); getting a job; undergoing specific treatment or counseling; avoiding delinquent peers; refraining from the possession of firearms, dangerous weapons, or an automobile; refraining from drinking or use of drugs; living at home and obeying parents; living in a foster or group home; restoring damage to victims (Box 8.4); doing volunteer public service work or chores; enrolling in special classes for vocational training; and regularly reporting to the probation officer.

restitution A court-ordered condition of probation that requires the offender to repair the financial, emotional, or physical damage done (a reparative sentence) by making financial payment of money to the victim or, alternatively, to a fund to provide services to victims

BOX 8.4 **RESTITUTION**

Restitution is a court-ordered condition of probation that requires the offender to repair the financial, emotional, or physical damage done (a reparative sentence) by making financial payment of money to the victim or, alternatively, to a fund to provide services to victims. In addition, restitution programs are frequently ordered in the absence of a sentence to probation. It is an example of a community service alternative that is designed to make the offender directly accountable for crime while simultaneously protecting the public. It is based on the concept of restorative justice—that the offender will make amends to both the victim and the community.

Almost every state has restitution programs in operation, although Florida, Minnesota, and Michigan seem to be leaders in the development of American restitution programs. (Restitution programs have been extensively implemented and evaluated in Great Britain.) In Minnesota, parolees may also be required to reside in a residential center and pay part of their wages to victims. Other jurisdictions require victim–offender conferences to establish the amount of financial compensation to be given the victim.

A new model in this area is the Balanced Approach and Restorative Justice (BARJ) philosophy. It emphasizes the establishment of closer ties between community agencies and granting equal status to needs of the offender, the victim, and the community. Victim–offender mediation is a strong component of these models. The BARJ model is a part of juvenile legislation in Pennsylvania and Indiana.

Research findings on juvenile restitution programs report a small but significant impact on recidivism. They also demonstrate that restitution program participants, both offenders and victims, express strong support regarding their participation and involvement in them.

Sources: David M. Altschuler, "Community Service Initiatives: Issues and Challenges," *Federal Probation*, Vol. 65 (2001), pp. 28–32; Gordon Bazemore and Mark S. Umbright, *Balanced and Restorative Justice for Juveniles: A Framework for Justice in the 21st Century* (Washington, DC: Office of Juvenile Justice and Delinquency Prevention, 1997); Ronald J. Seyko, "Balanced and Restorative Justice Efforts in Allegheny County, Pennsylvania," *The Prison Journal*, Vol. 81 (2001), pp. 187–205; Bruce A. Arrigo and Robert C. Schehr, "Restoring Justice for Juveniles: A Critical Analysis of Victim–Offender Mediation," *Justice Quarterly*, Vol. 15 (1998), pp. 629–666; Office of Juvenile Justice and Delinquency Prevention, *Guide for Implementing the Balanced and Restorative Justice Model* (Washington, DC: U.S. Department of Justice, 1998).

The purpose of these conditions is to alter the juvenile's environment of past delinquent behaviors in the hope that by removing those factors that were a negative influence, the youth will be less likely to misbehave. It can also be argued that conditions of probation may cause more misbehavior than they prevent. By imposing conditions on a youth that do not constrain his or her nonprobationer peers, the juvenile may feel picked upon, alienated, or left out. Examples of such arbitrary conditions could include curfews, not driving, obeying all laws (including such minor infractions as crossing a street against the light), or going directly home after school. For some youths on probation, the conditions of their probation are so arbitrarily restrictive that to live normal lives, they have no choice but to violate these conditions.

Probation should have conditions, but these conditions should be studied carefully before being mandated. They should be realistic and tailored as much as possible to fit a workable plan for both the youth and the community. They should also be flexible enough to allow for special circumstances, such as letting a youth with a curfew go to a special school function, maintain employment that may keep him or her out after curfew, and so forth. Conditions should be stated in a fair and comprehensive manner. The youth involved should know exactly what is or is not expected of him or her and what he or she can expect from the court, including how to, and under what circumstances the youth can, approach his or her probation officer regarding negotiation of conditions. Probation conditions can also apply to the parents, guardians, or custodians of the youth on probation. For example, the court may order that the parents maintain closer control over the juvenile, undergo family therapy at a community mental health center, or participate in other suggested treatment programs. Similar considerations regarding the imposition of conditions on parents as discussed regarding youths should be followed.

If the child (or parents) violates the conditions of probation, he or she may be returned to the court for a new disposition based on the latest misbehavior. Because probation is a means of retaining the youth in the community (and thus a means of eliminating the problems of reintegration after being in an institution), every effort is usually made to refrain from removing the child from the family and community. It is not uncommon for a youth to be returned to probation status time and time again. The courts tend to look for things such as current violations, their impact on the community, the child's past record, his or her attitude toward probation and society, and other factors. It is important to note that these factors were considered when the original disposition of probation was granted. The informal probationer who violates the condition of probation may expect to go before the court for a formal hearing and be adjudicated as either a delinquent or an incorrigible. For the youth on formal probation, the conditions of that probation may be made tighter. Often, the youth is required to report more often to his or her probation officer and the hours under curfew are increased significantly.

If it seems that the youth may have to be brought before the court again, the probation officer can assume disciplinary control over the client. If the officer has a large and unmanageable caseload, disciplinary control has little or no impact. In such a situation, the threat of return to the court becomes an arbitrary action, based on infrequent or totally negative contact with the juvenile.

If one accepts that youths should remain in their communities, if at all possible, it is not surprising to see that some courts bend over backwards to avoid sending youths to institutions, even if they repeatedly violate the conditions of their probation. There is a limit, however, to the tolerance of even the most concerned courts. The violation of probation can and often does result in an order remanding the youth to a correctional facility.

There are those who interpret a violation of probation as a failure of the individual officer. This tends to force many officers to make sure that if a violation does occur, the blame falls on the juvenile and not the officer. To deflect the blame, however, the probation officer must resist committing him- or herself to the youth. Thus, if the probationer does fail, the officer can exonerate him- or herself of any responsibility and say that it is entirely the juvenile's fault. Pressure of this sort certainly does not strengthen the effectiveness of the correctional concept of reintegration.

DURATION OF PROBATION

As in the case of conditions of probation, the length of time a youth must spend on probation varies from state to state where statutes exist or from court to court within each state. Some statutes limit the maximum time of the probation. And in some states, the maximum term of probation may be extended one or more times after required notice and a court hearing. If a statute is either nonspecific about the limit or does not establish one at all, the maximum extended length is usually considered to be until the juvenile reaches majority, usually age 18 years.

If the juvenile has proven that he or she can responsibly meet the conditions of probation, including no further law violations, the courts can shorten the term of probation and release the youth to the community with an unsupervised, normal citizen status.

ORGANIZATION AND ADMINISTRATION OF PROBATION

Administratively and organizationally, juvenile probation has traditionally been a local function. In general, there are three major types of organizational structures used by the states in their provision of juvenile probation services:

1. A centralized, statewide system;
2. A centralized county or city system supported by state supervision, consultation, standard-setting, staff development assistance, and partial state subsidies; and
3. A combined state–local structure, with the largest jurisdictions operating their own probation departments and the state providing services in other areas.

Local courts or the state administrative office of the courts in twenty-three states and the District of Columbia administer probation services. Fourteen other states administer probation through a juvenile court in urban counties and a state executive system in smaller counties. Ten states administer probation through a statewide executive branch department. In the remaining three states, the county executive is in charge of probation services.[23] These organizational structures create complex intergovernmental problems, chiefly because, as mentioned previously, most states place the administrative responsibility for juvenile probation services on the shoulders of the juvenile courts.

Juvenile probation has suffered and continues to suffer because there is no uniformity of standardization of administrative procedures. Administration by more than one level of government is a major cause of trouble. If juvenile probation administration continues to be divided among several units of government, a strong, centralized state-level agency should be responsible for setting goals and standards in probation services for those departments that are unable to set their own.

Where the question of state versus local administration of juvenile probation services is raised, the best solution, from an organizational standpoint, is to have supervision from the state and administration through the counties. Such a plan has the following advantages:

1. It has greater potential for assuring uniformity of standards and practice, including provision of services to rural areas.

2. It makes more feasible certain kinds of research, statistical and fiscal control, and similar operations.

3. It best enables recruitment of qualified staff and provision of centralized or regional in-service training and staff development programs.

4. It permits staff assignment to regional areas in response to changing conditions.

5. It facilitates relationships with other aspects of the state correctional program.[24]

However, even if everyone agreed that the administration of probation services belongs at the local level, this consensus would not completely solve the problem of intergovernmental relations. County or city probation services are administered by either the court or an administrative agency that is a separate function of the local government.

Some system professionals feel that the probation function should be part of the local corrections component; conversely, others maintain that the responsibility for probation services should remain with the juvenile court because of the court's legal jurisdiction (the sentence is suspended while the offender is on probation, yet the court maintains legal control and can revoke the suspension, if warranted, and commit the offender to an institution).[25]

Major police organizations contend that the administration of juvenile probation should be the function of the county or district courts and not at the community level. This is part of the movement toward consolidating such services at more cost-effective levels.

THE PROBATION OFFICER

Even with proper administration, sound organizational structure, and the commitment of state and local governments to providing competent probation services, probation still requires one more ingredient: the dedicated, well-trained, and concerned juvenile or probation officer.

"All juvenile courts have an auxiliary staff to provide the court's social service function. The same staff usually operates the intake and adjustment service, the predispositional investigation and report service, and the probation supervision service."[26] These staff members are sometimes called juvenile counselors, but more frequently they are known as juvenile probation officers. This name originated because of their traditional role of supervising juveniles on probation. In general, state statutes spell out the specific powers and duties of the juvenile probation officer.

Duties

The duty and responsibility of the juvenile probation officer is to carry out the functions of juvenile probation: (1) intake and screening, (2) investigation, and (3) supervision. How much success the officer has in fulfilling these functions will be determined by several factors, some of which are beyond the officer's control. For example, the number of probation officers a court can hire will be limited by the court's budget, and the number of officers has a direct bearing on the size of each caseload. The training (when there is training) an officer receives is the prerogative of the court under its mandate to provide staff to oversee probation.

Although considered low in professional standing within the juvenile justice system, the probation officer generally receives the necessary court backing to enable him or her to do the job effectively. In many respects, the probation officer may be viewed as being second only to the juvenile court judge in the degree of power he or she holds within the juvenile justice system. The probation officer has the power to direct cases to and from the court system, decide whether a juvenile is to be kept in detention, influence the court's disposition through his or her ability to color the court's picture of the child and the child's family, and exert a general influence over the outcome of a case.

Qualifications

Community supervision staff (this includes juvenile probation officers) should possess the necessary educational background to enable them to implement the dispositional orders of the court effectively. Staff members should possess a minimum of a bachelor's degree in one of the helping sciences (e.g., social work, psychology, counseling, criminal justice).[27] The juvenile probation officer should also have emotional maturity and integrity, a belief in the ability of youths to change, an interest in working with and helping children, a basic respect for the law, an ability to work well with other professionals and community members, a desire to grow professionally, and a firm belief in the dignity and worth of young people.

These qualities are an essential part of a prospective juvenile probation officer. Persons who meet these requirements or standards should receive extensive on-the-job training regarding the diagnosis and treatment of the juvenile probationer. They should be encouraged to avoid the trap of the routine administration of social services at the expense of support and treatment.

Survey results indicate that there are an estimated 18,000 juvenile probation officers at work in the United States. The majority of them (85 percent) are involved in the delivery of basic services (intake, investigation, supervision) at the line officer level. The remaining 15 percent administer probation offices or manage probation staff.[28]

Training

There should be forty hours of initial and eighty hours of ongoing training each year in the subject areas in which community supervision staff members, including juvenile probation officers, are required to work. This training should begin with an orientation program for new workers to enable them to become familiar with court or agency policies, attitudes, and demands. In-service training, casework supervision, and procedures for educational leave should be included in on-the-job training.

In-Service Training.   In-service training should be designed to meet the needs of the staff at various levels, including supervisory and administrative. Larger agencies should assign a full-time person to conduct in-service training; appropriate state departments in organizing training regionally should assist smaller agencies.

Casework Supervision.   Casework supervision involves instruction for the probation officer in the proper use and application of diagnosis and treatment. Without specific instruction of this kind, it is difficult for the untrained worker to apply what has been learned in the training program to practical situations involving juveniles, their families, and the community.

Educational Leave.   The probation department should not only offer but actively encourage educational leave and stipends so that both part- and full-time staff members have the opportunity to broaden their education, meet desired qualifications, and improve their professional abilities and competence.

It is unrealistic to assume that all the educational and training needs of the probation officer can be met during an in-service training period. For this to happen, there must be well-prepared personnel to carry out the necessary supervision and training of those who need it; unfortunately, this is seldom the case. Maximum contributions to the field of probation will not be realized unless staff members are encouraged to advance, learn, and grow. Graduate professional training is an excellent way to accomplish this goal. Advanced professional training can be pursued by taking a master's degree in social work, which normally requires two full years' work beyond a bachelor's degree, or a graduate degree in sociology, psychology, criminology, or public administration. These degrees require one year or two years' study beyond the undergraduate degree.

A survey of juvenile probation officers in all fifty states and the District of Columbia reflected their views regarding training. Nearly one-half of the respondents indicated that their jurisdiction was considering the certification of juvenile probation officers, making it a professionally credited position with certain stated requirements. The survey also revealed that organizations tended to emphasize pre-service training but more in-service training was now required.[29]

Method of Appointment

Probation staff should be selected in accordance with civil service laws where there is an organized civil service system. Where these laws do not apply, the staff should be selected on the basis of the merit of the applicants. The selection process should include a thorough review of the applicant's education, experience, and training. A merit examination should be used in making appointments. It should be open to all persons who meet the qualifications.

The evaluation and/or examination should test basic skills and knowledge required for good performance. It should not involve matters that are meant to be learned on the job. When appointed, the new probation officer should be given a reasonable period of time in which to become acquainted with his or her new duties and responsibilities.

Salaries

Salaries for newly appointed probation officers are as nonstandardized as the function and terms of probation itself. In a survey of juvenile probation officers, more than one-half (53 percent) of the line officers reported earnings of less than $40,000/year; 13 percent earned $40,000/year or more. About 30 percent of the administrators reported annual earnings of more than $49,999. Regarding job concerns, 42 percent of the probation officers surveyed expressed fear that their job was becoming more dangerous. About one-third of the officers reported that they had been assaulted on the job in their career.[30] It is apparent that the job of a probation officer is not lucrative. The desire to serve the public and juvenile clients is the driving force in this profession.

Probation standards call for salaries commensurate with employment in similar positions of trust and responsibility. Because of low salary rates, most of the nation's probation departments cannot compete with other government agencies in recruiting the caliber of staff member that they need and want. It is little wonder that the majority of probation departments identify lack of staff as their biggest problem in administering and conducting juvenile probation services.

Caseload Size

As mentioned previously, a decisive factor in the quality of probation services is the size of the officer's caseload. All facets of the probation officer's work, from preliminary investigation to supervision, are affected by the caseload. An overcrowded caseload will usually result in a cursory investigation, in which many pertinent and potentially crucial facts may be overlooked.

Recent survey results of juvenile probation officers indicate that the size of caseloads in departments ranged from 2 to 200. The median (midpoint) of active caseload size was 41, but the officers suggested that the optimal caseload size should be 30 clients.[31]

Supervision—other than formal reporting and infrequent checks at school, work, and home—is literally impossible with a large caseload. Large caseloads not only limit supervision to a cursory police-type function, but also tend to move probation services further away from professional social casework standards for diagnosis and treatment to a more authoritarian role.

INNOVATIONS IN JUVENILE PROBATION

Several programs and supervision supplements have been devised to supplement juvenile probation. A sample of these different strategies is presented in the following sections.

Probation Subsidy

No discussion of juvenile probation would be complete without a discussion of what has come to be known as the probation subsidy program (see Box 8.5). It has been pointed out that the lack of staff and overload

probation subsidy Money
provided to counties and
local jurisdictions for not
committing offenders to
prisons

BOX 8.5 **PROBATION SUBSIDY**

A **probation subsidy** is a program run by a state. The subsidy provides money to counties and local jurisdictions for not committing offenders to prisons. The intents of subsidies are to bolster local probation services, encourage expansion of probation services, develop innovative probation strategies, and lessen the prison overcrowding problem.

Probation subsidies originated in California and, for a period before the resurgence of neoclassical ideology, forced sharp changes in an otherwise enlightened environment and reduced the proportion of felon offenders sentenced to California penal institutions. Increasing probation service strength also saved the California prison system millions of dollars in the interim. Coupled with intermediate punishments, particularly intensive supervised probation, such subsidies could form the backbone of a correctional reform in many states suffering from prison overcrowding.

---

of case assignments can greatly lessen the impact that probation might otherwise have on diverting juveniles from the formalized system. The probation subsidy program was started to alleviate this situation; it is used in several states today.

Simply stated, probation subsidy provides funding and guidance necessary to enable participating courts to develop and implement community-based treatment programs as alternatives to institutionalization. Usually, funding is provided by the state to the local courts. It is based on the number of youths that each court is able to divert from the state system.

The aim of the subsidy program, therefore, is to reduce the necessity for commitment of juveniles to state correctional facilities by strengthening and improving the supervision of juveniles placed on probation by the juvenile courts. The program encourages the courts to develop a wide range of special programs that may include counseling and placement services; contracts for psychiatric, psychological, and medical services; special day care centers; vocational and educational programs; family and group counseling; tutoring services; extensive use of volunteers; and use of case aides, work and recreational programs, educational counseling, and myriad other services integral to effective probation supervision programs.

The functions of probation (i.e., intake, investigation, and supervision) are also functions of probation subsidy workers. Essentially, except for funding base and allocations, regular probation and probation subsidy officers operate in a similar manner. Staff assignments and caseload sizes may vary, however, for probation subsidy officers. For example, some states have regular, local probation officers who handle the nonsubsidy probation caseloads and probation subsidy officers who handle nothing but subsidy caseloads.

Because probation subsidy is meant to go beyond regular probation in diverting children from the correctional program, in general, subsidy officers have caseloads comprising youths who are on informal probation or have not yet reached the formal hearing stage. This type of caseload, which usually requires less routine paperwork, enables the subsidy workers to spend more of their workday providing or coordinating direct services for youths on their caseloads.

The probation subsidy program, where it has been tried, has had a far greater success rate than anticipated. It has reduced the social and individual cost of juvenile delinquency by reducing treatment costs, reducing the pattern of institutional commitments, and meeting the treatment needs of delinquent youths within the community.

Some states have also tried what is called a negative subsidy (see Box 8.6).

Volunteers in Probation

The use of volunteers to supplement the efforts of paid correctional and juvenile justice system personnel are an increasingly common practice. Most probation department administrators endorse it enthusiastically. Recall that probation itself actually began as a volunteer service in the nineteenth century. In recent years, rising probation caseloads, lack of staff, and increased costs have brought about a renewed dependence on the assistance of community volunteers in probation. With the emphasis today on community-based programs for both adult and juvenile offenders, community volunteers are especially useful, and in the courts, the number of volunteers has increased significantly in the past fifteen years. Voluntary work in probation is a documented subject, and several works have been written that explain all facets of volunteer programs in probation. In a volunteer program, the probationer remains under the supervision of the probation department after having been placed on probation. However, the youth's primary contact is with a volunteer, usually on an individual basis within the community setting.

Case assignments are made on a commonsense basis. Volunteers and children should be matched for the most rewarding relationship.

BOX 8.6 NEGATIVE SUBSIDY

In addition to the policy option of subsidizing probation services in counties that commit fewer than expected offenders to prison every year, or for meeting state requirements and standards, some state lawmakers have decided that certain types of offenders ought to be kept in their local community under probation control. To encourage such retention, Oregon charges each county $3,000 for every committed offender whose crime falls in the "least severe" category. This means that a check for $3,000 must accompany the commitment papers when the least risky case offender is transported to prison. This is a **negative subsidy**, designed to encourage local communities to accept responsibility for providing correctional care and control for their own residents.

negative subsidy Fees or charges designed to encourage local communities to accept responsibility for providing correctional care and control for their own residents

The matching should be based on the needs of the probationer and the skills and interests of the volunteer. Both the youth and the volunteer must feel comfortable with each other or nothing will be accomplished. Many of the larger probation departments have a volunteer coordinator who oversees and supervises the pairing of youths and volunteers and the supervisory responsibilities during the probation period.

There are risks involved in matching probationers and volunteers. One of the risks involves matching that ends in failure. This is a major problem because the professional staff member must pick up the pieces and attempt to keep the youth interested in the program and out of trouble. The youth may already be badly alienated from the system and may cause the regular probation officer more concern and problems than if the child had been assigned to his or her caseload in the first place. Under these circumstances, regular professional probation officers become resentful or extremely skeptical of volunteers who may undermine the system through their inexperience, lack of professional training, or inability to perform probationary tasks.

Intensive Supervision

intensive supervision Increased contact between the officer and the client by decreasing caseload size

Intensive supervision is designed to address several different systemwide supervision problems and issues. First, its aim is to generate increased contact between the officer and the client by decreasing caseload size. This increased contact will benefit society through the close monitoring of high-risk offenders. It will also provide improved service delivery and more effective treatment for clients. Lundman defines intensive supervision programs as:

> . . . an example of the United States' current "get tough" policy with respect to adolescent crime. Intensive probation and intensive parole programs are *tough* ways of doing time in the community. Small caseloads allow for the strict enforcement of the routine conditions of probation and parole. Officers have time to make sure clients are in school or at work each weekday and home each night and weekend. [Italics in original][32]

It typically features small caseloads of ten to fifteen clients with officers working in teams of two. It is combined with such program features as education, community service, restitution, employment, and electronic monitoring.[33] Intensive supervision also targets high-risk offenders who would be incarcerated if the program were not available.[34] The hope is that intensive supervision will lead to a reduction in the institutional population and lower recidivism rates.[35] However, research finding on several intensive supervision programs fail to demonstrate any appreciable difference in recidivism rates between intensive supervision clients and other juvenile offenders in the community.[36] Yet, the ability of intensive supervision to achieve a break-even result with reduced costs of incarceration is a positive finding.[37]

Electronic Monitoring

Another "get tough" approach to the community supervision of juvenile offenders is electronic monitoring. **Electronic monitoring** tracks movement using a tracking device worn by the client. It can be used to monitor curfews imposed by the court or take the place of institutional confinement, using the home as the site of punishment.[38]

Evaluations of electronic monitoring programs cite several beneficial aspects of this program. First, it is less costly than incarceration. Second, it can easily be combined with other forms of treatment because the juvenile is in the community. Third, the offender is not removed from social supports—school, family, churches, and so on. Participants did not complain that electronic monitoring was overly intrusive and a violation of their privacy.[39]

Juvenile Supervised with an Electronic Ankle Monitor

electronic monitoring Tracks movement using a tracking device worn by the client

School Probation

Historically, schools have been recognized as a delinquency prevention institution. The hope was that education would open up opportunities for juveniles and give them a stake in conformity. Thus, schools have been a focal point of recent violence prevention and restitution efforts.[40]

As a result, like their police counterparts, juvenile probation officers have moved their offices directly into middle and high school buildings to have closer contact with their clients. This move provides more effective monitoring and also increases communication between the officer, the client, other community agencies, and teachers and school authorities. Pennsylvania has widely adopted school probation with programs in fifty of its sixty-seven counties. Some 150 officers working in 300 schools have served more than 16,000 juveniles. Preliminary research evidence demonstrates that school probation has a desirable impact on both school attendance and behavior.[41]

DIVERSION

Initially, the purpose of the development of the juvenile court was to divert juveniles form the adult criminal system. Ironically, in the 1960s, the diversion of juveniles from formal processing within the juvenile justice system became a prominent goal of juvenile justice. However, as discussed in previous chapters, this movement essentially was reversed in the 1980s and 1990s (see Box 8.7 Scaring Juveniles Straight!).

BOX 8.7 **SCARING JUVENILES STRAIGHT!**

Juvenile crime prevention programs are often based on commonsense assumptions and fail to refer to the lessons provided from previous attempts or criminological theory. Searches for panaceas (quick-fix cure-alls) for delinquency are sought and readily embraced. Realistic expectations can get lost in a rush for a definitive solution. One example of such a "get tough" program is the Juvenile Awareness Program at the Rahway State Prison in New Jersey (known as "Scared Straight!"). The history of the program and initial evaluation results are presented in frank detail by James O. Finckenauer. His book provides an in-depth examination at the evaluation process surrounding a delinquency prevention program.

There were several commonsense assumptions behind the Scared Straight program. First, the program took a page from deterrence theory and exposed juveniles who were headed for trouble to the realities of prison life from hardened, veteran, long-term inmates—the Lifers' Group. These inmates shared their experiences in the criminal justice system with the visiting juveniles in stark detail. Mirroring aversion therapy and behavior modification, the inmates adopted a rough, confrontational approach. The hope was that this exposure would literally scare the juveniles straight: The tough façade of street kids would crumble into tears under the onslaught of the Lifers' presentations. Awareness of what was in store for them if they continued along their present path would steer the juveniles away from delinquency.

The program would also benefit the inmates—the initial sponsors of the program. Apparently, they wished to make a contribution to society and put their long prison sentence to constructive use. The public became aware of this program in 1979 through a documentary that received wide exposure and won both an Emmy and an Academy Award. The film, grimly narrated by actor Peter Falk (well-known at the time as television's Detective Columbo) was peppered with statements claiming widespread effectiveness. These claims were repeated in a long-term follow-up of the juveniles in the original film (1999's *Scared Straight 20 Years Later*, narrated by actor Danny Glover). Fueled by the public perception of increasing juvenile crime, declining support for rehabilitation, and a dramatic promise of a new solution to delinquency, the program spurred other states to call for the immediate adoption of this approach.

Finckenauer examines Scared Straight as a program and phenomenon common to delinquency prevention programs: the search for a cure all. He states that such programs fall victim to a four-stage, cyclical process in which (1) a cure-all is proposed, (2) the hype surrounding the program grows and spreads dramatically, (3) frustration caused by the failure of the program crushes hopes and even the program itself, and (4) the cycle begins anew with a different approach. The way out of this quagmire is to sponsor realistic expectations about delinquency prevention programs. They are difficult to design and to implement successfully, and thus require careful planning, persistence, and hard work.

As originally designed by the Lifers' Group, the Scared Straight program targeted three types of at-risk juveniles: the good (no involvement in crime), the bad (guilty of minor infractions), and the ugly (serious involvement in crime). However, the implication was that the program would be most effective with the ugly group—serious juvenile offenders who were truly on the road to prison. However, Finckenauer's evaluation determined that 41 percent of the juveniles who visited Rahway had no prior record of delinquency. Nevertheless, the program appeared to obtain referrals with great ease. In fact, the program expanded very rapidly. In September 1976, the first group of juveniles visited Rahway prison. By January 1977, the number of visits to the prison had increased from the original one trip per week to two per day, five days a week. The type of juvenile client who would best benefit from such exposure was never determined from these visits. In fact, the belief that the program was suitable for all juveniles was an early indication of the unrealistic expectations surrounding this approach.

Because the prisoners themselves conceived this program, it was necessary for them to obtain approval from the superintendent of the prison and then get referrals from outside agencies. Judge George Nicola was approached, and he soon became a firm supporter of the program. The format of the sessions evolved over time from a simple tour to the shock-oriented, confrontational approach that was presented in the film.

Was Scared Straight an effective form of delinquency prevention therapy? Despite its ability to demonstrate the realities of prison life, the program was little more than a field trip of horrors. First of all, Scared Straight was never a program in the truest sense. The goals of the intervention strategy were not clearly specified, planned, and developed. The implementation of the program was spontaneous rather than strategically developed to meet the risk and needs faced by juveniles. Moreover, there were little or no follow-up services provided for the juveniles after they returned to their homes and communities. The program was founded on the good intentions of the Lifers' Group and a judge who wished to do something constructive about the problem of juvenile delinquency. Delivery of services beyond the prison visit was not a part of the program.

In terms of the impact of the program on juvenile recidivism rates, Finckenauer describes his difficulties in establishing an experimental design for the program evaluation and obtaining data. His design was not perfect, and the results must be judged accordingly. However, he did attempt to consider several outcome measures of recidivism. First, recidivism was simply dichotomized as success or failure. Also, the type of delinquency was weighted by seriousness (success = 0), juveniles in need of supervision (status offenses = 1), or a juvenile delinquent (criminal = 2) offense. Finally, fifteen members of the group that visited Rahway were interviewed to obtain their impressions about the program and information on their behavior following their trip.

Overall, the results were not encouraging. In summary, the experimental group (juveniles who visited the prison) had a much higher rate of failure than the juveniles who did not take part (41.3 versus 11.4 percent). Again, some of this disparity in failure rates might have been because the juveniles targeted for the program were those already perceived to be headed for trouble. Yet, this result did not change when prior record was taken into account. Experimental group members with a prior record had a higher recidivism rate (48.2 percent) than did the members of the control group, who had committed past crimes (21.4 percent). In terms of the seriousness of the new offense, the experimental group also did significantly worse than the control group.

Finally, the results of the self-report study revealed that several of the juvenile program graduates who seemed to be successful in terms of the official record did commit some delinquent offenses. Of the seventeen experimental group members, fifteen were officially considered successful. In reality, all of them had committed some type of minor offense (e.g., skipping school, drinking alcohol, destroying property, smoking marijuana). On the basis of this information, Finckenauer concluded that the experimental group was more seriously delinquent than the control group. The program failed to reduce delinquency. As could be expected, the outcry from Scared Straight supporters was vociferous. Finckenauer's findings were attacked and questioned on the basis of his methodology, his intentions, and even his interest in conducting the study. Nevertheless, evaluation programs from similar programs seem to support Finckenauer's contentions about the Scared Straight approach.

Some reviews of juvenile awareness programs did record positive results. For example, Homant and Osowski conducted a program evaluation of the Juvenile Offenders Learn Truth (JOLT) program at the Southern Michigan State Prison in Jackson. In spite of findings that demonstrated that the JOLT program failed to reduce juvenile recidivism, the program continued to be supported by practitioners. The authors suggested that the program had little cost for the Michigan Department

(continued)

of Correction, had some positive impact on the inmate counselors, and no harmful effects on the juveniles involved. Thus, they recommended the continuation of the JOLT program despite its limitations.

The SHAPE UP (Showing How a Prison Experience Undermines People) program was established in Canon City, Colorado, in response to the popularity of Scared Straight. Again, the main program premise was that descriptions of the harsh realities of prison life from veteran inmates would "shape up" juveniles. The program evaluation was based on participant observation and interviews. One group that was affected by the program was the inmates themselves. Many of them became youth counselors and adopted that perspective in dealing with juveniles involved in the program. This new role overshadowed their negative status as prisoners and led to the development of a new, positive self-image.

However, most evaluation findings involving this approach were negative. The effectiveness of the oldest juvenile awareness program in the United States, the San Quentin (California) Squires program, was evaluated by Lewis. The procedures followed in the Squires program were very similar to Scared Straight with some exceptions: "Scare tactics" were not utilized and juveniles who participated were enrolled in three sessions with the inmates. The Lewis evaluation followed an experimental design. Males between 14 and 18 years of age with an average number of 7.4 previous arrests were assigned at random to experimental (N = 53) and control (N = 55) groups. The analysis revealed that there were no significant differences in arrest rates between the groups after a twelve-month follow-up period. In fact, the juveniles who participated in the program had a higher arrest rate than those who did not (experimentals = 81.2 percent, controls = 67.3 percent). It was also determined that the older members of the experimental group were arrest-free longer than the older controls, but they committed more serious delinquent offenses than the controls. Lewis concluded that "seriously delinquent youth cannot be turned around by short term programs such as Squires and Rahway" and that a "pattern for high-risk youth suggested that the Squires program may have been more detrimental to them." There was some evidence that the program was sponsoring rather than preventing delinquency.

Similar findings were reported by Buckner and Chesney-Lind in their evaluation of Hawaii's Stay Straight program. Like the Squires program, Stay Straight did not feature scare tactics by inmates. It stressed the "experience of prisoners" using factual storytelling and advice rather than intimidation. Only youth with one prior arrest were referred to the program. The research design featured 300 juveniles: 100 males and 50 females in both the experimental and control groups. The members of these groups were then matched on the basis of sex, age, race, and prior record to ensure comparability. A one-year follow-up was utilized, and recidivism was defined as at least one subsequent arrest. Rearrests were reported as follows: experimental males = 41 percent; experimental females = 22 percent; comparison group males = 37 percent and comparison group females = 32 percent. None of the differences were statistically significant. Closer examination revealed some damaging findings about the program. Females who attended sessions had a significantly higher number of arrests. Experimental males had a significantly higher number of arrests that resulted in a formal charge. The authors cautioned that these findings could be due to factors other than program participation. Program youth may have had a "higher delinquency" potential. In addition, deterrence theory tells us that the lesson of the prisoners' experience could best describe the severity and not the certainty of punishment to these juveniles. Buckner and Chesney-Lind reached the same basic conclusion about this type of program as the previous findings: "It is unrealistic to expect that any single experience, no matter how profound, would have a significant and long-lasting impact on a problem so complicated and intractable as juvenile delinquency."

Petrosino and his colleagues conducted a meta-analysis from the research findings from nine well-designed studies of Scared Straight programs. They concluded that these interventions were likely to have a harmful effect and actually increase delinquency in comparison with doing nothing at all. Moreover, other Petrosino work noted the reasons these commonsense panaceas continue to thrive: (1) They make sense to a public eager for quick, easy solutions; (2) It is difficult to stop programs after they have become institutionalized; (3) The program seemed to benefit the inmates as well as the juveniles; and (4) Policy makers believe so strongly in such programs that they refuse to let them die. Ignoring research evidence can only lead to the survival of poor programs that cause more harm than good.

Sources: J.C. Buckner and Meda Chesney-Lind, "Dramatic Cures for Juvenile Crime: An Evaluation of a Prison-Run Delinquency Prevention Program," *Criminal Justice and Behavior,* Vol. 10 (1983), pp. 227–247; Gray Cavender, "Scared Straight: Ideology and Media," *Journal of Criminal Justice,* Vol. 9 (1981), pp. 431–439; James O. Finkenauer, *Scared Straight! and the Panacea Phenomenon* (Englewood Cliffs, NJ: Prentice Hall, 1982); J. Heeren and David Shichor, "Mass Media and Delinquency Prevention: the Case of 'Scared Straight,'" *Deviant Behavior,* Vol. 5 (1984), pp. 375–386; Robert J. Homant and J. Osowski, "Evaluation of the 'Scared Straight' Model: Some Methodological and Political Considerations," *Corrective and Social Psychiatry and Journal of Behavioral Technology Methods and Therapy,* Vol. 27 (1981), pp. 130–134; R. V. Lewis, "Scared Straight—California Style: Evaluation of the San Quentin Squires Program," *Criminal Justice and Behavior,* Vol. 10 (1983), pp. 209–226; Anthony Petrosino, Carolyn Turpin-Petrosino, and J. Buehler, "'Scared Straight' and Other Juvenile Awareness Programs for Preventing Juvenile Delinquency," *Cochrane Database of Systematic Reviews,* Issue 2 (2002), Art. No.: CD002796. DOI: 10.1002/14651858.CD002796; Anthony Petrosino, Carolyn Turpin-Petrosino, and James Finckenauer, "Well Meaning Programs Can Have Harmful Effects! Lessons from Experiments of Programs Such as Scared Straight," Vol. 36 (2000), pp. 353–379.

The impetus that brought about the widespread use of diversion is not too different from the philosophy that led to the creation of the juvenile court—that is, the belief that official processing has negative consequences for juveniles. Official processing tends to stigmatize or label them as "bad," resulting in serious consequences for the juveniles. The basic tenets of this orientation toward diversion are as follows:

1. Responses to many juvenile offenses are excessive; most juvenile delinquency involves nonserious acts.

2. When a child is officially processed, he or she is stigmatized.

3. The stigma has a negative effect on the child's self-concept and on the way others treat him or her. This, in turn, is assumed to have lasting negative effects on the child's behavior.

4. The effect on self may be to alter the child's self-concept to that of a bad or criminal person. The child may then seek out similar peers and may act in ways that confirm his or her self-depreciation.

5. The stigma may also limit the child's opportunity for conformity, because the community will respond negatively to the child. Consequently, some support systems that might aid in altering the child's behavior may be removed.

Diversion is not limited to any one segment of the juvenile justice system or to agents and agencies of the system. For example, citizens failing to report crimes is the main mechanism through which juveniles are diverted from the justice process. Although nonreporting of crimes is certainly not an "official" form of diversion, diverting offenders from official processing is nonetheless the effect. Police may divert many, if not most, juveniles with whom they have contact before they perform an arrest or take the juvenile into custody. However, after a juvenile is arrested, more than 75 percent are referred to juvenile or adult court.[42]

Among those juveniles who are referred to a diversion program, it is not uncommon for them to be "generally well functioning, mostly attending school or working, and yet they have each committed a trouble-some, minor offense."[43] All in all, with the decreased use of diversion programs, today it tends to be only the "cream of the crop" among juvenile offenders who go to such programs. The result is the widening reach of the juvenile justice system. Rather than using diversion programs to keep some juveniles from being officially processed, juvenile justice systems use diversion today to bring more juveniles under some form of control. This is commonly referred to as a "net-widening" effect. Although all units of the juvenile justice system have the capacity to divert, one unit (intake) is usually viewed as the formal diversionary unit. As discussed previously, intake is usually performed by juvenile probation officers. The function of this unit is to determine whether a juvenile will be sent before the juvenile court and, if not, into whose custody the juvenile should be released (e.g., parents, foster care, a halfway house) and any programs in which the juvenile should participate (e.g., drug and alcohol abuse education, various treatment programs, school, or mental health programs). Even though this unit functions as the designated diversion mechanism, it is important to note that many—in fact, most—juveniles are never processed to this point. Most acts of diversion, then, are informal and occur prior to the involvement of any unit of the juvenile justice system. In many ways, this is similar to the functioning of the adult criminal justice system. That is, the majority of criminal offenses are never referred to law enforcement, and among those offenses that are reported, many offenders are warned but not arrested or processed for lack of evidence.

The decision to divert a juvenile or to process him or her through juvenile court depends on several issues, some legal and some extralegal. The deeper into the juvenile justice system a person is processed, the greater the likelihood that demographic factors (e.g., race, gender, social class) can be identified as influential.[44] This may be an important part of the reason the majority of juveniles involved in the juvenile justice system are minority (mostly African-American), lower-income, urban males. However, it is not only demographic factors that are associated with being more thoroughly processed. Neighborhood of residence, family background, and school record also have been shown to be important factors.[45]

The further one proceeds in the system, the more formal the process of diversion. However, each unit within the system has the capability to decide to remove the child from further formal processing. In fact, the emphasis on diversion in the 1960s and 1970s created numerous public and private organizations and facilities to which a juvenile may be diverted. Some examples are family counseling programs, halfway houses, Outward Bound, drug and alcohol rehabilitation and treatment centers, and restitution and community service programs. Other diversion-type programs that have been started in recent years in many urban areas are not so much programs as they are grassroots, community-based efforts to "put delinquents on the right track." Churches and community-based organizations stepped forward in the 1990s to offer their services and members as "mentors" for troubled youth. These efforts are not without precedent. John Augustus, the father of the concept of probation for adults, did the same thing starting in 1841 in Boston.

The Problem with Diversion

Several rationales have been used to justify the creation and continued support of various diversion programs and practices. The theoretical rationale, described previously, is that drawn from labeling theory.

The rationales offered in support of diversion efforts are centered on both the theoretical implications of such a process and what some observers believe are the practical implications (or lack thereof) regarding diversion. These rationales can be summarized as follows:

- Juveniles who are diverted can avoid the stigma associated with formal processing and the resultant change in self-image, associations, and behavior associated with the negative societal reaction to the stigma. Diversion, then, at least in theory, "prevents" secondary deviance and criminal career progression.

- Diversion allows juveniles to receive help when they might otherwise not have access to various treatment opportunities. A diversion program can place children in agencies and programs that provide treatment not available in juvenile corrections.

- Diversion allows agents of juvenile justice to use their discretion and make referral or release decisions on the basis of criteria that might otherwise be ignored by the court.

- Diversion can reduce the caseload of the juvenile court by diverting nonserious cases and so allow the court to concentrate its resources on more serious juvenile crime.

- Diversion is a less expensive alternative to court processing.

Although these rationales are legitimate and seemingly appropriate, a great deal of concern has been expressed by various scholars and practitioners over the large-scale and almost unquestioning acceptance of diversion and the consequent explosion of diversion agencies and programs in the early 1970s. As a result of these questions and concerns, the use of diversion programs has been significantly scaled back in recent years. This is not to say that diversion has ceased to be an important part of juvenile justice; rather, diversion programs have been seriously reconsidered, and today they are one option among many. Diversion is still a common practice and still seen as valuable for some juveniles. However, more restrictive and harsher responses have gained support since the 1970s, when diversion efforts dominated juvenile justice.

Concerns regarding diversion generally center on the belief that the rationales for and effectiveness of diversionary programs may not be as valid as they were previously believed to be. Consequently, those who voice these concerns have been instrumental in promoting harsher responses on the part of the juvenile justice system. Most of the objections to diversion fall within the following categories:

1. **Absence of evidence to prove stigmatization increases delinquency or diversion eliminates stigma.** Little empirical evidence exists to suggest that the tents of labeling theory are valid—that is, that stigma produces further delinquency. Therefore, the effect of labeling by the criminal court may be overstated. Evaluations of juvenile diversion programs have led one observer to conclude that "diversion of juveniles accused of status and property crimes is at least as effective as further penetration of the juvenile justice system."[46] However, this is not to say that there are not costs involved in such actions. Lundman points out that although diversion compels juveniles into treatment programs without formal processing, it also acts as a net-widening action, drawing some juveniles who would otherwise have been "left alone" into supervision and treatment. The result may be that the diversion of a juvenile simply substitutes one stigma for another. Rather than bearing a delinquent label, the child may bear the stigma associated with treatment by a mental health or drug abuse agency or the stigma of affiliation with social welfare agencies.[47]

2. **Increased discretion may mean increased abuse of discretion.** Although some jurisdictions set standards for diversion, many do not, and when standards do exist it is not mandatory that they be followed. Diversion decisions, because of their discretionary nature, may lead to overemphasis on extralegal factors such as age, race, and social class. Lundman concludes that diversion programs have the potential to magnify rather tan reduce problems.[48]

3. **Diversion may increase rather than decrease the number of juveniles under control of the state.**   There is evidence to suggest that diversion results in referrals of juveniles who otherwise might have been released without conditions. The number of juveniles under some form of official supervision or in diversion programs is difficult to estimate. However, knowing that in 1993 at least 36,488 juveniles were in the custody of state officials suggests that there are a very large number of juveniles under some form of supervision or treatment.[49]

4. **Diversion may subvert due process.**   Diversion from juvenile court is never completely voluntary. In some instances, it may, on the face, seem to be so, but some element of state coercion is always involved. This is because the diversion is always in lieu of court processing—a strong coercive agent. Because diversion naturally involves coercion of the state, concern over the due process rights of juveniles is present. The nature of diversion requires the removal from the system prior to a determination of guilt or innocence. The programs and agencies to which juveniles are diverted restrict their liberties and attempt to change their behaviors, yet the juveniles have not been found guilty and have none of the protections a court adjudication can provide. In addition, many diversion decisions, as well as decisions within the agencies and programs to which juveniles are diverted, are administrative determinations. These actions are not very visible, nor are legal mechanisms available to review these decisions.[50] Consequently, the harsh consequences that diversion is meant to avoid may actually occur in a different form as its result.

5. **Diversion diverts attention away from needed reforms in the juvenile justice system.**   Diversion has provided a panacea in the form of an alternative to juvenile court processing. The proponents of diversion saw many problems in the formal juvenile justice system and so created an alternative that would bypass or avoid formal processing. The problems identified by reformers are still present, however, because diversion has only pacified a concerned constituency. Therefore, the necessary changes in juvenile court have not occurred and are not likely to occur as long as attention is distracted from the real problem.[51]

6. **There is no solid evidence that diversion reduces recidivism.**   Evaluative research on diversion programs has not been done to any great extent. Existing research does not yield any conclusive results.

What, then, do we do about diversion? Surely there is a need to divert juveniles who might be harmed by formal processing. Yet placing juveniles under state control without due process, especially when they otherwise might have been released, and using questionable selection criteria only create new problems. What seems to be required is, first, an assessment of diversion procedures and the efficiency and effectiveness of these procedures. Second, diversion policies and procedures should be standardized, regulated, and made more visible and open to review. Third, some application of due process and clarification of juvenile rights in this area is necessary to ensure fairness. Fourth, every effort should be made to ensure that the "net" is not "widened" and thus more children brought under state control. Finally, our attention should not be drawn away from needed reforms of the juvenile justice system. Both the formal and the informal systems of disposition can and should exist, though they should undergo much-needed reform.

SUMMARY

There is one major problem facing the success of probation: careless overuse. Probation supervision tends to be a dumping ground for all those difficult juveniles whom the judge may be afraid to send back into the community without some protection from future misgiving or criticism. He or she does not wish to place them, and yet the judge "must do something" with them. Mentally challenged children, who are in need of very specialized types of services, also are often placed on probation because there is no other place for them. The effect is the dilution and misapplication of limited resources. For many juveniles, then, the circumstances of probation invite failure.[52]

The trend in corrections is increasingly toward community-based programs, which are being asked to offer diagnosis, diversion, and treatment, and to reduce stigma. As this trend continues, greater use will be made of probation as an alternative to institutionalization. With this increased use comes the threat of overuse of the program as an effective means of dealing with youth in trouble.

The nationwide use of probation is the preferred disposition, preferably without the subsequent adjudication of guilt within the particular case. It is also recommended that volunteers serve in all capacities in the probation process. Richard Lundman says it best: "It is recommended that routine probation remain as the first and most frequent sentencing option for moderately delinquent juveniles convicted of index crimes against property."[53]

There are persuasive arguments in favor of probation over institutionalization: (1) a reduced stigma for the youth involved, (2) the advantage of remaining in the community, (3) the availability of a wealth of resources offered in the community that are generally absent in the institution, (4) the number of youth served and diverted from the formal system, and, most important, (5) the reduced costs of probation as compared with those of institutionalization. We must ensure, however, that reduced cost does not just make probation cheaper without also making it better.

KEY TERMS

- benefit of clergy
- electronic monitoring
- intensive supervision
- John Augustus
- judicial reprieve

- negative subsidy
- probation
- probation subsidy
- recognizance
- restitution

DISCUSSION AND REVIEW QUESTIONS

1. Define the term *probation*. Explain what is meant by formal and informal probation.
2. What are the functions of probation today? How are they best administered?
3. What is a petition and how is it filed? Why is it filed?
4. What qualities are important in an applicant for the job of probation officer? Are these qualities or qualifications being met?
5. Go to the Web site for *Easy Access to Juvenile Court Statistics*, http://ojjdp.ncjrs.org/ojstatbb/ezajcs and update the figures on the number of probationers contained in this chapter.
6. Which of the new forms of supervision discussed in this chapter do you think is the most promising? Why?
7. What should be the dominant philosophy of juvenile probation officers? Why?

VIDEO PROFILES

The *Diversion 1* video profile in MyCrimeKit presents Judge Bonaventura, Joshua's mother, the Director of Alternative House, and the Probation Officer description of the behavioral (e.g., actions during thirty-day ward of state), psychological and sociological (e.g., divorce of his parents) factors as precursors to the current alleged offense. Discuss whether consideration of these factors grounds the hearing in *parens patriae* or in due process for Joshua. Provide specific examples from the video to support your discussion. Using the information provided in this chapter related to probation, intensive supervision, and diversion discuss which, as a possible alternative to detention, might be a "best method" for dealing with Joshua's case and why. Use specific examples from the chapter and the video to support your discussion. Ms. Morensic, Director of the Alternative House, provides an overview of the services of Crisis Center Alternative House as well as their early challenges with Joshua. As it relates to her comments, compare and contrast the benefits of Joshua's placement at Alternative House with the arguments that favor probation over institutionalization as presented in this chapter.

The *Diversion 2* video profile in MyCrimeKit shows Morris, a juvenile offender, interviewed and shown at various points in the juvenile system. Morris discusses why he failed to appear in court. At one point during his testimony, he says that "he can't sit still." There is also discussion of anger management and family relationships. Is this behavior and action delinquent? What are the potential implications for probation supervision? What's the court's ruling?

MYCRIMEKIT

mycrimekit Go to MyCrimeKit.com to explore the following study tools and resources specific to this chapter:

- Practice Quiz: Test your knowledge with multiple-choice, true-false, fill-in-the-blank, and essay questions.
- Flashcards: 20 flashcards to test your knowledge of the chapter's key terms.
- Web Quest: Review the Web sites of the Office of Juvenile Justice and Delinquency Prevention as well as your state's Juvenile Justice probation agency.
- Web Links: Check out sites related to the content presented in this chapter.

ENDNOTES

1. U.S. Department of Justice, *Juvenile Justice: A Century of Change* (Washington, DC: Office of Juvenile Justice and Delinquency Prevention, 1999), p. 2.
2. U. S. Department of Justice, *Juvenile Offenders and Victims: 2006 National Report* (Washington, DC: Office of Juvenile Justice and Delinquency Prevention, 2006) http://ojjdp.ncjrs.org/ojstatbb/nr2006/downloads/chapter6.pdf

3. Ibid.

4. A. Stahl, T. Finnegan, and W. Kang, *Easy Access to Juvenile Court Statistics: 1990–1999*, http://ojjdp.ncjrs.org/ojstatbb/ezajcs; *OJJDP Statistical Briefing Book*. Online. Available: http://ojjdp.ncjrs.gov/ojstatbb/probation/qa07103.asp?qaDate=2005. Released on September 12, 2008; Sarah Livsey, 2006, *Fact Sheet: Juvenile Delinquency Probation Caseload, 1985–2002* (Washington, DC: U.S. Department of Justice Office of Juvenile Justice and Delinquency Prevention.

5. Patricia McFall Torbet, *Juvenile Probation: The Workhorse of the Juvenile Justice System* (Washington, D.C.: Office of Juvenile Justice and Delinquency Prevention, 1996), p. 1.

6. Ibid, p. 2.

7. W. S. Holdsworth, *A History of English Law*, Vol. 3, p. 294, quoted in *Probation and Related Matters* (New York: United Nations, Department of Social Affairs, 1951), footnote, p. 17.

8. Robert M. Carter and Leslie T. Wilkins, eds. *Probation, Parole, and Community Corrections* (New York: John Wiley & Sons, 1976), p. 83.

9. Board of State Charities of Massachusetts, *Sixth Annual Report* (Boston: State of Massachusetts, 1869), p. 269.

10. Sheldon Glueck and Eleanor Glueck, *Delinquents and Nondelinquents in Perspective* (Cambridge, MA: Harvard University Press, 1968), pp. 151–152.

11. U.S. Department of Justice, Law Enforcement Assistance Administration, *Annual Report of National Institute for Juvenile Justice and Delinquency Prevention* (Washington, DC: Government Printing Office, March 1980), p. 21.

12. Texas Public Policy Foundation, *Policy Primer: Juvenile Justice Reform in Texas: Thinking Outside the Cell*. Available online: http://www.texaspolicy.com/event-details.php?event_id=139; Peter W. Greenwood, Karyn E. Model, C. Peter Rydell, and James Chiesa, *Diverting Children from a Life of Crime: Measuring Costs and Benefits* (Santa Monica, CA: RAND Corporation, 1996).

13. Department of Social and Health Services, *Juvenile Rehabilitation Program, Budget Report* (Olympia, WA: Revised Code of Washington 13.06, 72.05, 1974), p. 268.

14. R. W. Kobetz and B. B. Bosarge, *Juvenile Justice Administration* (Gaithersburg, MD: International Association of Chiefs of Police, 1973), p. 325.

15. Patrick Griffin, "Rethinking Juvenile Probation: *The Desktop Guide to Good Juvenile Probation Practice* Revisited," *NCJJ in Focus*, Vol. 2 (November 2000), p. 2; Joseph B. Sanborn, "The Juvenile, the Court, or the Community: Whose Best Interests Are Currently Being Promoted in Juvenile Court?" *Justice System Journal*, Vol. 17 (1994), pp 249–266; Gordon Bazemore and Lynette Feder, "Rehabilitation in the New Juvenile Court: Do Judges Support the Treatment Ethic," *American Journal of Criminal Justice*, Vol. 21 (1997), pp. 181–212; W.D. Burrell, "Juvenile Probation and Prevention: Partners for the Future?" *Community Corrections Report on Law and Corrections*, Vol. 6 (1998), pp. 3–4, 16.

16. President's Commission on Law Enforcement and Administration of Justice, *Task Force Report: Juvenile Delinquency and Youth Crime* (Washington, DC: U.S. Government Printing Office, 1967), p. 16.

17. President's Commission on Law Enforcement and Administration of Justice, *Task Force Report: Corrections*, (Washington, DC: U.S. Government Printing Office, 1967), p. 132.

18. Douglas J. Besharov, *Juvenile Justice Advocacy, Practice in a Unique Court* (New York: Practicing Law Institute, 1974), p. 383.

19. Adopted from Lloyd E. Ohlin, Herman Piven, and D. M. Pappenfort, "Major Dilemmas of the Social Worker in Probation and Parole," *National Probation and Parole Association Journal*, Vol. 2 (1956), pp. 21–25; Daniel Glaser, *The Effectiveness of a Prison and Parole System* (Indianapolis, IN: Bobbs-Merrill, 1969); Carl Klockars, "A Theory of Probation Supervision," *Journal of Criminal Law, Criminology, and Police Science*, Vol. 63 (1972), pp. 550–557.

20. Richard D. Sluder and Frances P. Reddington, "An Empirical Examination of the Work Ideologies of Juvenile and Adult Probation Officers," *Journal of Offender Rehabilitation*, Vol. 20 (1993), pp. 115–137.

21. Jeffrey P. Rush, "Juvenile Probation Officer Cynicism," *American Journal of Criminal Justice*, Vol. 16 (1992), pp. 1–16; Russell L. Curtis, William A. Reese, and Michael P. Cone, "Cynicism among Juvenile Probation Officers: A Case of Subverted Ideals," *Journal of Criminal Justice*, Vol. 18 (1990), pp. 501–517.

22. Harry E. Allen, Chris W. Eskridge, Edward J. Latessa, and Gennaro F. Vito, *Probation and Parole in America* (New York: The Free Press, 1985), pp. 132–133.

23. Torbet, *Juvenile Probation*, p.2.

24. Kobetz and Bosarge, *Juvenile Justice Administration*, pp. 333–334.

25. Ibid, p. 335.

26. Besharov, *Juvenile Justice Advocacy*, p. 159.

27. See Lori Colley, Robert G. Culbertson, and Edward J. Latessa, "Juvenile Probation Officers: A Job Analysis," *Juvenile and Family Court Journal*, Vol. 38 (1987), pp. 1–12.

28. Torbet, *Juvenile Probation.*

29. Frances P. Reddington and Betsy W. Kreisel, "Training Juvenile Probation Officers: National Trends and Practice," *Federal Probation*, Vol. 64 (2000), pp. 28–32.

30. Torbet, *Juvenile Probation*, pp. 2–3.

31. Ibid, p. 3.

32. Richard J. Lundman, *Prevention and Control of Juvenile Delinquency* (New York: Oxford University Press, 2001), p. 166.

33. B. Stanton, *Juvenile Intensive Probation Surveillance Techniques* (Washington, DC: Office of Juvenile Justice and Delinquency Prevention, 1992).

34. Todd R. Clear, "Juvenile Intensive Probation Supervision: Theory and Rationale," in Troy L. Armstrong, ed., *Intensive Interventions with High-Risk Youths*, (Monsey, NY: Criminal Justice Press/Willow Tree Press, 1991), pp. 29–44; R. G. Wiebush and Donna M. Hamparian, "Variations in 'Doing' Juvenile Intensive Supervision: Programmatic Issues in Four Ohio Jurisdictions," in Troy L. Armstrong, ed., *Intensive Interventions with High-Risk Youths*, (Monsey, NY: Criminal Justice Press/Willow Tree Press, 1991), pp. 153–188.

35. Allen, Eskridge, Latessa, and Vito, *Probation and Parole in America*, pp. 194–196.

36. William H. Barton and Jeffrey A. Butts, "Intensive Supervision Alternatives for Adjudicated Juveniles," in Troy L. Armstrong, ed., *Intensive Interventions with High-Risk Youths*, (Monsey, NY: Criminal Justice Press/Willow Tree Press, 1991), pp. 317–340; Henry Sontheimer and Lynne Goodstein, "An Evaluation of Juvenile Intensive Aftercare Probation: Aftercare versus System Response Effects," *Justice Quarterly*, Vol. 10 (1993), pp. 197–227.

37. Lundman, *Prevention and Control*, p. 180.

38. I. Montgomery, "Electronic Monitoring: Overview of an Alternative to Incarceration for Juvenile Offenders," *Journal for Juvenile Justice and Detention Services*, Vol. 10 (1995), pp. 26–28.

39. Michael T. Charles, "Electronic Monitoring for Juveniles," *Journal of Crime and Justice*, Vol. 12 (1989), pp. 147–169; John S. Clarkson and James J. Weakland, "A Transitional Aftercare Model for Juveniles: Adapting Electronic Monitoring and Home Confinement," *Journal of Offender Monitoring*, Vol. 4 (1991), pp. 1–15; Melvyn C. Raider, "Juvenile Electronic Monitoring: A Community Based Program to Augment Residential Treatment," *Residential Treatment for Children and Youth*, Vol. 12 (1994), pp. 37–48.

40. Scott H. Decker, *Increasing School Safety through Juvenile Accountability Programs* (Washington, DC: Office of Juvenile Justice and Delinquency Prevention, 2000).

41. Patrick Griffin, "Juvenile Probation in the Schools," *NCJJ In Focus*, Vol. 1 (Winter 1999), pp. 1–11.

42. H. N. Snyder, *Violent Crimes Cleared by Juvenile Arrest* (Washington, DC: Office of Juvenile Justice and Delinquency Prevention, 1994).

43. S. R. Rose, "Analysis of a Juvenile Court Diversion Program," *Journal of Offender Rehabilitation* Vol. 24 (1997, 3/4), pp. 153–61.

44. Studies include D. M. Bishop and C. E. Frazier, 1996, Race Effects in Juvenile Justice Decision-Making: Findings of a Statewide Analysis. *The Journal of Criminal Law and Criminology*, 86(2): 392–414; R. D. Hoge, D. A. Andrews, and A. W. Leschied, 1995, Investigation of Variables Associated with Probation and Custody Dispositions in a Sample of Juveniles. *Journal of Clinical Child Psychology*, 24: 279–86.

45. Studies include: E. J. Latessa, L. F. Travis, and G. P. Wilson, "Juvenile Diversion: Factors Related to Decision Making and Outcome," in S. H. Decker, ed., *Juvenile Justice Policy: Analyzing Trends and Outcomes* (Beverly Hills, CA: Sage Publications, 1984), pp. 145–65; Rose, "Analysis of a Juvenile Court Diversion Program."

46. R. J. Lundman, *Prevention and Control of Juvenile Delinquency*, 2nd Ed. (New York: Oxford University Press, 1993), p. 110.

47. M. W. Klein, "Issues and Realities in Police Diversion Programs," *Crime and Delinquency*, Vol. 22 (1976, October), pp. 421–27.

48. Lundman, *Prevention and Control.*

49. Office of Juvenile Justice and Delinquency Prevention, *Juveniles Taken into Custody: Fiscal Year 1993* (Washington, DC: U.S. Department of Justice, 1995).

50. P. Nejelski, "Diversion: The Promise and the Danger," *Crime and Delinquency*, Vol. 22 (1976), pp. 393–410.

51. Ibid.

52. Besharov, *Juvenile Justice Advocacy*, p. 384.

53. Lundman, *Prevention and Control*, p. 303.

9

Juvenile Institutions: The Success of Failure

*I*n theory, detention of youth fulfills three primary objectives. First, youth are detained if there is reason to believe that in the absence of such external controls the juvenile would be free to commit additional serious crimes, thereby posing a threat to the safety and security of the community. In this situation the child is incarcerated primarily for the benefit of the community. Second, juveniles also are detained in cases where the bad influences of a home environment necessitate placing the child in a more protective setting. In this case, children are viewed as being endangered and detention is construed a temporary measure until a more permanent home placement can be arranged. Finally, detention parallels the function of the bail system in adult criminal court, and ensures the appearance of the youthful offender at subsequent court dates.

BARRY KRISBERG AND JAMES F. AUSTIN[1]

LEARNING OBJECTIVES

1. Define and differentiate between male and female detention and institutionalization.
2. Describe the purpose of juvenile institutions.
3. Discuss the major aspects of *Morales v. Turman* and how that case may have had an impact on the national juvenile justice system as a whole.
4. Define and discuss unauthorized leave, isolation, and institutional alternatives.

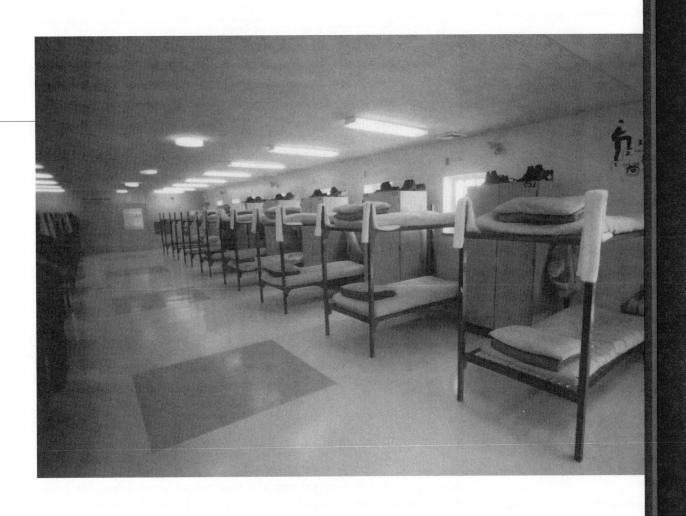

5. Discuss the issue of punishment versus treatment as the most realistic goal of the juvenile institutions of the past, today, and the future.

6. Discuss the importance of disproportionate minority confinement.

7. Describe the pros and cons of boot camps.

CHAPTER OVERVIEW

No matter what it is called—juvenile institution, training school, correctional facility, detention center, shelter, youth camp, ranch, halfway house, jail, reformatory, or prison—each of these places is an institution in which a delinquent and dependent youth can be held.

Commenting on the rising number of commitments to juvenile correctional institutions, Marler and Scoble state:

> While high-profile incidents of youth violence have gained national headlines during the past few years and politicians have vowed to "get tough" on juvenile offenders, the majority of adolescents in juvenile justice systems throughout the country are not violent offenders. In fact, more than half—about 70 percent—of juvenile offenders have been incarcerated for property offenses, multiple misdemeanors or controlled substance violations, and have substance abuse problems. Clearly, with this much variation, a one-size-fits-all approach to juvenile justice cannot work.[2]

Juvenile administrators must be prepared to counter the emotional reactions of the public to high-profile, juvenile crimes. They fuel the search for "quick-fix" solutions to delinquency that do not produce long-term results.[3]

The per capita operating expenditure by juvenile detention and correctional facilities has changed over the past twenty years. There has been a definite trend toward **privatization** (see Box 9.1). Smith reports that total operational expenditures for juvenile facilities increased from $2.4 billion in 1974 to $3.8 billion in 1994.[4] This rate of increase was greater for private facilities (136 percent) than public facilities (25 percent) during this time period.[5] Methods, features, and benefits of privatization are listed in Box 9.1.

However, there are substantial differences between public and private institutions. A juvenile institution is intended to provide specialized programs for children who must be under some form of restraint to be treated. Accordingly, it normally houses the more hardened, unstable, or nontreatable youths who do not even meet the liberal standards for juvenile probation. The institution program is an attempt to prepare the youth for return to the community. Whether this reintegration with society will work depends on several interrelated factors, one of which is the quality of aftercare services, which are necessary to strengthen and reinforce changes begun in the institution that can be tested and proved only

privatization The movement to have some institutions operated by corporate (nonpublic) entities

during the course of normal community living. These types of programs are more likely to be run by public agencies. Private juvenile facilities are more likely to be ranches, forestry camps, farms, halfway houses, and group homes that feature rehabilitation services and greater contact with the community.[6] Despite the fact that more juveniles were held in private facilities during this period, the number of private juvenile facilities increased more than their public counterparts.[7]

BOX 9.1 **PRIVATIZATION**

With lease purchase, government officials have created a nonprofit entity that acts on behalf of their agency. With *privatization*, a profit-making company actually owns the institution because private investors have put up money to build it.

Financing provided by a private company is almost always more costly because a unit of government can obtain a lower interest rate than a private company. A major reason for the higher cost is that lease payments on a privately owned institution must be treated as taxable income. In the recent past, the higher cost of private financing continued has been somewhat reduced because special tax benefits may be available to a company raising capital for construction. When tax benefits are available, private owners of a facility may pass their savings through to the governmental entity in the form of reduced lease payments.

Private owners of correctional facilities have been eligible to claim such tax benefits as depreciation and investment tax credits. However, federal legislation passed in 1986 disallows most of the tax advantages of private ownership. Accordingly, the cost of private financing will probably be even greater than in the past.

Privatization may also involve private sector management and operation of a correctional facility. Although private firms may offer contracts for both operations and financing, these issues should be examined separately. Although costs of operation may be discretionary, costs of private financing are necessarily greater when raising capital for construction.

Other features of private sector participation may be of interest to state and local officials. Many firms now offer a comprehensive package of services called *turnkey* or *design–build* contracts in which a single company provides a variety of services ordinarily divided among several different firms. Depending on the laws of each jurisdiction, consolidation into one contract may be an efficient approach that results in faster completion of the correctional facility.

Industrial development bonds represent a public–private partnership. This approach offers tax-exempt income to investors because securities are issued with the authorization of a governmental entity. However, total financing must be limited to $10 million, and the unit of government must pay full, fair market value for the facility on termination of the lease. Use of industrial development bonds is tightly restricted by federal law, and it is expected that Congress will impose further limitations on this approach in the future.

The number of juveniles held in private facilities is on the rise. In 1999, the number of juvenile offenders in residential placement in private facilities numbered 31,599—an increase of 7 percent over the number in 1997. The number of juveniles in residential placement in public facilities numbered 76,355 but they only increased by 1 percent over 1997.

Sources: National Institute of Justice, *Ohio's New Approach to Prison and Jail Financing* (Washington, DC: U.S. Department of Justice, November, 1986), p. 9; Melissa Sickmund, "Juvenile Offenders in Residential Placement: 1997–1999," *Juvenile Offenders and Victims—National Report Series* (Washington, DC: Office of Juvenile Justice and Delinquency Prevention, March, 2002), p. 1.

The Inside of a Detention Center

Despite the vast expansion and growth of community-based facilities, there has still been no major decline in the use of juvenile institutions. In the *Gault* decision, the Supreme Court emphasized the reality of institutionalization for a juvenile:

> Ultimately, however, we confront the reality.... A boy is charged with misconduct. The boy is committed to an institution where he may be restrained of liberty for years. It is of no constitutional consequence...and of limited practical meaning...that the institution to which he is committed is called an Industrial School. The fact of the matter is that, however euphemistic the title, a "receiving home" or an "industrial school" for juveniles is an institution of confinement in which the child is incarcerated for a greater or lesser time. His world becomes "a building with whitewashed walls, regimented routine and institutional hours...." Instead of mother and father and sisters and brothers and friends and classmates, his world is peopled by guards, custodians, state employees, and delinquents confined with him for anything from waywardness to rape and homicide.[8]

Video Profile: Life Inside

HISTORICAL ORIGINS OF JUVENILE INSTITUTIONS

America's early juvenile institutions were patterned after nineteenth-century European models. In 1817, the London Philanthropic Society was founded and included in its purpose and practice the reformation of juvenile offenders.

This organization opened the first English house of refuge for children, which became the prototype of similar houses of refuge in the United States.

Houses of Refuge

One of the first prisons in history was specifically designed for juvenile offenders. In 1704, Pope Clement XI built the Hospice of San Michele in Rome. It was designed to accomplish the aim of **expiation**—the atonement of sins through suffering. Its strict regimen could be summarized as follows:

expiation Atonement of sins through suffering

> The young offenders worked in association in a central hall at tasks in spinning and weaving. Chained by one foot and under a strict rule of silence, they listened to the brothers of a religious order while they droned through the Scripture of religious tracts. The incorrigible boys were separated, day and night, in little cubicles or cells. Large signs, hung throughout the institution, admonished "Silence." Floggings were resorted to as penalties for "past mistakes."[9]

Houses of refuge were the next organized attempt to control and treat juvenile delinquency. These institutions marked a major shift away from family-oriented discipline and toward treatment administered by society in specialized facilities. As houses of refuge spread throughout Europe and America, they retained a reformatory atmosphere, associated with education and with mechanical labor, as in the trades. Rauhe Haus, founded in Hamburg, Germany, in 1833 by Dr. John Henry Wichern, served as a model for the institution combining reform and refuge.[10]

New York, Boston, and Philadelphia were the centers of urban population in the early 1800s. The woeful plight of wayward youths confined with adults in jails in these cities prompted groups to study the ways in which juveniles were being handled in Europe. The philosophy on which early American juvenile institutions were founded was, therefore, not an indigenous one. It can be traced to several European leaders and educators such as Johann Heinrich Pestalozzi (1746–1827), who established a school for orphans at Neuhoff, Switzerland, in 1775.[11] Unfortunately, Pestalozzi's legacy to American school children—the reduction of physical abuse and punishment in common schools—made little impression on those who ran the houses of refuge or the reform schools.

The New York Society for the Reformation of Juvenile Delinquents, founded in 1823, organized the first of the institutional movements. Originating from a movement within the Society of Friends, the New York Society opened the first reformatory in the United States, the New York House of Refuge, in 1825. The New York house and those opened in Boston and Philadelphia generally accepted destitute and orphaned children as well as youths convicted of crimes in state and/or local courts. Life was hard for the children who grew up in these special houses. Their parents were looked down on as too poor or degenerate to provide them with the basic necessities of life. The refuge house managers considered immigrant youths, white female delinquents, and blacks of both sexes (generally, blacks were totally excluded from the refuges) inferior to white, American-born males.

The New York City House of Refuge experienced a rapid growth rate, and similar growth occurred in other houses of refuge. Before long, they became overcrowded and filled with a mixture of hard-core juvenile delinquents and orphans. New York's answer was Randall's Island institution in the East River. Randall's Island allowed the Society for the Reformation of Juvenile Delinquents to apply a more systematic reformatory regime; one that society members believed was the answer for dealing with delinquent and wayward youth.

The first public juvenile institution was a municipal reformatory for boys, established in New Orleans in 1845. Prior to that, the operation and maintenance of the institutions was a joint effort responsibility of state and private agencies. The first state reform school for boys was opened in 1845 in Westboro, Massachusetts. Known as the **Lyman School for Boys**, it was closed only in 1972.

The prevailing philosophy and educational practice of the times had a great deal of influence on the operation of juvenile institutions. During this time, it was believed that behavior was entirely a matter of self-control; thus, related influences were given little consideration. The early methods used in institutions involved strict discipline, the inculcation of regular work and school habits, and the extensive use of punishment.

In 1835, Pennsylvania enacted legislation to add incorrigibility as a reason for commitment. The new law was challenged as unconstitutional after an incorrigible child had been committed to the House of Refuge without a jury trial. In *Ex parte Crouse*, the Pennsylvania Supreme Court upheld the commitment, ruling that "the House of Refuge is not a prison, but a school, where reformation, not punishment, is the end." This case upheld the authority of the state to act in *parens patriae* for the benefit of juveniles.[12]

New York established a state agricultural and industrial school in 1849, and Maine, a training center in 1853. By 1870, Connecticut, Indiana, Maryland, Nevada, New Hampshire, New Jersey, Ohio, and Vermont could boast separate institutions or training schools for delinquents. By 1900, thirty-six states had followed suit, and today they are located in every state.

The original functions of the houses of refuge, reformatories, and juvenile institutions were threefold: (1) to get poor, wayward, and delinquent youths off the streets; (2) to separate youths from adult criminals; and (3) to save juveniles from crime through a regimented lifestyle, education, and training. Although juvenile institutions were an attempt to

Lyman School for Boys The first state reform school for boys, opened in 1845

Ex parte Crouse Decision by Pennsylvania Supreme Court that upheld the authority of the state to act in *parens patriae* for the benefit of juveniles

protect the children from the negative influence of adult institutions, the courts were still permitted to commit juvenile offenders to adult prisons if they desired.

Although the efforts to rescue juveniles in the early 1800s were crude and haphazard, they did offer a beginning. The religious environment and training of the early houses of refuge was largely Protestant, in keeping with the religious affiliation of early settlers in the eastern United States. To counter this Protestant influence, several private sectarian institutions were established. The Roman Catholic order of the House of Good Shepherd established institutions for girls, and the Christian Brotherhood assumed responsibility for parochial schools and for institutional care of delinquent Catholic boys. Protestant denominations also established institutions for delinquent youth of both sexes. After the major Jewish migrations near the end of the nineteenth century, American Jews began to build orphanages and training schools as well.

Reform Schools

During the period 1859–1890, the movement to set up houses of refuge was replaced by the reform school and preventive agency movement. The Boston House of Reformation was one of the more notable reform schools. Juvenile asylums were established, and the practice of "placing children out" became popular. By 1890 nearly every state outside the South had some type of reform school for delinquent youths that was also responsible for the care of numerous destitute children. One of the major problems facing the reform schools then still exists today: the problem of agreeing to a legal definition of juvenile delinquency. Because of this, youths who had committed a crime, youths who had neither committed nor been convicted of a crime, and youths who were convicted of a crime for which the law had no penalty were all held together in the same school. Also housed there were children who had been abused or abandoned by their parents as well as youths who had been committed by their parents for being unruly or unmanageable.

Although the reform schools devoted more time to schooling (usually half a day or more), many of them were otherwise indistinguishable from the early refuges. Most were large congregate institutions with regimented workshop routines. Many reformers sought to change the routines of these reform schools by introducing a more varied and aesthetic institutional life for the children, with guidance aimed at bettering the total child and not simply making the child conform to the rigors of strict discipline, work, and training.

Cottage Reform School

The **cottage reform school** plan, founded by Wichern at Rauhe Haus, offered an opportunity to break away from the congregate placement

cottage reform school Designed to give a home interest and attachment for institutionalized juveniles

of children in the institutions. Wichern's cottage plan is described as follows:

> Each house is to be a family, under the sole direction and control of the matron, who is the mother of the family. . . . The government and discipline are strictly parental. It is the design to give a home interest, a home feeling and attachment, to the whole family."[13]

Cottage reform schools spread widely throughout the United States. New Jersey (1864) and Indiana (1866) opened cottage schools, and some older institutions converted from the congregate to the cottage plan. The cottage system for housing institutionalized juveniles continues to be the most popular form in use today.

State Reformatories

The 1870s were marked by the beginning of yet another type of institution: state reformatories for young men 16 to 30 years of age who were first offenders. This development aided in resolving the category of children referred to as juvenile delinquents. American penal reformers, influenced by European innovations, established the New York State Reformatory at Elmira in 1877, the Massachusetts Reformatory for Men in 1884, and a reformatory for women and girls convicted of misdemeanors, chiefly those involving sex offenses, in New York in 1893. With the growth of the reformatory movement, some juvenile delinquent institutions were relieved of their older and often more troublesome inmates, a relief that was welcomed.[14]

Deficiencies of the Reform Movement

Early juvenile institutions had many failings. In the Eastern states, they were located in the large metropolitan cities, and these locations afforded the juveniles little change from the conditions that had so much to do with their being delinquent. With a vast amount of open land, Western states overcame this shortcoming by locating their schools in the countryside and organizing their institutional programs around agricultural work. By the 1890s, most Western reform schools had introduced vocational education, along with military drill and organization, into their routines. But they were otherwise very similar to the older Eastern institutions and were bound toward a common destiny.

In the South, no provision was made for juvenile lawbreakers until long after the Civil War. The Populist political movement ushered in badly needed reforms. Prior to that time children were put in jail, in convict camps, in the country road gangs, or in prison farms along with adults.

As quoted by H. W. Charles in the last half of the nineteenth century, A. O. Wright of the Wisconsin Board of State Charities summarized the feeling of child-saving philanthropies of the time:

> If I were to classify the order of places, best or worst, in which people may be placed, especially children or young people, I say first of all, a good home; second best, a small institution rightly managed under proper persons, meaning by a small institution, one or two hundred inmates or less; thirdly, a large institution; fourth, a bad home.

Punishment in reform schools was often brutal, and reformatory institutions became known, in the words of one superintendent, as "not the first aid to the injured ... the forlorn hope." At the Illinois Reformatory a boy was hung by chains on the wall for nearly three days. He was alternately beaten and given the "water cure" until he died with his back broken in three places.[15]

Noncriminal youth who did not attend school regularly or were unruly in school were spared the unhappy fate of reform school when parental or truant schools were started in 1900 just for those children. Thus youths who did not belong among the populations of juvenile institutions were kept out of them.

Strongly influenced by popular scientific notions about juvenile delinquency and its probable causes, reform school managers and institutional superintendents emphasized everything from physical conditioning, strict military discipline, and the learning of a trade to the attainment of "decent" moral standards.[16] Little progress has been made beyond the attempts of early correctional administrators. Today, basically the same problems are being faced: overcrowding, lack of public support and proper legislation, and a continuous debate on the link between cause and treatment of delinquency. The systems and practices started in the early houses of refuge, reform schools, reformatories, and juvenile institutions have remained intact. Throughout the United States, many institutions are relics of the nineteenth century. In many cases, their programs have changed little since the founding date was put on their cornerstones.

FACILITIES FOR JUVENILES

Schools built to house the homeless and dependent children who roamed the streets of Europe in the nineteenth century became the model for many later established in the United States. In England, the Reformatory School Acts of 1854, 1857, and 1866 offered methods whereby courts could send offenders under the age of 16 years to reformatories and, later, industrial schools. In 1825, the New York City House of Refuge became the first real American response to the juvenile problem. These early facilities were prison-like structures, and the courts were still allowed to send juvenile offenders to adult prisons instead if they so desired. Juvenile institutions were an attempt to protect the children from the bad influence of the adult institutions, even though the system was crude and decentralized. Most of these schools were established by private organizations that recognized the need for special attention to both juvenile offenders and neglected or dependent children. The first cottage housing systems for juveniles, now the most popular systems, were founded in Massachusetts (1854) and Ohio (1858). Not until 1899, however, in Chicago, was the juvenile court system coordinated within a political jurisdiction as an integral part of the criminal justice system in the United States. Since that time, the juvenile court system has extended to cover every jurisdiction in the country, and a fairly standard pattern of juvenile confinement has ensued.

JUVENILE INSTITUTIONS TODAY

detention center Secure institutions often housing a mixture of juvenile offenders, victims, and status offenders

The primary kinds of institutions for juveniles in the present-day United States are detention homes and training schools (see Box 9.2).

Detention Centers

The main type of facility for juveniles today is the **detention center**, where juvenile victims of crime and juvenile offenders are often kept in the same facilities, with the same treatment afforded to both, under *parens patriae*. The Census of Juvenile Placement reported in 1997 that one in five (20 percent) juveniles was held in facilities with fewer than 31 residents and a similar proportion was held in facilities with more than 350 residents. In terms of security status, the majority of juveniles in residential placement (71 percent) were confined after school hours by at least one locked door or gate.[17] Many states have statutory provisions for the detention of juveniles in jails so long as they are segregated from adult offenders. Some states have statutes or policies prohibiting such detention, but practical problems frequently require the violation of these statutes.

Facilities designated exclusively for juvenile detention are usually not the best examples of how an ideal juvenile correctional facility should be designed and operated. Most of these structures were originally built for some other purpose and converted to their present

The Inside of a Detention Center

BOX 9.2 **TYPES OF JUVENILE FACILITIES**

Juvenile facilities are classified by the term of stay and type of environment.

Term of Stay
Short-term   Facilities that hold juveniles awaiting adjudication or other disposition.
Long-term   Facilities that hold juveniles already adjudicated and committed to custody.

Type of Environment
Institutional   Environments impose greater restraints on residents' movements and limit access to the community. Most detention or diagnostic centers, training schools, and ranches are classified as having institutional environments.
Open   Environments allow greater movement of residents within the facilities and more access to the community. Facilities with open environments mainly include shelters, halfway houses, group homes, and ranches, forestry camps, or farms.

---

use with as little expense as possible. Most are overcrowded before they reach their rated capacities. In the adult institutions, the emphasis is on custody, and the same preoccupation with security shapes the programs and general environment in the juvenile facilities. Most are located in urban areas and are virtually sealed off from the community by their physical structure and other security measures. The youths are placed in dormitory-style housing, or single cells in some cases, often with the fixed furniture and dreary interiors that are typical of adult institutions. Most juvenile detention centers lack services and programs that might improve the residents' chances of staying away from crime. These juveniles are denied most of the good aspects of adult programs and are subject to the worst aspects of institutional programs (see Box 9.3). More than twenty years ago, the National Advisory Commission on Criminal Justice Standards and Goals made specific recommendations for juvenile detention facilities. These recommendations remain sound and deserve review:

- The detention facility should be in a residential area and near court and community resources.

- The population of detention centers should not exceed thirty residents. When the population significantly exceeds this number, separate components should be developed under the network system.

- Living areas should not house more than ten or twelve youngsters each, with single rooms and programming regarded as essential. Individual rooms should be pleasant, adequately furnished, and homelike rather than punitive and hostile.

- Security should not be viewed as an indispensable part of the physical environment but should be based on a combination of staffing patterns, technological devices, and physical design.

BOX 9.3 **SUICIDE PREVENTION IN JUVENILE FACILITIES**

Suicide in juvenile detention and correctional facilities is more than four times greater than youth suicide overall. According to the Centers for Disease Control and Prevention (CDC), the suicide rate of adolescents ages 15 to 19 years has quadrupled from 2.7 suicides per 100,000 to 11 suicides per 100,000 in 1994. The CDC has also reported that more teenagers died of suicide during 1994 than of cancer, heart disease, acquired immune deficiency syndrome, birth defects, stroke, pneumonia and influenza, and chronic lung disease combined.

The U.S. Bureau of the Census has been collecting data on the number of deaths of juveniles in custody since 1989. In the first year of the survey, juvenile officials self-reported seventeen suicides in public detention centers, reception and diagnostic centers, and training schools during 1988. Fourteen such suicides were reported during 1993. Given the epidemiological data regarding adolescent suicide, coupled with the increased risk factors associated with detained and confined youth, the reported number of suicides in custody seems low. The National Center for Health Statistics, in contrast, reported that 30,903 persons committed suicide in the U.S. in 1996. Of these, approximately 7 percent (2,119) were youth age 19 years or younger. For youth younger than age 15 years, suicides increased 113 percent between 1980 and 1996. Because of statistics like these, many juvenile justice experts and practitioners believe that suicides are underreported. To date, no comprehensive study of deaths in custody has been undertaken.

Source: Office of Juvenile Justice and Delinquency Prevention, *Juvenile Justice: Youth with Mental Health Disorders: Issues and Emerging Responses* (April 2000), http://www.ncjrs.org/html/ojjdp/jjjnl_2000_4/sui_1.html

---

- Existing residential facilities within the community should be used in preference to building new facilities.

- Facility programming should be based on investigation of community resources and the possible use of them before determining the facility's in-house program requirements.

- Any new construction and renovation of existing facilities should be based on consideration of the functional interrelationships between program activities and program participants.

- Detention facilities should be coeducational and should have access to a full range of supportive programs, including education, library, recreation, arts and crafts, music, drama, writing, and entertainment. Outdoor recreational areas are essential.

- Citizen advisory boards should be established to pursue development of in-house and community-based programs and alternatives to detention.

- Planning should comply with pertinent state and federal regulations and the Environmental Policy Act of 1969.[18]

It would be well for administrators and legislators to dust off these documents and see where they stand two decades later in their implementation.

The issue of whether it is productive to place juveniles in institutions is being hotly debated in correctional circles. Jerome Miller mounted the most extensive attempt at decarceration when he served as Youth Commissioner for Massachusetts in 1969. Faced with official criticism of the operations of training schools in the state, Miller took the radical step of closing all reform schools and placing juvenile offenders on community supervision.[19] Although initial research indicated that juveniles under community supervision had slightly higher recidivism rates, the Massachusetts reform has proven effective. The small size of these community programs, coupled with secure confinement, has influenced the development of similar reforms in Utah, Missouri, Maryland, and other states.[20]

Institutions are the most expensive and least successful method of handling juvenile offenders.[21] However, until the services needed for supervision and treatment in the community are forthcoming, judges often have no other choice but to commit offenders. The junior prisons are not all bad, but the custody philosophy is the prevailing model, and it creates the same problem at this level that exists at the adult level. The dangers that these institutions present to the civil rights of the juvenile offender were forcefully brought to public attention in a series of landmark court decisions, outlined in Chapter 7.

TODAY'S APPROACH TO INSTITUTIONS

Directors of early juvenile institutions were concerned chiefly with the protection of society. Youths confined within institutional walls were judged enemies of society, and their custody was looked on as a disciplinary measure. How far have things advanced since then? Has there been measurable progress in the search for an answer to the problem of juvenile delinquency? For the past several decades, juvenile institutions have been subscribing, at least superficially, to a philosophy of social responsibility for the rehabilitation of deviant youth. As a consequence, today's institutions call for greater emphasis on education, vocational and personality training, and the inculcation of socially accepted living habits. Although recent Supreme Court decisions, such as *In re Gault*, have moved away from the *parens patriae* concept, it is still a widely held belief that society is responsible for juvenile delinquency. The collective social conscience of America has reacted with an incredible variety of programs meant to alleviate the problem.

Society has a way of placing its concerns in an order of priority, concerns that are social and technological. One often hears the inquiry, "If we can put a man on the moon, why can't something be done about crime?" Social problems that lead to, cause, or are associated with crime and delinquency might be solved if top priority were given to solving these problems using the finest minds in the world and an unlimited budget. Such efforts are not likely in the near future, however, so debate, half-measures, and temporary solutions will have to do for the foreseeable future.

Video Profile: Professional Perspective

In the meantime, juvenile crime increases, public schools cease to function, and organized and armed youth gangs reemerge as a menace in the community. A return to the extensive use of imprisonment, which stigmatizes youthful criminals as the enemies of society, may well be the future for juvenile corrections. Although not all youths belong in juvenile correctional institutions (e.g., status offenders, mentally or emotionally disturbed youth, first-time offenders), economic pressures may force a line to be drawn.

The data in Table 9.1 reveal that there were 108,931 juvenile offenders in residential facilities on October 27, 1999. More than one-third of these

Table 9.1
JUVENILE OFFENDERS IN RESIDENTIAL PLACEMENT, 1997–1999

Most Serious Offense	Number of Offenders	Percent	Percent Change, 1997–1999
Delinquency	104,237	96	5
Person	38,005	35	7
Homicide	1,514	1	−21
Sexual Assault	7,511	7	34
Robbery	8,212	8	−13
Aggravated Assault	9,984	9	5
Simple Assault	7,448	7	12
Other Person	3,336	3	50
Property	31,817	29	−1
Burglary	12,222	11	−3
Theft	6,944	6	−5
Auto Theft	6,225	6	−5
Arson	1,126	1	23
Other Property	5,300	5	13
Drug	9,882	9	6
Drug Trafficking	3,106	3	2
Other Drug	6,776	6	9
Public Order	10,487	10	8
Weapons	4,023	4	−4
Other Public Order	6,464	6	17
Technical Violations*	14,046	13	12
Status Offense	4,694	4	−32
Total Juvenile Offenders	**108,931**	**100**	**3**

*Technical violations include violations of probation, parole, and valid court orders.

Source: Melissa Sickmund, "Juvenile Offenders in Residential Placement: 1997–1999," *Juvenile Offenders and Victims: National Report Series* (Washington, DC: Office of Juvenile Justice and Delinquency Prevention, March 2002), p. 1.

offenders had committed an offense against the person. Although the percentage of juveniles held for some personal offenses had actually declined between 1997 and 1999, the number of these juvenile offenders had increased 7 percent overall. Also note that the trend in residential placement of status offenses is decreasing. The percentage of juveniles in residential placement for status offenses declined between 1997 and 1999 (a 32 percent decrease). Between 2000 and 2008, there continued to be a steady decline in residential placements, with fewer than 81,000 juvenile offenders housed in 2008. This is the fewest amount of juveniles housed in juvenile facilities since 1993 when the number was approximately 79,000.[22]

The proponents of community-based programs and treatment for troubled youth may argue against it, but a return to old-fashioned discipline, large congregate institutions, and the reform school-style institutions, although not the most desirable response, may be unavoidable. However, if the increased use of institutions and the "Get Tough" policy is to be effective, the public will be faced with staggering costs for new and bigger institutions with more staff, and an increasing drain on limited resources.

Detention

The National Juvenile Detention Association defines *detention* as follows:

> Juvenile detention is the temporary and safe custody of juveniles who are accused of conduct subject to the jurisdiction of the court who require a restricted environment for their own or the community's protection while pending legal action. Further, juvenile detention provides a wide range of helpful services that support the juvenile's physical, emotional, and social development. Helpful services minimally include: education; visitation; communication; counseling; continuous supervision; medical and health care services; nutrition; recreation; and reading. Juvenile detention includes or provides for a system of clinical observation and assessment that complements the helpful services and reports findings.[23]

In addition, the American Correctional Association Detention Committee defined the seven essential characteristics of juvenile detention:

- **Temporary custody.** Of all the methods of incarceration within the criminal justice system, only juvenile detention stresses its temporary nature. Detention should be as short as possible.
- **Safe custody.** The safe custody concept implies freedom from fear and freedom from harm for both the juvenile and the community. This definitional theme refers to a safe and humane environment

with programming and staffing to ensure the physical and psychological safety of detained juveniles.

- **Restricted environment.** The nature or degree of restrictiveness of the environment is generally associated with the traditional classifications of maximum, medium, or minimum security or custody.

- **Community protection.** In addition to the factors listed previously, the court has a legitimate right to detain juveniles for the purpose of preventing further serious and/or violent delinquent behavior.

- **Pending legal action.** Pending legal action includes the time spent awaiting a hearing, disposition, a placement, or a return to a previous placement.

- **Helpful services.** Programs are available to detained juveniles to help resolve a host of problems commonly facing detained juveniles. Because detention has the potential of creating a tremendously negative impact on some juveniles, it is important that programming have the depth of services required to meet the needs of a wide range of juvenile problems.

- **Clinical observation and assessment.** Most juvenile codes specifically refer to this theme as a purpose for detention. The controlled environment of juvenile detention often provides the opportunity for intense observation and assessment to enhance decision-making capabilities. Properly credentialed people who coordinate and conduct the observation and assessment process provide competent clinical services.[24]

Authorities generally agree that only certain youths should be detained involuntarily. They include those who would probably disappear prior to their hearing, those with a high probability of committing a dangerous offense while awaiting court disposition, and those who must be held for another jurisdiction. Federal guidelines emphasize that no youth should be detained unnecessarily, and those who can remain safely in their homes should be allowed to do so. These guidelines also specify that juveniles needing diagnostic evaluations should be able to receive them without being subjected to detention. In all, open facilities should be used for all youth not explicitly requiring a secure custodial setting.

Guidelines and recommendations, no matter how well intended or thought out, are useless unless they are put into practice. They are, however, useful as a yardstick against which to measure the real-life findings encountered by students of the juvenile justice system. Detention facilities can include jails, centers located above the juvenile court, converted mental wards, or anyplace in which youth can be imprisoned pending a hearing or transfer.

The emphasis on custody, which pervades the adult institutions, also shapes the general environment of juvenile detention facilities. Most of these facilities are located in urban areas and are virtually sealed off from the community by their physical structure and other security measures. The youths are placed in dreary single cells or barracks-type housing with fixed furniture.

The chance of leaving a detention facility to return to a nondelinquent lifestyle is remote when one considers the lack of services and programs for youths in detention. They are denied most of the good in the adult programs and are subjected to the worst aspects of institutional living.

Placing a Youth in Detention

There are several critical factors that have been linked with the courts' decision to place a youth in a detention facility:

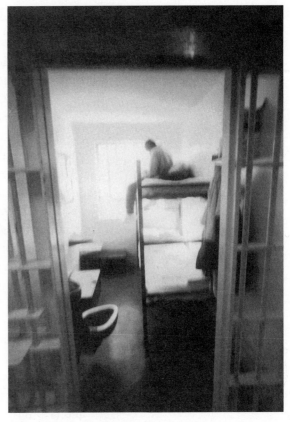

The Inside of a Jail Cell

1. Location of the detention unit,
2. The time of the youth's apprehension,
3. The location of that apprehension,
4. Availability of intake personnel to screen referrals,
5. The credibility of the referring source, and
6. The degree to which the court sees its detention policies as an area of community interest.[25]

For example, it has been observed that:

1. The further the detention unit is from the referring police units, the lower the rate of placement.
2. If a juvenile is apprehended after court office hours, he is more likely to be held in detention.
3. Youth are more likely to be detained if apprehended on the street or in public buildings where parents or concerned adults are less likely to be available to intervene.
4. When intake personnel are available for thorough screening and for detention hearings, juveniles are less frequently held in detention.
5. The higher the credibility of the referring source with court personnel, the greater the likelihood that a juvenile will be detained.
6. Time of year...especially as related to the school calendar, public attitudes, and interorganization relations of the court with other community agencies also affect how detention policies are implemented.[26]

INSTITUTIONS: FUNCTIONS AND THEORIES

Although the stated purposes of the juvenile detention facility and the juvenile institution (or state training school) are ideologically different, what they produce is quite similar. Adult prisons and juvenile institutions have been criticized repeatedly for their inherently degrading and dehumanizing effects on inmate populations. However, the continued use and survival of institutions indicates that they are performing functions and purposes acceptable to society, which continues to tolerate them.

In an article titled "Tear Down the Walls? Some Functions of Prisons," the authors, Charles Reasons and Russell Kaplan, suggest that the actual survival of prisons and institutions depends on their "fulfilling four important manifest functions in varying degrees: (1) reformation, (2) incapacitation, (3) retribution, and (4) deterrence." However, Reasons and Kaplan also suggest that there are eleven latent functions of institutions more significant than the four manifest functions that also serve various interests and needs:

> "(1) maintenance of a crime school, (2) politicization, (3) self-enhancement, (4) provision of jobs, (5) satisfaction of authoritarian needs, (6) slave labor, (7) reduction of unemployment rates, (8) scientific research, (9) do-gooderism, (10) safety valve for racial tensions, and (11) birth control. These latent functions, largely unintended and generally unrecognized, suggest that abolition of the prison may not be as assured as some reformers suppose."[27]

Because institutions are considered the most expensive and least successful method of handling juvenile offenders, one must question whether these functions of institutions (or ones similar to them) are preserving them despite the costly operations and lack of success attributed to juvenile institutions. Alternatives to institutionalization, such as the provision of supervision and treatment in the community, are under close scrutiny to prove themselves. It no longer suffices simply to state that these services exist. With less tolerance for crime and criminals, adult and juvenile, these community services will have to prove effective almost immediately to be continued. All juvenile programs are under such scrutiny today; however, programs that break with tradition and contemporary innovations are usually most suspect and subject to early curtailment.

It seems, then, that the manifest and latent functions of institutions do outweigh their high cost and their lack of success with offender populations. This contention assumes that their purpose is custody as opposed to treatment. Unfortunately, the emphasis on custody as the prevailing model creates the same problems of civil rights at the juvenile level as it does at the adult level. The dangers that juvenile institutions hold for the civil rights of the offender were forcefully brought to public attention in the *Gault* decision.

The theory (that incarceration is an effective device for changing people and at the same time deterring others) is debatable, despite the *Gault* decision. Unfortunately, national statistics on recidivism after incarceration are generally not available to refute this theory substantively. Accurate statistics on the rate of recidivism of juvenile institutional populations after release would certainly provide useful information on the supposed deterrent effect of institutions. The incarceration of youths, in fact, can reach a point of diminishing returns. Studies have indicated that communities spend enormous sums of money keeping juveniles locked up longer than is necessary—so long, in fact, that the chances of realizing rehabilitation are greatly decreased. Findings emphasize the absence of a positive correlation between time served in institutions and subsequent criminal or delinquent behavior.

The juvenile justice system suffers from some basic mistaken notions regarding the functions of institutionalization: First, punishment is of little importance, and, second, punishment and rehabilitation can occur in the same setting. In an article "When to Punish, When to Rehabilitate," Ellsworth Fersch suggests a two-step process: First punishment, then rehabilitation. He contends that this would restore faith in the criminal justice system and respect for the individual and society. "We need to separate these critical functions and provide short, swift, and humane punishment, followed by voluntary rehabilitation."[28] Fersch may be right, although the effects of punishment on a frightened youthful offender may well neutralize his or her receptivity to rehabilitative programs. Even voluntary participation by the youth may be consent merely to gain release from the institution or rehabilitative setting. If a system such as Fersch's is adopted, those responsible should take care to maintain the fine difference between being viewed as "prison screws" or "rehabilitative agents."

In review, there are four manifest and eleven latent functions that are attributable to juvenile institutions. The continued existence of juvenile institutions may be the result of their successful fulfillment of the latent functions, whereas fulfillment of the functions of reformation, incapacitation, retribution, and deterrence are of secondary consequence. However, it is apparent that today's juvenile institutions have fallen far short of providing conclusive proof that theory in their favor is, in fact, valid.

INSTITUTIONAL TREATMENT AND REHABILITATION

The National Advisory Commission on Criminal Justice Standards and Goals offered extensive guidelines and standards to assist the juvenile institutions in their reexamination of educational and vocational training programs. Unfortunately, despite these standards and guidelines, actual experience has shown that most youths committed to juvenile institutions are simply "doing time." Their release is more often based on such non–treatment-related factors as overcrowding, administrative decisions, and, incredibly, nontreatability. Instead of being a constructive and maturing experience, incarceration in a juvenile institution is often harmful for the juvenile. Nonconstructive time spent away from family and community leads to a lessening of the sense of belonging and responsibility.

Both the public and the juvenile justice professional view institutionalization as a last resort, an alternative to be used when nothing else is available. In fact, there has been a recent decrease in the rates of institutionalization of juveniles at a time when juvenile court delinquency cases—the primary source of commitments to institutions—seem to be increasing. The decrease in institutional care, therefore, may reflect the recent emphasis on finding alternatives for the treatment of youthful offenders, using incarceration only where it is absolutely necessary to the child's welfare and/or to the protection of the community.

Services in Institutions

Institutionalized juveniles, for whatever reason they are in institutions, must be provided access to services required for individual growth and development. These services include meaningful, high-quality education and adequate vocational training programs.

Irving Kaufman suggests that to accomplish this end, all sentences should be fixed terms. On show of good cause, the court should impose any subsequent change.

> Indeterminate sentences have been rejected by the commission as a game of chance based on arbitrary decisions. Frequently in the past the most violent juveniles were released from institutions because they were, ironically, difficult to control. Power to determine the actual length of stay of a juvenile is thus removed from the hands of correctional authorities. To encourage good behavior, correctional administrators are allowed to reduce a youth's sentence by no more than 5 percent. The maximum term of incarceration should not exceed two years for any offense.[29]

Currently, even when the treatment staffs do plan a potentially meaningful program, they can seldom be assured of how long they have with their "client." As long as release is possible at any time, training programs are practically worthless. To believe, therefore, that youths are released from juvenile institutions only when they are successfully rehabilitated or "cured" is to believe a fantasy.

The use of fixed-length sentences would allow the juvenile to complete useful training programs. One must keep in mind, however, that the length of time a youth spends in an institution and the degree to which he or she is rehabilitated are not always related. To assume, for example, that the longer a youth spends incarcerated, the more he or she will be rehabilitated, and vice versa, is not always true. To justify the use of fixed-length sentences, therefore, on the basis of allowing enough time for the completion of adequate training programs and then not to provide these programs would be in violation of the principle of "right to treatment." Under a system of fixed-length sentences, it would be necessary for the institutional staff to tailor treatment programs to fit the varying periods of time youths could spend in the institution. It would defeat the purpose of the treatment plan, for example, if a youth sentenced to from two to four months were placed in a treatment program that required at least ten months to complete.

Morales v. Turman

Many people have assumed that a juvenile has the right to treatment after he or she comes under the auspices of the juvenile justice system, or at least that treatment does exist. However, the *right* of a juvenile to rehabilitation and/or treatment (regardless of whether treatment actually exists) in a correctional institution has until very recently gone uncontested. Most court cases regarding rights to treatment have involved adults, but in 1974, the U.S. District Court for the Eastern District of Texas in *Morales v. Turman* determined that constitutional rights of incarcerated minors had been violated and ordered the parties involved to submit a comprehensive plan for righting these violations.[30] This case has raised a wide range of issues regarding the nature and adequacy of procedures and programs adopted by the Texas Youth Council (TYC). The TYC has the responsibility under Texas law for minors adjudicated delinquent and involuntarily committed to its custody. In this case, the court withheld issuing a permanent order of relief in favor of the plaintiffs to give TYC a chance to make amends and to present a treatment plan favorable to all parties involved. This was done because the granting of requested relief could quite possibly entail extensive changes in virtually every phase of the TYC operations.

What the plaintiffs in this case accomplished was nothing less than an exhaustive attack on a set of policies and programs that, when taken as a whole, represent no less than a state's entire juvenile correctional system. The assurances requested by the plaintiffs should serve as examples to be followed by similar court action throughout the United States. *Morales v. Turman* and its implications for correctional attitudes, settings, and treatment rights are crucial to the future of the juvenile justice system. Although this case applied specifically to Texas, the conditions described therein are similar to those in a large number of other states in this country. It is hoped that these systems that have been or are moving in the direction of providing requests and assurances similar to those contained in the *Morales* case will continue to do so and that states that find their programs sadly behind the times and lacking in humane treatment practices will soon follow suit. If not, court action similar to that brought against the TYC may leave them no choice.

The whole concept of treatment or the lack thereof within U.S. juvenile institutions raises this basic question: "Is it our intention to punish youth who violate the law or to rehabilitate them?" Put another way: "Are we for justice, or are we for laws?" According to Rossi:

> In the juvenile area, the system for training criminals throughout the United States is complete. Hardly a course is overlooked in the education of youth when they enter this exceptional and unequalled academy of learning. Quickly and proficiently they develop into criminals. Yet, juveniles are not brought into this world as potential, hard-core criminals. A criminal, like a surgeon, requires training and enlightenment, growth and extension. The manner and means of training and development a juvenile receives will determine whether or not he or she will become a criminal. Crime is not a talent! It is a means of survival and self-preservation and a way of life for many young individuals. It's not an artistic, creative endeavor such as music, painting, or architecture.[31]

If law is to be upheld, a juvenile who violates the law should be accorded every right currently granted to adult offenders, including the right not to be detained or incarcerated for status offenses or incorrigible acts. If justice is to be served, the optimal solution is that only those youths for whom no alternative exists other than incarceration are committed to juvenile institutions and at the same time accord them all rights granted adults. Furthermore, incarcerated youths should be guaranteed humane rehabilitative treatment, and nonincarcerated youths should be placed in community-based treatment programs that promote their remaining in society as useful citizens.

Escape and Unauthorized Leaves

Among the many serious problems confronting juvenile correctional administrators and staff is escape or unauthorized leave from juvenile institutions. Unauthorized leaves both disrupt and destroy a juvenile's participation in residential treatment programs designed to make possible a successful reentry into the community. In the past few years, professional staffs at institutions have become increasingly aware of this problem.

Increasing rates of unauthorized leaves apply nationwide. It is the authors' belief that the frequency and length of unauthorized leaves should be controlled. Reduction in the frequency of unauthorized leaves should reduce the rate of criminal behavior committed by juveniles in the community and should make the juvenile more available for treatment. A long-range reduction in delinquency is also probable.

An interstate agreement for juveniles (called the Interstate Compact on juveniles) was formulated in the early 1950s to cope with the many problems involved in supervising and controlling juveniles and juvenile delinquents. A major purpose of this agreement is to provide for a way to return captured escapees to the state from which they had escaped. Under the compact, when the runaway child is apprehended in another state, the arresting agency usually contacts the institution or agency from whose jurisdiction the child ran. If problems are encountered, the Interstate Office may assist whenever possible.

The constitutionality of the compact has been challenged on the grounds that it has not received the consent of Congress and that it violates the protection privileges and immunities and due process clauses of the Fourteenth Amendment.[32] Ruling in a case that challenged the compact *(Chin v. Wyman et al.)*, a New York court said that with respect to the possible violation of due process, a hearing should be held in the state to which the youth had fled, on the question of whether he or she should be returned to the home state. Such a hearing, the court said, was necessary to satisfy due process requirements.[33]

Before leaving the subject of escape and unauthorized leave, the reader should consider two things: (1) The granting of full constitutional protection to juveniles carries potential hazards unrealized by many. For example, adult convicts attempting to escape from an institution can be legally shot. How acceptable would it be to allow a 13-year-old joyrider to be subjected to the same sort of life-endangering threat? And (2) Of the thousands of young people who escape or take unauthorized leave from juvenile institutions each year, many are never caught and are not heard from again. Could it be that perhaps they have found their own successful means for rehabilitation outside the world of institutional treatment programs? (At least one juvenile institution recognizes this possibility and calls it "self-placement.")[34]

INSTITUTIONAL PUNISHMENT

Horror stories of brutal punishment, sexual abuse and assault, and convict child labor were once commonly reported in newspapers, magazines, and other media. For the most part, the juvenile justice system has overcome these abuses; however, children still may suffer many dehumanizing acts when they are locked away in jails, institutions, and "kid prisons."[35]

Often funds and resources that could be used for education, health care, and positive treatment of youth are used up on negative programs. Many institutions continue to emphasize punishment or the threat of punishment as their primary means of controlling their youthful populations. Bizarre corporal punishments are common in juvenile institutions and detention facilities. A Harvard student, for example, who posed as a 16-year-old inmate of the John J. Connally Youth Center in Roslindale, Massachusetts, reported that one commonly used punishment was to hold a boy's head under water, and for minor infractions of the rules, youths were beaten by the fists of teenagers forced to participate under threat of a beating themselves.

The use of solitary confinement or isolation is as widespread in juvenile detention facilities and institutions as is corporal punishment and the administration of calming or tranquilizing drugs. Its use continues despite condemnation from the theoreticians and practitioners.

Within juvenile correctional institutions, organizational traditions exist that compound the problems caused by mixing treatment and punishment. In treatment philosophy as in punishment philosophy, the primary source of the delinquent or incorrigible behavior is sought within the offender. As a consequence, the treatment philosophy has never challenged the social functions of institutional punishment, nor has it indicated the extent to which caste-like correctional organizations may seriously hamper efforts at rehabilitative treatment. There is a tendency for youths to view whatever is done to them as punishment rather than treatment.

> Part of the reason for this perception lies in the fact that treatment personnel, even if highly trained (and they are in short supply in most juvenile training schools), have a symbiotic relationship with clients which is subtle and paradoxical. The status of the professional, his helping role, his very place in the whole scheme of things depends heavily upon the client remaining in a subordinate relationship to him. The paradox is, therefore, that although the professional role ostensibly exists to help the client, it is, in fact, one which relies upon a super ordinate-subordinate relationship. As a result, it is difficult for the client to change unless his relationship to those above him changes also. Organizational arrangements are not available by which to encourage him to stop conceiving of himself as delinquent, inmate, or patient, and to conceive of himself, instead, as non-delinquent, employee, or student.[36]

Although some institutions are taking steps to move inmates step by step into new roles, there are still too few organizational structures within correctional institutions that allow the youth to be anything but an inmate and a delinquent. There are, therefore, two types of punishment practiced within our juvenile institutions: (1) actual physical punishment such as beatings, isolation, restraints, and so forth; and (2) a psychological attitude that causes the youth to view everything happening to him or her, while at the hands of an adult power structure, as punishment—even if that action is intended to be treatment oriented and in the youth's best interest.

THE FUTURE OF JUVENILE INSTITUTIONS: PROGRAMS AND ISSUES

In recent years, delinquency has increased, and this has stimulated the development of numerous kinds of programs for the juvenile institutional field. Four of the most significant of these new programs are described briefly as follows:

1. **Community-based treatment.** **Community-based treatment** includes various methods of handling juveniles in a community setting as alternatives to commitment or for reducing the number of commitments. They are of special interest because of their relative economy compared with institutional commitment and because of the advantages of treatment in a setting as normal or "close to home" as possible.

   The principal vehicles include intensified and selected probation and parole caseloads offering special counseling and community help plus "in and out" and trial furloughs; group homes and agency-operated residential treatment programs; "day care" in specialized institutional programs that return youngsters home at night and on weekends; regional detention centers with diagnostic service intended to reduce "dumping" into institutions; special "closed" local facilities with intensive counseling; and family involvement.

   community-based treatment Methods of handling juveniles in a community setting as an alternative to an institutional commitment

2. **Group treatment.** **Group treatment** techniques offer essentially the advantage of economy over one-to-one counseling relationships, plus treatment advantages gained from insights on behavior through viewpoints expressed from several sources. In the institutional setting they have included families of the trainees. Their common goal is acceptance of responsibility rather than satisfaction with shallow conformity.

   group treatment The treatment of juveniles in a group setting versus an individual setting. Group treatment may also include the family of the juvenile.

3. **Diversification.** Development toward **diversification** is represented by the growth of small camp programs, halfway houses, group-treatment centers, reception and screening centers, vocational training centers, and special short-term programs. The goal of the breadth of these programs is to address the different problems faced by juveniles.

   diversification The breadth of juvenile commitment programs represented which attempt to address the different problems faced by juveniles

4. **Decriminalization and Deinstitutionalization.** Detention of juveniles would be drastically reduced if persons in need of supervision and dependency-neglect cases were removed altogether from juvenile court jurisdiction. Decriminalization of conduct that is prohibited "for children only" would remove thousands of children from court-controlled institutions. This shift would work only if alternatives were available to respond to neglected and troubled children. One such mechanism is the system of "Youth Service Bureaus" advocated by the President's Crime Commission in 1967.[37]

In the future, juvenile justice administrators must guarantee that alternatives to institutionalization are as readily available to the children of the poor as to middle- and upper-class children. One may argue that poor children commit more wrongs, but the unequal handling of criminal cases may be because upper- and middle-class families are more often allowed to deal with the problem outside the system. Ironically, poor children are often placed in juvenile institutions for their own protection and good, regardless of the seriousness of their offense(s), whereas children from prosperous backgrounds are usually released—also for their own good—even though they may have committed more serious offenses.

Boot Camps for Juvenile Offenders

boot camps Programs modeled after military basic training in an attempt to balance punishment with treatment and education

Boot camps developed in the 1990s as a means to punish offenders while limiting institutional crowding (see Box 9.4). They are defined as follows:

Boot camp programs are modeled after military basic training. Offenders often enter the programs in groups that are referred to as platoons or squads. They are required to wear military-style uniforms, march to and from activities, and respond rapidly to the commands of "drill instructors." The rigorous daily schedule requires youths to wake up early and stay active throughout the day. Although programs differ somewhat, the schedule usually includes drill and ceremony practice, strenuous physical fitness activities, and challenge programs (e.g., ropes courses) as well as required academic education. Frequently, youths in the camps receive summary punishments, such as having to do pushups for misbehaviors.[38]

Thus, boot camps satisfy the popular demand for punishment while recognizing the youth's need for treatment and education.

Boot camps are perhaps the most visible means of showing the public that those responsible for trying to curtail juvenile crime are taking the initiative. One question might be: do we use boot camps simply because they appeal to the public's image of "getting tough" on juvenile crime rather than because we believe they will accomplish the goal of reducing juvenile crime and recidivism? Phrased differently, we must ask ourselves if juvenile boot camps are so popular because of their political appeal rather than because they work.[39]

Boot Camp

By 1996, forty-eight residential boot camps for juveniles were operating in twenty-seven states.[40]

Evidence of the effectiveness of these programs is mixed and limited. Juveniles who take part in the camps report positive responses to their institutional environment and its programs.[41] In addition, juvenile boot campers recorded improvement in their reading and math skills.[42] However, across the board, boot camp participants have similar, if not higher, rates of recidivism than other juvenile, nonparticipant counterparts.[43]

The problem in sustaining the program gains from boot camp programs is tied to the availability and quality of aftercare programs. On release, the juvenile needs community-based programs to address his or her individual concerns.

> Aftercare programs must be broad-based and flexible enough to meet the particular educational, employment, counseling, and support needs of each participant. The aftercare component should form dynamic linkages with other community services, especially youth service agencies, schools, and employers.[44]

Boot camps are not the ultimate answer to juvenile delinquency, but they seem to have the potential to be a part of the "response matrix in corrections."[45]

Disproportionate Minority Confinement

Disproportionate minority confinement is the overrepresentation of minority youth in juvenile institutions. It has been recognized as a problem in almost every state. This problem is usually a cumulative one—the result of decisions made at every stage of the juvenile justice system, from arrest to confinement to release.[46] Official figures indicate that minority group juveniles, especially African Americans, make up a higher percentage of

disproportionate minority confinement The overrepresentation of minority youth in juvenile institutions

BOX 9.4 **JUVENILE BOOT CAMPS**

Yet another commonsense program designed to deal with juvenile delinquency is the correctional boot camp, which is modeled after military basic training. They were designed to appeal to the public's desire for "getting tough" on juvenile crime. One aim was to boost the discipline and self-concept of juvenile offenders. They are often placed in platoons or squads, wear military-type uniforms, and take part in rigorous physical activity and marching at the direction of drill instructors. This military routine was coupled with rehabilitation methods such as: drug counseling, GED preparation and testing, mentoring, community service. and aftercare programs (intensive supervision on return to the community) and involvement with police, the judiciary system, and community groups on release. They were also designed to serve as an alternative to incarceration. Young, first-time, nonviolent offenders were typically targeted for boot camps in the hope that they would go straight. The shock of incarceration, coupled with the disciplined environment of the boot camp, would remove the juvenile from prison, reduce the cost of incarceration, and discourage recidivism. Although originally designed for adults, boot camps were adapted for juveniles. It was believed that they provided a balanced approach to juvenile justice by integrating offender accountability, punishment, rehabilitation, and delinquency prevention. By 1996, forty-eight residential boot camps for juveniles were operating in twenty-seven states.

Evidence of the effectiveness of these programs is mixed and limited. Bourque and her colleagues conducted one evaluation of the effectiveness of boot camps in Ohio, Colorado, and Alabama in 1991. The research focused on 300 male youths entering the programs during their first year of operation. The three programs had a graduation rate of more than 80 percent. Graduates who were interviewed on their release believed that they had changed considerably as a result of the experience. However, the graduates in all three programs registered high rates of rearrest, ranging from 20 percent to 33 percent. The conclusion was that the boot camp model could be adapted for juveniles as long as treatment elements such as education were required. It was also recommended that future juvenile boot camps should develop an effective program rationale, balance militaristic with rehabilitative elements, select youths appropriate for the program, provide continuous training for staff, and carefully structure the aftercare component of program.

Research indicates that graduates consider the boot camp a positive experience. Some graduates reported improvements in physical fitness and education. One study indicated that educational programs increased participants' reading, math, language, and spelling grades by at least one grade level. Moreover, employment following release seemed to be at acceptable levels. Some findings suggest that intensive supervision following release from boot camp led to lower reincarceration rates. For these benefits to be maintained, community services must be provided to boot camp graduates when they return to the community.

Yet, studies consistently report negligible improvement in recidivism rates for boot camp graduates. A meta-analysis by Wilson and his colleagues of forty-three boot camp studies (forty from the United States, one from Canada, and two from the United Kingdom) on almost 120,000 juvenile participants determined that boot camps were neither worse nor better than typical imprisonment. There was also some indication that boot camp graduates are more likely to recidivate than probationers. The crucial absence of aftercare programming following incarceration has an effect on recidivism rates. The boot camp experience must be supported by such programs. The boot camp example again emphasizes that there are no easy answers to the delinquency problem.

Sources: Joanne Ardovini-Brooker and Lewis Walker, "Juvenile Boot Camps and the Reclamation of Our Youth: Some Food for Thought," *Juvenile and Family Court Journal*, Vol. 51 (2000), pp. 21–29;

J. Bottcher and M.E. Ezell, "Examining the Effectiveness of Boot Camps: A Randomized Experiment with a Long-Term Follow Up," *Journal of Research in Crime and Delinquency*, Vol. 42 (2005), pp. 309–322; J. Bottcher and T. Isorena, "First Year Evaluation of the California Youth Authority Boot Camp," in Doris L. MacKenzie and E.E. Herbert, eds., *Correctional Boot Camps: A Tough Intermediate Sanction*. (Washington, DC: National Institute of Justice, 1996), pp. 159–178; Blair Bourque, R. C. Cronin, F. R. Pearson, M. Han and S. M. Hill, *Boot Camps for Juvenile Offenders: An Implementation Evaluation of Three Demonstration Programs* (Washington, DC: National Institute of Justice, 1996); Thomas C. Castellano and E. L. Cowles, *Boot Camp Drug Treatment and Aftercare Intervention* (Washington, DC: National Institute of Justice, 1995); R.C. Cronin, *Boot Camps for Adult and Juvenile Offenders: Overview and Update*. (Washington, DC: National Institute of Justice, 1994); Francis T. Cullen, Kristie R. Blevins, Jennifer S. Trager, and Paul Gendreau, "The Rise and Fall of Boot Camps: A Case Study in Common-Sense Corrections," *Rehabilitation Issues, Problems and Prospects in Boot Camps*, pp. 53–70 (2005), http://www.haworthpress.com/web/OR. Retrieved on July 7, 2008; Elizabeth L. Grossi, ed., "Prison and Jail Boot Camps," *Journal of Contemporary Criminal Justice*, Vol. 13 (1997), pp. 93–205; M. C. Kurlychek and C. A. Kampinen, "Beyond Boot Camp: The Impact of Aftercare on Offender Reentry," *Criminology and Public Policy*, Vol. 5 (2003), pp. 581–606; Doris Layton MacKenzie, Angela R. Gover, Gaylene Styve Armstrong, and Ojmarrh Mitchell, "A National Study Comparing the Environments of Boot Camps with Traditional Facilities for Juvenile Offenders," *National Institute of Justice: Research in Brief* (Washington, DC: U.S. Department of Justice, August 2001); Michael Peters, David Thomas, and Christopher Zamberlan, *Boot Camps for Juvenile Offenders: Program Summary* (Washington, DC: Office of Juvenile Justice and Delinquency Prevention, 1997); Eric Peterson, "Juvenile Boot Camps: Lessons Learned," *Office of Juvenile Justice and Delinquency Prevention Fact Sheet# 36* (Washington, DC: U.S. Department of Justice, June 1996); J. B. Wells, K. I. Minor, E. Angel, and K. D. Stearman, "A Quasi-Experimental Evaluation of a Shock Incarceration and Aftercare Program for Juvenile Offenders," *Youth Violence and Juvenile Justice*, Vol. 4 (2006), pp. 219–233; David B. Wilson, Doris L. MacKenzie, and Fawn Ngo Mitchell, "Effects of Correctional Boot Camps on Offending," *The Campbell Collaboration* No. 10 (2006), www.campbellcollaboration.org. Retrieved on July 9, 2008.

juvenile arrests and were disproportionately held in detention centers and training schools.[47] Figures also indicate the following:

- Although proportions are declining, African American juveniles are overrepresented at all stages of the juvenile justice system compared with their proportion in the population.

- Minorities accounted for 67 percent of juveniles committed to public facilities nationwide—a proportion nearly twice their proportion of the juvenile population.

- Interview data reveal that white boys were less likely to have been in a gang than African American and Hispanic boys but more likely to have carried a gun.

- African American youth accounted for 15 percent of the juvenile population in 1997 but 26 percent of all juvenile arrests and 44 percent of arrests for violent offenses.

- African American juveniles accounted for 38 percent of the crimes against persons in 1996.

- All racial groups had large increases in drug case rates between 1991 and 1996: 116 percent for whites, 132 percent for African Americans, and 167 percent for youth of other races.

- Between 1987 and 1996, the increase in the number of African American juvenile cases involving detention was nearly four times the increase for whites.
- Minorities accounted for seven in ten youths held in custody for a violent offense.
- In 1997, half of the girls in residential placement were minorities.[48]

In 1988, the Juvenile Justice and Delinquency Prevention Act of 1974 was amended to require states to meet four mandates:

1. Remove juveniles from adult jails.
2. Keep juveniles separated from adult offenders.
3. No longer incarcerate status offenders.
4. Reduce disproportionate minority confinement.

Legislation in 1992 required states to reduce the proportion of minority juveniles confined in secure facilities or face reduction in federal funds available for their juvenile programs.[49] Subsequent federal legislation required local law and justice council advisory committees to submit an annual report on the proportionality of rehabilitative services, their effectiveness in relation to community supervision and parole, and citizen complaints regarding disproportionality in the county juvenile justice system.[50] The Office of Juvenile Justice and Delinquency Prevention provides training, grants supporting training, and technical assistance to develop and test approaches to reduce disproportionate minority confinement.[51]

Explanations for disproportionate minority confinement follow two trends. One falls short of calling the system racist and refers to the treatment of minorities as "differential treatment."[52] Another indicates that the greater involvement of minorities in violent and serious crime is the cause of disproportionality. A related theory notes the extended exposure of minority groups to socioeconomic, family, and educational problems that contribute to their involvement in crime and delinquency.[53]

Those studies that found that race made a difference have examined several stages of the juvenile justice process. Conley finds that African American youths were severely over-represented at every stage of the process.[54] McGarrell observes trends in juvenile court processing from 1985 to 1989 in 159 counties from seventeen states. Nonwhite referrals increased significantly in juvenile court processing. Some of the increase was fueled by the rise in drug cases.[55] A cohort study of 50,000 youths followed from intake to judicial disposition found that race was a significant factor in determining outcome. Bishop and Frazier conclude that African American youths were placed at a considerable disadvantage by the cumulative effect of differential treatment.[56] Another study followed a random sample of jurisdictions through three points of the juvenile justice system and finds that race had a significant and independent effect on detention.[57] A Washington state study reports that minority youths were much more likely to be confined than white youths even when the violent crime rate was high. Negative stereotypes of minorities drove perceptions of dangerousness and led to confinement.[58]

Several studies indicate that a long arrest record and the seriousness of the present offense had more influence on sentencing decisions than race. Bell and Lang find that the number of prior offenses influenced sentencing decisions and that white juveniles were consistently treated more leniently than other offenders.[59] A Florida study reported that minority overrepresentation in the commitment process was due to the seriousness and number of prior adjudicated offenses.[60] Finally, extensive and comprehensive research by Michael J. Leiber and his colleagues documents that minorities (African Americans, Native Americans, and Hispanics) are more likely to receive serious sanctions for their delinquent acts than whites throughout the juvenile sentencing process.[61]

Several states have attempted to develop innovative solutions to deal with disproportionate minority confinement. In response to research findings that minority juveniles accounted for 48 percent of all youths formally charged in juvenile court, Pennsylvania developed prevention and intervention strategies. They included youth clubs and truancy and dropout prevention projects. These projects had mixed results, reporting low levels of truancy, suspension, and recidivism in some areas.[62] In 1991, five states (Arizona, Florida, Iowa, North Carolina, Oregon) developed pilot programs addressing the issue that minority representation was the result of the scarcity of resources for minority youth programs. To resolve this problem, programs that address the problems that lead to delinquency must be developed and made available to all juveniles.

Juveniles in Adult Jails and Prisons

Juveniles are being held in adult facilities. This is largely the result of new sentencing policies holding juveniles accountable for their offenses and trying them as adult offenders. Table 9.2 documents the rate of increase in this occurrence. Between 1983 and 1998, the number of juveniles held in adult jails more than tripled.

Table 9.3 indicates the attributes of juveniles admitted to state prisons in 1985 and 1997. Although the number of admissions has increased, it seems that fewer of these juvenile inmates had been admitted for a violent offense, whereas juveniles convicted of drug offenses increased dramatically. Although the proportion of white juveniles had decreased, increases

Table 9.2
JUVENILES IN ADULT JAILS, 1983–1998

Year	Juveniles
1983	1,736
1984	1,482
1985	1,629
1986	1,708
1987	1,781
1988	1,676
1989	2,250
1990	2,301
1991	2,350
1992	2,804
1993	4,300
1994	6,700
1995	7,800
1996	8,100
1997	9,105
1998	8,090
% Change, 1983–1998	**366%**

Source: James Austin, Kelly Dedel Johnson, and Maria Gregoriou, *Juveniles in Adult Prisons and Jails—A National Assessment* (Washington, DC: Bureau of Justice Assistance, 2000), p. 5.

were noted for both African American and Hispanic offenders. Males make up the majority of these inmates, and they seem to be getting younger. Although the average maximum sentence has decreased, the average minimum sentence increased by nine months.

On the basis of this information, Austin and his colleagues made the following recommendations to the Bureau of Justice Assistance

Table 9.3
ATTRIBUTES OF JUVENILES ADMITTED TO STATE PRISONS, 1985 AND 1997

Attribute	1985 Prison Admissions	1997 Prison Admissions
Total Admissions	3,400	7,400
Offense Type		
Violent	82%	61%
Property	42%	22%
Drug	2%	11%
Public Order	4%	5%

Race/Ethnicity		
White	32%	25%
African American	53%	58%
Hispanic	14%	15%
Other	1%	2%
Gender		
Male	97%	97%
Female	3%	3%
Age at Admission		
17	80%	74%
16	18%	21%
15	2%	4%
14 and younger	0%	1%
Average Sentence		
Maximum	86 months	82 months
Minimum	35 months	44 months

Source: James Austin, Kelly Dedel Johnson, and Maria Gregoriou, *Juveniles in Adult Prisons and Jails—A National Assessment* (Washington, DC: Bureau of Justice Assistance, 2000), p. 6.

and correctional administrators who manage juveniles held in adult institutions:

- Ensure that classification instruments are valid for this subset of the adult correctional population and that risk and needs instruments reflect maturation issues and special needs of the juvenile population.
- Develop specialized programs responsive to the developmental needs of youthful offenders, including: educational and vocational programs, sex offender and violent offender programs, and substance abuse programs that take into account the roles these issues have in adolescent development.[63]

SUMMARY

Juvenile institutions are as good or as bad as those in the adult system. Most people dislike seeing youths detained in jails and lockups, but this practice still persists in jurisdictions where there are either no or limited alternatives. In one southeastern Ohio community, for example, it is not uncommon for parents with unruly children to call the local sheriff. He obliges by locking them up for a few days to "teach them a lesson." This is done without the knowledge of the court and is a clear violation of the juvenile's rights to due process.

From numerous research projects conducted over the years, it is clear that detention and incarceration in juvenile institutions harm many youths. Despite the failures of the adult corrections system, society seems to prefer using a similar type of system for the youths who come in contact with the juvenile justice system. To counter this attitude, standards of treatment and guidelines for handling the problems of delinquents must be applied carefully to these youths in trouble. Otherwise, the impact on society can be more negative than positive.

Just as important as the institutions are the alternatives to institutionalization offered by juvenile corrections administrators. The rights and recourses available to adults in the adult corrections system will probably soon be accessible to juveniles as well. Although the two systems are not yet equal, the movement toward equalization seems irreversible. It is the job of the juvenile justice professional to ensure that these similarities are more on the positive side than the negative.

KEY TERMS

- boot camps
- community-based treatment
- cottage reform school
- detention center
- disproportionate minority confinement
- diversification
- *Ex parte Crouse*
- expiation
- group treatment
- Lyman School for Boys
- privatization

DISCUSSION AND REVIEW QUESTIONS

1. Define *detention* and *institutionalization*. What is the basic difference between them?
2. What is the purpose of juvenile institutions? Is that purpose realistic, given the structure of today's society? Why or why not?
3. What is meant by "right to treatment"? Discuss the major aspects of *Morales v. Turman* and how that case may have an impact on the national juvenile justice system as a whole.
4. Define and discuss the following terms:
   a. Unauthorized leave
   b. Isolation
   c. Institutional alternatives
5. Discuss the issue of punishment versus treatment as the most realistic goal of the juvenile institutions of the past, today, and the future.
6. Why is the issue of disproportionate minority confinement so important?
7. What do boot camps have to offer? Should the practice be continued and expanded?

VIDEO PROFILES

The *Life Inside* video profile in MyCrimeKit describes the juvenile institution as presented by (1) the juvenile and (2) the "contents" and features of the "cell." Discuss whether the juvenile facility presented in the video centers on rehabilitation or retribution. Use specific examples from the video.

During the interview of two juveniles, they suggest, "the facility is willing to help you out if you want to be helped out." How do the institutional programs described in this chapter correspond to the reasons the juveniles give for facility assistance? Finally, which type of institution (public or private) most closely corresponds with the reasons that the juveniles noted?

The *Professional Perspective* video profile in MyCrimeKit is an interview with the superintendent and shows sites from inside the facility. Compare the expectations the superintendent has for the staff and for the juveniles. What are the similarities and differences? Discuss the superintendent's perceptions on the facility, working in it with the staff and juveniles, and what it means for overall success of the juveniles. What are his perceptions on recruiting and retaining staff? What does he do to assist with retention efforts? The superintendent cites many characteristics of "good" officers, which the video also highlights. What are some of these?

The *Peace Learning Program* video profile in MyCrimeKit highlights a program in a girls' facility. What is peace learning? What is challenge learning? The program coordinator discusses goals of peace learning. What are they and how might these be applied in the real world or to curtail delinquent behavior? Finally, compare and contrast the Peace Learning Program with the Future Soldiers Program video presented in Chapter 12.

MYCRIMEKIT

mycrimekit™   Go to MyCrimeKit.com to explore the following study tools and resources specific to this chapter:

- Practice Quiz: Test your knowledge with multiple-choice, true-false, fill-in-the-blank, and essay questions.
- Flashcards: 20 flashcards to test your knowledge of the chapter's key terms.
- Web Quest: Go to the Web site for OJJDP's Census of Juveniles in Residential Placement and update the figures contained in this

chapter. Also, look up the figures for your state and see how the trends there compare with those of the entire nation.

- Web Links: Check out sites related to the content presented in this chapter.

ENDNOTES

1. Barry Krisberg and James F. Austin, *Reinventing Juvenile Justice* (Newbury Park, CA: Sage Publications, 1993), p. 74.

2. Betty Marler and Marc Scoble, "Building a Juvenile System to Serve the Majority of Young Offenders," *Corrections Today*, Vol. 63 (April 2001), p. 86.

3. Charles J. Kehoe, "Juvenile Corrections in a Changing Landscape," *Corrections Today*, Vol. 63 (April 2001), p. 6.

4. Bradford Smith, "Children in Custody: 20-Year Trends in Juvenile Detention, Correctional, and Shelter Facilities," *Crime and Delinquency*, Vol. 44 (1998), p. 537.

5. Ibid., p. 538.

6. Ibid., p. 539.

7. Ibid., p. 530.

8. *In re Gault*, 387 U.S. 1, 27 (1967).

9. Harry E. Barnes and Negley K. Teeters, *New Horizons in Criminology* (Englewood Cliffs, NJ: Prentice Hall, 1959), p. 334.

10. Robert W. Mennel, *Thorns and Thistles: Juvenile Delinquents in the United States, 1825–1940* (Hanover, NH: University Press of New England, 1973), pp. 52–54.

11. Ibid., pp. 25–26; S. Schlossman, "Delinquent Children: The Juvenile Reform School," in Norval Morris and David J. Rothman, eds., *The Oxford History of the Prison: The Practice of Punishment in Western Society* (New York: Oxford University Press, 1995), pp. 363–389.

12. David W. Roush, *Desktop Guide to Good Detention Practice* (Washington, DC: Office of Juvenile Justice and Delinquency Prevention, 1996), p. 27.

13. Horace Mann, "Account of the Hamburgh Redemption Institute" (n.p. 1843).

14. Mennel, *Thorns and Thistles*.

15. H. W. Charles, "The Problem of the Reform School," *Proceedings of the Conference for Child Research and Welfare 1* (1910); Clarissa Olds

Keller, *American Bastilles* (Washington, DC: Carnaham Press, 1910), pp. 8–9.

16. David Rothman, *Conscience and Convenience* (Boston: Little Brown, 1980); Alexander W. Pisciotta, *Benevolent Repression: Social Control and the American Reformatory-Prison Movement* (New York: New York University Press, 1994).

17. *OJJDP Statistical Briefing Book.* Online. Available: http://www.ojjdp. ncjrs.org/ojstatbb. 28 February 2001; Joseph Moore, "Innovative Information on Juvenile Residential Facilities," in *OJJDP Fact Sheet* (Washington, DC: Office of Juvenile Justice and Delinquency Prevention, 2000).

18. National Advisory Committee on Criminal Justice Standards and Goals, *Report of the Task Force on Juvenile Justice and Delinquency Prevention* (Washington, DC: U.S. Government Printing Office, 1976), p. 695.

19. Jerome G. Miller, *Last One over the Wall: The Massachusetts Experiment in Closing Reform Schools* (Columbus, OH: The Ohio State University Press, 1991).

20. Robert B. Coates, Alden D. Miller, and Lloyd E. Ohlin, *Diversity in a Youth Correctional System: Handling Delinquents in Massachusetts* (Cambridge, MA: Ballinger, 1978); Barry Krisberg and James Austin, "What Works with Juvenile Offenders: The Massachusetts Experiment," in Dan Macallair and Vincent Schiraldi, eds., *Reforming Juvenile Justice: Reasons and Strategies for the 21st Century* (Dubuque, IA: Kendall/Hunt Publishing, 1998), pp. 173–196.

21. See Travis C. Pratt and Melissa R. Winston, "The Search for the Frugal Grail: An Empirical Assessment of the Cost-Effectiveness of Public vs. Private Correctional Facilities," *Criminal Justice Policy Review,* Vol. 10 (1999), pp. 447–471; Jeffrey Butts and William Adams, *Anticipating Space Needs in Juvenile Detention and Correctional Facilities* (Washington, DC: Office of Juvenile Justice and Delinquency Prevention, 2001); M. J. McMillen, "Planning Juvenile Detention Facilities: The Real Costs," *Journal for Juvenile Justice and Detention Services,* Vol. 13 (Spring 1998), pp. 44–57.

22. Office of Juvenile Justice and Delinquency Prevention, *Juveniles in Residential Placement: 1997–2008* (Washington, DC: U.S. Department of Justice, 2010).

23. Roush, *Desktop Guide to Good Detention Practice,* p. 83.

24. Ibid., pp. 83–84.

25. Rosemary C. Sarri, *Under Lock and Key: Juveniles in Jail and Detention* (Ann Arbor: University of Michigan, 1974), p. 21.

26. Ibid., pp. 21–22.

27. Charles E. Reasons and Russell L. Kaplan, "Tear Down the Walls? Some Functions of Prisons," *Crime and Delinquency,* Vol. 21 (1975), pp. 360–372.

28. Ellsworth Fersch, "When to Punish, When to Rehabilitate," *American Bar Association Journal,* Vol. 61 (1975), pp. 1235–1237.

29. Irving R. Kaufman, "Of Juvenile Justice and Injustice," *American Bar Association Journal,* Vol. 62 (1976), pp. 730–734.

30. *Morales v. Turman,* E.D. Tex., 1974, 383 F. Supp. 53.

31. J. Rossi, *Hard Cores Don't Come from Apples* (Pasadena, CA: Ward Ritchie Press, 1976), pp. 51–52.

32. For further discussion on the subject of escapees and/or runaways, the reader is referred to: *Smallwood v. Hindle* (District Court of Iowa, Black Hawk County, October 11, 1964); and the Runaway Youth Act, Title III of the Juvenile Justice and Delinquency Prevention Act of 1974 (P.L. 93–415).

33. *Chin v. Wyman et al.* (N.Y. Supreme Court Westchester County, December 31, 1963), 246 N.Y.S. 2d. 306.

34. The institution referenced is Training Institute of Columbus, Ohio.

35. Clemens Bartollas, Stuart J. Miller, and Simon Dinitz, *Juvenile Victimization: The Institutional Paradox* (New York: Halstead Press, 1976): Clemens Bartollas and Christopher M. Sieverdes, "Juvenile Correctional Institutions: A Policy Statement," *Federal Probation,* Vol. 46 (1982), pp. 22–26; John M. MacDonald, "Violence and Drug Use in Juvenile Institutions," *Journal of Criminal Justice,* Vol. 27 (1999), pp. 33–44.

36. President's Commission on Law Enforcement and Administration of Justice, *Task Force Report: Corrections* (Washington, DC: U.S. Government Printing Office, 1967), p. 149.

37. Ronald Goldfarb, *Jails: The Ultimate Ghetto* (Garden City, NY: Anchor Press, 1976), p. 315.

38. Doris Layton MacKenzie, Angela R. Gover, Gaylene Styve Armstrong, and Ojmarrh Mitchell, "A National Study Comparing the Environments of Boot Camps with Traditional Facilities for Juvenile Offenders," *National Institute of Justice: Research in Brief* (Washington, DC: U.S. Department of Justice, August, 2001), p. 1.

39. Jerry Tyler, Ray Darville, and Kathi Stalnaker, "Juvenile Boot Camps: A Descriptive Analysis of Program Diversity and Effectiveness," *Social Science Journal,* Vol. 38 (2001), p. 458.

40. Mac Kenzie, Gover, Armstrong, and Mitchell, "A National Study."

41. Ibid.

42. Michael Peters, David Thomas, and Christopher Zamberlan, *Boot Camps for Juvenile Offenders: Program Summary* (Washington, DC: Office of Juvenile Justice and Delinquency Prevention, 1997), pp. 19–20.

43. Ibid., pp. 21–22.

44. Eric Peterson, "Juvenile Boot Camps: Lessons Learned," *Office of Juvenile Justice and Delinquency Prevention Fact Sheet# 36* (Washington, DC: U.S. Department of Justice, June, 1996), p. 2.

45. Joanne Ardovini-Brooker and Lewis Walker, "Juvenile Boot Camps and the Reclamation of Our Youth: Some Food for Thought," *Juvenile and Family Court Journal,* Vol. 51 (2000), pp. 21–29.

46. Karen B. Shepard, "Understanding Disproportionate Minority Confinement," *Corrections Today,* Vol. 59 (1995), pp. 114–115.

47. Heidi M. Hsia and Donna Hamparian, *Disproportionate Minority Confinement: 1997 Update—Juvenile Justice Bulletin* (Washington, DC: Office of Juvenile Justice and Delinquency Prevention, 1997); Wayne N. Welsh, Phillip W. Harris, and Patricia H. Jenkins, "Reducing Overrepresentation of Minorities in Juvenile Justice: Development of Community-Based Programs in Philadelphia," *Crime and Delinquency,* Vol. 42 (1996), pp. 76–98.

48. Office of Juvenile Justice and Delinquency Prevention, *Minorities in the Juvenile Justice System—1999 National Report Series, Juvenile Justice Bulletin* (Washington, DC: U.S. Department of Justice, 1999).

49. Vicky T. Church, "Meeting Disproportionate Minority Confinement Mandates," *Corrections Today,* Vol. 58 (1994), pp. 70–72.

50. Bernard C. Dean, *Juvenile Justice and Disproportionality: Patterns of Minority Over-representation in Washington's Juvenile Justice System* (December, 1997) http://www.sgc.wa.gov/JJD/JJD%20 Report.htm

51. Hsia and Hamparian, *Disproportionate Minority Confinement.*

52. Darlene J. Conley, "Adding Color to a Black and White Picture: Using Qualitative Data to Explain Racial Disproportionality in the Juvenile Justice System," *Journal of Research in Crime and Delinquency,* Vol. 31 (1994), pp. 135–148.

53. Patricia Devine, Kathleen Coolbaugh, and Susan Jenkins, "Disproportionate Minority Confinement: Lessons Learned from Five States," *OJJDP Juvenile Justice Bulletin* (Washington, DC: Office of Juvenile Justice and Delinquency Prevention, 1998),

p. 8; Charles J. Kehoe, "Juvenile Corrections in a Changing American Landscape," *Corrections Today*, Vol. 63 (2001), p. 6; Darnell F. Hawkins, John H. Laub, Janet L. Lauritsen, and Lynn Cothern, "Race, Ethnicity, and Serious and Violent Offending," *OJJDP Juvenile Justice Bulletin* (Washington, DC: Office of Juvenile Justice and Delinquency Prevention, 1998).

54. Conley, "Adding Color."

55. Edmund F. McGarrell, "Trends in Racial Disproportionality in Juvenile Court Processing: 1985–1989," *Crime and Delinquency*, Vol. 39 (1993), pp. 29–48.

56. Donna M. Bishop and Charles E. Frazier, "The Influence of Race in Juvenile Justice Processing," *Journal of Research in Crime and Delinquency*, Vol. 25 (1988), pp. 242–263.

57. Madeline Wordes, Timothy S. Bynum, and Charles J. Corley, "Locking Up Youth: The Impact of Race on Detention Decisions," *Journal of Research in Crime and Delinquency*, Vol. 31 (1994), pp. 149–165.

58. George S. Bridges, D. J. Conley, R. L. Engen, and T. Price-Spratlen, "Racial Disparities in the Confinement of Juveniles: Effects of Crime and Community Social Structure on Punishment," in Kimberly Kempf-Leonard, Carl E. Pope, and William H. Feyerherm, eds., *Minorities in Juvenile Justice* (Thousand Oaks, CA: Sage Publications, 1993), pp. 128–152.

59. Duran Bell and Kevin Lang, "The Intake Dispositions of Juvenile Offenders," *Journal of Research in Crime and Delinquency*, Vol. 22 (1985), pp. 309–328.

60. Florida Department of Juvenile Justice, "Seriousness of Delinquency History Relative to Disproportionate Minority Confinement," *Bureau of Data and Research: Research Digest*, Issue 18 (April 1998). http://www.djj.state.fl.us/RnD/r_digest/Issue18/issue18.htm

61. Michael J. Leiber and Jayne M. Stairs, "Race, Contexts, and the Use of Intake Diversion," *Journal of Research in Crime and Delinquency*, Vol. 36 (1999), pp. 56–86; Michael J. Leiber and Katherine M. Jamieson, "Race and Decision Making within Juvenile Justice: The Importance of Context," *Journal of Quantitative Criminology*, Vol. 11 (1995), pp. 363–388; Michael J. Lieber, "Toward Clarification of the Concept of 'Minority' Status and Decision-Making in Juvenile Court," *Journal of Crime and Justice*, Vol. 18 (1995), pp. 79–108; Michael J. Leiber, "A Comparison of Juvenile Court Outcomes for Native Americans, African Americans, and Whites," *Justice Quarterly*, Vol. 11 (1994), pp. 257–279.

House of Corrections, Zebulon Brockway. Brockway pressed for the use of parole and the indeterminate sentence mainly because of the large number of prostitutes who were being shuttled in and out of his institution.

Indeterminate sentencing and parole as advocated by Crofton and Brockway were introduced in 1876 at the Elmira Reformatory in New York. In the form of parole worked out at Elmira, the prisoner was kept under the supervision and control of the prison authorities for an additional six months following release. By 1891, eight states had authorized the indeterminate sentence but only for first-time offenders. New York excluded first-time female offenders altogether.

For adult prisoners, true indeterminate sentencing has won acceptance more slowly than has parole. However, a genuine indeterminate sentence (one having no minimum or maximum length) has been used in the juvenile justice system for some time. One might question, however, if the juveniles are not released because of their willingness to conform to the model used to determine their ability to return to a free society (as is the case in a genuine indeterminate sentence). Another question is whether they are not released periodically merely because of overcrowded conditions, lack of sufficient funds and resources, or other shortcomings of the system.

The American Law Institute's Model Youth Correction Authority Act of 1939 introduced the practice of granting the court the right to commit delinquent or dependent youths to the local youth authority for diagnosis and placement. This act is significant because it focused much attention on the youth authority model in the 1940s and 1950s. The model promoted the concept of parole release and aftercare supervision for committed youths. Today, every state has statutory provisions for both juvenile and adult parole.

Parole for juveniles can be traced back to the early houses of refuge established for children in the latter half of the nineteenth century. "Juvenile parole developed for several years as part of the general child welfare field, but recently, while still retaining a close involvement with child welfare programs, has assumed a more distinct status."[2] The concepts of foster care and group homes have also led to the emergence of parole as a specific practice. However, juvenile parole still remains one of the least developed of all aspects of the juvenile justice system.

JUVENILE PAROLE TODAY

After release from correctional institutions, most juveniles eventually go back to the neighborhoods from which they came. The basic functions of juvenile aftercare are three: (1) classifying the offender to determine readiness for release and the risk factor upon release, among other things; (2) the rehabilitation and reintegration of the juvenile into the community; and (3) the reduction in the likelihood of the juvenile's committing further delinquent acts, that is, reduction in recidivism.

Experts in the field of juvenile aftercare agree that the aims of parole are based on two separate though not mutually exclusive objectives: (1) the protection of the community and (2) the proper adjustment of the offender. With a growing emphasis on the integration and coordination of institutional and parole services, it becomes increasingly evident that the most important objective of the total correctional process is the protection of society. It seems that the question should not be the protection of society versus the rehabilitation of the delinquent but, rather, the protection of society through the offender's rehabilitation.

The immediate purpose or objective of parole is to assist the parolee in understanding and coping with the problems faced after release, to get used to the status of being a parolee. The long-range goal of parole is to assist in the development of the juvenile's ability to take independent action and make correct choices regarding behavioral standards that will be acceptable to society. This latter goal is essential, for it is of permanent benefit to both the parolee and the community.

Overall, the usefulness and effectiveness of parole in achieving its goals and purposes depend on whether it performs two social tasks. The first is sound case disposition. This encompasses the selection of those juveniles from among the institutionalized offender groups who, at a certain point, would benefit from return to the community instead of remaining in the institution. Because most juveniles are eventually paroled, the primary concern becomes more one of when to release, as opposed to whom. The second social task is social treatment, which includes providing the offender with access to adequate community resources to aid in reintegration.

Both these social tasks place immense responsibility on the correctional system within juvenile justice. Case disposition involves "people processing" to select the right course of action to meet the needs of each individual youth, and social treatment necessitates intervention (sometimes welcomed, often not) into the social situation in which the person functions in an attempt to change attitudes and behaviors. The final outcome is often nothing less than the actual shaping of the present and future lives of human beings.

THE PAROLE DECISION PROCESS: WHO DECIDES AND HOW?

Parole services in the juvenile justice system should be administered by the same state agency that is responsible for the institutional and related services to delinquent and dependent children. This agency is called the juvenile paroling authority.

Juvenile parole services as administered vary widely among the states and Puerto Rico. Unlike other programs for youths, such as public education, which is nearly always administered by a state educational agency, juvenile parole has no clear-cut organizational pattern. A youth authority, a child welfare agency, an adult correctional agency, a lay board, or the correctional institution staff may administer it.

Differing patterns of local jurisdiction have emerged for various reasons. Some state officials have chosen to give jurisdiction to local agencies, on the assumption that youth would receive better care from them than from the centralized, state-operated programs. In other states, the jurisdiction for parole has fallen to local agencies by default; there were simply no state agencies that could provide the needed supervision at a local level.

To ameliorate such nonstandardized organizational arrangements for the administration of aftercare services, the law under which the youth is committed to a juvenile correctional institution should provide that the agency granted legal custody also is given the right to determine when the youth shall leave the institution. For purposes of this text, the administering agency of juvenile parole will be referred to as the "juvenile paroling authority."

mycrimekit™

Video Profile: Juvenile Probation and Parole 2

When to Release

Unlike the adult parole boards, most juvenile paroling authorities do not determine the length of time (at the postsentencing stage) of an offender's prison term. Some juvenile paroling authorities do, however, require that the juvenile remain incarcerated for a certain period before release on parole. The period varies among states and jurisdictions. In most instances, however, the youth's length of commitment is determined by what is called "the progress toward rehabilitation." Progress is sometimes measured by a token system that awards a specific number of points for various positive actions. In most states, the criterion for measuring successful rehabilitation (and therefore, time of release) is whether the juvenile conforms or causes problems. Unfortunately, there exists no valid measure of a genuine rehabilitation or change of attitude. The youth's behavior may be tempered by knowledge of the release date or may be motivated solely to please "the man." By seeming to have been reformed, the youth receives the quickest release possible.

Institutions with the most adequate treatment services are the best prepared to judge the youth's readiness for parole. In these institutions, staff members should have the opportunity to come to know the juvenile as an individual person, so that

Juvenile Released from Boot Camp

they can judge more accurately the progress, risk, and potential for successful reintegration into the community. In institutions in which the process model has replaced the treatment model, the decision as to when a particular youth is ready for parole can be based on little more than the behavior shown by that youth while institutionalized. In this case, factors to consider are the number of times isolation had to be used and the number of fights, or other behavioral problems, caused by the youth. If the process model is to become the model used within juvenile correctional institutions, guidelines based on criteria other than good behavior are needed in determining preparedness for release.

For purposes of parole, there is general agreement that the youths should be released as soon as operative criteria determine they are ready. The use of the fixed sentence, with a minimum and a maximum, could well interfere with this conceptual approach.

Gains made by the youth in the institution (if any) must be strengthened when they are returned to the community by the basic functions of the parole process. Good release planning is a key to the success of the youth's "return life" in the community. Institutional staff, working in conjunction with parole staff, should prepare the juvenile for any negative reactions or other stumbling blocks to reintegration that may be encountered in the community. This prerelease planning should include the utilization of community resources during incarceration, if possible, and discussion of postrelease problems, thus helping to bridge the gap between the institution and the community.

The question of when to release a juvenile on parole depends on the youth's future behavior and how far one can predict that behavior. There are several policy considerations that should be evaluated prior to granting parole:

- Whether the juvenile has profited by his or her stay in the institution;
- Whether reform has taken place so that it is unlikely that another offense will be committed;
- Whether behavior in the institution has been acceptable;
- Whether suitable employment, training, or treatment is available on release;
- Whether the juvenile has a home or other place, such as a group home, to which to go;
- Whether the youth's perception of his or her ability to handle reintegration into the community is viewed as acceptable;
- Whether the seriousness of past offenses and the circumstances in which they were committed are not sufficiently severe as to preclude release;

- Whether the juvenile's appearance and attitude prior to release are acceptable;
- Whether behavior on probation and/or former parole, if applicable, are acceptable; and
- Whether institutional staff workers' perception of the youth's successful return to the community is positive.

In making parole selection decisions, the paroling authority generally runs the risk of making one of two types of errors. The first is granting release to a juvenile who will commit new offenses or parole violations. The second is not granting release to a youth who would have completed parole without violation. Because more than 98 percent of all juveniles committed to institutions are eventually released, the chances are that, sooner or later, both of these errors will occur, perhaps often. A thorough evaluation of the policy considerations previously mentioned, coupled with a good knowledge of the youth, the system, and the setting to which the juvenile will be returned, will certainly aid the paroling authorities in their decision of when to release.

PAROLE SERVICES

Parole services consist of all the various components of the juvenile justice system required to facilitate the goals and basic purposes of parole. These include institutional efforts at classification, the efforts of the parole staff and juvenile paroling authority to assist the youth in reentry to the community, and efforts of the community on the juvenile's behalf.

parole services All components in the juvenile justice system that facilitate the goals and basic purposes of parole

Juvenile parole services begin with preparole investigations to establish the groundwork for parole supervision and obtain the necessary background information on the child and family. Parole services continue until the discharge of the parole case. The average length of time the juvenile will spend on parole status varies from state to state. Some states keep their juveniles in active aftercare supervision programs for an average of one year or less; others give aftercare supervision for an average of one year or more. Girls generally are maintained on parole longer than boys; the reason may lie in society's attitude that the young female offender requires protection through supervision for a longer period than does the young male.

The service of supervising a paroled youth is a form of social work; thus, it is helpful if the parole officer has had some social work training. Unfortunately, as is the case with probation and institutional staff, many of them do not. Parole officers experience many of the same problems as their probation counterparts: too many children to supervise, too large a territory to cover, and too much time spent in travel.

It is unrealistic to assume that the parole officer can be all things to all youths. Community involvement in the youth's rehabilitation is paramount to the success of any aftercare services program. Even though the parole agent can identify the juvenile's problems, developing solutions to these problems ultimately lies within the community. The community must be willing to reaccept the child and, through its acceptance, facilitate the primary goal of individual rehabilitation. Juvenile aftercare services should therefore act as an agent of community change.

Caseload Size

caseload size The number of parolees supervised by an aftercare officer/probation officer

Caseload size is an important factor in the ability to deliver effective parole services. The report of the President's Commission on Law Enforcement and Administration of Justice called for a maximum caseload of fifty juveniles for the aftercare counselor (active supervision cases). One prerelease investigation was held to be equal to three cases under active supervision.

Aftercare programs should be set up for proper counseling and direction for all categories of offenders. It is preferable for the juvenile to maintain personal contact with the parole officer to ensure adequate supervision. Caseload sizes should not be so large that routine contact between the parolee and the parole agent is conducted only through telephone calls.

Although it is claimed that a reduction of the size of a parole officer's caseload would result in greater success for parolees, there is no evidence to prove it. Proposals to reduce caseload size still gain wide acceptance on the basis of promised improvement in success rates, even though research suggests that reducing the caseload size alone is not the answer.

> The institutionalization of the fifty-unit concept is now firmly entrenched. Budgets for operating agencies, testimony before legislative bodies, standards of practice, and projections for future operational needs all center about this number. There is no evidence of any empirical justification for fifty, nor for that matter, any other number.[3]

Parole Staff

Without adequate staff, aftercare programs are likely to remain a neglected component of the juvenile system. The President's Commission on Law Enforcement and the Administration of Justice stated that the juvenile justice system spends ten times more money and resources to incarcerate a juvenile than it does for probation or aftercare. Low salaries, large caseloads, and lax professional standards are not conducive to attracting highly trained and qualified professionals to enter into a career of juvenile aftercare.

Parole Officer Working One-On-One with Juvenile

Ideally, parole staff should possess a master's degree in social work or a related field because of the nature and complexity of their tasks. This standard has proven virtually impossible to attain, however. To compensate for the lack of formal professional training in the diagnosis and treatment of behavioral problems, extensive in-service training and other methods of staff development are highly recommended.

Adherence to this recommendation would help to solve many problems currently facing juvenile aftercare staff. Furthermore, the staff could get down to the business of supervising and helping youths in need. This would be a clear improvement over simply trying to survive in a system that often seems not to care.

CONDITIONS OF PAROLE

Although the **conditions of parole**, under which a juvenile is released in the community, are not quite as stringent as those for adults, they are complex. Among the specifications generally included in the conditional release of the juvenile are (1) not committing further offenses, (2) staying off drugs and away from alcohol, (3) not hanging around with the old gang or other persons who are known offenders or could have a potentially damaging effect on the youth on parole, (4) reporting on a regular basis to the parole officer or other designated person, (5) staying in a specified geographical area, and (6) getting a job or obtaining training that will lead to gainful employment. Several states have an actual parole contract that the youth is required to read, understand, and sign prior to release.

conditions of parole
Requirements that the paroled juvenile not commit certain behaviors (e.g., new offenses), as well as conform to others (e.g., attend school) to prevent revocation

Conditions may be changed and renegotiated after consultation with the juvenile parole counselor. This provision, practiced by other states as well, is an attempt to make the terms of a juvenile parole as flexible as possible, adjusting realistically to changing needs, desires, and opportunities. Violation of the conditions of parole can result in revocation by the parole authority. However, the only valid reason for parole revocation is clear evidence that the youth simply cannot function properly in the community.

After the decision to grant parole is made, the specifications attached to that conditional release often become the measure of a youth's freedom and responsibility. Because failure to observe a condition of parole may result in revocation, its legal significance is clear. The value of such conditions is that both the youth and the community are made to understand that parole, although a mechanism for release from the institution, is not absolute freedom. The right to decide parole conditions within individual jurisdictions, the way in which these conditions are actually imposed, and the discretionary right of an individual parole officer to enforce these conditions are crucial continuing legal safeguards in both adult and juvenile corrections.

The basic legal issues associated with parole conditions may be summarized as follows:

1. Conditions often affect such basic constitutional freedoms as religion, privacy, and freedom of expression;

2. Too often they are automatically and indiscriminately applied, without any thought given to the necessities of the individual case;

3. In many instances, conditions lack precision and create needless uncertainty for the supervised individual and excessive revocation leverage for those in authority; and

4. Some conditions are extremely difficult, if not impossible, to comply with.[4]

Revocation of Parole

revocation of parole The decision to revoke a juvenile's parole

Ordinarily, **revocation of parole** is within the purview of the juvenile paroling authority (if one exists). In most jurisdictions, the paroling authority must issue a warrant, or order, if its intent is to detain a juvenile suspected of violating parole. A few states permit detention for parole violation without such a warrant. The discretionary powers of the paroling authority are very broad regarding its decision to revoke the juvenile's parole. Irregularities and failure to provide legal representation at revocation hearings have received careful scrutiny by appellate courts and, most recently, the U.S. Supreme Court.

In late June 1972, the U.S. Supreme Court decided a most important case regarding parole revocation and revocation hearings. The case of *Morrissey v. Brewer* contained facts that were fairly typical of the standard practices regarding parole revocation as it existed in approximately twenty states where no hearings were held to determine the appropriateness of revoking the offender's parole.

Morrissey v. Brewer U.S. Supreme Court case enhancing the rights of parolees

The petitioners in *Morrissey* were two parolees originally sentenced to prison in Iowa for forgery. Approximately six months after being released on parole, their parole was revoked for alleged violations. The two men appealed an appellate court's decision on the grounds that the revocation of the paroles without a hearing had deprived them of due process of law guaranteed by the Fourteenth Amendment.

The appellate court, in affirming the district court's denial of relief, reasoned that parole is only "a correctional device authorizing service of sentence outside a penitentiary" and concluded that a parolee is still "in custody"[5] and not entitled to a full adversary hearing, as would be mandated in a criminal proceeding. The Supreme Court reversed the court of appeals decision and held that

> the liberty of parole, although indeterminate, includes many of the core values of unqualified liberty and its termination inflicts a "grievous loss" on the parolee and often on others. It is hardly useful any longer to try to deal with this problem in terms of whether the parolee's liberty is a "right" or a "privilege." By whatever name, the liberty is valuable and must be seen as within the protection of the Fourteenth Amendment. Its termination calls for some orderly process, however informal.[6]

The Supreme Court has since guaranteed the "orderly process" when it laid down guidelines establishing minimum standards of due process regarding parole revocation. In referring to these guidelines, the Court stated that

> they include (a) written notice of this claimed violations of parole; (b) disclosure to the parolee of evidence against him; (c) opportunity to be heard in person and to present witnesses and documentary evidence; (d) the right to confront and cross-examine adverse witnesses (unless the hearing officer specifically finds good cause for not allowing confrontation); (e) neutral and detached hearing body such as a traditional parole board, members of which need not be judicial officers or lawyers; and (f) a written statement by the fact finders as to the evidence relied on and reasons for revoking parole.[7]

Although these requirements refer to the actual revocation hearing, the court required substantially the same requirements at a preliminary hearing conducted at a time prior to the revocation hearing and shortly after arrest or detention. The court said that this preliminary hearing should be "conducted at or reasonably near the place of the alleged parole violation or arrest and as promptly as convenient after the arrest while information is fresh and sources are available... to determine whether there is probable cause or reasonable ground to believe that the arrested parolee has committed acts that would constitute a violation of parole conditions."[8] There is no doubt that the Supreme Court's ruling in reviewing *Morrissey v. Brewer* has enhanced the rights of a parolee, but it has also left several questions unanswered.

Revocation Rates

The rate of parole revocation is often used to measure the effectiveness of various parole programs. Prus and Stratton suggest that

> if one is to use revocation rates as a measure or program success, one should be highly conscious of the processes by which decisions to revoke parolees are made. While known infractions draw attention to the parolee and make his status as a parolee problematic, violations are subject to multiple interpretations and the seriousness of a given offense can be readily defined away. The decision to revoke a parole reflects the agent's personal orientations and his perception of self-accountability to the goals and personnel of the system in which he works. Revocation is not a structured response to parole violations; it is a socially influenced definition.[9]

It cannot be stressed too strongly that parole revocation rates are meaningful only when the reasons and procedures by which parole may be revoked are clearly understood.

DISCHARGE FROM PAROLE

discharge from parole
Discretionary decision that reasonable assurance exists that the parolee will continue to adjust in the community without supervision

In most jurisdictions, the parole officer may recommend the juvenile on parole status for **discharge from parole** at any time after the juvenile's release from the correctional institution. Release from parole is, however, conditional and is based on criteria similar to those used in determining release from the institution. Keeping in mind that the major goal of parole is the protection of society *through* the rehabilitation of the offender, it is paramount that there is a reasonable assurance that the parolee can continue to adjust satisfactorily in the community after the parole supervision is removed. In many states, the discharge of the juvenile from parole jurisdiction is reserved for the juvenile paroling authority or its agent. The juvenile's parole counselor is responsible for recommending discharge and for submitting this recommendation in writing to the paroling authority prior to the actual discharge of the parolee.

The decision to discharge a juvenile from parole can have as many potential pitfalls as the decision to place him or her on parole in the first place. For some youngsters on parole, survival in the community is possible because they can depend on their parole counselor. At least the officer is supposed to have some interest in their existence. When this crutch is removed, the parolee may regress in both behavior and attitude and may well end up back on the road to crime. Most jurisdictions are reluctant to discharge a juvenile from parole for at least one year after release from the institution. It is hoped that this is enough time for the competent and observant agent to recognize and work on the youth's long-range needs and to help him or her achieve independence from the juvenile justice system.

We state previously that juvenile aftercare is the often neglected component of the juvenile justice system. Similarly, post-aftercare services are the abandoned component. After discharged from parole, most juveniles are left to their own devices until they either become 18 years of age (and are considered adults) or commit crimes and are returned to the courts for yet another trip on the juvenile justice merry-go-round. This is too often a ride they must take because somewhere someone failed to prevent the circumstances leading to their original delinquent acts.

Research on post parole success rates is generally scant, even though there is a definite need for it. In the absence of solid data, juvenile justice officials continue to play youth and society against one another.

JUVENILE RECIDIVISM

Attention on juvenile recidivism rates during aftercare have been sparked by such concerns as the following:

- Escalating juvenile crime rates,
- Dramatic increases in the number of youth entering secure care,
- Spiraling institutional costs,
- The juvenile correctional system's demonstrated ineffectiveness in controlling or reducing delinquent behavior among aftercare populations, and[10]
- The increased use of juvenile incarceration has not demonstrated measurable reductions in juvenile arrests following the release of incarcerated offenders.[11]

Traditionally, juveniles have demonstrated high recidivism rates on parole (from 55 percent to 75 percent).[12] Similarly, a study of juveniles released from Wisconsin institutions between 1986 and 1990 indicates that 37 percent were reincarcerated within two years. On average, youths were in the community for only seven months between commitments.[13] Research on community supervision programs for juveniles has also yielded disappointing results. In her research review, MacKenzie is unable to reach definitive conclusions regarding the effectiveness of such programs.[14] In response to these problems, new models of supervision and treatment of juvenile aftercare have been developed.

The Intensive Aftercare Program (IAP Model)

IAP Model Program emphasizing a highly structured and intensive supervision with follow-up services in the community

Developed by David Altschuler and Troy L. Armstrong, the **IAP Model** addresses the documented failure of juvenile incarceration and aftercare by emphasizing the following:

1. Preparatory institutional services that can be reinforced in the community,
2. A highly structured transitional experience that bridges the institution and the community, and
3. The use of intensive supervision and follow-up services in the community.[15]

The IAP Model stresses juvenile case management in five components:

1. **Assessment, classification, and selection criteria.** High-risk youth are identified through the use of a validated risk-screening instrument.
2. **Individualized case planning that incorporates family and community perspectives.** Specific attention is given to youth problems in conjunction with families, peers, schools, and other social networks.
3. **A mix of intensive surveillance and services.** Staff must have small caseloads and provide services not only during the daytime and during the week but also during weekends and in the evenings.
4. **A balance of incentives and graduated consequences.** Violations are dealt with in proportion to their seriousness. In addition, good performance should be recognized within a graduated system of meaningful rewards.
5. **The creation of links with community resources and social networks.**[16]

The Office of Juvenile Justice and Delinquency Prevention has funded projects based on the IAP Model in four states (Colorado, New Jersey,

Nevada, and Virginia) that will be subject to intensive research by the National Council on Crime and Delinquency.

SUMMARY

In this chapter, the concepts of juvenile parole and juvenile aftercare are used interchangeably. Probation, which takes place before the institutionalization of a juvenile as a diversionary procedure, is separate from parole. Juvenile parole (aftercare) is used to bridge the gap back to the community after incarceration. The juvenile under the guidance of the juvenile parole officer is more likely to be a problem than the juvenile reporting to the juvenile probation officer. Parole for juveniles has a dual purpose: protection for the community and proper adjustment of the parolee.

Many attempts have been made to classify youths in correctional institutions as potentially good risks on parole. Here, *classification* refers to the prediction of behavior after release. Classification, if applied properly, contributes significantly in the assignment of parolees to the appropriate type of parole officer.[17] More effort must be expended in this area if juvenile parole is to be maximally effective.

The juvenile parole decision-making process is fragmented and varied throughout the states. Fragmentation is a major problem and one that must be addressed squarely in determining the kind of organizational structure for a juvenile paroling authority. Organizational muddle, combined with excessive rhetoric and little action, has tended to push juvenile parole into the same model as the adult systems. Whether this movement will prove useful or harmful remains to be seen.

KEY TERMS

aftercare

caseload size

conditions of parole

determinate sentence

discharge from parole

good time law

IAP Model

indeterminate sentence

juvenile parole

Morrissey v. Brewer

parole services

revocation of parole

DISCUSSION AND REVIEW QUESTIONS

1. Describe the difference between probation and parole.
2. How does the historical background of parole differ from that of probation?

3. List and discuss the major goals and three basic purposes of aftercare. How are these being realized?

4. Discuss the importance of the decision of the U.S. Supreme Court in *Morrissey v. Brewer.*

5. What factors should be considered for the successful release from an institution to parole status and for the discharge of a youth from parole? Are these considerations similar? Why or why not?

6. Explain how parole fits into the juvenile justice system and how it relates to the rest of the system.

7. Who decides when to parole and on what basis?

VIDEO PROFILES

The *Juvenile Probation and Parole 1* video profile in MyCrimeKit shows one juvenile's interaction with the Administrative Review Committee that will make the decision about parole. What is the role of the members of the Administrative Review Committee? Discuss Abel's response to some of the committee member's questions in terms of the Committee's initial release decision. Do you agree? Why/why not?

The *Juvenile Probation and Parole 2* video profile in MyCrimeKit shows Andy's interaction with the Administrative Review Committee. What are Andy's charges? Compare Andy's responses to the Committee with Abel's responses in the previous video. Do Andy's responses to the Committee align with the goals of the Committee as described by the Superintendent and as described by some of the committee members? Discuss.

MYCRIMEKIT

mycrimekit™   Go to MyCrimeKit.com to explore the following study tools and resources specific to this chapter:

- Practice Quiz: Test your knowledge with multiple-choice, true-false, fill-in-the-blank, and essay questions.

- Flashcards: 20 flashcards to test your knowledge of the chapter's key terms.

- Web Quest: review your state's Juvenile Justice Web site for information about parole/aftercare.

- Web Links: Check out sites related to the content presented in this chapter.

ENDNOTES

1. Harry E. Barnes and Negley K. Teeters, *New Horizons in Criminology,* 3d ed. (Englewood Cliffs, NJ: Prentice Hall, 1959), p. 568.

2. President's Commission on Law Enforcement and Administration of Justice, *Task Force Report: Corrections* (Washington, DC: U.S. Government Printing Office, 1967), p. 60.

3. Robert M. Carter and Leslie T. Wilkins, eds., *Probation, Parole, and Community Corrections* (New York: John Wiley, 1976), p. 212.

4. Ibid., p. 667.

5. *Morrissey v. Brewer,* 408 U.S., 471 (1972).

6. Ibid., p. 489.

7. Ibid.

8. Ibid., p. 486.

9. Robert Prus and John Stratton, "Parole Revocation Decision Making: Private Typings and Official Designations," *Federal Probation* (March 1976) 48.

10. Richard G. Wiebush, Betsie McNulty, and Thao Le, "Implementation of the Intensive Community-Based Aftercare Program," *OJJDP Juvenile Justice Bulletin* (July 2000), p. 1.

11. David M. Altschuler and Troy L. Armstrong, "Reintegrative Confinement and Intensive Aftercare," *Juvenile Justice Bulletin* (July 1999), http://www.ojjdp.ncjrs.org/bulletin/9907_3/reintegrate.html

12. Barry A. Krisberg, James Austin, and Paul Steele, *Unlocking Juvenile Corrections* (San Francisco: National Council on Crime and Delinquency, 1991).

13. N. Troia, *Correctional Institutional Recidivism among Youth Released from DYS Institutions, 1986 to 1990* (Madison, WI: Wisconsin Department of Health and Social Services, 1993).

14. Doris Layton MacKenzie, "Commentary: The Effectiveness of Aftercare Programs—Examining the Evidence," *Juvenile Justice Bulletin* (July 1999), http://www.ojjdp.ncjrs.org/bulletin/9907_3/comment.html

15. David M. Altschuler and Troy L. Armstrong, "Intensive Juvenile Aftercare as a Public Safety Approach," *Corrections Today,* Vol. 60 (1998), pp. 118–123.

16. Wiebush, McNulty, and Le, "Implementation," p. 2.

17. Ryan M. Quist and Dumiso G. M. Matshazi, "The Child and Adolescent Functional Assessment Scale (CAFAS): A Dynamic Predictor of Juvenile Recidivism," *Adolescence,* Vol. 35 (2000), pp. 181–192; Robin A. Lemmon and Sharon K. Calhoon, "Predicting Juvenile Recidivism Using the Indiana Department of Correction's Risk Assessment Instrument," *Juvenile and Family Court Journal,* Vol. 49 (1998), pp. 55–62.

JUVENILE VICTIMIZATION

As presented in Chapter 2, juvenile victimization patterns are somewhat unique to children's age, race, sex, place, and living situations. This means some juveniles are more likely to become victims of certain types of crime. However, these standard definitions of crime are not the only hazards that juveniles face.

The Developmental Victimization Survey

Conducted by the Crimes Against Children Center at the University of New Hampshire, the Developmental Victimization Survey (DVS) is a longitudinal study designed to assess a comprehensive range of childhood victimizations across gender, race, and developmental stage. Using the Juvenile Victimization Questionnaire, research from the DVS on a representative sample of 2,030 children ages 2–17 years determined the following victimization patterns in 20022:

- **Physical Assaults, Bullying, and Teasing**
  - More than one-half of the respondents (530/1,000) were the victims of assault in the past year. One in 10 was injured in the assault. The offender in these assaults was mostly likely either a family member or an acquaintance.
  - One-fifth of the youths were the victims of bullying.
  - One-fourth were the victims of teasing.
  - For juveniles 13–17 years of age, the rate of dating violence was 36/1,000.[3]

Juvenile Assault

- **Sexual Victimizations**
  - One in 12 of the respondents were the victims of a sexual assault in the past year; 22 in 1,000 were the victims of a completed or attempted rape.
  - Sexual victimization was most common among girls and disproportionately occurred among teenagers.[4]

- **Child Maltreatment**
  - This category includes emotional (name calling or denigration by an adult) and physical abuse as well as neglect. One in 7 respondents was the victim of child maltreatment.
  - Teenagers were the most likely to be physical abuse victims.
  - Neglect was fairly equal across all youth age groups.[5]

- **Property Victimization**
  - One-fourth of the children were property crime victims in the past year, including robbery (40/1,000), vandalism (96/1,000) and theft (140/1,000).[6]

- **Witnessed and Indirect Victimization**
  - This category included domestic violence, the physical abuse of a sibling, assault with (138/1,000) or without (209/1,000) a weapon, household theft (209/1,000), having someone close to them murdered (29/1,000), being near a riot or other civil disturbance where shooting and bombing was occurring (55/1,000), and being in a war zone.
  - Adults were the perpetrators in most of these events.[7]

- **Demographic Differences**
  - African American respondents had the highest rates of aggregated property victimization and were also most likely to witness crimes. They were also most likely to be victimized by flashing and to be the targets of emotional abuse.
  - Whites and Hispanics had higher rates of assaults without injury and by siblings.
  - Whites had the highest rate of bullying.
  - Hispanics suffered the greatest rates of sexual assault and harassment as well as family abduction.[8]

- **Multiple Victimizations**
  - 71 percent of the children and youth reported multiple victimizations in the past year. The mean number of separate and distinct victimization incidents was three.
  - Victims of any type of sexual offense were most likely to be victimized again (97%). In particular, they were likely to suffer an assault (82%) or to witness or experience indirect victimization (84%).[9]

These results present an alarming picture and "confirms the pervasive exposure of young people to violence, crime, maltreatment and other forms of victimization as a routine part of ordinary childhood in the United States."[10]

Some administrators operate on the "conventional wisdom" that the juvenile's own home, no matter how bad, is better than no home at all. However, too often a bad or abusive home environment has contributed to juvenile victimization; moreover, a bad or abusive home environment may have contributed to the very behavior of an offending juvenile that has resulted in involvement with juvenile justice in the first place. To return juvenile victims and/or offenders to such a home is analogous to patching a flat bicycle tire and then riding the bike over nail strips. Some parents are not physically, mentally, emotionally, or financially capable of providing their children with proper care and supervision. In such cases, the problem can often be resolved with professional treatment or case-work intervention. However, it may still be necessary to remove children from the home during rehabilitation, and a temporary placement may be the proper environment in which to carry this out.

GROUP HOMES

Group homes are a relatively recent development in the United States. There are those who contend that today's group homes, both private and public, are simply an extension of the halfway house concept. At their onset, in the early 1960s, group homes may indeed have been halfway houses. At the time, they were perceived as a way to ease the rehabilitated youth's reentry into the community. In fact, they could be viewed as a kind of halfway-out house. The group home was responsible primarily for providing additional direction and support to the child, support needed to make the final adjustment to community living.

At first, group homes placed emphasis on making a youth self-sufficient, self-responsible, and self-reliant. To ensure the likelihood of success, institutions were often discouraged from referring to group homes boys or girls who had serious behavioral problems. This practice tended to rule out such offenders as the repeat automobile thief, the sexually deviant offender, or those who might commit extreme acts of violence to themselves or others.

In short, early group homes looked after the "low-risk" youth who could be eased into the community from the institution with the minimum amount of treatment or trouble. It was rare for the group homes to accept a youth who had not gone through the institutional "softening up" process.

Today, those responsible for group home operations shy away from the term **halfway house**. It is believed that this label connotes imperma-nence, both to those who find themselves as residents and those on the

---

mycrimekit

Video Profile: Residential Facility Tour

group homes Alternative placement for juveniles as a means of easing the youth's reentry to the community

halfway house One type of group home; the term *halfway* has a negative connotation, but the focus remains on easing delinquent reentry outside. In fact, for many residents the state group home has become a more permanent home than they have ever known. In this situation, the name "halfway" becomes disturbing to those who may be experiencing their first feeling of belonging.

Group homes exist throughout the country in one form or another. Most states sign contracts with private group homes and do not run the homes directly. A few states run, own, and operate the homes themselves. In the 1970s, group homes broke out of the image of "transition warehouses" of the 1960s. In the 1980s, many provided extensive treatment programs. These new group homes are willing to work with youths from institutions, those rejected by institutions, and those assigned directly from a centralized diagnostic center. Their main purpose is the same—to ease the youth's re-entry to society—but they also provide group care, counseling, and/or treatment for whatever period seems to be appropriate.

Purpose of the Group Home

The group home is generally a small residence for six to fifteen youths. It is meant to be a place where adequate peer relationships can be formed but affectional ties to and demands from adults are kept at a minimum. Group homes impose needed external controls, but youths are not required to accept "substitute parents," as is the case in the foster home setting. Acceptance of a dependent role can be particularly difficult for the youth who, in his or her normal course of maturing, is in the process of achieving emotional independence from parental figures. Because in most cases those considered for group home placement are children

Group Homes Promote Socialization Through Small-Group Interaction

between ages 13 and 18 years, group homes can promote the socialization process through small-group interaction, interaction that does not involve a father or mother figure.

The group home, which was introduced in 1916, offers interaction in small groups in which confidence in and conflicts with a limited number of people provide the requisite emotional support and opportunities for growth. The group home concept is the result of the findings of interrelated studies conducted in various settings in which socialization takes place (i.e., the family, community treatment centers, and institutions) and of theoretical insight into what makes a person develop into a mature member of society (i.e., the normal development process).[11]

There are seven characteristics generally accepted as common to group homes:

- They are residential,
- They provide group care,
- They contain between six and fifteen residents,
- They are community based,
- They provide social services,
- They have a full-time staff, and
- They serve youths who are capable of living in the community but who need, for a variety of reasons, an alternative to other natural homes.

The following is a workable definition of a group home from 1973, still valid today:

A group home is a small, community-based residential facility for a group of youths for whom a community-living situation is desirable, but who need an alternative to their natural homes. A full-time staff supervises the youth's activities and is responsible for coordinating the provision of social services, whether these services come from staff members themselves or from the community.[12]

Group homes are not a family enterprise. Professional and custodial staffs are employed to run group homes (state or private) on a salaried basis. Unlike foster homes or adoptions, a "normal" or "normative" family atmosphere does not generally exist in a group home. Instead, members often receive community services in a fragmented or piecemeal way from several unrelated agencies. With this kind of setup, the youth is not overburdened with outside involvement, involvement that is not only unrelated but also sometimes not well coordinated and in which victimization of the juvenile clients can be a problem.[13]

School Facilities and Education

School facilities in the larger, more institutionalized group homes may be on the grounds of the home. The teaching staff is drawn from the group home staff. However, children in group homes often attend public schools in the community in which the home is located. Successfully integrating youths from group homes into the public schools depends partly on the cooperation and coordination efforts of group home staff, children, the public schools, and the community. Through their efforts, children with problems can be assimilated smoothly into schools designed to serve the average child.

Group homes with sufficient funds can hire a community intervention specialist, whose task it is to facilitate the transition of the group home children into local community activities such as schooling. Many states have Title I teachers who conduct classes for group home children at either the local public school or, in situations that warrant it, the individual group home. Classrooms may be set aside for Title I teachers to use as they require them. Group home youth can be given credit for work completed at school or carried out at the group home level, with credit being granted by the local school officials in coordination with Title I teachers. Every school-age child in a group home should receive a fundamental and meaningful education, whatever his or her point of entry into the program, tested ability, behavioral difficulties, and motivation.

Youths who enter group homes often come from an institutional educational program, where positive reinforcement methods are likely to be used. Positive reinforcement provides rewards, such as privileges and good grades, for exhibiting desired behavior. When youths from this environment are placed into a public school in the community near the group home, they suffer from a form of educational shock. The more stringent demands of the public school system often cause these youths to become discouraged, and their motivation wanes. Past experience has shown that some of these youths create disciplinary problems in the classroom, problems that result in their being removed from school. Sometimes dismissal is what they wanted in the first place.

Title I teachers can also act as tutors, guidance counselors, and overall educational coordinators for group home residents. In these capacities they can ease the overall educational shock syndrome experienced by many youths and help them to solve motivational shortcomings and ease tensions leading to disruptive behavior in the classroom. Relieved of this responsibility, the public school classroom teacher has more time to teach, time that might otherwise be wasted in overcoming administrative and/or behavioral problems.

Title I teachers, or their facsimiles, ensure that the educational needs of the group home youth are met in a meaningful and compatible way, for not only the individual child but the community as well. If neither is available, it becomes crucial that the group home either have its own internal educational system or an excellent working relationship with the local public school.

Group Home Admissions

In recent years, group homes have become increasingly popular within the juvenile justice system. In most states, a youth must be under court order or jurisdiction on entering a group home. It is not uncommon for youths entering group homes do so on a *parole status*. This means that if they do something wrong, their parole could be revoked and they might be returned to the institution or incur other disciplinary action. To avoid red tape and waste of staff time normally involved in a parole revocation, some states have changed the status of state group home youth from parole status to continued "institutional" status. Instead of revoking a youth's parole, the juvenile can simply be transferred back to the institution.

Licensing

Most states have the authority to license group homes as a specific category of childcare services. Licensing requirements also provide a description of the children and young expectant mothers that the group home serves. They are those

- who need foster care but who cannot ordinarily adjust to the close personal relationships normally required by a foster family home;
- who leave an institutional setting for a transitional period of care prior to returning to their own home or prior to achieving independence (e.g., job, armed services, college);
- who need emergency placement pending more permanent planning or during temporary disruption of a current placement; or
- who are emotionally disturbed or physically or mentally handicapped, or whose behavior is so bizarre as to be unacceptable to most foster parents; provided that the supervising agency, through its own program or by the marshaling of appropriate community resources, can provide the necessary specialized services that may be required by the group which the facility serves.[14]

Many states stipulate that group home operators must become licensed by the state. Licensing of operators ensures that professional standards are applied to group homes to prevent abuse and the existence of group homes of poor quality. There are some precedents that offer guidance to those concerned with the licensing of group home operators. Each state, for example, has a Nursing Home Administrator's License Board. This board interviews prospective operators, gives them a written test regarding their abilities as nursing home operators, and generally evaluates their capabilities, training, and experience. The problem with developing a written test for group home operators, however, is that there is no agreement among those in the field on a common body of knowledge that all group home operators require. This may reflect the fact that there has been no sufficient definition of the group home's role and responsibilities.

Program Services

The adequate provision of program services to juveniles is perhaps the single most important issue facing group homes today. These program services include educational counseling, tutoring, job placement, individual counseling, and life skills counseling. They are essential to the group home's goal of successfully reintegrating juveniles into the community. Those in the group home field should have a common understanding of what services group homes should offer and how those services fit into existing community resources.

The provision of services needed to treat juveniles adequately instead of "warehousing" them has emerged as a genuine concern of group home professionals in recent years. Problems with the provision of needed services to group home youths may arise if such factors as (1) whether youths with varying needs and problems can be accommodated successfully within the same group home setting and (2) whether youths in different age groups are compatible and able to be treated together are not taken into consideration.

Program evaluation is essential to the provision of program services and any treatment that may result. Proper evaluation can answer such questions as these: (1) What is the best way of ensuring that a group home is actually providing high-quality services as efficiently and effectively as possible? and (2) Which client assignments, staffing patterns, and interfacing with outside service agencies are in the best interests of the juveniles being served? The proper evaluation of group home services will move group homes a major step forward in their realization of their full potential as a childcare resource.

Group Home Referrals

What a group home program evolves into may be a far cry from what that program was actually intended to do. One reason for this is that inappropriate referrals are frequently made, referrals that often redefine the role and purpose of the group home and thus endanger its survival.

Staffing of Group Homes

The program of rehabilitation at a group home is determined by the kinds of residents in that home and their particular needs. It is the staff's function to see to it that the program meets those needs and that there are sufficient personnel resources to support it. In general, there is no single staffing pattern that will fit the needs of all group homes.

Group home staff and supplementary volunteers should be suited for the job, and they should be fully aware of and trained for the demands of the particular home's program. Although not a prerequisite for group home house parents, a college degree is an asset because of the semiprofessional aspects of the job.

Personal characteristics and attitudes such as sincerity, maturity, concern, patience, and an empathy with youth are extremely important attributes for group home house parents. However, group home administrators often find it difficult to recruit good house parents because of the low salary levels. Few people with the desired character traits of good group home house parents can afford to take the job.

In addition to the personal characteristics mentioned, the operators of group homes should have administrative skills and the ability to act as liaison between the home and the community. Group home operators may find that they are required to provide in-service training for new staff. Finally, if the group home claims to provide a therapeutic service for its youth, then at least one person on the staff should have the credentials to act as a counselor.

Future of Group Homes

The following recommendations for future action in the group home field were made in 1973 by the state of Washington. These suggestions are still valid goals for group home operations:

- As a prerequisite for licensing, each group home should provide a comprehensive description, in writing, of its proposed service delivery plan.
- Copies of all new or updated description packages should be made available to all potential child-placing agencies and/or people. Such descriptions can often provide useful knowledge for the determination of an appropriate placement and can save the referral agency and the child time and trouble.
- To involve the community and to limit responsibilities for group home operations to a few people, each group home should be required to appoint a board of directors.
- To facilitate the functions listed, no member of the board of directors should be in a position to benefit financially from the group home's operation.
- Each group home should be evaluated on the basis of the development of a sound methodology.

- The evaluation of the group home should take place at least every six months.

- State-sponsored training should be provided for all group home staff personnel. Diversification in programs offered by group homes is beneficial to both the juveniles being served and the community.

- As a means of evaluating success rates and tracking the post-placement progress of former group home residents, those former residents should be subjects of appropriate follow-up studies.

- Coordination of the development of all group home programs, including future programs, should be strongly considered. Such a centralized group home planning function is essential to the provision of high-quality services that appropriately meet the needs of juveniles placed in a group home setting.[15]

Because of their general nature, the group home operators of other states could adopt these recommendations readily.

With regard to the role of the group home in the juvenile justice system of any particular state, the state must define that role. Of special importance is the relationship between institutions and group homes. When the purpose of the group home is defined clearly and programs are funded and begun, only then can the group home programs realize their full potential as community-based juvenile corrections alternatives.

FOSTER CARE

The concept of *parens patriae* contains the doctrine that society shall have the ultimate parental responsibility for all children in the community. Thus, when a youth cannot or will not remain at home, society must provide a substitute living arrangement. One such alternative is foster care. **Foster care** is a generic term applied to any kind of full-time substitute care for children outside their own homes by persons other than their parents. Although this generic term could also be used to describe institutional care, group home care, adoptive care, and so forth, here it will mean specifically foster home care.

A foster home, unlike the group home, offers services to the youth who still has fairly strong dependency needs, rather than to the young person who is struggling to be free of adult control.

A *foster home* is a family paid by the state or local government to board a neglected, abused, or delinquent child. If the court believes that the child does not need the controls of a correctional institution but is not yet ready for the move to independence offered in a group home, the child will most likely be placed in a foster home. In 1933, a total of 47.2 percent of the dependent, neglected, and emotionally disturbed

foster care Any kind of full-time substitute care for children outside their own home by people other than their parents

children needing substitute care were placed in foster family homes, and the remaining 52.8 percent were institutionalized.[16] The trend in the past six decades has been away from institutional care to foster care.

Background of Foster Care Homes

The feudal practice of *indenture,* in which parents contracted to place their child with a master craftsperson to learn a trade, is the forerunner of foster home care. In return for teaching the child a trade, the craftsperson had his or her services for a given length of time. Although the feudal system vanished, the practice of indenturing youth remained in the form of private and public placements of dependent or destitute children. Delinquent children were also indentured. From 1853 to 1879, the Children's Aid Society of New York placed 48,000 children in homes in Southern and Western states. These placements were unpaid; that is, the family agreed to feed, house, clothe, and educate the child at its own expense. In 1866, Massachusetts started placing children who were charged with delinquent acts with families who were paid board.[17] The Massachusetts plan was the first systematic attempt at providing foster home care for delinquent youths.

With the rise of the juvenile court movement in 1899 and the consequent effort to remove the stigma of delinquency, the use of foster home care emerged as a preferred alternative to correctional placements. In Boston and Buffalo in the 1930s, foster homes were used to provide care for youths who needed secure custody. Foster parents were guaranteed a flat sum with an additional per capita rate for each child in residence.

The use of foster care homes has shown a steady growth in the second half of the twentieth century. But in the 1960s, concern was voiced about the effectiveness of foster care programs. During that period, professionals were becoming aware that the supply of foster homes was limited, that the needs of children coming into care were changing, and that the sheer number of youths in need of service was growing at an alarming rate.

Foster family care also came under attack in the 1970s as widespread reports of foster parent child abuse were publicized. Because of these reports, the National Council of Juvenile and Family Court judges recommended a federal law requiring agencies receiving federal foster care funds to make plans for each child's removal, if possible, from foster care. In a similar stand, the staff of the National Commission for Children in Need of Parents has urged mandatory reviews, by a court or other outside authority, of every agency's plans for every child each sixty days. However, despite these shortcomings, foster care continues today to be the most frequently used alternative home placement for children of all ages.

The Need for Foster Care

Specific reasons why foster care may be needed can be grouped into two main categories: (1) *parent*-related problems and (2) *child*-related problems.

The most frequent **parent-related problems** are as follows:

parent-related problems
Specific reasons associated with the parents (e.g., parental rejection, child abuse) that might place a child in foster care

- Parental inadequacy,
- Parental rejection,
- Mental illness,
- Child abuse,
- Child neglect,
- Abandonment,
- Addiction to drugs,
- Alcoholism,
- Imprisonment, and
- Inability to cope.

The most frequently observed **child-related problems** are as follows:

child-related problems Specific reasons associated with children (e.g., mental handicap, delinquent behavior) that might place a child in foster care

- Parent-child conflict,
- Delinquent behavior,
- Incorrigibility,
- Emotional disturbance,
- Physical handicap,
- Mental handicap,
- Child–sibling conflict, and
- Sociopathic behavior.

If one or more of these problems does exist, the following questions then arise: What type of child can be expected to benefit from an experience in a foster care home? What type of child would not be suitable for foster care placement? Although these questions are difficult to answer, experience and common sense do offer some basic clues for the right course of action.[18]

Separation of a child from its parents can become necessary for a wide range of reasons according to family problem. Some of these are as follows:

- The physical condition of the mother,
- Mental illness of the mother,
- Emotional problems of the children,
- Severe neglect or abuse, and
- Family problems.

Providing adequate income, medical care, housing, or child supervision could avert many separations. However, a residual group seems to be prone to separation because of severe psychological problems.

If there were a profile of the "average" child in foster care, it would indicate that most children entering foster home care come from broken homes with either one or both parents absent. The children are usually from lower-class, chronically deprived families that are living a crisis-oriented existence. The principal source of referrals for the children coming into foster care is their parents, followed by social service agencies, the courts, and the police. The average length of stay for children in foster family care is less than one year. However, many children placed in foster family care remain for three years or more.

The Decision to Remove

The removal of children from their home and their subsequent placement in foster family care should occur only as a last resort, when such intrusive means of intervention cannot be avoided. Although removal may be the only practical answer for some children, evidence from several states indicates that such removals result all too frequently in inadequate foster care placements. In essence, the social system ends up substituting poor care and neglect by the parents for poor care and neglect by the state.

Video Profile: Child Abuse

The removal of endangered children from the home is authorized in almost all states when the court determines that such action is in the best interests of the child. The burden of proof should be on the court and/or the intervening agency to demonstrate the actual need for the removal of a child. Cases involving nonaccidental physical harm to the child should be determined by a preponderance of evidence. All other cases should be determined by clear and convincing evidence. In any event, the court should determine that the available foster home placement would not endanger the child or children.

Selecting the Foster Home

After the decision to separate the child (or children) from the parents is made and all the pertinent placement information is gathered, the process of choosing a home to meet the child's specific needs should begin. The range of homes available to the child-placing agency home realistically determines the criteria for an appropriate, whether private or public. In the past, the majority of foster homes were located in low-income urban areas. The need to supplement income with the money received for taking in a foster child has often been criticized in cases in which it seems the sole reason a family will take a foster child in the first place. In these cases, the benefit to the child being placed should be questioned. In recent years, social agencies have been focusing their home-finding efforts in higher-income suburban areas.

Assuming that delinquents from various ethnic backgrounds have a better chance of adjusting in a familiar environment, efforts have also been made of late to place minority children in ethnically appropriate homes. A good foster home, regardless of location, generally has the following characteristics:

- The foster father has a high degree of participation in the minor's care;
- The foster parents accept the natural parents as significant persons in the minor's life;
- The foster family is well accepted in the neighborhood and the community;
- The foster parents' own children seem secure and well adjusted;
- Relationships within the family are characterized by mutual respect;
- The foster parents help the minor understand that he or she can be loved;
- The foster parents give affection without expecting immediate returns; and
- The foster family has a clear set of "ground rules" for behavior, but a teenager's need for privacy and group activities is recognized.[19]

Foster Family Care: A Changing Image

Foster family care has recently come under severe criticism by experts in the field of childcare. These professionals are now somewhat more reluctant to favor foster family care as an alternative placement service than they once were. Foster family care has been used so widely (nobody keeps an accurate count) that it has become looked on as the panacea for the ills of delinquent, dependent, incorrigible, and neglected and/or abused youngsters. Under the current system that allows these placements, children spend their formative years (onset of most placements is 5 years of age) in a state of "nonidentity," being shifted from one foster home to the next. They grow up without roots, uncertain of their futures, and with callous outlooks on life. Authorities in the field say that they will reach adulthoods filled with more welfare, unemployment, and crime than will their non–foster care counterparts.

Assuming this to be true, one could make the further assumption that children being placed in foster family care come from families in which parents will not or cannot respond to the array of services being offered, services such as day care, homemaker help, protective services, and appropriate financial and medical care, all of which may make it possible for the child or children to remain in their own homes as opposed to being added to the ranks of foster care cases. Many youths, therefore, are coming from homes that are beyond rehabilitation. Consequently, the temporary nature of foster care has been greatly changed. More youths are apt to spend all their minority years in foster families. The longer a child remains in foster care, the more likely he or she is to remain there. One solution to this problem is to ensure that maximum efforts at providing these needed services are made early in the case history.

This solution is aimed at the top of the foster care funnel—the own home–to–foster home route. If, however, foster care placement cannot be avoided, the next solution is aimed at the middle of the funnel. This is where the juveniles remain captive due to incredible amounts of bureaucratic bungling and red tape. The middle of the foster care funnel must be unclogged to allow for free flow out the other end, so that juveniles can either go back to their own homes or go into permanent adoptive placements. Unfortunately, children are kept in foster care by outmoded laws and the self-preservation instincts of the social service industry, an industry that would rapidly move away from status quo if foster children were put into permanent homes. This situation could possibly be remedied by adopting the provisions of the Federal Adoption Assistance and Child Welfare Act of 1980. It was designed to provide families with preplacement services to prevent the need for children to enter the foster care system, provide proper care for children who are in the system, and move children through the system and back into home or adoption as quickly as possible.[20]

Focusing on the Problem

Traditional emphasis in foster care has been on the children. Focus must now be centered on the failures of our social and economic systems, which lead to the family dysfunctions that can result in the need for foster care.

A child research project carried out at the Columbia University School of Social Work clearly pinpointed where changes should take place:

> Knowledge about the kinds of family situations that lead children to enter foster care has implications for both practice and policy. It would, of course, be an oversimplification to consider all the families of children in placement as constituting a homogeneous group. But with the exception of some families of emotionally disturbed children, there are many characteristics common to this parent population. These common areas include pervasive poverty, high incidence of minority group membership, frequent receipt of public assistance, one-parent families, and physical and mental illness.
>
> It is apparent that the social service system as presently structured does not have the capability to provide basic preventive services to strengthen family life. A majority of the families in the study were

Positive Family Relationships Improve a Juvenile's Success in the System

known to social agencies before the placement crisis. Yet these agency resources did not prevent the movement of these children into foster care. The child welfare system is forced to operate like firemen arriving after the house was burned.... Fulfillment of its service task is hampered by the extent of damage done prior to agency intervention. Disadvantaged circumstances, extreme pathology, and inadequate parenting are common precursors of placement, thus handicapping the most sincere professional efforts to give such children a chance before they reach adulthood.[21]

The characteristics that are common to the parent population in this study are also those often linked with the causes of crime and delinquency. It seems clear that programs that would be effective in curbing the movement of children into foster care could prove useful in preventing delinquency. Basic preventive services to strengthen family life would, therefore, serve the juvenile justice system as a whole, including the families of children who must enter foster care.[22]

There are no complete solutions to the child-rearing dilemma. "In any society there will always be ... children in need of substitute parenting. But enlightened social policies designed to improve living conditions of the urban poor could effect significant reductions in the number of children entering care."[23]

Until such time as social and/or economic resources are made available to those who must now rely on foster care, foster home placement as an alternative to institutionalization will remain ever present within the juvenile justice system. As such, it is incumbent upon the power structure to make necessary improvements in the foster care system.

ADOPTION

adoption The social and legal process for becoming a parent

The third and final alternative to institutionalization to be discussed in this chapter is adoption. "**Adoption** is the social and legal process of becoming a parent. After adoption, parents and children have essentially the same reciprocal rights and responsibilities as if they were biologically related."[24] The problems that face natural parents and children are much the same, therefore, as those facing adoptive parents and adopted children. This is true in all aspects of family life, including those that could bring the children and parents in contact with the juvenile justice system. Children from group homes or foster homes may end up being adopted, and adopted children may end up being placed in a group or foster home.

Historical Background

To acquire heirs to their thrones, the ancient Assyrians, Egyptians, Babylonians, Greeks, and Romans instituted the practice of adopting children. Actually, adoption can be traced to the beginning of recorded history. The adoption of Moses by Pharaoh's daughter and Esther by Mordecai are both recorded in the Bible. The ancient Chinese considered ancestor worship so significant that they established the custom of allowing a childless male to claim the first-born son of his younger brother. More than 4,000 years ago, the Babylonians, in the code of Hammurabi, emphasized the importance of perpetuation of the family in the following section of their code:

> If a man take a child in his name, adopt him as a son, this grownup son may not be demanded back.[25]

Primitive tribes were known to have used the practice of adoption to settle quarrels with one another. One tribe would adopt a child, usually a male, belonging to a member of high status in another tribe.

Modern adoption law has its beginnings in the Roman Empire, where adoption became very popular for both social and religious reasons. The Roman father had total authority over his children and descendants, including the power of life and death. This dominance had a crucial effect on the development of adoption; it meant that the adoptive father had complete control over his adopted children. All previous family ties—biological, legal, religious, and economic—were severed. When an adoption was formalized, there was no possibility of it being reversed.

The adoption of children was practiced in European countries during the Middle Ages. However, it was unknown to the common law of England, from which much of American law is derived. The emphasis on blood lineage was the major reason English common law lacked regulations regarding the adoptive process. Feudal tradition was such that only a biological male child born during wedlock could inherit his parents' rights and property. A child born out of wedlock or one who was adopted was not a legal heir.

That is not to say the English were not concerned with the plight of homeless, parentless children. They were, but until the Adoption of Children Act of 1926, they chose means other than adoption to meet those needs. Apprenticeship and indentured servitude were two methods in common use, and when the English founded colonies overseas, these practices went with them. In the seventeenth century, a vast number of destitute English children became apprenticed as child laborers in Virginia, Massachusetts Bay, and other colonies. "The apprenticing of poor children to the Virginia Company began as early as 1620.... A record of 1627 reads: 'There are many ships going to Virginia and with them 1400 to 1500 children which they have gathered up in diverse places.'"[26]

During the eighteenth and nineteenth centuries in the United States, the apprenticeship system was still the preferred method of taking care of homeless children. No governmental or legal sanction existed for adoption. Blood relatives began taking complete responsibility for their family's orphaned or dependent children. Soon it became a common practice for them to specify in their wills the relative with whom the orphaned child should live. Mark Twain's Tom Sawyer illustrates this practice: An aunt raised Tom after his own parents died.

Apprenticing of children began to die out during the rapid industrialization of the United States in the mid-1800s. Machines replaced apprentice tradespeople and craftspeople. Child welfare agencies were formed, agencies that attempted to place needy children in institutions or in foster and adoptive homes.

Opponents of adoption often criticized the placement of homeless children in private homes. Responses to such criticism, however, were often overzealous and lent a decidedly paternalistic air to the subject. Unfortunately, the paternalistic attitude continues today. This attitude is well illustrated by the following quote from the founder of the New York Children's Aid Society:

> It is feared that these children would corrupt the morals of the families to which they are sent.... We must remind such persons [the critics of adoption] of the wonderful capacity for improvement in children's natures under new circumstances; and we assert boldly, that a poor child taken in thus by the hand of Christian charity, and placed in a new world of love and of religion, is *more likely to be tempted to good,* than to tempt others to evil.[27] [emphasis in original]

Early adoption laws were considered private laws—that is, laws made available only to those select persons to whom knowledge of a specific child to be adopted was made available. Members of the general public as a rule were uninformed of the adoption laws or of how they themselves could adopt a child. It was thought that only a member of the elite society could be entrusted with the duty of converting a poor, ignorant little child into a God-fearing member of decent society. The very notion that others less fortunate than themselves could be good, loving parents to adopted children probably never even entered the minds of the lawmakers of the day or those for whom the laws were made.

Adoption Today: Why and Who

In Western society, a childless family has generally been thought to be an incomplete family. Consequently, the inability to conceive or bear children has been one of the primary reasons that people adopt. A new sense of so-cial responsibility and a growing concern and awareness about overpopula-tion is leading many who are already natural parents to adopt children in need of parents. They are inclined to believe that it is better to adopt a child who is already here than to have a new child and add to the popula-tion of the world.

Adoption is open today for children of any age, not only infants. Furthermore, more attention is being paid to children who traditionally were difficult to place, such as older children; siblings; mentally, emotion-ally, or physically handicapped children; and children of a minority or mixed racial background.

In the United States, adoption statutes vary from state to state. In general, however, any unmarried adult, single parent, or married couple in which both are adults may file for the adoption of a child. If either of the prospective parents is a minor, the parties may jointly adopt the other spouse's child. In many states, anyone who is a resident of that state is allowed to adopt. Other states require that the adopting parents be a specific number of years older than the person to be adopted.

Rights and Responsibilities in Adoption

Every child has the right to have his or her own parents, and no child should be unnecessarily deprived of this right. A child has a right to grow up in a reasonably wholesome family setting that should offer affection, security, and the desire to see that the child develops in the best manner possible by providing all the necessities of childhood, including adequate medical care. As for responsibility, the child is obligated to obey the adoptive parents and perform any other duties that would be expected of a child by his or her natural parents.

> Natural parents of children who may be adoptable have rights, too. In our culture and under our law, the natural parents or, if they are not married to each other, the mother, have the right to custody and control of children born to them. They also have the responsibility for their support, care, and upbringing. This right of the parents must be exercised for the child's benefit, and if not, must yield to the child's interest and welfare. A parent may not be deprived of his rights nor divest himself of his responsibility for the care of a child except through process of law with full protection of the child.[28]

Natural parents also have the right to have counseling in arriving at a decision of whether to give up their child for adoption, and they must have a full understanding of their rights and the consequences of their decision, especially of the irreversibility of such a decision after the adoption is made final in court.

Problems in Adoption

In an adoption placement, several problems can slow or hinder its success. Some of these follow:

- **Adoptions arranged primarily for the convenience of the natural parents, to meet the need of the adoptive parents, or for the profit of the intermediary parties.** In all such arrangements the welfare of the child is a secondary objective, if it is an objective at all.

- **Delay in placement.** Loss of time in making permanent, adequate placement for an infant endangers his or her opportunity for healthy development and deprives his or her adoptive parents of their share of an interesting and significant period of his life.

- **Multiple home placements.** When a child is subjected to multiple placements, whether by plan or default, his emotional development is jeopardized.

- **Placement in a home that ultimately proves incapable of providing the wholesome atmosphere considered to be the child's right.** A poor emotional environment is destructive to the child's development. Competent casework with the child's prospective parents prior to placement reduces the incidence of the abuse represented by gross misplacement.

- **Failure to resolve problems of the natural parents.** The lack of able counsel at the proper time contributes to the persistence of unresolved conflicts in the parents that may affect their lives for a long time. Such trauma most often occurs when the decision to relinquish a child is made without a careful exploration of alternatives. Difficulties can be minimized by competent counseling.[29]

- **Unnecessary social or economic poverty, including a lack of medical care for the unmarried mother and her child.** Well-developed social services for unmarried mothers exist in many metropolitan areas and offer help that prevents impoverishment and degradation through misfortune.

- **Failure to provide and interpret significant medical information, including behavioral, emotional, and developmental needs, to prospective adoptive parents.** This failure may put both child and parents at a disadvantage. It is important when counseling families to interpret and communicate the implications of medical information for the future life and development of the child.[30]

If it is decided that the adoption of a child is a desirable and acceptable alternative to institutionalization, whether to prevent placement in an institution or as a postinstitutional placement, the problems noted here must be resolved for that placement to work.

Because a large number of children in our juvenile delinquent or dependent populations come from broken homes, homes with both parents missing, abusive or neglecting homes, and no homes at all, the goal of matching a child with a family that can provide a permanent home, love, and proper care can be beneficial in many ways. Fulfilling this goal could lead to a significant reduction in the number of children who are out on the streets, committing delinquent acts, or wandering aimlessly through life with no hope for a secure future and who have a good chance of coming in contact with the juvenile justice system.

Follow-up studies of adopted children tend to indicate that 70 percent to 80 percent of adoptions are successful. A stable and secure home environment has consistently been shown to be a major factor in forming a child's ego, personality, and social competence. It has also been shown that such an environment is best provided by the parent–child relationships and role exchanges within the traditional family setting. Unfortunately, many children in the United States are denied the love and security of a family of their own, and as a result, thousands are forced to spend their entire childhoods in foster homes and/or institutions. As cited earlier in this section, statistics show that there are children to be adopted (the supply). And, partly because of lower birth rates and the increased use of abortions in the 1980s, there is also the demand. Demand has even jumped from once highly coveted "white infants" to now include older, problem, and handicapped children who previously were almost always consigned to foster care.

If there is both supply and demand and there are still far too many available children remaining unadopted, then there is a problem with the system. Critics of the system tend to pin this blame on two major types of legislation that seem to be fairly consistent nationwide. The first set of laws tends to preserve the rights of the biological parents and thus prevent the adoption of their children. This is the case even though these children are often the victims of past beatings and other abuses that were the cause for their removal from their parents' home in the first place. This also applies in cases in which the biological parents have made no attempt to see their children in several years.

The other set of laws centers on financial aid made available to people who take in foster children. This aid is taken away from these people as soon as or shortly after the foster children are adopted. For some foster parents, this can mean losing more than $200 per month in expense allowance per child, and this cutoff of aid can keep those foster parents who have the desire to adopt their foster children from doing so. Even if they could survive the removal of the expense allowance, they probably could not afford to keep up the costly medical, dental, and mental health care that these children typically need; the government in the past has paid for such care only for children under foster care. The cutoff of the aid affects the helping professionals as well and creates a vast conflict of interests among them. It is estimated that more than one-half of the cost per year paid by taxpayers to support foster care is allocated for administrative salaries. Thus, by encouraging adoptions, social service workers and agencies would be putting themselves out of business. And although "working one's self out of a job" may be a noble concept, it is seldom seen in practice.

Effects of Early Family/Parent Training on Delinquency

One meta-analysis has documented the effectiveness of this early intervention method. Here, parent education (home visitation programs to improve health and parenting skills) and parent management programs (basically how to raise children effectively) were the focus of research.

In all, 55 studies of such programs passed the researchers' scientific criteria for inclusion (i.e., studies that featured a randomized, controlled experimental design). The dominant feature of these parent training programs was to strengthen the parents' ability to monitor and discipline the behavior of the child to promote parental involvement in the child's school experience. The basic aim was to teach parents when to reward desired behaviors and when to sanction misbehavior in the most appropriate and effective manner.

In summary, it was determined that early family/parent training had an effect on both juvenile delinquency and later adult crime, including the following:[31]

- Fewer instances of running away;
- Fewer arrests, convictions and probation violations;
- Fewer smoked cigarettes per day;
- Fewer days having consumed alcohol;
- Fewer behavioral problems related to the use of alcohol and other drugs at age 15 years;
- Lower rates of juvenile and violent arrests at age 18 years; and
- Lower prevalence of arrests for violent, property, drug and other crimes up to age 27 years and also up to age 40 years.

These findings document the effectiveness of these early intervention programs. They can provide the tools for proper child rearing and thus prevent future problem behaviors that can reduce future crime and delinquency.

SUMMARY

In this chapter we discuss juvenile victimization and three of the more common alternatives to institutionalization of children. Under ideal conditions, any of these alternatives may be the right one for a child, depending on his or her needs and the circumstances of the individual case. Group home living has been utilized traditionally as a placement for children who have already been in contact with the juvenile system and for whom an alternative to home living is generally mandated.

Ideally, the duration of foster care placement should be as short as possible. It is a temporary solution to the problems of a dysfunctional home, whether the dysfunction is parent or child related. Foster care is often used as an interim placement. Good foster homes may enable some youths to remain outside the institutional experience altogether. For others, it may speed their release by offering them someplace to go.

For the child who should be removed from the influence of adults in parental authority roles, the group home is often a better solution than foster care. Foster care is intended mainly for the child who needs the guidance and care of his or her parents but who cannot get that care from the present home situation.

Because it can provide a permanent, loving, caring home that offers the child a substitute family, adoption is actually more of a preventive measure than it is an alternative to institutionalization. By providing such a home to children who may otherwise have none—children who could end up drifting from one foster home to another—adoption helps prevent these children from being exposed to environmental conditions, lifestyles, and experiences that often lead to crime or incorrigibility.

The adopted child can develop a permanent sense of belonging and security about where he or she will be from day to day. The foster child, however, is not quite as fortunate. For example, it is not uncommon to remove a child who has problems from a foster home when these problems appear to be settled and signs of progress are evident. The child then finds him- or herself back in his or her own home, where the problems often occur all over again. If this experience is repeated often enough, the child will soon learn that to succeed in a foster placement is a disadvantage. Such frustrating experiences for an already troubled young mind can only jeopardize the chances of the child's having a healthy outlook about him- or herself and society.

Whether the choice is to place the child in a group home, foster home, or adoptive home, the procedures in each of these placements must be based on pursuing the best interests of the child.

KEY TERMS

adoption

child-related problems

foster care

group homes

halfway house

parent-related problems

DISCUSSION AND REVIEW QUESTIONS

1. Define the following terms:
   a. Group home
   b. Foster home
   c. Adoption
   d. Alternative placement.
2. Discuss the following questions:
   a. What types of children are served best by each of the alternatives discussed in this chapter? Why?
   b. What characteristics differentiate these placements from one another?
3. What is the historical background of each of the following childcare alternatives?
   a. Group homes
   b. Foster care
   c. Adoption.
4. What factors cause inappropriate referrals to group homes?
5. What characteristics are generally found in a good foster home?
6. What are some of the problems that may be encountered in the adoption of a child?
7. How does each of the three childcare alternatives discussed in this chapter fit into the present-day juvenile justice system?

VIDEO PROFILES

The *Residential Facility Tour* video profile in MyCrimeKit highlights describes the important features of the residential facility related specifically to the juvenile as presented by (1) the social worker's description of the juvenile's needs, (2) the judge's placement of the juvenile at the residential facility, and (3) the Director of Admissions at the residential facility. Compare and contrast the residential facility (e.g., the look/contents of a "cell/room," programs) with the facility presented in Chapter 9's *Life Inside* video profile. Describe the differences and similarities as it relates to *parens patriae*. How does the residential facility described in the video correspond to the reasons for juvenile group homes as described in this chapter, especially when there is family support for some of the juveniles at the residential facility?

The *Child Abuse* video profile in MyCrimeKit highlights the two-year involvement of a specific family with the juvenile/family court. Describe the situation in the household. What is the decision of the social worker during the meeting with the father in the home? Does the decision align with the discussion presented in the text? What is the judge's decision? Discuss this in terms of the text's presentation of children in need of supervision, as well as the interaction between the social worker and the father.

MYCRIMEKIT

mycrimekit™ Go to MyCrimeKit.com to explore the following study tools and resources specific to this chapter:

- Practice Quiz: Test your knowledge with multiple-choice, true-false, fill-in-the-blank, and essay questions.
- Flashcards: 20 flashcards to test your knowledge of the chapter's key terms.
- Web Quest: Review the Web sites of the Office of Victims Assistance for juvenile-related information, as well as your state's Juvenile Justice Web site for the types of alternative placements discussed in this chapter.
- Web Links: Check out both public and private agency sites related to the content presented in this chapter.

ENDNOTES

1. Gwen A. Holden and Robert A. Kapler, "Deinstitutionalizing Status Offenders: A Record of Progress," *Juvenile Justice* (Fall/Winter 1995), p. 5.
2. David Finckelhor, Richard Ormrod, Heather Turner, and Sherry L. Hamby, "The Victimization of Children and Youth: A Comprehensive, National Survey, "*Child Maltreatment*, Vol. 10 (2005): 5–6.
3. Ibid., p. 8.
4. Ibid., p. 10.
5. Ibid., p. 8.
6. Ibid., p. 14.
7. Ibid.
8. Ibid.
9. Ibid., pp. 16–17.
10. Ibid., p. 18.

11. Edward Eldefonso and Alan R. Coffey, *Process and Impact of the Juvenile Justice System* (Encino, CA: Glencoe Press, 1976), p. 172.

12. Northwest Regional Council, "Comprehensive Analysis of Major Program Components: Specific Finding and Recommendations," *State of Washington Group Home Study,* Vol. I (Zaring Corporation, October 1973), pp. 19–20.

13. Robert J. Mutchnick and Margaret Fawcett, "Group Home Environments and Victimization of Resident Juveniles," *International Journal of Offender Therapy and Comparative Criminology,* Vol. 35 (1991), pp. 126–142.

14. Washington Administrative Code 388-64-055.

15. *State of Washington Group Home Study,* p. 105.

16. Alfred Kadushin, "Child Welfare: Adoption and Foster Care," in *Encyclopedia of Social Work,* Vol. I (New York: National Association of Social Workers, 1971), p. 104.

17. Herbert D. Williams, "Foster Homes for Juvenile Delinquents," *Federal Probation* (September 1949), pp. 46–51.

18. See Burt Galaway and Richard W. Hudson, "Specialist Foster Care for Delinquent Youth," *Federal Probation,* Vol. 59 (1995), pp. 19–27; Mary I. Benedict, Susan Zuravin, Mark Somerfield, et al., "The Reported Health and Functioning of Children Maltreated While in Family Foster Care," *Child Abuse and Neglect,* Vol. 20 (1996), pp. 561–571.

19. Leslie W. Hunter, "Foster Homes for Teenagers," *Children* (November/December 1964), p. 234.

20. S. Robinson, "Remedying Our Foster Care System: Recognizing Children's Voices," *Family Law Quarterly,* Vol. 27 (1993), pp. 395–415.

21. Shirley Jenkins and Elaine Norman, *Filial Deprivation and Foster Care* (New York: Columbia University Press, 1972), p. v.

22. See also James W. Davis, Peter J. Pecora, Charley Joyce, et al., "The Design and Implementation of Family Foster Care Services to High Risk Delinquents Transitioning from Correctional Confinement," *Juvenile and Family Court Journal,* Vol. 48 (1997), pp. 17–32; James M. Gaudin and Richard Sutphen, "Foster Care Versus Extended Family Care for Children of Incarcerated Offenders," *Journal of Offender Rehabilitation,* Vol. 19 (1993), pp. 129–147; Jaana Haapasalo, "Young Offender's Experiences of Child Protection Services," *Journal of Youth and Adolescence,* Vol. 29 (2000), pp. 355–371.

23. Jenkins and Norman, *Filial Deprivation and Foster Care,* p. 258.

24. Kadushin, "Child Welfare: Adoption and Foster Care," p. 107.

25. Albert Kocourck and John C. Wigmore, *Source of Ancient and Primitive Law, Evolution of Law, Select Readings on the Origin and Development of Legal Institutions* (Boston: Little, Brown, 1951), p. 425.

26. Arthur W. Calhoun, *A Social History of the American Family,* Vol. I (New York: Barnes and Noble, 1960), pp. 306–307.

27. Charles L. Brace, *The Best Method of Disposing of Pauper and Vagrant Children* (1859), pp. 13–14.

28. Child Welfare League of America, *Child Welfare League of America Standards for Adoption Service* (New York: 2 Child Welfare League of America, 1968), p. 17.

29. See E. V. Meeker, "Termination of Parental Rights: Constitutional Rights, State Interests and the Best Interests of the Child," *Journal of Juvenile Law,* Vol. 17 (1996), pp. 82–93.

30. Committee on Early Childhood, Adoption, and Dependent Care, "Families and Adoption: The Pediatrician's Role in Supporting Communication," *Pediatricians,* Vol. 112(6) (2003), pp. 1437–1441.

31. Alex R. Piquero, David P. Farrington, Brandon C. Welsh, Richard Tremblay, and Wesley G. Jennings, *Effects of Early Family/Parent Training Programs on Antisocial Behavior & Delinquency* (Stockholm, Sweden: The Swedish National Council for Crime Prevention, 2008), p. 42.

12

Juvenile Gangs[1]

S *treet gangs are by-products of partially incapacitated communities. Until we dedicate the state and federal resources necessary to alter these community structures, gangs will continue to emerge despite value transformation, suppression, or other community efforts. Jobs, better schools, social services, health programs, family support, training in community organization skills, and support for resident empowerment. That's easy to say but obviously not easy to do.*

MALCOLM W. KLEIN[2]

LEARNING OBJECTIVES

1. Identify the nature and extent of the gang problem.
2. Determine the definition and attributes of gang structure.
3. Identify the risk factors for gang involvement and participation.
4. Identify the attributes of gang member recruits.
5. Identify the attributes of female gangs.
6. Identify racial and ethnic differences in gang structure and attributes.
7. Identify methods of gang entry.
8. Identify the attributes of the G.R.E.A.T. program.
9. Identify the attributes of the Office of Juvenile Justice and Delinquency Prevention Comprehensive Gang Model.
10. Identify the attributes of Gang Suppression programs.

CHAPTER OVERVIEW

Gangs have traditionally attracted a great deal of attention throughout the juvenile justice system. They are viewed as a major cause of delinquency, crime, and violence. Indeed, research on youths in Seattle, Denver, and Rochester has shown that gang members commit a large proportion of crimes. Youths are more likely to engage in delinquent behavior when they are members of a gang compared with the periods before and after gang membership.[3] While they are gang members, juveniles are more likely to engage in violent behavior, property crime, drug sales and substance use.[4] Understanding why and how juveniles join gangs can lead to the development of gang prevention strategies and reduce crime.

This chapter addresses gang issues by defining the term and discussing the theories pertaining to the causes of gang membership. We review of the identified risk factors that predict gang entry. Finally, current programs and policies that provide gang prevention, intervention and suppression are also discussed and the effectiveness of gang prevention programs is considered.

Magnitude of the Gang Problem

Youth gangs are not a new phenomenon in the United States. Although the precise year in which they appeared cannot be accurately determined, the consensus is that they surfaced in large urban centers, as the country was recovering from the Revolutionary War.[5] Other historical analyses suggest that gangs emerged in the southwest part of the country in the early 1800s as a result of the plight of young Mexican immigrants coping with the difficulties of adapting to the American culture. As the Industrial Revolution spread across the country, creating population booms in the larger cities, youth gangs surfaced within them.[6] Gangs thrived in cities such as Boston, New York, and Chicago, which were experiencing surges in population from new immigrants as well as from relocations from rural regions of the country. Gang members during that time were mostly Irish, Jewish, and Italian; the same ethnic groups that made up the lower socioeconomic class of that time period.

In the early part of the twentieth century, gang activity and violence usually were associated with protecting territory. Gang violence was controlled by, directed toward, and limited to gang members, with rival gangs being the target. Gang activity briefly subsided in the 1960s but resurfaced in the 1970s with increased vengeance. Gang members no longer were directing their energies solely toward protecting their own turf; drugs and weapons had begun to play a major role in their activities. In fact, large profits from the sale of illegal drugs motivate many youth to join gangs.

Based on their annual surveys of police departments, the National Youth Gang Center (NYGC) reports that annual estimates of total gang membership nationwide has averaged about 750,000 over a ten-year period (1996–2006).[7] The estimated number of gangs over this period averaged approximately 25,000. This survey also reported that 29 percent of the jurisdictions that city (populations of 2,500 or more) and county law enforcement agencies serve experienced youth gang problems in 2004. Gang problems were also concentrated in larger cities. Specifically, 99 percent of law enforcement agencies serving cities with populations of 100,000 or more have reported multiple years of gang problems.

However, few law enforcement agencies reported that their gang problem was "getting worse" between 2002 and 2004. Instead, the majority of agencies noted a fluctuating trend in which the local gang problem alternated between periods of increasing and decreasing serious-ness. For example, more than one-half of the agencies reporting to the 2006 survey indicated that gang-related aggravated assaults and drug sales had increased.[8] These "gang cycles" demonstrate that changing patterns of gang activity and violence are likely to occur at the local level. However, these variations at the local level do not lend themselves to developing nationwide generalizations about the gang problem.

Lewis Yablonsky offers the following summary of gang attributes based in part on his fifty years of research:

1. Gangs have a fierce involvement with their territory in their hood or barrio and will fight and to protect their turf;

2. Gangsters have different levels of participation—partially based on age—and can be characterized as core or marginalized participants;

3. Different gangs have diverse patterns of leadership;

4. Many gangs and gangsters participate intensely in the commerce and the use of various drugs; and

5. Gangs are, in part, generated by their cultural milieu in a response to a society that blocks their opportunity to achieve the success goals of the larger society.[9]

Together, these conclusions stress that a gang is not a singular entity that is easily defined and that gang involvement varies.

WHAT ARE GANGS?

The Gang Defined

Although there is agreement among law enforcement, researchers, and lawmakers that gangs are a problem, there is little agreement in accept-ing a uniform definition of what a gang is.[10] Media depictions of gangs and their associated violence and culture have provided the general public with a loose definition of what gangs are, how they operate, and what types of crime they are responsible for. Law enforcement tends to rely on stricter, legal definitions of the term gang. Law enforcement measurement is based on definitions specific to the reporting jurisdiction. Neither method is particularly accurate. These definitions may be very narrow, resulting in gang activity not being captured. Law enforcement tends to group together criminal acts committed collectively by a gang, as well as a crime committed independently by a member of the gang, which may not have been propelled by the gang, categorizing the latter as gang related. The accuracy of such illustrations may be questionable and may reflect a certain underlying purpose. For example, definitions of gangs have been crafted to facilitate the prosecution of youth gang crimes. Los Angeles lawmakers included a broad, encompassing definition of gangs into their penal code to include any formation of a group of more than two persons, formal or informal, which may have a common name or use identifying signs and whose members engage in a pattern of criminal activity.

In addition to Yablonsky, prominent criminologists have offered several definitions of a gang. Albert Cohen describes gangs as groups involved in deviant, disruptive, antisocial, or criminal activity.[11] Walter Miller characterizes the gang as a self-formed association of peers with an organizational hierarchy who conduct illegal activities within a certain territory.[12] Irving Spergel offers a similar definition but adds that these members either perceive themselves or are perceived by the public as

Gang Members

aggressive and territorial.[13] Klein and Maxson have three criteria to define a street gang[14]: the community's recognition of the group, the gangs' self identification as a distinct group, and the gang's involvement in illegal activities that result in a consistent negative response from the police and citizens. Others such as Morash disagree that criminal activity should be an element of the definition.[15] However, if criminality and delinquency are not used to define the gang, then other youth groups such as college fraternities, Boy Scouts, and athletic teams may also fall under the definition of a gang.[16] Overall, the common elements found in most definitions are that gangs are self-formed groups of peers that have a gang name, leadership, territory, recognizable symbols and signs, and collectively carry out illegal activities.[17]

Recently, Klein reported the Eurogang Consensus Nominal Definition of Street Gangs: "A street gang is any durable, street-oriented youth group whose own identity includes involvement in illegal activity."[18] Here, *durability* refers to the ability of gangs to continue to exist despite turnover of members. *Street-oriented* implies spending a lot of group time outside home, work, and school—often on streets, in malls, in parks, in cars, and so on; and *youth* means that its members are more adolescent than adult. Youth gang members typically range between 10 years of age and early twenties.[19] The acts that they commit are delinquent or criminal, not just bothersome. Their identity as a group, not their individual self-interest, is the final determining characteristic.

Klein and Maxson note how dynamic of the group process of the gang operates. Crime and cohesiveness build on each other. Gangs develop "group esteem" in place of self-esteem.

Territoriality serves to separate in-group from out-group, reinforcing all of the "specialness" of one's gang. When a member of his or her territory is attacked, the event calls for a payback. If the attack is with firearms, this desire is especially pronounced.[20] Thus, the group identity of the gang becomes greater than that of its individual members. The "group ego" substitutes for the weak, individual ego-identity.[21]

Self-Report Method. Measurement of gang crime is accomplished through law enforcement accounts as well as from self-reports from gang members. The self-report method allows members to claim gang membership and participation in crimes. This method began being used in the early 1900s and continues to be often used, although its validity is often questioned. Gang members may conceal their membership and their criminal activity from the police as well as from researchers conducting surveys. Alternatively, others may exaggerate their involvement. The advantage of using self-report methods is that researchers may capture wide information from a variety of gangs. However, those who may self-identify with gang membership may be drawing on a very loose definition of the "gang" concept that does not fit within the traditional definition. To minimize the misreporting, Bjerregaard suggests creating a more restrictive definition of the "gang" by posing additional screening questions limiting possible responses to the more customary definitions of gangs.[22]

The differing definitions of gangs and gang membership create vagueness and the possibility of erroneously estimating the problem. Jurisdictions and scholars that use a narrow definition may underestimate their gang crisis. Alternatively, those who use broader definitions may overestimate their problems. These estimates have implications for both research and public policy. A universal definition would allow a better understanding of the magnitude of the problem as well as provide jurisdictions with better data to efficiently allocate their resources and measure the success of their programs.

RISK FACTORS

Various risk factors have been identified which may influence a youth's propensity to join a gang. Studies have examined the effects of gender, race, and age as predictors of gang entry. In addition, family factors such as structure, income, socioeconomic status, and parental attachment also influence gang membership. Other factors including attachment to school, association with delinquent peers; and geographic characteristics such as neighborhood type and population levels, all have bearing on a child's chances of joining a gang. By identifying which factors predict future gang membership, "at risk" populations can be identified and targeted with appropriate prevention strategies in order to control gang membership.

Why do juveniles join gangs? Delinquent peer networks and negative peer influences are consistent predictors. Characteristics of peer networks are important and should receive attention in most gang problems. Other factors that have been identified include reactivity, aggressiveness, impulsivity, and negative life events. When these behaviors are evident, close parental supervision may be the best method of curtailing gang involvement.

Klein also offers a "minimal list" of the attributes of potential gang member recruits:[23]

- **Low self-concept.** Low self-esteem, high tolerance for deviance.
- **Admitted involvement in violence.** Gang members are disproportionately involved in offending and are especially responsible for the majority of serious and violent crimes committed by juveniles. Their gang membership facilitates this type of involvement in crime. There is something unique about gang membership itself that increases their participation in serious and violent crime.[24]

Video Profile: Former White Supremacy Member

- **Defiance of parents.** Poor family management strategies, low family involvement, inappropriate parental discipline, low parental control or monitoring, poor affective relationships between parent and child, and parental conflict contribute to gang membership. Lower levels of parental supervision result in reduced levels of informal social control to which the child is exposed. This reduced level of self-control increases levels of delinquency as well as the odds of the child entering a gang.[25] Youths who were not closely monitored by their parents were found to be more involved in gangs than youths who received closer parental supervision. Similarly, youths with lower supervision also possessed lower levels of self-control.[26] Neighborhoods that are composed of many single parent households also result in higher delinquency rates for youths who reside within that community, regardless whether the child comes from a one-parent family. Anderson claims that this occurs because informal social control weakens because there are fewer overall parents to supervise the neighborhood's children.[27]

- **Deficits in adult contacts.**

- **Social disabilities or defects.** Adolescents who associate with deviant peers are more likely to join gangs. Gang members are more likely to engage in precocious sexual activity, have friends who are involved in delinquency and loiter, or hang out with peers in unsupervised groups. Research from the Pittsburgh Youth Study indicates that younger adolescents with delinquent gang member peers had greater odds of entering gangs.[28]

- **Deficient school performance, both academic and disciplinary.** Gang membership is more likely among adolescents whose parents have low educational expectations for them, who demonstrate poor school performance, who have a low commitment to and involvement in school, who experience educational frustration, who have low school self-esteem, and who experience educational marginality and school stress resulting from such factors as getting into trouble in school or getting poor grades. Childhood school attachment levels predict future gang entry as do low educational aspirations. Youths with low attachment were found to be more at risk for adolescent gang membership. In addition, those who were rated as learning disabled and those with poor academic achievement also had increased odds of joining gangs.[29]

- **Limited repertoire of skills and interests.**

- **Poor impulse control.**

- **Early conduct disorder.**

- **Early onset of delinquency.**

- **Perceptions of barriers to jobs and other opportunities.**

Curry and Spergel also point out that gang members have higher rates of delinquency than nongang members.[30] Furthermore, gang members have been found to be more involved in gun-related crimes and are more likely to possess concealed weapons.[31] In terms of neighborhood characteristics, gang members are more likely to live in socially disorganized, high crime areas where drugs are available. Hispanic and African American subjects are more likely to be gang members than are White subjects. Low family socioeconomic status or poverty is related to gang membership. Of course, exposure to and possession of multiple risk factors increases the probability of gang membership.[32]

Certain features of gang life are very attractive to juveniles with these attributes. Belonging to a gang and sharing its identity is not only a strong incentive, it also gives the sense that in the gang there is protection from attack. The gang's emphasis on territoriality also gives its members something tangible to identify with and call one's own. Finally, there is the promise of material rewards: Gang members have always found ways to have pocket money.[33] As one gang member noted: "A gang is a bunch of brothers hooked up, trying to make money. The gang is really about making money, it's holding your own neighborhood so nobody can come into your neighborhood and try to take the bread out of your mouth."[34] Thus, the reasons for joining are both psychological and economic.

Female Gangs

Most of the research on gang membership focuses on the attributes of young males. However, female gangs and female gang membership have gradually been rising even though most gangs are still predominately male. Most gang estimates are based on member self-reports. Bjerregaard indicates that estimates of female gang membership fluctuate greatly among the many studies that attempt to determine them. She contributes to the differing type of data that are used in the calculations. Studies that use official data show limited female participation. Studies that use self-report methods have considerably higher percentages of female gang membership.[35] In their study of the data from the Denver Youth Study, Esbensen and Huizinga estimate that between 20 percent and 46 percent of gang members were female.[36] Similarly Bjerregaard and Smith found that 22 percent of respondents in the Rochester Youth Development Study were females.[37] Therefore, the experience of female gang members has attracted much attention.[38]

Survey results from an eleven-city evaluation of the G.R.E.A.T. program confirm that "gang membership appears to be an equal opportunity promoter of delinquent behavior." Researchers found that 38 percent of the gang members surveyed were female. Gang girls reported committing the same variety of offenses at a slightly lower frequency than gang boys. However, gang girls were two to five times more delinquent than nongang boys.[39] A further analysis of the G.R.E.A.T. program data of Hispanic female gang members revealed that peers influenced their decision to join, especially when parental supervision was absent or inadequate.[40]

Miller notes that these girls have typically experienced multiple family problems. They were more likely to have witnessed physical violence between and to have been abused by adults in their homes. These family problems, coupled with exposure to neighborhood gangs, often through the introduction provided by gang-involved family members, make girls more likely to look up to and become involved with gangs.[41]

Moore and Hagedorn agree that female gang members have different offending patterns than males. They tend to commit fewer violent crimes than male gang members and are more likely to engage in property and status offenses. Female involvement in violent and drug-dealing offenses seems to be on the rise. They also report that most females join gangs for friendship and self-affirmation but also to work in an informal economy to generate income due largely to their economic marginality. They often see the gang as a refuge from victimization (typically sexual) at home.[42]

Unfortunately, there is also some evidence that female gang members are often the victims of sexual violence and exploitation at the hands of male gang members.[43] A multiyear field study of 74 female gang members revealed that their rates of violence dramatically increased in the period between joining the gang and their first pregnancy and then decreased with pregnancy and childbirth. Gang affiliation also occurred at the age when teenage girls face conditions of high stress.[44]

A study based on focus groups and life history interviews with Mexican American adolescent girls associated with male gangs in San Antonio, Texas, indicates that they were likely to engage in sexual relations, partying, substance use, and crime with male gang members. Excessive use of drugs and alcohol promoted these behaviors, and early sexual activity was especially damaging to these adolescent girls.[45]

Taken together, these findings demonstrate that girls are involved with gangs and that their experience with gang involvement and its impact are substantially different from those of boys. Ethnic differences between female gang members must also be considered in the development and implementation of gang prevention models. It is clear that "females clearly do participate in gangs and should be prominent in any discussion of gang programs and policies."[46]

Racial and Ethnic Differences

Another pertinent research question regarding gangs, their membership, and operation is the determination of racial and ethnic differences. If there are differences across gang members by race and ethnicity, then policy and program efforts must address them. One study found that

Hispanic/Latino gangs were more likely to have national affiliations and thus enhanced mobility. Such national gangs were also found to be more organized, criminally active, and larger than local gangs. The local gangs were somewhat more likely to be more visible at the area level, more turf oriented, and more likely to engage in drug dealing.[47]

Historically, African American gangs are more separated from society due economic marginality than White gangs.[48] Hagedorn also determines that social disorganization and economic marginalization contributed to the formation of gangs among African American youth. These effects promoted unemployment, drug use, and decreased the control of community institutions in Milwaukee.[49] However, another G.R.E.A.T.-based study determines that low self-control had a closer link to delinquency for Whites rather than African Americans.[50] Another study determines that the sale and use of methamphetamines was lower among African American gang members than other groups.[51]

Asian gangs have also demonstrated differences across gang members. Both African American and Asian American gangs are more likely to engage in violent activities (simple assault, shootings, and robbery). This tendency is especially pronounced among Chinese gang members.[52] Asian gangs represent a particular threat because they present cultural and linguistic barriers to law enforcement. Primarily, Asian gangs are heavily involved in the drug trade, illegal weapons smuggling, fraudulent commercial goods, and computer products.[53]

Field research on Asian gang members in Southern California revealed that they believed society treated them unjustly and that they would have to work harder than others to succeed. They also had friends and family members in gangs and admit that they had behavior problems in school. Although they were more likely to engage in crime and delinquency than nongang members, they were surprisingly more likely to be college students whose families earned more than $60,000 a year.[54] Taiwanese gang members were found to be from privileged social and economic backgrounds. They engaged in criminal behavior because they believed that it was easier to succeed in the more lucrative illegal marketplace.[55]

Gang Entry Methods

gang entry models Selection, Socialization, Enhancement models were developed to explain how gang joining works

Gang scholars have developed several **gang entry models** to explain how gang joining works.

The Selection Model. Scholars have attempted to determine whether antisocial youth seek out one another or if by joining a gang a youth's level of antisocial behavior becomes elevated. The selection model explains that delinquent and antisocial adolescents will seek to associate with others who are also delinquent and antisocial, thereby forming delinquent groups and gangs: "Birds of a feather flocking together."[56]

The implication is that gangs do not cause delinquency; members bring high-offending profiles with them and are in fact recruited for this reason.[57] Several delinquency studies have supported the selection model to explain gang entry.

In the Denver Youth Study, Esbensen and Huizinga find that those boys who eventually joined gangs had exhibited increased antisocial behavior in the years prior to gang membership.[58] Using data from the Rochester Development Youth Study, Thornberry and his colleagues report that a high level of antisocial behavior prior to gang entry was a predictor for future gang membership. They also find that other factors such as lower parental supervision, availability of drugs, and association with delinquent peers to increase probability for future gang entry.[59] An analysis of data from the Seattle Social Development Project echoes the findings of the prior studies and adds that African American youth had higher rates of gang membership than did youths from families with poor structure and management problems, and youths who lived in areas with easy accessibility to drugs.[60]

Socialization Model. The second model to explain gang entry is the socialization model. That is, that the gang attracts adolescents not because of their tendency to be delinquent. Rather, the gang lures adolescents seeking a source to acquire self-esteem, power, or protection. When indoctrinated into the gang, the youth's level of delinquency increases due to socialization effects. This suggests that antisocial and delinquent behavior is developed through one's association with other antisocial youths.[61] A youth's rate of delinquency would therefore be higher while a gang member than it would be before entering and after leaving the gang.[62]

The socialization model explains that those youths who join gangs develop antisocial behavior through association and social learning from other delinquent youth. This model posits that gang joiners' offending profiles are similar to other youths' before they join the gang but increase later due to the group processes of the gang.[63] Whether an adolescent is attracted to the gang or whether the gang attracts the adolescent has been of great interest to the field.

Enhancement Model. Although selection and socialization models offer conflicting explanations as to why youths join gangs, another explanation merges the two theories into an enhancement model. This model suggests that delinquent youths are recruited by gangs with similar delinquent tendencies. Socialization processes within the gang promote further antisocial behavior and criminal acts among its members.[64]

A study from the Seattle Social Development Project compares the delinquency rates of three groups of youths. The first group consisted of youths who were gang members and associated with other delinquent gang members. The second group included nongang members who associated with delinquent peers. The third group was of nongang members who did not associate with delinquent peers. Their study's conclusion is consistent with the enhancement model, in that the group that demonstrated the highest rates of delinquency and drug use was the first group, which consisted of gang members who associated with other delinquent peers.[65]

A similar study using data from the Pittsburgh Youth Study finds that boys who join gangs are more delinquent prior to gang membership than are other boys who do not join gangs. The study also indicates that during the gang membership, the boys' level of delinquency increased. This effect was attributed to delinquent peer association. These peers, other gang members, have a socializing effect on the boys' behaviors by being role models and mentoring the boys in how to engage in criminal activity and what is acceptable to the other peers.[66]

Of course, what factors influence when juveniles leave gangs should also be considered. In their field studies of St. Louis gang members, Decker and Lauritsen find that they left gangs because of the fear of violence and its effect on them, their friends, and families. Therefore, they recommend that interventions occur immediately following acts of violence when gang members are separated from their gang or at least when they are in small groups apart from the gang—in hospital emergency rooms, at the police station, or in family settings.[67]

GANG PROBLEMS AND ISSUES

Gangs cause several problems for their members and the communities in which they live and operate. Drug abuse among gang members has been cited as a major problem. Gang members use and sell drugs. Both behaviors contribute to gang violence by affecting behavior and further aggravating gang turf battles. One study reveals that marijuana and cocaine use were higher (as revealed by urinalysis) among current than past gang members.[68] Another study of Puerto Rican and Dominican gang members confirms that joining a gang increases an adolescent's risk for substance abuse. Even in the small city setting of the study, the study indicates that gang members had a young age for drug use onset (11.2 years) with rapid progression to more dangerous drugs occurring within 6 years.[69] In a San Francisco area study of three gangs, marijuana is found to play a central role in the everyday life and activity of gang members as the recreational drug of choice.[70] A multivariate study of data from the 1991 National Longitudinal Study of Youth determines that gang members who sold drugs were significantly more likely to engage in violent behavior than either gang members who did not sell drugs or drug sellers who were not gang members.[71]

Another salient issue is gang violence. Violent norms are often transmitted to gang members through socialization. In depth interviews

Drug Dealer

with incarcerated gang members revealed that they emphasized the functionality of guns. Not only do they provide protection, they help to project and maintain a reputation for toughness that gang members find desirable.[72] Societal forces also contribute to gang homicides. A three-year field study of St. Louis gang members indicates that socialization had a role in gang homicides. Most often, it was used in retaliation against rival gangs thus increasing the group's cohesion against a common enemy. Excessive violence, however, had the negative impact of splitting the gang into subgroups and leads some members to leave the gang.[73] An examination of gang homicides in Newark, NJ over a five and a half year period agrees with Decker's findings as well.[74] It also seems that gang membership fails to provide protection against violent victimization. Using data from the national G.R.E.A.T. evaluation, researchers have found that gang membership exacerbated rather than provided protection against violent crime. Thus, gangs do not provide a safe haven for its members and actually places them in harm's way.[75]

Finally, gang migration (the movement of gang members from one city to another) has been cited by governmental task forces as a major problem. In her 1992 survey of law enforcement personnel in 1,100 U.S. cities, Maxson finds that just under half (47 percent) of the 597 cities that responded - an estimated arrival of no more than 10 migrants in the prior year. Only 34 cities (6 percent) estimated the arrival of more than 100 migrants during this period. Her conclusion is that "gang member migration, although widespread, should not be viewed as the major culprit in the nationwide proliferation of gangs."[76]

GANG PREVENTION PROGRAMS

Youth involvement in gangs poses a threat to communities and a challenge for the juvenile justice system. As juveniles' participation in gangs increases, so does the need to develop more effective ways to prevent and suppress gang activity. In spite of the growing magnitude of the problem, until recently only limited programs and resources have been directed against juvenile gangs.

Gang Resistance Education and Training (G.R.E.A.T.)

The Gang Resistance Education and Training (**G.R.E.A.T.**) program is a school-based gang prevention program targeting middle school students. It was introduced in 1991 in a joint effort between the Phoenix Police Department and the Bureau of Alcohol, Tobacco, and Firearms. The program has since been expanded and is currently offered across the country. G.R.E.A.T. removes gang attractiveness by introducing children to the negative aspects of gang membership and providing them with skills to resist pressure to enter gangs. Eight lesson plans are taught by a uniformed police officer in the classroom, rather than individually, through instruction, dialogue, and role-playing. Typically, the curriculum features the following:

- An introduction to acquaint students with the G.R.E.A.T. program and presenting officer.
- Crime/Victims and Your Rights—Students learn about crimes, their victims, and their impact on school and neighborhood.

G.R.E.A.T. Gang Resistance Education and Training school-based gang prevention program targeting middle school students

Police Officer Talking to Students

- Cultural Sensitivity/Prejudice—Students learn how cultural differences impact their school and neighborhood.

- Conflict Resolution (two sessions)—Students learn how to create an atmosphere of understanding that would enable all parties to better address problems and work on solutions together.

- Meeting Basic Needs—Students learn how to meet their basic needs without joining a gang.

- Drugs/Neighborhoods—Students learn how drugs affect their school and neighborhood.

- Responsibility—Students learn about the diverse responsibilities of people in their school and neighborhood.

- Goal Setting—Students learn the need for all goal setting and how to establish short- and long-term goals.

In short, it is a classic, broad-based prevention strategy similar to those found in medical immunization programs. After exposure to the G.R.E.A.T. curriculum, juveniles will be inoculated against the attractions of gang membership.

However, the results from evaluations of this program were less than impressive. Their implementation was questionable and the ability of exposed students to resist gang involvement was minimal. One evaluation found a significant program effect for five of the outcome measures (victimization, negative views about gangs, attitudes toward the police, prosocial peers, and risk seeking) were positive although gang involvement was not impacted. Once again, given the immensity of the problem and its potential for damage, the G.R.E.A.T. programs are likely to continue. The estimated cumulative number of students who have received the G.R.E.A.T. program is more than 2 million.[77]

Klein and Maxson call G.R.E.A.T. "a remarkably failed program with a remarkably positive public relations image" and "a study in the application of conventional wisdom in the face of contrary empirical knowledge."[78] They attribute the failure of the program to four factors:

1. G.R.E.A.T. was built on a conventional piece of wisdom that had no empirical formulation, namely, that a D.A.R.E.-type program of police officers delivering didactic lessons was effective.

2. G.R.E.A.T. relied on unproven conventional wisdom that certain life skills or attitudinal variables underlie the attractiveness of gang membership.

3. The content of G.R.E.A.T. lessons did not take advantage of the accumulated empirical knowledge about gangs. The content was not gang-specific; it did not take adequate account of gang structures,

processes, or culture nor of the connections between gang members and their families and communities.

4. G.R.E.A.T. was not targeted at those more at risk of gang membership. Probably 90 percent or more of its student participants would not have joined gangs in any case; any positive effect on the most vulnerable could easily have been masked by the diffusion of effects over total participants.[79]

The G.R.E.A.T. experience documents that gang education programs must be carefully targeted and implemented to be effective.

The Office of Juvenile Justice and Delinquency Prevention's Comprehensive Gang Model

In 1987, the Office of Juvenile Justice and Delinquency Prevention began a project to prevent gang violence and delinquency. It began as a project under the direction of Dr. Irving Spergel at the University of Chicago and is now known as the OJJDP Comprehensive Gang Model.

This model is built on five core strategies and the overall premise that gang prevention must be based on a team approach by a number of social service agencies acting in conjunction. The five core strategies are

1. **Community Mobilization.** Involvement of local citizens, including former gang youth, community groups and agencies, and the coordination of programs and staff functions within and across agencies.

2. **Provision of Opportunities.** The development of a variety of specific education, training, and employment programs targeted at gang-involved youth.

3. **Social Intervention.** Youth-serving agencies, schools, grass roots groups, faith organizations, police, and other criminal justice organizations "reaching out" and acting as links among gang-involved youth, their families, and the conventional world and needed services.

4. **Suppression.** Formal and informal social control procedures, including close supervision or monitoring of gang youth by agencies of the criminal justice system and also by community-based agencies, schools, and grass roots groups.

5. **Organizational Change and Development.** Development and implementation of policies and procedures that result in the most effective use of available and potential sources within and across agencies to better address the gang problem.

This model is firmly based on the premise that "long term change would not be achieved without also addressing at-risk youth and the institutions which support and control youth and their families."[80]

The model promotes program strategies that hold gang members accountable for crime but also provide critical services to prevent their further involvement in delinquency. These strategies include

1. Understanding different gang structures, systems, and processes in the neighborhood;

2. Development of an interagency street-level team approach to prevention, intervention, and suppression that is supported by clear policy;

3. Targeting, monitoring, arresting, and incarcerating gang leaders and repeat violent offenders;

4. Referring gang members, including fringe members and their parents, to youth and family services for counseling and guidance;

5. Crisis intervention and prevention of gang fights or disputes;

6. Probation and police team patrols of community "hot spots";

7. Close supervision of gang offenders and those at high risk by criminal and juvenile justice and community-based agencies;

8. Remedial education for targeted gang members, especially middle or junior high school youth, and remedial or special education for older gang youth; and

9. Job orientation, training, placement and mentoring for older youth gang members, including those with criminal records.[81]

Again, the model stresses the need for a coordinated, integrated approach to dealing with gangs. Punishment and treatment must be combined to be effective. As Klein and Maxson note, "The Spergel Model wants to do it all – it aims to combine prevention, intervention, and suppression in a single package."[82]

The Little Village Gang Violence Reduction Project.   The Little Village Project was one of Spergel's original gang prevention and suppression operations. It took place in La Villita, Chicago; a low income Mexican American community with approximately 80,000 residents. La Villita was experiencing chronic turf wars between two local gangs: the Latin Kings and the Two Six. This Gang Violence Reduction Project (GVRP) involved interagency efforts combined with community based group involvement. The primary factor for the programs success as the targeting of hard-core gang members through close teamwork between community youth workers, law enforcement, area residents, and community based organizations. Although each of the entities involved was primarily concerned with fulfilling its own organizational goals, over time cohesion developed between the agencies as they collaboratively sought similar objectives. The Project employed several of the strategies listed above: Community mobilization, opportunities provision, social intervention, suppression, organizational change and development, and targeting of gang members.

The community mobilization component focused on the integration of community based groups, residents, law enforcement, probation officers and youth workers many of whom were former gang members. The opportunities provision of the project utilized specifically tailored programs to provide education, jobs and job training for gang members who may be ready to leave the gang. In addition, other programs for non gang members were offered to prevent future gang entry. The social intervention component reached out to problematic youths to assist them to get back on course through a variety of counseling programs, and provided referrals for required services such as for substance abuse treatment, employment opportunities and training. The suppression element attempted to control gang behavior through police surveillance, arrests, probation and incarceration. In addition, other informal control methods were used such as interagency information sharing and positive communication with gang members and non-gang members.

Targeting was achieved through collaborative input of agencies involved. Distinctions were made between those youths who were highly at risk for engaging in gang activity and those who were marginally at risk. The project targeted approximately 200 youths over a four year period, which were identified as being at high risk for engaging in gang activity between the ages of 17 and 24. The program involved the collaboration of police officers, tactical officers, interagency youth workers, and evaluators from the School of Social Service Administration (SSA), University of Chicago, and members of a locally based antigang organization, the Neighbors Against Gang Violence (NAGV). Although each of the entities involved in the project carried out its own organizational goals, all the entities developed a unified mission in their collaborative quest to resolve the gang problem. Interagency meetings were held bi-weekly to discuss general issues regarding project development and the identification of youths in need of supervision, counseling and support. In addition, these agencies met every so often to discuss case management issues, assess program progress, and exchange information. Data provided by the SSA included analysis of police crime reports and provided the interagency team with information regarding recent gang patterns and crime trends, which were used by the team for efficient redeployment of resources.

Youth workers were from the target communities and were either personally previously involved in gangs or were closely associated with gang members. These youth workers worked closely with gang members and at risk youths by offering guidance, by supplying them with referrals to services, and by helping them pursue employment opportunities. Also, these same youth workers provided the other agencies, including the police officers, with information about gang members, gang structures, and their activities, which helped control gang activity. Overall these youth workers were respected by gang members as well as by the community at large. Police officers, parole officers and community youth workers sponsored various events to engage members of the rival gangs in sporting activities, counseling sessions, and training workshops. Meetings were also held between gang members and other local community groups.

Spergel and Grossman reported that the overall effect of the Gang Violence Reduction Program was positive. Approximately 95 percent of the targeted youths received some type of outreach service. About 66 percent were involved in program sporting activities. 64 percent received job placement assistance and 31 percent were targets of suppression efforts. Gang crime decreased in the target group, compared to gang crime in a control group which was not receiving program services. Also, comparison citizen surveys indicated that resident satisfaction was greater in the targeted neighborhoods than in another similar neighborhood, Pilsen, which had not received the program services. Community residents in Little Village had a greater reduction in the perceived level of gang crimes in their neighborhoods than did residents in Pilsen. In addition, Little Village residents believed that their police officers were more effective in combating gang crimes than residents in Pilsen.[83] However, these positive results were not sufficient to continue the operation of this program. Spergel reports that Chicago Police Department was not prepared to manage the level of community involvement and integration of program strategies that were required to keep it operational.[84]

Recent Results.   Since 1995, the Spergel model has been implemented in several cities across the country including Bloomington, Illinois; Mesa and Tucson, Arizona; Riverside, California; San Antonio, Texas; and Louisville, Kentucky. Evaluation results from the program have been mixed. In San Antonio, research was conducted on a sample of 110 program and 120 comparison group youths who received no project services. There was no evidence that the program youth reduced their involvement with their respective gangs. In fact, slightly more program youth became gang members. Overall, there was no substantial evidence that the program reduced the level of gang crime at either the individual, gang, or community levels.[85] In Tucson, the project was plagued by implementation problems. Only a limited number of agencies and community groups were involved. Program services focused on early intervention with younger juveniles. Once again, arrest patterns were not modified at either the individual or community levels.[86] However, the evaluation of the Riverside program revealed that arrests for serious violent crimes were substantially lower for

Operation Ceasefire The Boston Gun Project. A problem-oriented policing initiative aimed at reducing homicides among juveniles in Boston

program youths and they had a lower ratio of repeat drug arrests. However, their membership and involvement in gangs were not reduced relative to that of the youths in the comparison group.[87] To obtain up-to-date information on this project, consult the National Youth Gang Center website at http://www.iir.com/nygc/acgp/model.htm and a summary report of recent findings.[88]

Gang Suppression Programs

Gang suppression includes many law enforcement programs, especially those that go beyond normal police and prosecution practices.[89] They are often "intelligence-based" approaches that use data to establish and then guide program operations. Typically, it features an intervention that combines suppression at a number of levels (federal, state, and local) with the both the provision of social services and broader based enforcement (police, probation and parole, prosecution).[90] Here, we consider one, well-known suppression program – the Boston Gun Project also known as **Operation Ceasefire.**

The Boston Gun Project was a problem-oriented policing initiative expressly aimed at reducing homicides among juveniles in Boston. Between 1987 and 1990, youth homicides in Boston increased from 22 to 73 victims in 1990 (a 230 percent increase). From 1991 to 1195, Boston averaged about 44 youth homicides per year. In response to this crisis, professors at Harvard University's John F. Kennedy School of Government developed the program. The Project included (1) assembling an interagency working group of largely line-level criminal justice and other practitioners; (2) applying quantitative and qualitative research techniques to create an assessment of the nature of, and dynamics driving, youth violence in Boston; (3) developing an intervention designed to have a substantial, near-term impact on youth homicide; (4) implementing and adapting the intervention; and (5) evaluating the intervention's impact. Agencies included in the operation included the Boston Police Department; the Massachusetts departments of probation and parole; the office of the Suffolk County District Attorney; the office of the United States Attorney; the Bureau of Alcohol, Tobacco, and Firearms; the Massachusetts Department of Youth Services (juvenile corrections); Boston School Police; and gang outreach and prevention "street workers" attached to the Boston Community Centers program. Other important participants included the Ten Point Coalition of activist black clergy, the Drug Enforcement Administration, the Massachusetts State Police, and the office of the Massachusetts Attorney General.

Operation Ceasefire began in 1996. It was based on the "**pulling levers**" deterrence strategy which focused criminal justice attention on a small number of chronically offending gang-involved youth responsible for much of Boston's youth homicide problem.[91] Suppression tactics

pulling levers A deterrence strategy targeting a small number of chronically offending gang-involved youth were designed to deter chronic offenders by serving warrants, enforcing probation restrictions, and using the Federal courts for prosecution. The aim was to increase the cost of doing violence through these measures.

The program features face to face meetings with gang members to spread the "zero tolerance" for violence message of the pulling levers strategy. The long sentences that offenders receive were publicized in high-crime neighborhoods. The program sent gang mediation specialists are deployed to hot spots of violent gang crime that were identified by crime mapping. Crisis intervention teams were also deployed and the hot spots were continuously monitored by the police. Another strategy aimed to reduce access to firearms by disrupting the illegal gun market to interrupt their use. Federal firearm laws were used to prosecute dangerous offenders and take them off the street.[92]

Evaluation results on program impact were impressive. Operation Ceasefire achieved 63 percent reduction in Boston youth homicide and similar large reductions in non-fatal serious gun violence that was sustained for the next five years.[93] It also recorded a 23 percent reduction in the monthly percentage of recovered crime handguns that were new. Ceasefire had a significant impact on the supply of new handguns to criminals in Boston.[94]

Authors of the program offered the following key ingredients its apparent success:[95] Recognizing that violence problems are concentrated among groups of chronic offenders who are often, but not always, gang involved.

1. At the core of much group and gang violence is a dynamic or self-reinforcing positive feedback mechanism. The "Firebrake hypothesis": If this cycle of violence among these groups can be interrupted, perhaps a new equilibrium at a lower level of risk and violence can be established.

2. The utility of the "pulling levers" strategy. The aim of this method was to deter violent behavior by chronic gang offenders by reaching out directly to gang members, setting clear standards for their behavior, and backing up that message by pulling every lever legally available when those standards were violated.

3. Drawing on practitioner knowledge to understand violence problems.

4. Convening an interagency working group with a locus of responsibility.

5. Researcher involvement in an action-oriented enterprise.

To these, it should be added that Operation Ceasefire was a collaborative effort between community and criminal justice agencies. Enforcement was not solely responsible for the success of the effort.

Attempts to transfer this model elsewhere has had mixed results.[96] Rand researchers examined the effectiveness of the approach in the south Los Angeles Hollenbeck area – pre and post police intervention strategies. They found that crime was not significantly reduced either before or after the suppression period. Gun crime was significantly reduced during the intervention period in one area. Gang violence decreased sharply for the first 4 months of the intervention receded to the same level as before the intervention began. The researchers concluded that the project's performance was hampered by the reorganization of the L.A. Police Department's gang crime units and the lack of local ownership of the project. Again, this experience underscores the necessity for a well managed, collaborative approach between agencies engaged in gang suppression.[97]

The implication for police practice in gang suppression is clear. The Spergel model requires that law enforcement agencies carefully assess local problems before implementing any anti-gang strategy. Approaches to gang problems should be framed very narrowly to address identified problems of concern to communities and police.[98] Police gang units do not always follow these ideas. In their analysis of police gang units in four southwestern cities (Albuquerque, NM; Inglewood, CA; Las Vegas, NV; Phoenix, AZ). Katz and Webb found that these units rarely used their own intelligence to help guide their agencies responses to gangs. Organizational responses were heavily influenced by external stakeholders. Operational strategies were based on officer beliefs rather than through use of strategic planning and operational intelligence. Instead, the police typically responded with intense and traditional crime fighting tactics and questionable practices (racial profiling to determine gang members) to deal with the crime problems caused by gangs. They were largely ineffective and only succeeded in displacing gang problems to different areas.[99]

Video Profile: Future Soldiers Program

BOX 12.1 **MARA SALVATRUCHA (MS-13)**

Considered one of the most dangerous gangs in North America, Mara Salvatrucha (or MS-13) operates in at least 42 states (including the District of Columbia) and has about 6,000 to 10,000 members nationwide.[1] MS-13 began when Salvadorans fled to Los Angeles from their country's civil war in 1980. In response to Mexican and other gangs already in the area, the newcomers formed a *mara* (posse) of street-tough Salvadorans (*salvatruchas*). The number 13 is associated with Southern California street gangs. As the gang grew, it added members with military training. They dealt in extortion and drug trafficking, quickly expanding to include auto and weapons smuggling,

[1]Federal Bureau of Investigation, *The MS-13 Threat: A National Assessment*, http://www.fbi.gov/page2/jan08/ms13_011408.html. Retrieved on 6/12/08

human trafficking and kidnapping. They responded to increased enforcement in the U.S. by establishing outposts at home in El Salvador as well as Honduras, Guatemala, and Mexico.[2]

Following deportation from the U.S., MS-13 members quickly adapted to life in other countries. These countries responded in traditional ways of dealing with gangs. In Honduras, President Ricardo Maduro introduced zero tolerance laws to crack down on gang members. Called *mano dura* ("strong hand"), these laws imprisoned gang members for up to 12 years for even suspicion of membership as evidenced by tattoos. This level of enforcement had a detrimental effect on prison conditions and populations. President Manuel Zelaya tried a different approach, aimed at getting youths to give up violence and re-enter society peacefully. But the police still maintained gang units and routinely rounded up members in high crime areas.[3]

In El Salvador, President Tony Saca advocated a Super Mano Dura approach ("Super Firm Hand") that featured tight gun ownership laws and joint military/police patrols. But it also included funds for anti-gang and rehabilitation programs. Despite this approach, violent crimes, especially murders, soared. In Guatemala, President Oscar Berger adopted organized crime legislation that featured wiretaps and undercover operations to attack gangs. MS-13 members responded to these get tough policies in both countries with violent retaliation. New leaders replaced the jailed ones. Panamanian President Martin Torrijos took a different approach called Mano Amiga ("Friendly Hand") to provide youths with positive alternatives to gang membership, such as theater and sports activities. In sum, these approaches follow a familiar line of gang suppression and an attempt at prevention. The more deep-seated problems of poverty, corruption and overpopulation are untouched by them.

In the U.S., the FBI created a special task force to deal with MS-13 that included an office in San Salvador to coordinate international efforts. It is coupled with TAG (the "Transnational Anti-Gang Initiative") it plans to[4]:

- Identify and track gang members in El Salvador, gleaning as much information as possible about each member: their tattoos, their street names, their associates, their families, and their typical hideouts and hangouts in the U.S. and Central America.

- Channel this information through the FBI agents assigned to TAG, then forwarded to the FBI task force headquarters. The task force will ensure the information is shared with appropriate field divisions as well as law enforcement leaders in Central America.

- Conduct joint investigations with Central American law enforcement and provide operational assistance to them as needed.

- The task force has also instituted the Central American Fingerprint Exploitation (CAFÉ) to acquire criminal fingerprints from Central America and merge them with other records into the FBI's Integrated Automated Fingerprint Identification System (IAFIS) database.[5]

It is clear that prevention, suppression and intervention must all be used to combat this problem. Education initiatives coupled with the targeting of hard-core gang

---

[2]Arian Campo-Flores and Andrew Romano, "The Most Dangerous Gang in America," Newsweek, Vol. 145 (March 28, 2005).

[3]Ana Arana, "How the Street Gangs Took Central America," *Foreign Affairs*, (May/June 2005) http://www.foreignaffairs.org/20050501/faessay84310/ana-arana/. Retrieved on 6/12/08. Clare M. Ribando, *Gangs in Central America – CRS Report to Congress* http://www.fas.org/sgp/crs/row/RL34112.pdf. Retrieved on 6/12/08.

[4]Federal Bureau of Investigation, *Going Global on Gangs: New Partnership Targets MS-13*, http://www.fbi.gov/page2/oct07/ms13tag101007.htm. Retrieved on 6/12/08

[5]Federal Bureau of Investigation, *Fighting Gang Violence*, http://www.fbi.gov/aboutus/transformation/gangs.htm. Retrieved on 6/12/08.

(continued)

members can lead to a comprehensive effort to defeat such gangs. The extent of MS-13's reach also calls for the use of an international approach across all levels of government.

At the local level, Los Angeles police have used the RICO (Racketeer Influenced and Corrupt Organizations) statute to dismantle such gangs as the Mexican Mafia. Chief William Bratton has supported the development of Community Impact Action Teams consisting of local, state and federal law enforcement agents coupled with citizen watchdog groups, clergy, school officials, probation and parole officers, and city and state prosecutors. The effort led to a 14 percent reduction in crime statistics in January 2005.

SUMMARY

Before strategies can be developed to address gang problems, there must be an acknowledgment that a gang problem exists or has the potential to develop within a neighborhood. Huff notes that some political leaders may deny that their jurisdictions are experiencing gang problems because that may reflect negatively on their ability to control crime and provide safety for their constituents.[100] This denial sometimes also exists within law enforcement agencies as well as within schools for similar image reasons and concerns that they will be criticized for failing to address their problems.

It is important for local governments to recognize the existence of gangs—the precursor to formulating strategies to address the problem. Recognizing gang problems is not always a straightforward science. Some gangs advertise their existence by dressing in particular colors, by gesturing hand signs to other members, and by writing their gang names on property in public view. Those gangs are easier to detect and identifying their members is a task that can be accomplished by local law enforcement at the patrol officer level. Other gangs however, are clandestine operations. They operate covertly in order to avoid detection by law enforcement. These gangs cannot be exposed as easily. More intense law enforcement efforts are necessary to identify their members. This can be better accomplished through the utilization of investigatory police units such as detective squads and special gang unit personnel.

Because gang membership continues to grow, strategies to control gang growth must be tailored to address potential gang members as well as current and past gang members. Prevention, intervention, and suppression should be directed toward the appropriate audiences. General prevention strategies can target the general population. Increased prevention strategies with personal contact can be directed to those persons who exhibit increased risk factors for gang membership.

People who possess multiple risk factors may be the best candidates for the more intensive prevention programs. High risk factors include living in areas with easy access to illicit drugs, association with delinquent peers and with other gang members, living in areas with high rate of single parent households, residing in a broken home, and being a male between the ages of 10 and 14 years. Research findings in this chapter conclude that early influences of antisocial behavior in childhood, as well as early initiation of violence and marijuana use were predictors of future adolescent gang entry.[101] Prevention methods should therefore begin prior to teenage years—as recommended by educators involved with the G.R.E.A.T. program.[102]

Rather than administering prevention programs to the entire youth population, consideration should be given to reduce the size of the target group that receives the program. The G.R.E.A.T. program was directed toward middle school students. Studies have shown that prevention programs may have a better effect if administered to a younger population between the ages of 10 and 12 years.[103]

When a community has many children residing in single-parent households or the community has many households with working parents, the children are left with a reduced number of people to monitor their activities. These communities may benefit by offering supervised after-school activities which can prevent children from engaging in delinquent behavior when adults are not around. The effectiveness of the supervisor is a very important factor. An adult supervisor who has little interest in the activities of the children will not monitor them effectively. Therefore, a dedicated person must be chosen for this responsibility.

Better communication among the residents of a community can foster closer relationships among the residents, which may lead to increased interest in the welfare of one's neighbors. Community groups and tenant associations can provide the avenue for communication between residents and encourage the sense of ownership in one's neighborhood.

Intervention programs target those people who are currently members of gangs. A youth's mere membership in a gang does not necessarily result in criminality. However, the odds are that it will because gangs are organized around delinquent and criminal conduct.[104] Programs that offer vocational training and job opportunities may be directed toward this group to provide this target audience with referrals to conventional institutions and guidance to join the mainstream society.

Suppression programs are used to combat persistent gangs and gang members. By targeting the hardcore gang members, a strong message is sent to the gang. Close cooperation between police agencies, prosecutors, courts, probation officers and community agencies and leaders increases the effectiveness of suppression efforts.

In their policy analysis and review of gang prevention programs, Klein and Maxson offer six selected goals for gang control:[105]

1. **Prevent gang joining.** Encouraging gang desistance by overcoming the group processes that reinforce gang membership. Crime reduction during gang membership.

2. **Group-level goals** for gang change similarly come in several forms. Disrupt the structural factors that reinforce gang existence. Reduce intergang violence and prevent gang formation.

3. **Community level goals** for gang control are based on the notion that it is communities that spawn street gangs. Getting the police involved is easy; getting the community involved is difficult. Examine how the community promotes gang involvement.

4. **Implement the Spergel Model.** Mount programs for the general youth population or aim at the at-risk group.

5. **Maximize the use of verifiable data,** both local and generic.

6. **Position independent evaluation** of program processes ahead of time. Research to determine the effectiveness of programs is crucial.

By analyzing gang membership risk factors and understanding why and how adolescents join gangs, law enforcement, social service providers, and community groups can collaboratively develop policies and tailor strategies to efficiently address youth crime.

KEY TERMS

G.R.E.A.T.	Operation Ceasefire
gang entry models	pulling levers

DISCUSSION AND REVIEW QUESTIONS

1. The delinquent subculture has many attributes. Choose one and give an example of how it is present in American culture.
2. What identifies the gang as a subculture? What evidence would you cite to support such a claim?
3. Why do people join gangs?
4. What are the risk factors for gang joining? Which one is the most important?
5. How does containment insulate against delinquency? Why are you a college student instead of a jail or prison convict?

6. How can improvements in gang prevention efforts be improved?
7. What elements in gang prevention should be stressed?

VIDEO PROFILES

The *Gang Counseling* video profile in MyCrimeKit shows a gang unit in a detention facility. How do the attributes of gang members listed by the officer and the psychologist correspond to Malcolm Klein's "minimal list of the attributes of potential gang member recruits"? How to the models of gang entry methods described in this chapter correspond to the reasons that the officer, psychologist and juveniles in the unit give for joining a gang? According to these three groups, which of the models most closely corresponds with the reasons that they noted? How do the methods proposed by the officer and the psychologist to deal with gang members correspond to the OJJDP's Comprehensive Gang Model? What elements do they have in common and how do they differ?

The *Former White Supremacy Member* video profile in MyCrimeKit highlights one gang member and provides an interview with the superintendent about his goals for the juveniles within the gang unit. What is Mike's story about how he got to be in a gang? Mike talks about the benefits of being locked up. What does he perceive them to be? The facility is highly structured, both in design and in activities for the juveniles. What are the pros and cons of the structure for juvenile gang members who will one day be released? Finally, what are the Superintendent's goals for the juveniles in the gang unit?

The *Future Soldiers Program* video profile in MyCrimeKit follows "Mike" in a highly specialized program. What is the Future Soldiers program? Compare and contrast the administrative review committee's interaction with Mike and those in previous videos. Finally, discuss any relationships you see between this program and any of the programs discussed in this or previous chapters.

MYCRIMEKIT

mycrimekit Go to MyCrimeKit.com to explore the following study tools and resources specific to this chapter:

- Practice Quiz: Test your knowledge with multiple-choice, true-false, fill-in-the-blank, and essay questions.
- Flashcards: 20 flashcards to test your knowledge of the chapter's key terms.

- Web Quest: Review the Web sites of the Office of Juvenile Justice and Delinquency Prevention's Comprehensive Gang Model.
- Web Links: Check to see whether your local and state law enforcement sites have gang-related content.

ENDNOTES

1. This chapter is co-authored with Dimitrios G. Roumeliotis of the New York City Police Department.

2. Malcolm W. Klein, *The American Street Gang* (New York: Oxford University Press, 1995) p. 153.

3. Finn-Aage Esbensen and David Huizinga, "Gangs, Drugs, and Delinquency in a Survey of Urban Youth," *Criminology*, Vol. 31 (1993), pp. 565–587.

4. Rachel A. Gordon, Benjamin B. Lahey, Eriko Kawai, Rolf Loeber, Magda Stouthamer-Loeber, and David P. Farrington, "Antisocial Behavior and Youth Gang Membership: Selection and Socialization," *Criminology*, Vol. 42 (2004), pp. 55–87.

5. James C. Howell, *Youth Gangs: An Overview.* (Washington, DC: Office of Juvenile Justice and Delinquency Prevention, 1998).

6. Irving A. Spergel, *The Youth Gang Problem.* (New York: Oxford University Press, 1995).

7. National Youth Gang Center (2007). *National Youth Gang Survey Analysis.* Retrieved February 4, 2008 from http://www.iir.com/nygc/nygsa/

8. OJJDP Fact Sheet, *Highlights of the 2006 National Youth Gang Survey* (Washington, DC: U.S. Department of Justice, July 2008), p. 1.

9. Lewis Yablonsky, *Gangsters: Fifty Years of Madness, Drugs, and Death on the Streets of America* (New York: New York University Press, 1997), p. 184.

10. Richard A. Ball and G. David Curry, "The Logic of Definition in Criminology: Purposes and Methods for Defining Gangs," *Criminology*, Vol. 33 (1995), pp. 225–245.

11. Albert K. Cohen, *Delinquent Boys: The Culture of the Gang.* (New York: Free Press, 1955).

12. Walter B. Miller, "Gangs, Groups and Serious Youth Crime," in David Schichor and Delos H. Kelly, eds., *Critical Issues in Juvenile Delinquency.* (Lexington, MA: Lexington Books, 1980), p. 85.

13. Spergel, *Youth Gang Problem.*

14. Malcolm W. Klein and Cheryl L. Maxson, *Gang Structures, Crime Patterns, and Police Responses.* (Washington DC: U.S. Department of Justice. National Institute of Justice, 1996).

15. Mary Morash, "Gangs, Groups, and Delinquency," *British Journal of Criminology,* Vol. 23 (1983), pp. 309–331.

16. Finn-Aage Esbensen, L. Thomas Winfree, Jr., Ni He, and Terrance J. Taylor, "Youth Gangs and Definitional Issues: When is a Gang a Gang, and Why Does It Matter?" *Crime and Delinquency,* Vol. 47 (2001) pp. 105–130.

17. Howell, *Youth Gangs.*

18. Malcolm W. Klein, *Chasing After Street Gangs: A Forty-Year Journey* (Upper Saddle River, NJ: Prentice Hall, 2007), p. 18.

19. Esbensen, Winfree, He, and Taylor, "Definitional Issues."

20. Klein and Maxson, *Street Gang Patterns and Policies*, p. 207.

21. Klein, *The American Street Gang*, pp. 59–60.

22. Beth Bjerregaard, "Operationalizing Gang Membership: The Impact Measurement on Gender Differences in Gang Self-identification and Delinquent Involvement," *Women and Criminal Justice,* Vol. 13 (2002), pp. 79–100.

23. Klein, *The American Street Gang*, p. 80.

24. Terence P. Thornberry, "Membership in Youth Gangs and Involvement in Serious and Violent Offending," in Arlen Egley, Jr., Cheryl L. Maxson, Jody Miller, and Malcolm W. Klein, eds., *The Modern Gang Reader* 3d ed. (Los Angeles, CA: Roxbury, 2006), pp. 224–232.

25. A. L. Anderson "Individual and Contextual Influences in Delinquency: The Role of the Single-parent Family," *Journal of Criminal Justice*, Vol. 30 (2002), pp. 575–587.

26. Dana Peterson-Lynskey, L. Thomas Winfree, Jr., Finn-Aage Esbensen, and D. Clason, "Linking Gender, Minority Group Status and Family Matters to Self Control Theory: A Multivariate Analysis of Key Self-Control Concepts in a Youth Gang Context." *Juvenile and Family Court Journal*, Vol. 51 (2000), pp. 1–19.

27. Anderson "Individual and Contextual Influences in Delinquency."

28. Lahey and Gordon et. al. "Boys Who Join Gangs."

29. Hill and Howell, et. al. "Childhood Risk Factors."

30. G. David Curry and Irving A. Spergel, "Gang Involvement and Delinquency Among Hispanic and African-American Adolescent Males," *Journal of Research in Crime and Delinquency,* Vol. 29 (1992), pp. 273–299.

31. Ronald Huff and K.S. Trump, "Youth Violence and Gangs: School Safety Initiatives in Urban and Suburban School Districts," *Education and Urban Society*, Vol. 28 (1996), pp. 492–503.

32. Terence P. Thornberry, Marvin D. Krohn, Alan J. Lizotte, Carolyn A. Smith, and Kimberly Tobin, "The Antecedents of Gang Membership," in Arlen Egley, Jr., Cheryl L. Maxson, Jody Miller, and Malcolm W. Klein, eds., *The Modern Gang Reader* 3d ed. (Los Angeles, CA: Roxbury, 2006), pp. 31–33.

33. Klein, *The American Street Gang*, pp. 78–79.

34. Deborah Lamm Weisel, "The Evolution of Street Gangs: An Examination of Form and Variation," in Arlen Egley, Jr., Cheryl L. Maxson, Jody Miller, and Malcolm W. Klein, eds., *The Modern Gang Reader* 3d ed. (Los Angeles, CA: Roxbury, 2006), p. 94.

35. Bjerregaard, "Operationalizing Gang Membership."

36. Esbensen and Huizinga, "Gangs, Drugs, and Delinquency."

37. Bjerregaard and C. Smith, "Gender Differences in Gang Participation."

38. A.M. Grascia, "Girls, Gangs and Crime: Profile of the Young Female Offender," *Journal of Gang Research*, Vol. 13 (2006), pp. 37–49.

39. Finn-Aage Esbensen and L. Thomas Winfree, Jr., "Race and Gender Differences Between Gang and Nongang Youths," in Arlen Egley, Jr., Cheryl L. Maxson, Jody Miller, and Malcolm W. Klein, eds., *The Modern Gang Reader,* 3d ed. (Los Angeles, CA: Roxbury, 2006), pp. 171–172.

40. D.D. Sule, "Correlates of Hispanic Female Gang Membership," *Journal of Gang Research*, Vol. 12 (2005), pp. 1–23.

41. Jody Miller, "Getting Into Gangs," in Arlen Egley, Jr., Cheryl L. Maxson, Jody Miller, and Malcolm W. Klein, eds., *The Modern Gang Reader* 3d ed. (Los Angeles, CA: Roxbury, 2006), pp. 43–59.

42. Joan Moore and John Hagedorn, "Female Gangs–A Focus on Research," in Arlen Egley, Jr., Cheryl L. Maxson, Jody Miller, and Malcolm W. Klein, eds., *The Modern Gang Reader* 3d ed. (Los Angeles, CA: Roxbury, 2006), pp. 192–194.

43. George W. Knox, "Females and Gangs: Sexual Violence, Prostitution, and Exploitation," *Journal of Gang Research*, Vol. 11, (2004), pp. 1–15.

44. Mark S. Fleisher and J.L. Krienert, "Life-course Events, Social Networks, and the Emergence of Violence among Female Gang Members," *Journal of Community Psychology*, Vol. 32 (2004), pp. 607–622.

45. Alice Cepeda and Valdez Avelardo, "Risk Behaviors among Young Mexican American Gang-associated Females: Sexual Relations,

Partying, Substance Use, and Crime," *Journal of Adolescent Research*, Vol. 18 (2003), pp. 90–106.

46. Klein and Maxson, *Street Gang Patterns and Policies*, p. 34.

47. D.L. Yearwood and A. Rhyne, "Hispanic/Latino Gangs: A Comparative Analysis of Nationally Affiliated and Local Gangs," *Journal of Gang Research*, Vol. 14 (2007), pp. 1–18.

48. Christopher Adamson, "Defensive Localism in White and Black: A Comparative History of European-American and African-American Youth Gangs," *Ethnic and Racial Studies*, Vol. 23 (2000), pp. 272–298.

49. John Hagedorn, "Gangs, Neighborhoods, and Public Policy," *Social Problems*, Vol. 38 (1991), pp. 529–542.

50. George E. Higgins and Melissa L. Ricketts, "Self-control Theory, Race and Delinquency," Journal of Ethnicity in Criminal Justice, Vol. 3 (2005), pp. 5–20.

51. Curtis J. Robinson, "Methamphetamine Sales and Use among Gang Members: The Cross-over Effect," *Journal of Gang Research*, Vol. 9 (2001), pp. 39–52.

52. Glenn T. Tsunokai and Augustine J. Kposowa, "Asian Gangs in the United States: The Current State of the Research Literature," *Crime, Law and Social Change*, Vol. 37 (2002), pp. 37–50.

53. John Z. Wang, "Asian Gangs: New Challenges in the 21st Century," *Journal of Gang Research*, Vol. 8 (2000), pp. 51–62.

54. Glenn T. Tsunokai, "Beyond the Lenses of the "Model" Minority Myth: A Descriptive Portrait of Asian Gang Members," *Journal of Gang Research*, Vol. 12, (2005), pp. 37–58.

55. K. Kei-ho Pih and J. Mao, "Golden Parachutes and Gangbanging: Taiwanese Gangs in Suburban Southern California," *Journal of Gang Research*, Vol. 12 (2005), pp. 59–72.

56. Terrence P. Thornberry, Marvin D. Krohn, Alan J. Lizotte, and D. Chard-Wierschem, "The Role of Juvenile Gangs in Facilitating Delinquent Behavior," *Journal of Research in Crime and Delinquency*, Vol. 30 (1993), pp. 55–87; Benjamin B. Lahey, Rachel A. Gordon, Rolf A.Loeber, Magda Stouthamer-Loeber, and David P. Farrington, "Boys Who Join Gangs: A Prospective Study of Predictors of First Gang Entry," *Journal of Abnormal Child Psychology*, Vol. 27 (1999), pp. 261–276.

57. Klein and Maxson, *Street Gang Patterns and Policies*, p. 75.

58. Finn-Aage Esbensen and David Huizinga, "Gangs, Drugs, and Delinquency in a Survey of Urban Youth," *Criminology*, Vol. 31 (1993), pp. 565–587.

59. Thornberry and Krohn et. al., "The Role of Juvenile Gangs."

60. Karl G. Hill, James C. Howell, J. David Hawkins, and S.R. Battin-Pearson, "Childhood Risk Factors for Adolescent Gang Membership: Results from the Seattle Social Development Project," *Journal of Research in Crime and Delinquency,* Vol. 36 (1999), pp. 300–322.

61. Thornberry and Krohn et. al., "The Role of Juvenile Gangs."

62. Lahey and Gordon et. al. "Boys Who Join Gangs."

63. Klein and Maxson, *Street Gang Patterns and Policies*, p. 76.

64. Sara R. Battin, Karl G. Hill, Robert D. Abbott, Richard F. Catalano, and J. David Hawkins, "The Contribution of Gang Membership to Delinquency Beyond Delinquent Friends," *Criminology*, Vol. 36 (1998), pp. 93–115.

65. Battin and Hill, et. al. "The Contribution of Gang Membership."

66. Gordon and Lahey, et. al. "Antisocial Behavior."

67. Scott H. Decker and Janet L. Lauritsen, "Leaving the Gang," in Arlen Egley, Jr., Cheryl L. Maxson, Jody Miller, and Malcolm W. Klein, eds., *The Modern Gang Reader,* 3d ed. (Los Angeles: Roxbury, 2006), p. 69.

68. Charles M. Katz, Vincent J. Webb, and Scott H. Decker, "Using the Arrestee Drug Abuse Monitoring (ADAM) Program to Further Understand the Relationship Between Drug Use and Gang Membership," *Justice Quarterly*, Vol. 22 (2005), pp. 58–88.

69. M.R. De La Rosa, D. Rugh, and P. Rojas, "Substance Abuse Among Puerto Rican and Dominican Gang Members in a Small City Setting," *Journal of Social Work Practice in the Addictions*, Vol. 5 (2005), pp. 21–43.

70. K. MacKenzie, G. Hunt, and K. Joe-Laidler, "Youth Gangs and Drugs: The Case of Marijuana," *Journal of Ethnicity in Substance Abuse*, Vol. 4 (2005) pp. 99–134.

71. Paul E. Bellair and Thomas L. McNulty, "Gang Membership, Drug Selling, and Violence in Neighborhood Context," *Justice Quarterly*, Vol. 26 (2009), pp. 644–669.

72. P.B. Stretesky and Mark R. Pogrebin, "Gang-related Gun Violence: Socialization, Identity, and Self," *Journal of Contemporary Ethnography*, Vol. 36 (2007), pp. 85–114.

73. Scott H. Decker, "Collective and Normative Features of Gang Violence," *Justice Quarterly*, Vol. 13 (1996), pp. 243–264. See also, Scott H. Decker and Barrik Van Winkle, *Life in the Gang* (Cambridge, UK: Cambridge University Press, 1996).

74. J.M. Pizarro and J.M. McGloin, "Explaining Gang Homicides in Newark, New Jersey: Collective Behavior or Social Disorganization?" *Journal of Criminal Justice*, Vol. 34 (2006), pp. 195–207.

75. Dana Peterson, T.J. Taylor, and Finn-Aage Esbensen, "Gang Membership and Violent Victimization," *Justice Quarterly*, Vol. 21 (2004) pp. 793–815.

76. Cheryl L. Maxson, "Gang Members on the Move," in Arlen Egley, Jr., Cheryl L. Maxson, Jody Miller, and Malcolm W. Klein, eds., *The Modern Gang Reader*, 3d ed. (Los Angeles, CA: Roxbury, 2006), pp. 117–129.

77. Finn-Aage Esbensen, D. Wayne Osgood, Terrance J. Taylor, Dana Peterson, and Adrienne Freng, "How Great is G.R.E.A.T.? Results from a Longitudinal Quasi-Experimental Design," *Criminology and Public Policy*, Vol. 1 (2001), pp. 88–89; D. J. Palumbo, R. Eskay, M. Hallett, et. al., "Do Gang Prevention Strategies Actually Reduce Crime?" *Gang Journal*, Vol. 1 (1993), pp. 1–10; D. J. Palumbo and J. L. Ferguson, "Evaluating Gang Resistance Education and Training (G.R.E.A.T.): Is the Impact the Same as that of Drug Abuse Resistance Education (D.A.R.E.)?" *Evaluation Review*, Vol. 19 (1995), pp. 597–619; Thomas L. Winfree, Finn-Aage Esbensen, and D. Wayne Osgood, "Evaluating a School-Based Gang Prevention Program," *Evaluation Review*, Vol. 20 (1996), pp. 181–203; Thomas L. Winfree, Dana P. Lynskey, and James R. Maupin, "Developing Local Police and Federal Law Enforcement Partnerships: G.R.E.A.T. as a Case Study of Policy Implementation," *Criminal Justice Review*, Vol. 24 (1999), pp. 145–168.

78. Klein and Maxson, *Street Gang Patterns and Policies*, p. 96.

79. Ibid., p. 101.

80. OJJDP Comprehensive Gang Model, *A Guide to Assessing Your Community's Youth Gang Problem* (Washington, DC: Office of Juvenile Justice and Delinquency Prevention, March 2001), pp. 8–9.

81. Ibid., p. 10.

82. Klein and Maxson, *Street Gang Patterns and Policies*, p.121.

83. Irving A. Spergel and S.F. Grossman, "The Little Village Project: A Community Approach to the Gang Problem," *Social Work*, Vol. 42 (1997), pp. 456–470.

84. Irving A. Spergel, *Reducing Youth Gang Violence: The Little Village Gang Project in Chicago*. (Lanham, MD: AltaMira, 2007).

85. Irving A. Spergel, S.M. Wa, and R.V. Sosa, *Evaluation of the San Antonio Comprehensive Community-Wide Approach to Gang Prevention, Intervention and Suppression Program: GRAASP* (Chicago: School of Social Service Administration, University of Chicago, 2004).

86. Irving A. Spergel, S.M. Wa, and R.V. Sosa, *Evaluation of the Tucson Comprehensive Community-Wide Approach to Gang Prevention,*

Intervention and Suppression Program: GRAASP (Chicago: School of Social Service Administration, University of Chicago, 2004).

87. Irving A. Spergel, S.M. Wa, and R.V. Sosa, *Evaluation of the Riverside Comprehensive Community-Wide Approach to Gang Prevention, Intervention and Suppression Program: GRAASP* (Chicago, IL: School of Social Service Administration, University of Chicago, 2003).

88. Office of Juvenile Justice and Delinquency Prevention, *Best Practices to Address Community Gang Problems: OJJDP's Comprehensive Gang Model* (Washington, D.C.: U.S. Department of Justice, Office of Justice Programs, 2006). http://www.ncjrs.gov/pdffiles1/ojjdp/222799.pdf

89. Klein and Maxson, *Street Gang Patterns and Policies*, p. 74.

90. Noelle E. Fearn, Scott H. Decker, and G. David Curry, "Public Policy Responses to Gangs: Evaluating the Outcomes," in Arlen Egley, Jr., Cheryl L. Maxson, Jody Miller, and Malcolm W. Klein, eds., *The Modern Gang Reader*, 3d ed. (Los Angeles, CA: Roxbury, 2006), pp. 321.

91. Harvard University, Kennedy School of Government (2007). *Operation Ceasefire/Boston Gun Project*. Retrieved February 9, 2008 from http://www.ksg.harvard.edu/criminaljustice/research/bgp.htm

92. Office of Juvenile Justice and Delinquency Prevention (2000). *Youth Gang Programs and Strategies*. Retrieved February 8, 2008 from http://www.ncjrs.gov/html/ojjdp/summary_2000_8/multiagency.html#twelve

93. Anthony A. Braga, David M. Kennedy, Elin J. Waring, et al, "Problem-oriented Policing, Deterrence, and Youth Violence: An Evaluation of Boston's Operation Ceasefire," *Journal of Research in Crime and Delinquency*, Vol. 38 (2001), pp. 195–225.

94. Anthony A. Braga and Glenn L. Pierce, "Disrupting Illegal Firearms Markets in Boston: The Effects of Operation Ceasefire on the Supply of New Handguns to Criminals," *Criminology and Public Policy*, Vol. 4 (2005), pp. 201–232.

95. Anthony A. Braga, David M. Kennedy, and George E. Tita, "New Approaches to the Strategic Prevention of Gang and Group-Involved Violence," in Arlen Egley, Jr., Cheryl L. Maxson, Jody Miller, and Malcolm W. Klein, eds. *The Modern Gang Reader*, 3d ed. (Los Angeles: Roxbury, 2006), p. 345.

96. Klein and Maxson, *Street Gang Patterns and Policies*, p. 252.

97. George Tita, K.J. Riley and G. Ridgeway, *Reducing Gun Violence: Results from an Intervention in East Los Angeles* (Santa Monica, CA: Rand, 2003).

98. Deborah Lamm Weisel, "The Evolution of Street Gangs: An Examination of Form and Variation," in Arlen Egley, Jr., Cheryl L. Maxson, Jody Miller, and Malcolm W. Klein, eds. *The Modern Gang Reader*, 3d ed. (Los Angeles: Roxbury, 2006), p. 102.

99. Charles M. Katz and Vincent J. Webb, *Policing Gangs in America* (Cambridge: Cambridge University Press, 2006), pp. 88–89.

100. Ronald Huff, "Youth Gangs and Public Policy," *Crime and Delinquency*, Vol. 28 (1989), pp. 524–537.

101. Hill, Howell, et. al. "Childhood Risk Factors."

102. Dana Peterson and Finn-Aage Esbensen, "The Outlook Is G.R.E.A.T.: What Educators Say About School-Based Prevention and the Gang Resistance Education and Training (G.R.E.A.T.) Program." *Evaluation Review*, Vol. 28 (2004), pp. 218–245.

103. Hill and Howell, et. al. "Childhood Risk Factors."

104. Terence P. Thornberry, "Membership in Gangs and Involvement in Serious and Violent Offending," in Rolf Loeber and David P. Farrington, eds., *Serious and Violent Juvenile Offenders: Risk Factors and Successful Interventions*, (Beverly Hills, CA: Sage Publications, 1998), pp. 147–166.

105. Klein and Maxson, *Street Gang Patterns and Policies*, pp. 234–245.

adjudicated Term used in juvenile court that means the same as *convicted* in the adult court.

adjudicatory hearing Hearing that includes witnesses and all facts of the case. Typically, the judge makes the final decision about the case.

adoption The social and legal process for becoming a parent.

aftercare Aftercare and parole are interchangeable terms referring to the conditional release of a juvenile from a correctional institution.

bail Money or property presented to the court for release of the accused from custody; The U.S. Supreme Court has not determined if juveniles have a constitutional right to bail.

battered child syndrome A disease that impacts children due to persistent physical abuse.

benefit of clergy An early form of suspended sentence.

boot camps Programs modeled after military basic training in an attempt to balance punishment with treatment and education.

Cambridge (UK) Study of Delinquent Development Included working-class males from age 8 to 32 years, beginning in 1961–62 to identify predictors of prevalence, onset of offending, and persistence versus desistance of offending.

caseload size The number of parolees supervised by an aftercare officer/probation officer.

Cesare Beccaria Founded the "classical" school of criminology.

child savers Before the start of the modern era, these individuals crusaded for children's rights and for treatment of children different from that accorded adult criminals.

child-related problems Specific reasons associated with children (e.g., mental handicap, delinquent behavior) that might place a child in foster care.

children in need of services (CHINS) Abused, neglected, abandoned, and other victimized children.

classification Administrative controls utilized to manage delinquents for treatment.

classification of the act Classification of the delinquent behavior.

classification of the actor Classification of the juvenile.

classification systems for management Assessing the juvenile to determine classifications.

classification systems for treatment Assessing the juvenile for treatment needs.

cohort study Examines a selected group (cohort) of people who share a common experience in time (e.g., born in the same year).

Columbus Cohort Included all juveniles born between 1956 and 1960 in Columbus, Ohio, who had been arrested for a violent crime.

Community Assessment Centers (CACs) The intake point for the juvenile following arrest.

community policing Partnership between the police, neighborhoods, and the people they serve.

community-based treatment Methods of handling juveniles in a community setting as an alternative to an institutional commitment.

conditions of parole Requirements that the paroled juvenile not commit certain behaviors (e.g., new offenses), as well as conform to others (e.g., attend school) to prevent revocation.

containment theory Theory by Reckless that the tendency to commit unlawful acts is determined by the type, or quality, of the self-concept the person has and the person's ability to "contain" the act.

cottage reform school Designed to give a home interest and attachment for institutionalized juveniles.

criminological theory Attempts to explain why crime exists, how it takes place, and what can be done about it.

criminology Body of knowledge that represents attempts to determine the causes of crime.

custody assessment Assessment of the juvenile's supervision risk.

decarceration Removing as many juveniles as possible from custody and treating them in an open environment.

deinstitutionalization The act of removing nondelinquent juveniles from secure detention or institutions.

delinquency petition Formal petition seeking to adjudicate the juvenile delinquent that states the charges against the juvenile.

detention center Secure institutions often housing a mixture of juvenile offenders, victims, and status offenders.

Detention Risk Assessment Instrument (DRAI) Assessment of the juvenile's risk to the community.

detention The detaining of juveniles. Preventive detention of juveniles awaiting adjudication upheld in *Schall v. Martin*. However, holding accused status offenders in adult jails prior to adjudication is unconstitutional.

determinate sentence A fixed length sentence that must be served within a correctional institution.

Developmental Victimization Survey (DVS) Longitudinal study designed to assess a comprehensive range of childhood victimizations across gender, race, and developmental stage.

discharge from parole Discretionary decision that reasonable assurance exists that the parolee will continue to adjust in the community without supervision.

disproportionate minority confinement The overrepresentation of minority youth in juvenile institutions.

diversification The breadth of juvenile commitment programs represented which attempt to address the different problems faced by juveniles.

diversion Process of limiting the amount of involvement a juvenile has with the formal organization and procedures of the criminal and juvenile justice systems.

dual beneficiaries Due to the goal conflict in the juvenile justice system, it serves both delinquents and children in need of services.

Duke of Beaufort v. Berty Court decision (England, 1721) that children should be treated differently than adults.

electronic monitoring Tracks movement using a tracking device worn by the client.

elements of deterrence theory Identifying the aspects of punishment that are predicted to affect the future behavior of an offender or potential offender.

Ex parte Crouse Decision by Pennsylvania Supreme Court that upheld the authority of the state to act in *parens patriae* for the benefit of juveniles.

exclusionary rule Prohibition against the use of illegally obtained evidence in court.

expiation Atonement of sins through suffering.

face sheet Data recorded about the juvenile (e.g., prior arrests, current charges) during the intake process.

family group conferencing Model that many police diversion programs follow. The conference is aimed at resolving conflicts between all concerned parties (e.g., juveniles, parents, victims, community members).

folkways Socially acceptable behaviors.

foster care Any kind of full-time substitute care for children outside their own home by people other than their parents.

fundamental fairness The test of a juvenile's rights when considering whether the juvenile's statements were voluntary.

gang entry models Selection, Socialization, Enhancement models were developed to explain how gang joining works.

generality The breadth, depth, or limited nature of criminological theories.

"Get Tough" movement Movement featuring stricter penalties for youths—including the sentencing of juveniles as adults and the death penalty—that is focused on such issues as punishment, justice, and accountability. This terminology reflects the view that juveniles must bear individual responsibility for their crimes, particularly serious crimes, as adults do.

Gideon v. Wainwright Court decision (1963) allowing right to legal counsel in adult felony cases.

goal conflict The goals of the juvenile justice system include working with juveniles who have committed offenses as well as juveniles who are in need of services.

good time law Allows for the reduction of time to a sentence based on the person's good conduct or good behavior.

grand theories Criminological theories that are attempts to explain all types of criminal behavior.

G.R.E.A.T. Gang Resistance Education and Training school-based gang prevention program targeting middle school students.

grievance procedure Policy in place for a family to utilize when they think they are being treated unjustly or unfairly while in supervision.

group homes Alternative placement for juveniles as a means of easing the youth's reentry to the community.

group treatment The treatment of juveniles in a group setting versus an individual setting. Group treatment may also include the family of the juvenile.

halfway house One type of group home; the term *halfway* has a negative connotation, but the focus remains on easing delinquent reentry.

Hammurabic Code Dates from c. 2270 B.C., and is considered by many historians to be the first comprehensive attempt at codifying laws.

Hospice at San Michele One of the first prisons in the world; was designed to incarcerate juveniles and rehabilitate wayward youth.

House of Refuge A "group home" in London constructed in 1758 to rescue vagrant girls from almost certain lives of prostitution.

hulk Ships used to confine and transport delinquent children from England to Australia.

In re Gault (1967) Extended due process rights to juveniles, specifically right to a notice of charges, right to counsel, right to confront and cross-examine witnesses, and right of privilege against self-incrimination.

In re Winship (1970) To justify the finding of delinquency against a juvenile, there must be proof beyond a reasonable doubt.

incapacitation The action of holding an offender in secure detention or in jail or in prison so that the individual does not have the opportunity to commit any additional offenses against society.

indeterminate sentence A sentence having no minimum or maximum length; release is based on perceived rehabilitation of the individual person.

Index crimes Violent and property offenses for which data are collected in the Uniformed Crime Reports. Violent Index crimes include murder, forcible rape, robbery, and aggravated assault. Property Index crimes include burglary, larceny-theft, motor vehicle theft, and arson.

insulation The term used by Reckless to describe why some juveniles living in high-crime areas did not turn to crime.

intake The point at which the juvenile is "booked" into the juvenile justice system.

IAP Model Program emphasizing a highly structured and intensive supervision with follow-up services in the community.

intensive supervision Increased contact between the officer and the client by decreasing caseload size.

intervention strategy Refers to reports from the 1940s and early 1950s when some outside "intervening factor" was introduced into the life of a juvenile in an attempt to evaluate the influence of this intervening factor on the juvenile's future delinquent behavior.

John Augustus The father of probation.

judicial reprieve Temporary suspension of the imposition or sentence by the court.

juvenile court The first juvenile court was established in 1899 in Cook County, Illinois, and began the movement toward a truly separate system for juvenile justice.

juvenile delinquency A violation of a law by a person considered a juvenile (by age) in the jurisdiction.

juvenile parole The conditional release of a juvenile from a correctional institution.

Kent v. United States (1966) Provided due process rights to juveniles.

labeling theory No act is inherently criminal; it is the law that defines certain acts as criminal.

levels of deterrence Specific and general deterrence; both based on the idea that people act in ways that maximize pleasure and minimize pain.

limited extent The notion that juveniles' rights are not always recognized, acknowledged, or honored in society.

Lyman School for Boys The first state reform school for boys, opened in 1845.

Massachusetts Youth Screening Instrument (MAYSI) Assesses substance abuse and mental health at intake.

McKeiver v. Pennsylvania Court decision (1971) about whether juveniles have a constitutional right to a jury trial. The Court implied that the due process standard of "fundamental fairness" applied to juveniles, but the Court rejected the concept of trial by jury for juvenile cases.

middle-range theories Theories more limited in their approach and scope and that are attempts to explain a specific area or type of crime.

minors requiring authoritative intervention (MRAI) Juveniles who, depending on jurisdiction, meet criteria to be taken into custody until they can be served by a mandated crisis intervention agency.

Miranda Prior to any questioning, the juvenile is notified of his or her rights.

Morales v. Turman Court decision providing juveniles housed in institutions the right to treatment.

mores Societal norms and customs.

Morrissey v. Brewer U.S. Supreme Court case enhancing the rights of parolees.

mother image The practice of women dealing with delinquent and dependent youth before the start of the modern era. These women, including Jane Addams, Louise Bower, Ellen Herotin, and Julia Lathrop, were usually well traveled and well educated, and they had access to financial and political resources.

National Crime Victims Survey (NCVS) Survey conducted by the Bureau of Justice Statistics to uncover unreported crime by surveying households.

negative subsidy Fees or charges designed to encourage local communities to accept responsibility for providing correctional care and control for their own residents.

neglected Children whose parents fail them or whose parents inadequately meet their basic needs.

New York Reformatory at Elmira The first major correctional institution specifically for juveniles.

norms of the delinquent subculture The resulting norms of the delinquent subculture that form and emerge from reaction formation.

Old Bailey The central court in London, England, which also tried juveniles.

Operation Ceasefire The Boston Gun Project. A problem-oriented policing initiative aimed at reducing homicides among juveniles in Boston.

parens patriae The state has right and responsibility to take control over children from the natural parents when they prove to be unable to meet their responsibilities or when the child is a problem for the community.

parent-related problems Specific reasons associated with the parents (e.g., parental rejection, child abuse) that might place a child in foster care.

parole services All components in the juvenile justice system that facilitate the goals and basic purposes of parole.

Philadelphia Birth Cohorts Two birth cohorts; one included all males born in 1945 in Philadelphia from age 10 to 18 years, and one included all males and females born in 1958 that lived in Philadelphia from age 10 to 18 years. The two studies were designed to determine the effects of growing up in the 1960s and 1970s.

Positive Achievement Change Tool (PACT) Screening instrument at intake which uses a series of risk factors to assess whether a juvenile has a substance abuse or mental health problem.

privatization The movement to have some institutions operated by corporate (nonpublic) entities.

probable cause Evidence that would lead a reasonable person to believe that the accused juvenile may have committed a delinquent act.

probation A sentence not involving confinement that imposes conditions.

probation subsidy Money provided to counties and local jurisdictions for not committing offenders to prisons.

problem-oriented policing (POP) Law enforcement analyzes the problems they handle to determine a plan for handling the problems in a long term fashion.

procedural rights Rights pertaining to statutory laws and are accorded to juveniles during the fact-finding process of a juvenile case.

proof beyond a reasonable doubt Adjudication of delinquency burden of proof established by *In re Winship*.

proscribed Acts or behaviors that are universally forbidden. Some examples are rape, incest, murder, treason, kidnapping, and rebellion. These acts fall at the forbidden end of the behavioral continuum.

prosecutorial discretion Process by which serious cases involving juveniles are moved to adult court through the decision of the prosecutor.

psychic arrest Periods of continued tendencies toward crime. Forbush believed that if the period of his or her psychic arrest did not pass, a juvenile could be permanently locked into a life of crime.

pulling levers A deterrence strategy targeting a small number of chronically offending gang-involved youth.

Racine Cohort A longitudinal study that examined the criminal careers of persons born in Racine, Wisconsin, in 1942, 1949, and 1959.

radical nonintervention Schur's policy suggestion to leave kids alone whenever possible.

reaction formation Cohen's theory that a delinquent from a lower-class environment lacks self-respect and, in his or her frustration with class or social position, strikes out against middle-class values.

reasonable cause Evidence that would lead a reasonable person to believe that action is needed (e.g., evidence of abuse that would allow for a juvenile to be taken into temporary custody).

recognizance The obligation to appear in court.

reform schools Juvenile institutions that emphasized formal training and were administered by municipal and state governments in the mid-1800s.

remanding Waiving juvenile court jurisdiction over a youth and sending the case to the adult court.

restitution A court-ordered condition of probation that requires the offender to repair the financial, emotional, or physical damage done (a reparative sentence) by making financial payment of money to the victim or, alternatively, to a fund to provide services to victims.

revocation of parole The decision to revoke a juvenile's parole.

right of privilege against self-incrimination Accused juveniles' entitlement of the constitutional privilege against self-incrimination, the Fifth Amendment, established by *In re Gault*.

right to a judicial hearing Juveniles' right upheld by the *Kent* decision.

right to be left alone Juveniles' fundamental interest in privacy as expressed through substantive rights of all persons.

right to counsel Accused juveniles' right to legal counsel established by *In re Gault*.

right to a jury trial One of the few constitutional rights that are not provided to juveniles. Jury trials for juveniles in most cases are the exception rather than the rule, unless a motion specifically requesting the statutory provision of a trial by jury is made in the court jurisdiction.

right to treatment The U.S. Supreme Court has not addressed the constitutional right to treatment for juveniles. However, in *Morales v. Turman*, the court ruled that juveniles housed in detention had a constitutional right to treatment.

rights of confrontation and cross-examination Accused juveniles' right to confront and cross-examine witnesses was upheld in *In re Gault*.

risk assessment The juvenile's potential for recidivism.

risk factors Demographic characteristics (e.g., involvement in violent behavior prior to age 15 years) that identify juveniles "at risk" for offending.

Roper v. Simmons Decision (2005) outlawed the death penalty for juveniles in the United States.

screener The probation officer or intake officer who assesses the juvenile.

secondary deviation Theory developed by Lemert to explain how the legal process can make the crime problem worse through the official reaction to the act.

six focal concerns of lower-class delinquents Concerns identified by Miller include trouble, toughness, smartness, excitement, fate, and autonomy.

social bonds The form that social controls take; for example, the ties that people have to parents, school, peers, and others. When those bonds are weak, a person is freer to engage in criminal activity.

social controls The actual or potential rewards—either positive or negative, internal or external—for conforming to social mores.

social development model A comprehensive approach to preventing youth crime by addressing their risk factors and matching them to appropriate interventions at the correct stage of their lives.

Stanford v. Kentucky (1989) Decision by the Court that juvenile executions do not constitute cruel and unusual punishment.

status offender Conduct by the juvenile that would not be defined as a criminal act if committed by an adult; Nondelinquent youth, including those who commit offenses that would not be considered "criminal" if the youth were an adult (e.g., runaways), as well as dependent and neglected youths.

status offenses Acts committed by juveniles that would not be considered crimes if committed by adults.

statutorily excluded Offenses that, although committed by a juvenile, are so serious that state statute declares the juvenile will be treated as an adult.

stocks A wooden structure used in the 1600s for restraining criminals; usually used in a public setting.

street corner justice When police make "on-the-spot" adjustments when interacting with youth on the street.

substantive rights of minors Basic human rights such as life, liberty, and the pursuit of happiness.

Suicide Risk Screening Instrument (SRSI) Assessment of the juvenile's risk for suicide.

supervision risk Assesses the immediate level of supervision for the juvenile.

Thompson v. Oklahoma The U.S. Supreme Court ruled that Oklahoma's death penalty statute was unconstitutional because it failed to specify a minimum age for which the commission of a capital crime by a juvenile can lead to execution.

transfer of juveniles to adult court When the seriousness of the behavior and the nature of the acts committed warrant, juveniles are transferred to adult courts.

transportation In the late 1700s and early 1800s, there were delinquent children transported for crimes from England to Australia. During transportation, the children were kept in confinement on the various ships.

Uniform Crime Report (UCR) A cooperative statistical effort of among city, county, and state law enforcement agencies and represents the amount of crime reported to the agencies in a given year.

waived Legislative process by which serious cases involving juveniles are moved to adult court.

waiver petition Formal petition seeking to adjudicate the juvenile as an adult.

widening of the net Utilization of diversion has extended the jurisdiction of the juvenile justice system, thereby brining in juveniles who may not normally have entered the system.

zone in transition Identified by Park and Burgess as the major source of urban crime due to the social disorganization caused by conflicting norms and competing values; residents of this zone are in conflict and competing to survive.

credits

Chapter 12

p. 367: Alamy
p. 370: Alamy
p. 379: Shutterstock.com
p. 380: Alamy

index